STATISTICAL
PERSUASION

To Wilma

STATISTICAL PERSUASION

How to Collect, Analyze, and Present Data . . .
Accurately, Honestly, and Persuasively

Robert W. Pearson
University of Pennsylvania

Los Angeles | London | New Delhi
Singapore | Washington DC

For information:

SAGE Publications, Inc.
2455 Teller Road
Thousand Oaks, California 91320
E-mail: order@sagepub.com

SAGE Publications Ltd.
1 Oliver's Yard
55 City Road
London EC1Y 1SP
United Kingdom

SAGE Publications India Pvt. Ltd.
B 1/I 1 Mohan Cooperative Industrial Area
Mathura Road, New Delhi 110 044
India

SAGE Publications Asia-Pacific Pte. Ltd.
33 Pekin Street #02-01
Far East Square
Singapore 048763

Printed in the United States of America

Library of Congress Cataloging-in-Publication Data

Pearson, R. W. (Robert W.)

Statistical persuasion: How to collect, analyze, and present data . . . accurately, honestly, and persuasively Robert W. Pearson.

  p. cm.

Includes bibliographical references and index.

ISBN 978-1-4129-7496-7 (pbk.)

  1. Statistics. 2. Social sciences—Statistical methods. 3. Decision making—Statistical methods. I. Title.

HA29.P348 2011

519.5—dc22   2009031775

This book is printed on acid-free paper.

09   10   11   12   13   10   9   8   7   6   5   4   3   2   1

Acquisitions Editor:	Vicki Knight
Associate Editor:	Lauren Habib
Editorial Assistant:	Ashley Dodd
Production Editor:	Astrid Virding
Copy Editor:	QuADS Prepress (P) Ltd.
Typesetter:	C&M Digitals (P) Ltd.
Proofreader:	Ellen Brink
Indexer:	Diggs Publication Services
Cover Designer:	Candice Harman
Marketing Manager:	Stephanie Adams

CONTENTS

PREFACE

This book was born from a frustration (on both my part and my students') with available textbooks in statistics. Many of these texts do not fully meet the needs of the audience to whom I direct this book: graduate students in professional degree programs in public policy, education, social work, criminology, urban planning, and related schools or advanced undergraduates with an interest in these fields. Some texts are far too technical; others far too cute. Many give too little attention to the collection of data, procedures to generate the appropriate statistics, and the interpretation and presentation of results, especially for the types of diverse nonacademic audiences to whom their statistical analyses, conclusions, and recommendations are likely to be presented.

In short, this textbook distinguishes itself from, although it draws on, others by

- providing real examples and data concerning policy issues (in contrast to examples drawn from nonpolicy topics or from fabricated data that display properties unlikely to be found in the real world);
- demonstrating the steps used to generate the appropriate statistics and graphs in Excel and SPSS[1]/PASW 18.0 and then providing exercises to replicate and elaborate on these or other examples and data sets (these exercises are intended to create skills in and knowledge of applications that one might be required to complete in a position as policy analyst, advisor, supervisor, commissioner, or other elected or appointed public official or nonprofit officer);
- emphasizing the importance of presentation as much as analysis and research design, focusing on the needs, desires, and limits of one's audience(s) and the best ways of ensuring that statistics and graphical displays tell the story you want to convey while protecting your analysis from methodological criticism;
- focusing on the conceptual understanding of statistics and graphs, although the text refers (sparingly) to specific formulas when they help reveal a conceptual point about the statistics;

- combining a concern for the collection and management of data with attention to their analysis and presentation;
- learning something substantive about the real social issues in education, welfare, and public administration along the way;
- identifying the conditions under which statistics are used to confuse or deceive an audience and the "red flags" to look for in order to spot the unprincipled use of statistics;
- recognizing that statistics is a language that uses words and terms that depart from our everyday understanding of them; and
- (hopefully) bringing a sense of humor to the task without becoming silly or flip, and being clear without "dumbing down" the material.

The book presents the procedures necessary to produce statistical analyses and graphical displays in both Excel and SPSS. Excel is particularly useful in the input, analysis, and presentation of relatively simple statistics based on small data sets. It is not, however, designed to produce the more sophisticated data transformations, analyses, and diagnostic tests that a program such as SPSS easily performs. The procedural examples in this book, therefore, move fairly quickly away from the use of Excel and concentrate instead on SPSS, although we return to Excel when a quick and simple statistical solution is called for. The book is accompanied by a workbook with exercises that the reader will profit from completing with the data sets that are also available (http://www.sagepub.com/pearsonsp/). There is no substitute for learning by doing when it comes to understanding statistics. Granted, what one learns grows increasingly difficult to retrieve from memory when these skills aren't used. But the text is there to return to and refresh your recollection of the selection of the most appropriate statistical tool, the procedures for using that tool, and the interpretation of the output from that analysis. Hopefully, you'll find occasions in the future to return to the book in order to access the distant recesses of your brain into which you've stored the warehouse of statistical knowledge you'll acquire by reading the text and completing the exercises.

This textbook is less technical than many others. Its purpose, metaphorically, is to teach you how to drive a car. It's not a manual for becoming an automobile mechanic. I don't believe you need to know everything that's going on under the hood in order to be a good driver. Instead, you need to know how to start the engine, the rules of the road, and what are considered courteous and rude driving practices. You need to know the speed limit, when the driving conditions require you to slow down, when the open road and weather conditions allow you to let the throttle out. You need to know when to signal and who has the right of way. And you need to know when to call for help from the Automobile Association of America.

For the instructor teaching this course, I have developed a practical Instructor's Resource Manual that provides a Sample Syllabus, Handouts, a discussion of the objectives and how to conduct weekly lecture and lab sessions. Solution sets to the assignments are provided, that is, exemplary submissions, including a midterm and final essay assignment.

A set of PowerPoint slides is also provided, which include all of the graphs and figures that were used in the book. For those who choose to use Blackboard, all of these materials are available for use with Blackboard. In addition, there is an Electronic Testbank that contains the questions provided in the final exam and many others, organized by chapter. These materials can be accessed with a password at http://www.sagepub.com/pearsonsp/.

For the student, a student workbook is provided. The workbook contains nine exercises, a mid-term assignment, and a final assignment. Each exercise in the student workbook is followed by an assignment to be completed. The workbook is designed to aid the student in understanding the material. In addition, there are sample data sets that can be used with the exercises in the workbook. To access the workbook go to http://www.sagepub.com/pearsonsp/.

Brief videotapes of edited lectures will be made available on YouTube for instructors and students to help reinforce the understanding of concepts and the application and interpretation of statistical procedures.

As this book went to press, SPSS released a new version of its software, which we incorporated in the book and supporting instructional materials (Version 18.0). This version of the software has also transitioned to a new name: PASW. We toyed with the idea of describing the software as "PASW (formerly known as SPSS)," but thought this too awkward. Prior versions of SPSS are also clearly identified as SPSS (not PASW), and we thought it less confusing to students and faculty, especially the many who would be using prior versions of SPSS on their campuses, to continue to call the software "SPSS."

NOTE

1. SPSS was acquired by IBM in October 2009.

ACKNOWLEDGMENTS

My own interest in statistics began in graduate school at the University of Chicago in the 1970s. I had the opportunity to take statistics and methodological courses from outstanding scholars and teachers such as Kenneth Prewitt, Norman Nie, and James A. Davis. I also had the good fortune of receiving a work-study fellowship from the National Institutes of Mental Health. This fellowship not only sustained me financially through much of graduate school but also supported my work at the National Opinion Research Center (NORC), where I helped design questionnaires, supervise interviewers, analyze data, and draft reports for various clients. I learned much from working alongside dedicated and skilled professional practitioners of the art and science of survey research at NORC. Most important for my "upbringing" in this regard were Kenneth Prewitt, Norman Bradburn, Paul Sheatsley, and Celia Homans.

With a PhD in hand, I headed off to the Social Science Research Council's (SSRC) Center for the Coordination of Research on Social Indicators in Washington, D.C., where I became a member of another team of knowledgeable and skilled professionals, many of whom would distinguish themselves at SSRC and beyond in related fields of statistics, methodology, and data dissemination. These colleagues included Roberta Balstad Miller, Richard C. Rockwell, and David Myers. I had the privilege as a program officer at SSRC to work as staff to interdisciplinary committees of social scientists and statisticians working at the frontiers of both substantive and methodological problems. I learned much from these committees, such as The Comparative Evaluation of Longitudinal Surveys, Cognition and Survey Research, Social Indicators, and Confidentiality and Access to Federal Statistics. The scholars serving on these committees were my unwitting tutors and mentors. The most notable and remembered among them include Robert P. Abelson, Robyn M. Dawes, Stephen E. Fienberg, Robert M. Groves, Elizabeth F. Loftus, Judith M. Tanur, Eleanor Singer, George Duncan, Robert Boruch, Richard Berk, and Thomas Jabine.

Work on this book was encouraged by several scholars and administrators at the University of Pennsylvania. Among them are Lawrence W. Sherman, Donald Kettl, David Thornburgh, Chris Patusky, and Leigh Botwinik.

My students at Penn have been the ultimate source of inspiration and frustration, the prime movers behind the writing of this book. All deserve some measure of credit for any good this book may provide in helping others learn how to drive the statistical machinery that so many statisticians before us have developed. (Obviously, my students and teachers are absolved of any blame for any shortcoming the book may have.) Some of my students were the guinea pigs for test runs of the chapters in the book. But several students provided exemplary responses to the exercises I assigned and created a foundation for the solution sets available to instructors who adopt this textbook. Others provided helpful comments on earlier drafts of chapters and advice about important matters such as the phrasing of the book's subtitle. These students include Augustine Ayamga, Zach Blattner, Meliss Buck, Matt Closter, Laura Crotty, Melissa Field, Chris Kingsley, Casi Krot , Jack Higgins, Diona Howard, Maura O'Brien, Stephanie Odell, Br n Osbourne, Tracy Portle, Brian Quinn, Natalia Taggert, Natalie Vernon, nd David Zega. Zach's comments on the chapters were especially thoroug' and helpful.

I wish also to thank the following reviewers of the book who p vided detailed, constructive, helpful suggestions and welcome encour ,ement: Haiyan Bai, University of Central Florida; E. Helen Berry, Utah State University; Elizabeth M. Flow-Delwiche, Community College of Baltimore County; Allyson L Holbrook, University of Illinois at Chicago; Mack C. Shelley, Iowa State University; Rongjun Sun, Cleveland State University; and Yue Yin, University of Illinois at Chicago. Vicki Knight at Sage Publications was a thoughtful steward of the book from first drafts to final completion. And Shamila Swamy and Rajasree Ghosh at QuADS Prepress Pvt Ltd provided unfailingly adept editorial recommendations.

Finally, I want to thank my wife, to whom I dedicate this book. She's a model of professional integrity and hard work. Although she inspired me and encouraged me to write the book and her own long hours at work shamed me into spending similarly long hours in its writing, she can take neither blame nor credit for anything I have written in the pages that follow. She was too busy to read any of it. It's just as well probably. She's especially effective at arguing from an n of 1.

CHAPTER 1

INTRODUCTION

THE NEED FOR STATISTICS AND GRAPHICAL DISPLAY ●

Many of you are reading this book very likely because you're taking a course that some college administrator and/or faculty committee believes is important for you to suffer through. As in the other courses you're required to take, you're determined to grin and bear it for 12 to 15 weeks, have your passport stamped, and move on, perhaps to courses you actually *want* to take. Or you're an intrepid soul who wants to learn statistics on your own and apply best principles and practices in your job, generating and interpreting statistics or judging others' use of them.

Some of you are quite nervous about statistics. You've heard of or experienced statistics as formulas you loathed and soon forgot, as a mysterious language that you misapplied on more than one occasion, or as a pack of lies that others used to lead you away from the path of truth.

Some of you can expect in your current or future job to rely on others to complete the statistical analysis and graphical display. The wise among you will realize that you don't want to be captive to what these people tell you can and cannot be done. You've got to know enough to know what's possible even if you may not be able to or have the time to wield these tools yourself. Similarly, some of you want to learn enough about statistics and data collection strategies to know when those who criticize your efforts or your organization's actions are making a valid point and when they are inventing results behind a curtain of bewildering statistical language and gadgetry.

And then there are some of you (maybe even the same folks above) who believe that data and analysis can help humans make better and wiser decisions. They can. They have. We'll discuss these instances shortly and try to draw general guidelines for the conditions under which this is more or less likely to take place.

The policy analyst that this book hopes to help you become or to better communicate with is a broker between decision makers and social scientists and statisticians, whose language and methods are difficult for decision makers to fully understand. The policy analyst must integrate knowledge and insights from multiple disciplines and multiple methodologies. In seeking to cut through the clutter of messages that decision makers receive, in order to move bureaucracies, entrenched interests, and long-standing administrative cultures, the policy analyst, cum advocate, will be tempted to overstate his or her case and, in so doing, fuel the criticism of those who oppose those recommendations. This text is designed to help you spot when that enthusiasm gets the better of others and to check your own impulse to distort what the data say.

● THE POLITICS OF NUMBERS

That numbers matter is nowhere more tellingly validated than by the vast amount of money, time, and energy that go into collecting, analyzing, and presenting them and—on some occasions—by the conscious attempts to bend them to support someone's position (see, e.g., Prewitt, 1987). In these latter instances, data and statistics become the handmaidens of ideology or self-interest. It is as much the purpose of this book to enable you to spot these statistical charlatans as to create truthful, useful, and effective analyses and presentations yourself.

Solid and defensible statistical analysis can be important in moving policies in an effective direction. But you have to have your statistical house in order if you hope to promote positive change. If not, those who oppose the prescriptions that you draw from your evidence will attack your ideas through your methods. Don't give them the chance. Learn and apply statistics appropriately, lest disputes over them muddy the waters and immobilize the body politic. Learn to apply statistics—in Robert Abelson's (1995) terms—as principled argument.

Seek through sound analysis to mitigate disputes over methods. Such arguments—often noted more for their heat than for their light—simply befuddle the public, the media, and public officials. The exchanges between Paul Krueger and Paul Peterson and their colleagues (Howell & Peterson, 2004; Krueger & Zhu, 2004a, 2004b; Peterson & Howell, 2004) over the effects of school vouchers on inner-city minorities is a case in point. Arguments over how to handle missing values and how to code the race of a child have left the public, journalists, and many social scientists unsure of the actual effects of school vouchers and, thus, whether their implementation is a worthy goal. In so doing, they serve, according to the economist Henry Aaron (1978), the profoundly conservative purpose of undercutting the demand for policy innovation.

THE STRENGTHS AND WEAKNESSES OF THEORY, DATA, AND ANALYSIS

The good news is that good data, theory, and analysis have helped raise important problems on the public agenda and provided a road map for their solution. The bad news is that they don't always do this.

Evidence for the power of ideas can be found among the works of political scientists and sociologists of knowledge who have sought to understand the conditions under which ideas and sound reasoning (including statistical ones) make a positive difference in public and social policy. John Kingdon (2003), for example, has studied how issues rise on or fall from the public agenda at the national level. In his widely read book *Agendas, Alternatives, and Public Policies*, Kingdon persuasively demonstrates that sound analysis and good theories have made a substantial impact on bringing to national attention and providing solutions to a range of issues, from the deregulation of the airline industry to health care reform. That such analysis is more often at play in the primeval soup of policy alternatives than at the stage of setting the national agenda itself does not belie its importance.

Unfortunately, there's a flip side to this story. Consider, for example, the implementation of the Head Start program. Sheldon H. White and Deborah A. Phillips (2001) tell an interesting story about the role played by developmental psychologists and the research they brought to bear on this program's initial design. It's a story that illustrates the differences in cultures and operating procedures between the experts and practitioners in the evolution of Head Start and the limits of available data and analysis in answering the tactical questions that arise in the design and implementation of programs in specific local settings. As Jule M. Sugarman, Associate Director of Head Start in its early years, recollected,

> The Planning Committee had only established the policy. It was up to the administrators to set rules and guidelines.... [We] found that "experts" were not very deep in their knowledge. No one could tell us, based on real evidence, what the proper child-staff ratios or length of program should be. Despite their lack of depth, experts were vigorously committed to their point of view and often rejected other views in irrational and unproductive ways. Many of the decisions eventually had to be made by administrators because the professionals could not reach decisions among themselves. (Zigler & Valentine, 1979, pp. 118–119, as quoted in Featherman & Vinovskis, 2001, p. 89)

Tensions and differences in goals, as well as knowledge (or the lack thereof), also highlighted the relationships between the top-down, expert-guided central planners and the anti-elitist, local community action implementers. The objectives of developmental psychologists and pediatricians who saw child development as the program's purpose conflicted sharply with those who viewed Head Start in light of empowerment and mobilization of children's parents in poor communities.

Interestingly, White and Phillips (2001) alert us to another potential problem here as well. Developmental psychology at the time of the experiments that supported the creation of Head Start was heavily dominated by cognitive psychology and its focus on cognitive development in children (in contrast, e.g., to social and emotional development). On the other hand, preschool directors did not share this emphasis on cognitive development and, abetted by Head Start administrators who sought flexible and local adaptations, were cognizant of different local conditions among heterogeneous populations.

This is a point to which we will refer later, but one worth drawing your attention to now. That is to say, certain research designs—especially, sample surveys of individuals—have an often unrecognized tendency to focus explanations on the characteristics of individuals in contrast to the structure of circumstances and opportunities that broader social forces make available to some groups of individuals. This distinction—often referred to as the difference between agency and structure—runs deeply throughout the history of the social sciences and policy research. It will not be resolved in this book. I do, however, want to alert you to the fact that different research designs can unwittingly cause us to fall into one of these two camps, just as the fashion of a discipline at any point in time can lead us to explore some questions rather than others.

We can also approach the good news/bad news story about the influence of good theory, data, and analysis on the policy process as policy analysts by reframing this observation as a question. To wit, under what conditions is our analysis likely to make a positive difference?

● DESIGNING USEFUL RESEARCH

Judith Gueron, as head of the Manpower Demonstration Research Corporation, is one of the many analysts/administrators who have sought to draw lessons for those who wish to use sound research and analysis—in her case, social experiments—to inform public policy. Many of the lessons she has drawn from several decades of research on employment and training programs appear obvious, although they are often breached in practice (e.g., diagnose the problem correctly, devise a reasonable treatment). But her success is probably predicated on

- designing a real-world test,
- addressing questions that the public cares about,
- contextualizing the results in the face of what is known about effective and ineffective programs,
- actively disseminating the results without overstating the case, and
- soliciting key partners throughout the process.

In other words, the effectiveness of your analysis is as much a political process as it is a statistical one.

Peter Szanton (2001) addresses the question of how to increase the value of analysis through a different approach. He asks why policy prescriptions—based on appropriate designs and statistics—are so often ignored by public officials. More specifically, Szanton asks why the advice given to local public officials—whether from social scientists based in universities, think tanks, or consulting firms—was so often useless and unused in helping resolve the urban problem in the United States in the 1960s and 1970s. There's plenty of blame to go around in his account. But unlike most research that focuses on the supply side of advice, Szanton argues persuasively that the lion's share of the problem lies in city governments themselves. In short, they lack the incentives and capacities to accept and act on sound advice.

Although Szanton (2001) is careful to circumscribe the lessons he draws from cities, I believe that its lessons extend well beyond that arena, as the parallel between this work and Judith Gueron's attests. Szanton helps us better understand the conditions under which policy research is most (and least) likely to achieve the aim of "informing" the design and implementation of "better" public policies and programs.

Szanton (2001) draws several conclusions based on a variety of case studies in which scholarly advice was ignored (and, occasionally, followed). Ineffective advice was more likely to occur when

- structures and relationships between analysts and policymaker were formal (e.g., lodged in urban "centers" and "institutes") rather than personal or informal,
- goals were national and ambitious rather than specifically local, and
- efforts were funded directly and exclusively by third parties (e.g., foundations) rather than by local decision makers.

Efforts to impose a technical solution to a political problem were invariably doomed and short-lived.

Conversely, successful collaborations between a policy analyst and local government tended to be based on less visible, less formal, lower-level ad hoc relations. Under these conditions, advice was more likely to be acted on and more likely to endure. Success was also more likely to result when the advisor was nonthreatening, persistent, flexible, committed, and willing and able to take the blame for any shortcoming in results and, conversely, redirect the light of success on public officials. Success was also furthered by selecting problems that were amenable to quick and effective solutions, for which a demonstration or experiment could be conducted. They were problems that city officials or bureaucrats thought important.

These insights move Szanton (2001) to describe the following difficulties that the prospective consumers of advice face:

> Innovation in city agencies must negotiate an obstacle course of civil service regulations, line-item budgets, collective bargaining requirements, community sensitivities, an attentive press, and the charges of a political opposition. A local government agency, in short, is deeply embedded in a local social setting and tightly constrained by it. (p. 113)

Szanton (2001) concludes with nuggets of advice for the three sets of institutions in this drama. There are far too many to summarize here, but a selected few are listed:

- Advisors and foundations should seek to augment the capacity of local governments to accept and act on advice as much as provide advice (p. 125). Plenty of good ideas for change and improvement exist; it's the lack of political, managerial, or fiscal capacity that's the problem.

- Avoid the search for universal truths and generalities. Although this is helpful for building theory (and in securing tenure as a university professor), a community's needs are likely to be unique. They will want advisors to address their particular needs. When funders and advisors insist on searching for more universal truths, clients become disinterested, uncooperative, and resistant—characteristics that do not create a fertile bed for constructive change.

- Findings, advice, and recommendations will tend to favor the interests of some person or group at the expense of another and are, therefore, inherently political. Being political, those who give it should brace themselves for attacks against their results, motives, costs, and methods. If you can't take the heat, stay out of the kitchen!

- Advice, if calling for substantial change, will always require time to bring about that change.

- For consumers of advice, don't ask for it if you don't want it!

THE GRAMMAR OF STATISTICS •

Pick up any textbook in statistics, and you will soon realize why statistics seem so foreign. It is. The language for many is not only new but mysterious. This is so for several reasons. The language of statistics is

- paradoxically precise yet probabilistic;
- slightly askew from everyday usage and downright misleading in some instances;
- replete with instances in which the same word takes on substantially different meanings, even in a statistical context; and
- replete with double negatives (e.g., rejecting the null hypothesis is one of my favorites).

All these characteristics, of which there will be ample examples throughout, get in the way of understanding and communicating statistics, but they help make a decent wage for the statisticians who invent the jargon, use it, and criticize others' misuse of it. This book tries to ease your pain but won't eliminate it entirely. You will have to learn the language in order to understand what others are saying or writing and in order to translate that language for your colleagues who haven't read this book and completed the exercises that accompany it.

Statisticians appear to be a rather negative group on the whole. In addition to a preoccupation with rejecting the null hypothesis, they're also fond of focusing a great deal of attention on errors. Indeed, they've developed quite an assortment of them. They begin with "errors of observation" (see Groves et al., 2004). These are defined as differences between your conceptual or theoretical constructs (what you want to measure) and what you actually measure, say, in respondents' answers to your questions. You were asking about "profits." The respondent thought you were asking about "prophets"!

There are also "errors of nonobservation" (Groves et al., 2004, p. 60). How can I err in something I don't observe, you may ask? Such errors may be "sampling errors," that is, the differences between a statistic calculated from a sample of the population and its "true" value in the population as a whole (this true value is referred to as a population **parameter**,* in

---

*Words in bold font can be found in the glossary to this book.

contrast to a "statistic" or "estimate," which is based on a small set of observations taken from a population). These errors may also arise from coverage errors, where some members of the population of interest are excluded or underrepresented in the study, say, because they're less likely to be home during the hours in which interviews take place or less likely to have access to a phone in a telephone survey. And errors may arise because those people who did respond are unlike those who did not—the topic of **nonresponse bias**, to which we will return later. There are plenty of errors to go around.

All this attention on errors leads many readers to despair. You need not. If the errors are not systematic, they may behave much like "white noise." They'll surely reduce the size of some statistics that seek to explain the variation in the concept you would like to understand better. But a little noise never hurt anyone. It's the missed messages that are disguised by the noise that should concern us. We will return to this issue under the rubric of concepts such as **residuals**. Yes, it is a different language.

Errors of measurement are commonplace. Consider the task of measuring someone's height. You may not have precise tools for this task, or your angle for viewing your colleague's height may have led you to misread the ruler that you tape to the wall. You may measure her height with or without shoes, with or without the end of a level to rest on the top of your friend's head, and so on. But, on the whole, your measures aren't likely to be terribly wrong. For most purposes, they're probably quite good enough. It's the potential for systematic errors in measurement that might cause problems.

Can there be such errors in measuring someone's height? Yes. It turns out that we're all a little taller in the morning after a good night's sleep in a horizontal position than we are in the evening after having stood on our feet or sat on our butts for an entire day. Why? Our vertebrae are cushioned by intervertebral disks made up of fibers and a gel the consistency of Jello. These disks compress somewhat during the day and expand while we're asleep. Surely "errors" in measuring height caused by these small daily changes won't be too bad either, will they? Again, probably not. But it's something we should always think about.

The statisticians' preoccupation with errors can be a downer. Get over it. If you're led into such a funk by this text or others, remember the following three points:

1. Don't throw the baby out with the bathwater. Use common sense, even in the face of fancy statistics. A little error, especially in comparison with the magnitude of an actual effect and the uses to which you'll put the measure, may be quite alright.

2. Don't make the opposite mistake, however, of thinking that errors aren't all that bad. They can be, although not necessarily so.

3. Statistics may shroud themselves in a fog of apparent precision with, say, ***p* values** of .0134. This is an illusion. Decimal points do not confer precision. Don't be taken in by them or purposefully try to mislead others by overusing them yourself.

BE CAREFUL WHAT YOU WISH FOR: THE ● POTENTIALLY PERVERSE EFFECTS OF NUMBERS

As you well know, the need for quantifiable results can produce perverted outcomes. Many accuse the No Child Left Behind (NCLB) law of creating too great an emphasis on standardized tests, which lead teachers to "teach to the test." Some worry that teachers are repeatedly drilling students on standardized tests on subjects for which they and their principals are being held accountable (e.g., math and reading to the neglect of subjects such as history and science and activities such as art and physical exercise). Of course, teaching to the test need not be bad if the tests are well designed and push students to learn what is known to be useful and important.

Because the measurement of proficiency in NCLB is left to each state to determine, you can find some states dumbing down their tests to ensure that high percentages of their students achieve proficiency. The current winner of the award for statistical shame is Mississippi, which has designed a fourth-grade test of reading, for example, in which about 90% of their children score "proficient or better." This score ties Mississippi for the best score in the country with Nebraska. When Mississippi fourth graders, however, are tested by a national standardized reading test in the National Assessment of Educational Progress (NAEP), only about 18% of these children achieve reading proficiency or better. Mississippi's kids drop from 1st to 50th in rank among the states, falling 71 percentage points lower on the NAEP than on their home-grown tests (Wallis & Steptoe, 2007, p. 39).

Equally pernicious, tests and statistics can lead teachers and school administrators to cheat, as we will see later in our examination of test score data from school districts in Texas. And there is ample evidence that the high-stakes standardized tests have led some principals, whose jobs depend on showing high proficiency levels and/or improving scores, to hold back (i.e., "retain") children in, say, the 9th grade, knowing that the students face an important test in 10th grade. These students, stigmatized as "dropbacks," often drop out of school (McNeil, Coppola, Radigan, & Heilig, 2008).

The perverse incentives that numbers can create are not, of course, limited to public schools in the United States. A study of the length of telephone calls to a customer service center at a small bank demonstrates the unintended consequences of numeric goals and numeric measurement systems (Shen, 2003). Figure 1.1 (a histogram generated in Excel) shows a quite striking fact: A large number (and percentage) of calls to the service center were terminated in 10 seconds or fewer. You wouldn't think a service employee could satisfactorily respond to a customer in less than 10 seconds. Indeed, the most frequent length of response was 2 seconds! What's happening here?

It turns out that the bank had a policy when these data were collected to penalize service representatives if the average length of their calls was "too long." How would you make sure you didn't violate company policy if you were a customer service rep? Hang up quickly on a few callers, of course. "Oops, sorry about that. I hit the wrong key. May I help you?" After these data were shown to the bank, the bank changed its policy.

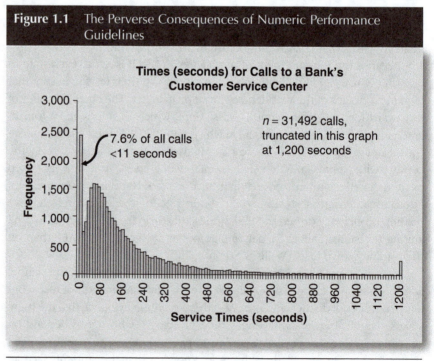

Figure 1.1   The Perverse Consequences of Numeric Performance Guidelines

SOURCE: Based on Shen (2003), as referenced in Moore and McCabe (2006, pp. 10–11).

The good news lesson of this example is that good data can chase away bad data (and associated behaviors). (Not always, of course. We're still waiting on Mississippi.)

A PREVIEW OF TAKEAWAYS FROM THE BOOK ●

I will shortly argue that you should begin your research at the point you want to end. That is to say, what decisions do you (or someone else) need to make for which statistics will matter? So let us begin with a preview of where you can expect to land at the end of this flight. As a result of reading the chapters and completing the exercises, you will become painfully aware of the following:

• **Correlation** is not causation, although you can come close with a little help from friends such as temporal order, strong theory, consistent evidence from multiple studies, and the elimination of competing alternative explanations.

• Single statistical measures can be misleading. Base important decisions on evidence that has been replicated and findings from a variety of studies and methods that converge on the same conclusions.

• Sound analysis begins by displaying the data and getting a feel of its shape, character, and idiosyncrasies.

• Variability characterizes every human process and the data we use to describe those processes.

• Don't mistake chance variation for causation, patterns, or trends. Chance can offer a "fool's gold" of apparent regularity.

• Statistics may help reduce uncertainty but not eliminate it. Become comfortable with probabilities.

• A statistically significant difference does not necessarily mean a meaningful difference.

• Research (i.e., data collection, analysis, and presentation) of the kind described in this book should be focused on helping people decide among alternative courses of action. Check your idle curiosity at the door. It's too expensive for most governments, public agencies, and nonprofit organizations.

• Research design is as important, if not more so, than statistical tests. Sophisticated statistics cannot overcome poorly designed and executed data collection efforts.

Intermediate statistics such as regression require a fairly extensive knowledge of the assumptions on which they are based and the consequences of and remedies for their violation. Equally important, they require special effort on the part of the policy analyst to translate their results into "stories" that others—not trained in their use—can readily understand.

- A great deal of what we think we know actually rests on assumptions for which we have no solid research.

- Two data points do not make a trend.

- Effective presentations begin with your message and follow with selected evidence to support it.

- Statistics may reveal the truth, but simple, unexpected, concrete, credible, emotional stories are more likely to persuade others to act or think differently (Heath & Heath, 2007).

- Statistics are often best communicated after you transform them into scales or analogies around which your audiences can wrap their hearts and minds. People have a harder time imagining what $2.3 trillion is (the costs of health care in the United States in 2007) than $7,600 (the average costs of health care for every man, woman, and child).

- Every research design has its strengths and weaknesses. Knowing them will help you use these tools to advance an argument, make a better decision, disarm an opponent, or spot a statistical charlatan.

- There are appropriate statistical tools for nearly every task. Use a hammer to drive a nail, a screwdriver to turn a screw.

- It's not only okay but sometimes a good idea to transform data and then reanalyze them. Some transformations are indispensable—for example, a percent.

- Nearly every statistic rests on one or more assumptions when making a statement about a process taking place in a population from which you only have drawn a sample (i.e., statistical **inference**). A careful statistician will check to see if these assumptions are met and then modify the data or select a different tool in response to that detective work. An even better statistician will help ensure that the right data are collected in the first place and the results presented in ways that target audiences can understand.

- The field of statistics includes a lot of polysyllabic terms (e.g., **heteroscedasticity**) that may impress friends, family, and colleagues, but get in the way of making points that "stick."

RHETORIC VERSUS PHILOSOPHY ●

As David Brooks wrote in an op-ed in the *New York Times* of March 2, 2006, philosophy is the search for truth, while rhetoric is the persuasive argumentation of a position. These two pursuits are often in conflict. It is the hope of this book that we can bring them into harmony.

Mark Twain attributes this quote to the British statesman Disraeli: "There are three kinds of lies: lies, damned lies, and statistics." An erudite American statistician, Fred Mosteller, quipped in response: "It's easy to lie with statistics, but it's easier to lie without them." Considerable research in cognitive psychology and decision theory has demonstrated repeatedly that our guts, hearts, and heads play tricks on us that good data and statistics can help protect us from. Our objective here is to learn how to make persuasive and principled statistical arguments and identify those that are not.

Note for those of you reading this text as part of an applied course on statistics: This book is part of a fully integrated instructional package that includes a student workbook (available at http://www.sagepub .com/pearsonsp/) in which you will find weekly exercises. The first one of these exercises is to be completed after reading the first three chapters of this book. This is pretty easy stuff so far. There's no need to stop here. Read on.

CHAPTER 2

RESEARCH DESIGN AND DATA COLLECTION

BACKWARD RESEARCH: IN MY END IS MY BEGINNING ●

We will turn shortly to the strengths and weaknesses of different research designs and data collection strategies that give us the raw materials that our statistical tools will craft into effective and honest arguments and presentations. But we will begin by considering where we want to end by using Alan Andreasen's (2002) principle of backward research.

Andreasen (2002) tells a story that shows us what can occur when an analyst works with a client in the public or nonprofit sectors. His example comes from a nonprofit performing arts organization, but it surely applies far beyond this case. In short, the executive director of the organization wants to know more about her organization's market and commissions a research agency to collect, analyze, and report on the several types of audience that attend performing arts programs in her city. The agency consults previous studies of this kind and then designs, say, a random digit dial (RDD) telephone survey of adult residents of the city, conducts interviews, creates data files, and applies the appropriate statistical tools to analyze the data. The agency then produces a glossy report, using the finest graphical tools available. It's filled with statistics.

The executive director reads the report and, having finished it, lays it aside with a sigh of disappointment. The report tells her what hundreds of similar studies have already reported: The audiences for the performing arts are largely female, well educated, urban, relatively young or old, and well-off economically. She already knew that.

Even the few new nuggets of knowledge in the report did not provide her with insights on which she could act. Why, for example, do men attend less often than women? Why are the middle-aged less likely to attend? How could she motivate these groups to come more frequently while sustaining her loyal market segments? How could she create and sustain loyal audiences in the future? The executive director, in Andreasen's telling of the story, explains in frustration, "When the researcher tried to explain the results, it was obvious he hadn't understood what I wanted. The results were all a bit off the mark" (pp. 60–61).

Clearly, part of the fault lies with the executive director in not communicating what she really wanted to know. As explained in the previous chapter, the most successful research is marked by a close collaboration between researcher and client, where the research is driven by the client's questions and needs (in contrast, e.g., to the questions that a scientific discipline strives to answer).

The story above is commonplace. A group of my students had volunteered to help the Graduate Student Association (GSA) draft a questionnaire to be administered to graduate students in professional degree programs in the School of Arts and Sciences at the University of Pennsylvania. I reviewed the draft questionnaire and asked the students, rather skeptically, what decisions the GSA planned to make on the basis of the answers to the draft survey's large number of questions about levels of satisfaction with issues ranging from advisors to debt. I couldn't see how they could put the data to any use. "Well," the response from one of the students came, "GSA surveyed the PhD students about a year ago, and they thought they should survey the professional degree graduate students too. GSA's president told us he'd figure out how to use the data after the results had come in." Ugh.

It is, of course, the case that a client does not always know exactly what he or she needs to know. But mindless fishing expeditions are unlikely ever to catch a fish worth eating. Be more "planful" and disciplined and help your client be so too by following a "backward research design."

Here are the 10 steps of a backward research design (modified from Andreasen) that will ensure more successful outcomes than the ones described above:

1. Ask your client what key decisions are to be made using the research's results.

2. Determine—in collaboration with your client—what information will help him make those decisions.

3. Prepare a prototype report or ask your client what actions or decisions would follow if you discovered x, y, or z. This exercise will also

help you determine what alternative explanations need to be considered (and perhaps discarded).

4. Determine what questions must be answered to complete the final report.

5. Ascertain whether these questions have already been answered in other research.

6. If not, design one or more studies that can be conducted within your time and financial constraints.

7. Implement the study(ies).

8. Write the report and present the results.

9. Help deflect or respond to any criticism the report might receive and direct any praise toward your client.

10. Evaluate the research process and contribution, and propose a new study to answer the new questions your client now comes up with but couldn't have foreseen before your brilliant study and presentation of results.

Interestingly, the first five of these steps do not require you to raise a statistical finger (although you may be required to know how to read and evaluate someone else's research, a skill that follows from doing research yourself).

Ideally, you also have a theory or model, a story that offers an explanation of the patterns of relationships you expect to find in answer to questions such as why middle-aged men tend not to attend the ballet, why homicide rates in the United States dropped in the 1990s, why poor children perform more poorly on standardized tests than wealthy ones, or why some women on welfare tend to stay on welfare for extended periods of time. Moreover, your theory and the questions you seek to answer—should you need to collect your own data—will build on research that has already established the plausibility of at least parts of your theory or model. If so, you're humbly following in the footsteps of Sir Isaac Newton, who, in a letter to a rival mathematician, Robert Hooke, wrote in 1676, "If I have seen further it is by standing on the shoulders of giants." (Newton may not have been beyond sarcasm here, as Hooke himself was rather short of stature.)

It is, of course, possible that extant research does not provide a solid foundation for what you seek to answer. You may find yourself in the situation of the two statisticians who were having a hard time solving a particular problem. "You know what our problem is Bill [Kruskal]?" asked Fred Mosteller. "We're standing on the shoulders of pygmies."

Hopefully, you've already picked up some skills about how to find existing research on the subject and questions of interest to you. Technologies such as the Internet and Google have made these tasks easier, and libraries at major research universities provide valuable resources and skilled reference librarians to help you in your search. These resources make the search and acquisition of statistics and data (observations on which statistics are based) relatively easy (although you may be surprised to discover that despite the vast amount of information and data that exist today, answers to your specific questions may not reside among these data). We will practice, in the exercise to be found at the conclusion of Chapter 3 of this book, how to bring data collected by someone else into Excel or SPSS for further analysis. There's plenty of data out there for your examination. A list of some of these possible sources can be found in Appendix A, "From Whence Do Data Come?"

Let's assume that you've made it through Andreasen's first five steps and have concluded that the available studies—although providing a portrait of the conditions in which you are interested and pointing toward a variety of causes and responses you may want to investigate—don't give you or your client the answers needed to make more informed decisions. You have to design a study or prepare a Request for Proposal (RFP) to the research community in order to conduct a study that will answer the questions you've posed. (Note here too that although someone else may actually conduct the study, complete the analysis, and submit report(s), you and your colleagues may be required to evaluate the credibility of the proposals for this research before awarding a contract and then assess the quality of the data and reports that others eventually produce.)

Not surprisingly, it turns out that different research designs have different strengths and weaknesses that you'll have to consider in conducting the study yourself or in outsourcing this task. This is the topic to which we now turn.

● STRENGTHS AND WEAKNESSES OF DIFFERENT RESEARCH DESIGNS

What are the basic types of research designs that you might turn to in order to answer the questions that will assist you or others in making more informed choices? They are as follows:

- Experiments
- Sample surveys
  - Mail, phone, face-to-face, Internet, computer assisted
  - Longitudinal, cross-sectional

- Administrative records
- "Actors," "confederates," "testers," and "audits"
- Observations (unobtrusive or participant)
- Focus groups

Whether any of these research designs draw a sample from a population of interest is a somewhat different, and central, concern of **inferential statistics**, a topic to which we will turn in Chapter 8. Suffice it here to note that there are occasions when it is possible to study an entire population in contrast to a sample drawn from it (e.g., all students in a school, all school districts in a state).

Beware as well that you are likely to draw the impression from the following pages that policy research is an impossible task, fraught with problems that produce errors at every stage. While it is true that no data collection strategy or design is perfect, don't allow these difficulties to lead you to despair of ever finding answers to questions that will help you or someone else make better decisions. Policy research actually does help (and, of course, sometimes it doesn't). There are better and worse ways to gather data. There are some data and statistical tools that will give you more or less confidence in your conclusions, despite knowing that your data harbor imperfections. And there are ways in which you can combine different research designs within the same study (e.g., embed an experiment within a cross-sectional survey), which helps mitigate the weaknesses of any one research design (Boruch, 1975).

Experiments

Some research and policy wonks admire experiments so much as to label them the "gold standard" of research. Those who champion the virtues of experiments are somewhat correct. But we can't always use gold or afford it, as we will note in our discussion of the weaknesses of experimental designs.

Figure 2.1 presents a diagram of a classical experimental design.

We begin with a population of interest to us. Let's say it's the noninstitutionalized adults in the United States. (*Noninstitutionalized* is a term used by survey researchers typically for the purpose of excluding from a study people who are difficult to reach and interview. These may include, for example, patients in hospitals, prisoners, and military personnel stationed abroad.) Let's further stipulate that we want to test whether the health insurance provided by the federal government results in greater

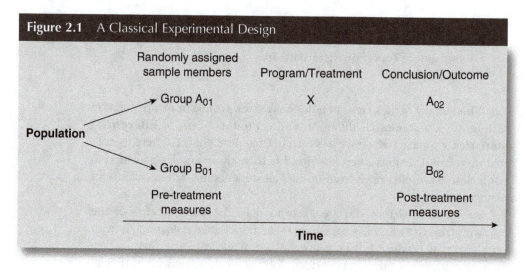

Figure 2.1   A Classical Experimental Design

access, better quality, and lower costs than the existing, employer-based, private health insurance plans. This is an important question for which no experimental data exist, although at least one social experiment in health care—the RAND health insurance experiment, which was conducted between 1974 and 1982—used randomized assignments to assess the consequences of different levels of copayment in private health insurance plans on the use of health care services. This research demonstrated, not surprisingly, that the more people had to spend directly out of their own pocket, the less health care service they consumed. What you may not have considered is that the experiment also showed that health among the sick poor was adversely affected with higher copays (Relman, 2007, pp. 101–103).

You've probably already identified some difficulties with assigning some randomly selected, noninstitutionalized adults for enrollment in a national health insurance program in our hypothetical example. You might, for example, decide to screen from your initial population those people currently receiving some form of national health insurance. Estimates range as high as 45% of the American public currently receiving such health insurance through Medicare, Medicaid, State Children's Health Insurance Program (SCHIP), or military and veterans' hospitals. Among other implementation problems, such a study would require nearly half of your subjects to drop their current private health care insurance. The currently uninsured—about 17% of the American population—might very well welcome participation in the experiment. (The RAND study provided "side payments" to participants in the experiment who suffered some financial loss as a consequence of their random assignment to different health insurance plans.) Our own hypothetical experiment would ask that the sample of respondents randomly assigned to a government health plan faithfully stay in the program—which statisticians refer to as the "treatment." In the diagram, Group A is a sample randomly drawn from the population that receives the treatment. (We will discuss random selection and sampling later, in Chapter 7.) Another group of people, Group B, are also randomly selected but receive nothing different from their current coverage (private or none). This is often called the "control" group.

We gather information about current health conditions from everyone who was randomly selected for the study, before the assignment to the treatment and control groups. If the assignment was properly executed, we can be confident that the two groups won't differ on these measures at their initial assignment to the treatment or control group (but it's good to check anyway). If we discover that they don't differ, we're also even more confident that the randomization has produced two groups that do not differ on things we did not measure. We administer the treatment and then, after an adequate amount of time elapses for effects to appear, remeasure the outcomes of interest. If Group A differs from Group B at the conclusion of the study (e.g., fewer emergency room visits, fewer deaths), we would conclude that it was the treatment that caused the difference. National health insurance is less expensive, more broadly accessible, and provides better care! Obviously, we should pass such national legislation. If only life were so simple!

As we'll also see in survey samples, random selection is important. In the case of experiments, it permits us to isolate the unique effects of the treatment from all other possible factors that influence health conditions. (You can test more than one treatment or program at a time using factorial designs, but these are beyond the scope of this book. For an intuitive understanding of such designs, see Almquist & Wyner, 2001.) If the randomization is properly executed, the two groups will differ only in that one received the treatment and the other did not. Any difference we observe in outcomes is attributable to the treatment because it is the only condition on which they differ.

Obviously, experimental designs are commonplace in areas such as the assessment of pharmaceutical products and medical devices. More than 1,000,000 randomized control trials (RCTs)—another term for "experimental design"—of medical treatments have been conducted since the late 1940s, when the first antibiotic treatment for tuberculosis, streptomycin, was evaluated through an experimental design (Sherman, 2003, p. 10). Many of these studies have been identified, cataloged, and themselves studied through the Cochrane Collection (www.cochrane.org/index.htm). Although much less frequent in the social sciences, more than 10,000 experiments are known to have been conducted and are referenced in the Campbell Collaboration (www.campbellcollaboration.org/). Experiments are especially useful in determining "what works."

Experiments face a variety of challenges, however. Opponents of experimental designs may argue that it is ethically unjustifiable to provide some benefits to one set of people while denying them to another. This objection does not always hold water, however. Surely, if we knew the precise effect and costs and benefits of a program, we wouldn't need to conduct an experiment. But rarely do we know this. Social scientists have also discovered that some programs that are believed to result in beneficial outcomes actually do not (e.g., many self-help programs) and, worse, have been shown in randomized controlled trials to do harm to the treatment group.

For example, RCTs on the program D.A.R.E. (Drug Abuse and Resistance Education) have shown the program to be ineffective (U.S. General Accounting Office, 2003), although a new D.A.R.E. curriculum for seventh and ninth graders, "Take Charge of Your Life," is currently undergoing a 5-year randomized trial evaluation by the University of Akron. Some studies have shown that kids exposed to the earlier D.A.R.E. program ended up taking more illicit drugs than the control group of randomly assigned youth who did not participate in the program. These "boomerang" effects, as they are sometimes called, arise when subjects interpret and/or evaluate the likelihood of an outcome differently than what the evaluation or program designer believes to be the case (Capella, Yzer, & Fishbein, 2003).

More generally, ethical/legal objections to social experiments can be mitigated through any one or more of the following strategies (Boruch, 2004, p. 5098):

● Include in the study only those groups of people for whom the treatment's effectiveness is uncertain or not legally or ethically questionable.

● Employ a wait-list in which those currently denied the treatment are given it later (assuming that it has been shown to be effective or, at minimum, not harmful after the initial results of the first set of assignments are known).

● Assign entire institutions (e.g., schools, hospitals) or geopolitical units (e.g., police precincts, counties) to treatment and control groups rather than assigning individuals within those units (see Boruch, 2005).

Moreover, if the treatment is in short supply relative to its demand, random assignment to a treatment can be seen as a fair means of allocating the treatment.

There are, of course, a large number of important questions that simply can't be assigned to an RCT. Questions in international relations do not lend themselves to random assignments of countries or their leaders to control and treatment groups. One cannot, for example, assign governments to be either democratic or authoritarian and then observe whether the democratic countries are less likely to engage in war than the authoritarian ones, a widespread hypothesis in international relations theory (Frieden & Lake, 2005).

Further questions arise concerning the "fidelity" of programs modeled on an RCT that have shown a treatment to produce a substantial and intended effect. An RCT of the effects of the mentoring provided by Big Brothers Big Sisters in a study by Public/Private Ventures (Tierney & Grossman, 1995), for example, demonstrated the positive effects of adult mentoring on the kids whom the program served. Another RCT of the long-term effects of early child care intervention—the Ypsilanti Perry Preschool experiment—found higher rates of high school graduation and employment and lower rates of teen pregnancy and arrest (Weber, Foster, & Weikart, 1978). Similar results to these were found in an RCT of black children in Harlem (Deutsch, 1967).

Other programs have been subsequently based ostensibly on these successful programs and cite one of these experiments to justify their own. This has been the case even when these subsequent programs lack key elements of the studied programs (e.g., they don't screen and train "Bigs" as rigorously as Big Brother Big Sisters or don't provide the range and depth of support services to kids and their families of the Ypsilanti study).

"Gold standard" research designs can also be perverted, either in their implementation or in their interpretation. This is especially likely to be the case when large amounts of money are at risk. The RCT that reported Vioxx to be a safe and effective treatment for pain, for example, demonstrated two fundamental flaws in its clinical trial. The first involved fraud. The second used the smoke screen of "statistical significance" to deflect attention from its real, and troubling, effects. The fraudulent action was the omission of three people from the study who took Vioxx and suffered heart attacks. The report said that only five of the treatment group suffered heart attacks in contrast to only one participant from the control group. The second flaw was more subtle. The comparison of five to one heart attacks was reported not to have achieved the status of "statistical significance," a term to which we will return in Chapter 8 and the remainder of the book. Suffice it to say that the differences between five (or eight) heart attacks and one could well be substantively meaningful if not "statistically significant" (Ziliak & McCloskey, 2008, pp 28–31).

Most of the examples noted above employ what we might consider a classical experimental design.[1] But departures from the design features of classical experiments are commonplace and predate RCTs. Several authors have sought to order and classify these departures from experimental designs under the rubric of "quasi-experiments" (Campbell & Stanley, 1963; Cook & Campbell, 1979), although one of these authors has subsequently admitted to have come to call many such designs "queezy-experiments" (Cook, 2003).

Such designs include the following (Shadish, 2004):

- Interrupted time-series designs, in which consecutive observations are compared before and after the introduction of a treatment, which can be a program intervention or a change in policy (we will turn in more detail to a variety of such designs in Chapter 13)

- The outcomes of two or more treatments or conditions are studied, but an investigator does not control the assignment to these conditions. An investigator, for example, may sample from a list of people known to have participated in a job training program and compare their characteristics with those of a sample drawn from people known not to have participated in such a program. Such a design would be analogous to comparing A_{02} with B_{02} in Figure 2.1, without the initial random assignment to treatment and control groups. The results from such designs can be strongly influenced by selection bias; that is, people who volunteer to participate in a job training program may have unmeasured characteristics (e.g., ambition) that could produce any observed differences (e.g., employment) in outcomes rather than the treatment itself. Some studies of this kind can also produce results that are an artifact of program administrators permitting only those people most likely to succeed to participate in the program (a process referred to as "creaming"). Such processes are inherent in performance evaluation systems that look only at outcomes (e.g., the number of participants who get jobs within a month of graduation from a training program, without regard to their characteristics at program intake). This type of **quasi-experimental design** is often called a nonequivalent control group design.

- Single-case designs, in which one or more participants' responses to different dose levels of a treatment are observed over time

- Case-control designs, in which a group with a particular outcome or condition (e.g., lung cancer) among a set of "cases" is compared retrospectively with those without this condition who are otherwise similar (the "controls")

- Similarly, a matched comparison research design is constructed by, say, first collecting information from and/or about a group of interest (e.g., youth in a particular neighborhood) and then finding a sample of individuals from the broader population whose characteristics match the characteristics of the members of the first group. Joan McCord (2003), for example, conducted a 30-year follow-up study of research originally launched in 1942 among a group of boys who lived in two congested urban neighborhoods in Cambridge and Somerville, Massachusetts. Information about the group of boys from these neighborhoods was collected from the boys themselves, their families, and the neighborhoods. A second group of boys was selected to match each member of the Cambridge-Somerville group on social background, temperament, and physique. A coin toss determined which boy from these matched pairs would receive weekly, and sometimes extensive, visits from caseworkers over a 3-year period. Thus, assignment to treatment and controls was random; selection for the sample itself was not. Selection for the second group depended on matching the characteristics of the members of the first group. (We will later see that this type of selection for a sample will require the use of a different set of tools to measure the strength and direction of a relationship from the tools used to analyze a survey where the participants are selected independently of each other.)

● Correlational designs, in which possible treatments, conditions, and outcomes are measured simultaneously without random assignment to treatment and control groups (this type of study often characterizes sample surveys, the design of which we will turn to shortly in more detail)

The point of this discussion on experimental designs, as well as the other research designs, is not that they can or cannot be trusted to produce sound and useful conclusions. The conclusions instead are that

- different designs have different strengths and weaknesses;
- the implementation of any design and the fidelity of its replication in later studies are the type of "devil in the detail" that can profoundly affect the results;
- one should take care in assuming that the results based on a sample from one kind of population (e.g., registered voters in Milwaukee) are applicable to a different population (e.g., registered voters in Philadelphia); and
- when the stakes are high, the incentives for manipulating the implementation of a study and distorting its interpretation are also high and require careful attention.

Sample Surveys

Surveys encompass a surprisingly wide variety of types. They vary, for example, by the methods for collecting responses: mail, phone, face-to-face, paper and pencil, or the Internet. They differ in that some capture responses on paper, others on the hard drive of a laptop. They vary by whether they collect information from a set of people at one point in time (often referred to as a "cross-sectional" survey) or whether they collect information from the same subjects repeatedly over time (i.e., "longitudinal" or "panel" studies). Surveys can also collect data from and about organizations and events.

Sample surveys also vary by the ways in which respondents are selected. Selecting respondents randomly and with known probabilities of selection enables you to employ the vast array of statistical tools that we'll explore later in making inferences about a population from data collected only from a subset of that population (i.e., a random sample). In contrast, convenience samples (e.g., asking people to complete a survey in a shopping mall) or snowball samples (e.g., asking your current respondent to identify the next person to interview) provide no known probability of selection. Snowball samples may, however, be useful in studies of migration chains and social networks (see, e.g., Massey, Durand, & Malone, 2002). Although you cannot draw inferences about the characteristics of the population from which such samples are drawn, they may be valuable in generating ideas or pretesting a questionnaire. Such is also the case with the other types of research designs described below.

Sample surveys are used to collect information about an incredible variety of topics, although we often don't realize that the information reported to us on a nearly daily basis comes from this form of data collection. Unemployment rates (Current Population Survey), job counts (Current Employment Statistics), inflation (**Consumer Price Index, CPI**), consumer confidence (Survey of Consumers), illicit drug usage (National Survey on Drug Use and Health), academic performance of 4th, 8th, and 12th graders (National Assessment of Education Progress), risk factors for chronic diseases (Behavioral Risk Factor Surveillance System), and crime victimization (National Crime Victimization Survey) are just a few social and economic indicators that surveys produce.

There are also many surveys conducted for specific purposes—say, to understand how the public in a county views its local government and whether these attitudes vary by demographic group, geographic area, or the number of encounters citizens have with government workers and officials. You will see such a survey in the Orange County Survey of Public Perceptions as part of the exercises that accompany the chapters of this book.

If you're responsible for issuing an RFP to organizations whose purpose is to collect survey data (e.g., the National Opinion Research Center [NORC] at the University of Chicago, the Survey Research Center [SRC] at the University of Michigan, or a private firm such as Westat or Mathematica),[2] you will want to know (and ask the bidders for this work) the answers to at least the following questions about the survey being commissioned (see Groves et al., 2004, p. 33):

1. *How will the potential sample members be identified and selected?* (The identification of prospective sample members is referred to as the sampling frame—that is, a list of all members or an identifiable subset of the population in which you're interested.) The selection can be a simple random sample (SRS) from a list, say, of everyone in the phone directory of a town or city. The SRS is the most easily understood method of selecting sample members. But one often doesn't have a handy list of all members of a population. We'll return in Chapter 8 to a fuller discussion of selection techniques, including stratified and clustered selection methods that get around the absence of a list of all members of a population.

2. *What approach will be taken to contact those sampled, and how much effort will be devoted to trying to collect data from those who are hard to reach or reluctant to respond?* That is to say, how many times will the data-collecting agency return to a house, call a phone number again, or send another mail questionnaire or reminder before chalking the case up to a nonresponse? Will especially persuasive interviewers be assigned to those who are selected but who are reluctant to respond? Will incentives be offered to increase the participation of reluctant respondents?

3. *How much effort will be devoted to evaluating and testing the questions that are asked?* We will return in the next chapter to the issue of pretesting, to which this question refers. To how many people will a draft questionnaire be administered during the pretest? How will the respondents' comprehension of the question be assessed? How will we determine whether the questions are actually measuring what we believe (hope?) them to be measuring?

4. *What mode will be used to pose questions and collect answers from respondents?* That is to say, will respondents be questioned via a face-to-face interview, a phone call, a self-administered paper-and-pencil questionnaire, a diary, a form on the Internet, or some combination of these modes? Groves and colleagues (2004, p. 140) depict all these data collection modes in a historical perspective in a graph (Figure 2.2), with an accompanying glossary for its various acronyms.

Glossary of Acronyms

ACASI Audio computer-assisted self-interviewing. Here, the respondent operates the computer and enters his or her answers.

CSAQ Computerized self-administered questionnaires. These include questions posed both via e-mail and on a Web site.

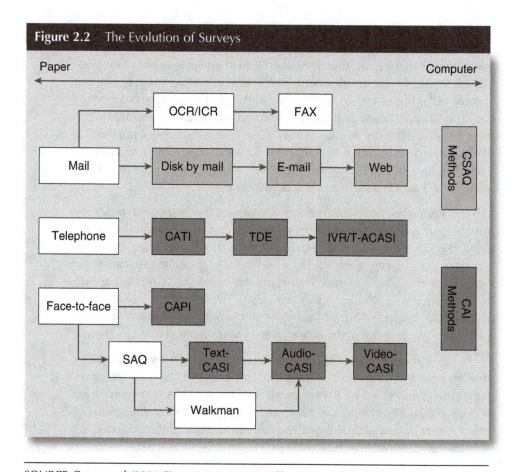

Figure 2.2 The Evolution of Surveys

SOURCE: Groves et al. (2004, Figure 5.2, p. 140). Used by permission. Copyright John Wiley & Sons.

CAPI Computer-assisted personal interviewing. A computer displays questions on a screen, which an interviewer reads and then uses to enter the respondent's answer.

CASI Computer-assisted self-interviewing. Questions and responses are written (text-CASI), questions are presented in audio form (audio-CASI), or graphs are used to present questions (video-CASI).

CATI Computer-assisted telephone interviewing. This is the same as CAPI except that the interview is conducted over the phone.

OCR Optical character recognition, a technology that permits answers to mail questionnaires to be machine read. This technology was further advanced with the development of ICR, or "intelligent character recognition," which permits machines to read and code handwriting.

SAQ Self-administered questionnaires. Such questionnaires could be handed to or distributed to respondents in a group setting or mailed to them. This mode, for a brief time, used Walkman audio cassette tape players to ask questions, which were then answered on a paper form.

TDE Touchtone data entry. This mode is used to collect limited amounts of data by asking respondents to call a toll-free number and respond to recorded voice questions via the phone's keypad.

IVR Interactive voice response. A computer plays recordings of questions to a respondent over the phone, and responses are given either by using the phone's keypad or by answering aloud. This is also sometimes called T-ACASI because it's like ACASI but uses a phone.

Note that such a wide variety of modes of survey data collection and their combination make it difficult to draw any conclusions about which is "best" for a particular situation (although we will make some simple comparisons below). Indeed, no single mode is best for all circumstances. Choices must be made in the context of the objectives of the study and the personal, technological, and financial resources available.

5. *If interviewers are involved, how much effort will be devoted to training and supervising them?*

6. *How much effort will be devoted to checking the data files for accuracy and internal consistency?* An interviewer or respondent can miss a question or record a numeric response that falls outside the range of legitimate answers, or someone entering the data into a file (other than a respondent or an interviewer) may strike the wrong key. Questions that should have been skipped might have been answered and vice versa. In other words, the data may be "dirty." To what lengths will the collecting organization try to "clean" the data during the editing stage?

7. *What approaches will be used to adjust the survey estimates to correct for errors that can be identified?* Will the data be weighted to compensate for the discovery that certain groups of one's population are underrepresented among the final respondents (e.g., the poor may be less likely to have access to phones; those who work evenings and weekends may not be as likely to be at home when an interviewer calls). Will any adjustments be made for people who refuse or fail to answer an entire questionnaire (e.g., unit nonresponse) or individual questions in it (e.g., item nonresponse)? Will missing responses to individual questions cause such respondents to be excluded from any analysis that uses the answers to that

question, or will the values for these missing observations be imputed from knowledge of other information in the survey? Will measures discovered to lack sufficient **reliability** be adjusted and, if so, how?

Survey Mode. The range of different modes of sample surveys is quite large. Although it is difficult to make general assessments about these modes, research does suggest that some consequences follow from your choice of design and administration. One of the earliest such studies by Hochstim (1967) compared face-to-face, telephone, and mail modes of survey administration. The study randomly assigned households in Alameda County, California, to one of these three modes and to one of two different questionnaires. Like other studies, the face-to-face interviews produced the highest response rates but also had the highest costs. Telephone and mail questionnaires were within 12% of each other in cost. There were few substantive differences across the three modes, although mail questionnaires produced higher levels of some behaviors, such as reported alcohol consumption, and higher levels of nonresponse to specific questions, findings that have since been replicated.

A more recent study of the comparative costs of an RDD telephone survey versus an address-based mail questionnaire using the 2005 Behavioral Risk Factor Surveillance System showed that they were similarly close. The telephone version of the survey cost $79,578 per 1,000 completed interviews, 12% greater than the $70,969 per 1,000 completed mail questionnaires (which included a follow-up questionnaire mailing and a postcard reminder; Link, Battaglia, Frankel, Osborn, & Mokdad, 2008, p. 21).

Although there is no list of all individuals or all households in the United States from which one could draw a sample, the U.S. Postal Service (USPS) has created the computerized Delivery Sequence File (DSF), which contains all delivery-point addresses serviced by the USPS (except for general-delivery addresses). A number of studies (Iannacchione, Staab, & Redden, 2003; O'Muircheartaigh, Eckman, & Weiss, 2003) have demonstrated that the DSF may include up to 97% of all U.S. households. In the same methodological study noted above (Link et al., 2008), the address-based mail survey produced response rates higher than those of an RDD survey in five of the six states in which the study was conducted: 33.9% versus 29.4% in California, 39.9% versus 35.8% in Illinois, 26.2% versus 22.5% in New Jersey, 36.5% versus 31.1% in Texas, and 40.3% versus 34.1% in Washington. Phone interviews achieved a 45.8% response rate versus 37.0% for the mail version of the survey in North Carolina.

Of course, different modes have different levels of coverage; that is to say, they vary in how likely they are to reach a target audience. The combination of area probability sampling frames (a topic to be covered in Chapter 8) with face-to-face interviews is typically the most likely to achieve the greatest level of coverage and completed interviews, although some trade-offs have to be made to minimize costs (e.g., members of the military, prisoners, or residents of Alaska and Hawaii are typically excluded from such samples because of the costs of accessing them).

Telephone coverage rates follow close behind, with computers and Internet access lagging behind in terms of the proportion of the U.S. public with access to these technologies, as displayed in Figure 2.3.

Note, however, that these numbers disguise differences in the prevalence of these technologies in U.S. households by important matters such as age, race, education, and income. While 96.6% of all U.S. households

Figure 2.3 Access to Phones, Computers, and the Internet in the United States

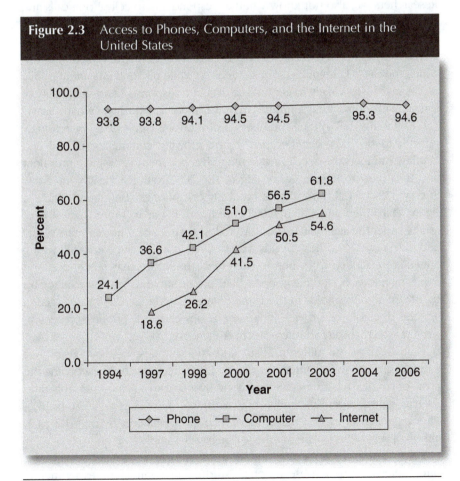

SOURCE: Bureau of Labor Statistics, Current Population Surveys. www.bls.gov/CPS

had access to a phone in 2006, only 87% of households with yearly income less than $10,000 did. In other words, a survey interested in the poor may potentially miss one of every eight such households if administered via telephone interviews, which is sometimes referred to as "coverage error." Similarly, while 54.6% of U.S households owned a computer in 2003, only 20% of households whose "head" did not complete high school owned one. On the other hand, 76.8% of households whose head had a bachelor's degree owned a computer.

Cell phones pose another challenge to research that relies on phone interviews because cell phones are often not included in telephone samples; a call to a cell can cost a respondent money. (This can be compensated by offering cell phone users proper remuneration for completing the survey.) Researchers will also not know whether respondents to cell phone calls are, say, driving a motor vehicle at the time the call is picked up, a condition that is illegal in some states and that has been shown to be associated with an increase in traffic accidents. Nor will a researcher know the environment in which the call is being taken. Those received while respondents are in public places may be less likely to get full and accurate responses. And the quality of transmissions through cell phones may also affect data quality: "Whatdyasay?"

Excluding cell phone numbers from phone surveys is increasingly difficult to do, however, because of the growing comingling of cell and landline numbers. Also, cell phone usage has become increasingly prevalent and thus hard to ignore. According to the 2006 National Health Interview Survey, 13% of U.S. households had only cell phones (Blumberg, 2007), a figure that Ehlen and Ehlen (2007) predict will soar to more than 40% of adults under the age of 30 (in contrast to less than 5% of adults 65 years of age and older) by 2009. These trends may well result in coverage errors if young adults are excluded from phone surveys in the future that rely entirely on sampling frames of landline phones. RDD phone surveys may now exclude up to 19% of all households in the United States (Link et al., 2008, p. 7). (For a general discussion of these and other issues that cell phones present in surveys, see Lavrakas, Shuttles, Steeh, & Fienberg, 2007.)

Finally, how do different data collection modes vary by costs? Not surprisingly, face-to-face interviews are typically the most costly, exceeding the costs of conducting interviews via phone by a factor of 2, although this ratio for national surveys may climb as high as 10 to 1 (Groves et al., 2004, p. 161). Phone interviews exceed the costs of mail questionnaires by only 1.2 to 1, although this varies by the number of callbacks, sample size, and so on.

No matter which mode of administration is used, sample surveys are often referred to as "observational" studies, in contrast to experimental designs. One of the most important weaknesses of such observational studies is their inability to firmly establish causal relationships, which so much of our research would like to establish. This is so for several reasons. First, all the statistics discussed in this book either assume no causal relationship (but merely establish whether "high" values of one variable tend to be found to coexist with high values of one or more other variables) or assume that one or more variables cause another. The operative word here is *assume*, because it may well be the case that Y causes X instead of X causing Y. Research that collects data about possible treatments and outcomes simultaneously is hard-pressed to demonstrate causation conclusively.

The joint association between two variables may, for example, be the **spurious** consequence of their shared association with a third variable, and they may therefore not be causally related at all. Perhaps the most famous instance of such a relationship is that found between ice cream consumption and crime. Although there is an empirical relationship between the two, one would be hard-pressed to argue that ice cream consumption causes crime. Indeed, their association appears to be the result of their joint occurrence with warm weather, which appears to cause, encourage, or enable both crime rates and ice cream consumption to rise.

It is also the case that observational studies don't introduce a treatment and assess its consequences but, rather, observe a consequence and then attempt to determine whether that consequence (e.g., unemployment) tends to vary with other measured characteristics (e.g., criminal record, education levels). To discover, however, that men who have been incarcerated have poor employment outcomes could well be the spurious consequence of characteristics of these men (e.g., alcohol/drug abuse, behavioral problems, poor interpersonal skills) that are likely to "cause" both poor employment outcomes and higher rates of incarceration (see, e.g., Pager, 2003). Similarly, it is difficult to conclude that participation in job training programs "causes" better employment outcomes by observing higher proportions of such participants with jobs than people who didn't participate in these training programs. Those with better employment opportunities may have self-selected into such job training programs and would have found employment even without having completed a training program (see, e.g., Winship & Morgan, 1999).

The final distinction to be made about surveys is that between cross-sectional and longitudinal surveys. Cross-sectional surveys measure the attitudes and behaviors of individuals at one point in time. Longitudinal or panel studies collect information about individuals (or whatever type of unit you're studying) repeatedly—that is to say, two or more times. A modest confusion may arise here because you can string together a series of repeated cross-sectional surveys that may look like a longitudinal study because it may be, say, responses of adults in the United States in 1970, 1971, 1972, and so on.

The distinction between cross-sectional and longitudinal designs is important for at least two reasons. First, as we will see again later in this book, observations in longitudinal studies are said to be "dependent." A response to a questionnaire in Year 2 in such a study is a function of being a respondent in Year 1 of that study. Dependent observations—in this particular meaning of the term *dependent* (we'll see other meanings later)—require different statistical tools or tests from those observations (such as those in cross-sectional surveys) that are said to be "independent" of one another. My random selection to participate in a cross-sectional survey has nothing to do with your random selection to participate. Thus, the observations in a cross-sectional survey are said to be independent. Second, longitudinal surveys—largely because of repeated measures over time—can provide somewhat more leverage in drawing cause-and-effect conclusions than can cross-sectional surveys (see, e.g., Singer & Willett, 2003). (Structural equation models, which are beyond the scope of this book, were developed to remedy this shortcoming of cross-sectional surveys, but they require some assumptions that can be difficult to defend.)

Administrative Records

Organizations collect data about themselves. Sometimes, a lot of data. They are often required to do so. Financial data, for example, are required by an organization's auditors and the Internal Revenue Service. Budgets are required for nearly all of an organization's planning processes. Universities are required to report crimes committed on campus. And many organizations collect data to assess and evaluate whether they are achieving their mission, although this is not always easy or inexpensive to do.

The types of administrative records are as diverse as the organizations themselves. They include, but are by no means limited to, orders, invoices, payments, receipts, insurance costs, the number of clients served, the number and level of donations received, employee data concerning employee backgrounds and absenteeism rates, fines and fees, customer complaints, and complaints responded to within specified periods of time.

This type of data has many of the same problems with quality and completeness as sample surveys. They are also not likely to include all the information one would like to have in order to test for a full range of possible explanations—say, for differences in the level of your employees' performance.

Administrative records, however, can be nonetheless indispensable for answering many questions about organizational performance. They can be made even more useful when combined with data explicitly drawn from a sample of an organization's members. Such information may also be strung together as part of a time series, say, of traffic fatalities in a state in a specified number of years. Such data can be used—for example, to assess the effects of changes in law enforcement practices (e.g., a crackdown on speeding violations, revocation of a driver's license for speeding)—in what is called an interrupted time-series analysis, to which we'll return in Chapter 13.

"Actors," "Confederates," "Testers," and "Audits"

Some research hires people to play a role that is intended to evoke a response that can be compared with responses to, say, different types of "actors." This type of research was first launched in a major, systematic way in studies by the U.S. Department of Housing and Urban Development to test housing discrimination (Wienk et al., 1979). The design has also been used, for example, to study the presence and consequences of racial stereotyping and discrimination in job markets.

One example of this type of study sought to understand the effects of incarceration on job opportunities and outcomes by conducting an experiment in Milwaukee between June and December 2001 (Pager, 2003). Pairs of white and black actors, also known as "testers" or "auditors," submitted applications for entry-level jobs advertised in a local newspaper and a state Web site for employment listings. Each member of the pair was randomly assigned to play the role of someone with a past felony conviction and 18-month prison sentence applying to randomly selected job listings. The testers were matched as best they could on personal qualities (although the vast majority of applications [76%] included no face-to-face interview, which made the possible differences between testers less important). Their applications differed otherwise only by race and criminal record.

The results were fairly dramatic if not unexpected, as represented in Figure 2.4 (from Pager, 2003, Figure 6, p. 958). The bars represent the percentage of these different categories of applicant who were called (in some cases, called back) for an interview. Both race and previous incarceration made a big difference in whether someone was asked for an interview.

Audits that combine experimental designs with "real-world" field settings are a powerful tool for uncovering actual behavior patterns, in contrast to intentions, expectations, attitudes, or opinions, on which many sample surveys focus.

There are, however, several potential shortcomings in such a design. First, the testers may not be precisely matched on the characteristics the investigator would like to hold constant, although alternating testers to take on different

Figure 2.4   Criminal Records, Race, and Employment Opportunities

SOURCE: Pager (2003, Figure 6, p. 958).

roles may well mitigate this problem. You cannot, however, easily have an actor change race from one setting to another. Second, audits are usually carried out in a specific location (e.g., Milwaukee) or small set of locations, thus raising the question of whether those locales are similar to or differ from the larger set of locations about which one would typically like to make inferences. Third, the testers, no matter how well rehearsed, may influence the results in nonrandom ways. It may be difficult to play the role of a drug felon in a job interview, and that discomfort might be communicated in such a way as to affect the likelihood of a callback. Finally, such designs are predicated on a lie or deceit in some way or another, ranging from the actors lying about their own backgrounds to the failure to disclose the fact that the activities are part of a research project that could potentially put the subjects at some risk of violating the law (see Heckman & Seligman, 1993, for a critique of this method).

The merits of this form of research design are apparent, however. These designs have been used to study questions that avoid the "social desirability" effect, where respondents give responses to place themselves favorably in the eyes of the questioner. This problem often troubles sample surveys as well as other study designs in which a respondent/participant is aware of being observed.

Other Observational Studies
(Unobtrusive and Participant)

Two more types of studies fall under the rubric of "observational" studies. The first is illustrated by a study that seeks to learn whether sports utility vehicle (SUV) drivers drive more aggressively than drivers of smaller automobiles. Observers would be instructed on what types of behaviors constituted "aggressive behavior" in the eyes of the principal investigators. The observers would position themselves on street corners and overpasses and look for the designated types of behavior in some sample of cars and SUVs that passed their observation points at designated (and randomly selected) times. Obviously, SUV and other automobile drivers are not being asked whether they drive aggressively. Their actual behavior is being observed instead (unobtrusively, you might say).

Although this type of study cannot be used to study all questions, it has the advantage of observing and measuring actual behavior instead of attitudes or intentions, which are only imperfectly related to behavior. Some attitudes and intentions are weakly held. Barriers and incentives can overpower them. "The road to hell is paved with good intentions," as the old proverb goes.

The second type of observational study embeds observers among the populations that are the object of study. This technique is commonplace in anthropology. It is often called participant observation or ethnography. Its methods were made famous by studies such as Margaret Mead's work with the Trobriand Islanders, but the method retains strong advocates among a wide range of researchers who study a variety of questions (see, e.g., Anderson et al., 2004). The method's strengths lie in the ability of observers to understand how others give meaning to their circumstances and interpret their realities and why others think and behave as they do.

The depth of meaning that these methods are capable of exploring comes at the expense of not being able to make estimates with a certain degree of certainty and precision about the prevalence of conditions in a population or the strength of the relationship among two or more concepts or differences between two or more groups. And some participant observers become so much a part of the population they're studying (i.e., "go native") as to color their ability to make unbiased observations.

Focus Groups

Focus groups are commonplace in market research. They typically involve the gathering of about a dozen people in relatively homogeneous groups who engage in semistructured, but highly open-ended, conversations. They are often used to test reactions to a new product or idea and, like ethnographic methods, to better understand how and why people hold certain attitudes or beliefs. One of the strengths of this method lies in the opportunity it provides to watch and observe nonverbal reactions as well as verbal responses. It can explore new ideas without implementing them. The group settings can trigger more ideas than a one-on-one interview. And this method can be used—like ethnographic research—to learn what questions to ask through more quantitative techniques (e.g., a sample survey).

Focus groups also have several potential and real weaknesses. Strong personalities can sway others' opinions (although this can be guarded against by a good facilitator). People may want to tell you what you want to hear (although this **social desirability effect** is present in many of the different research designs described in this chapter). And they cannot provide estimates about the prevalence of conditions in a population or the strength of the relationship among two or more concepts or differences between two or more groups with any degree of certainty and precision.

● NONRESPONSE MAY (OR MAY NOT) LEAD TO NONRESPONSE BIAS

Surveys of humans rarely, if ever, obtain completed interviews (question-naires) from every one who is sampled. Mail questionnaires to randomly selected members of lists often have response rates of no more than 5%. Telephone surveys such as the University of Michigan's Survey of Consumers, which measure consumer attitudes and expectations, complete interviews with only about 60% of the selected adults, and about 17% of sampled schools in the National Assessment of Educational Progress refuse to partic-ipate in the tests that produce "The Nation's Report Card." In general, face-to-face surveys produce the highest response rates, phone surveys the second, and mail questionnaires the lowest (Hox & de Leeuw, 1994), although Link and colleagues (2008) demonstrate a slight edge to an address-based mail questionnaire over an RDD survey. Among self-administered ques-tionnaires, paper-based formats tend to outperform e-mail and Web-based formats (Couper, 2001). Nonresponse and refusal rates have risen steadily across many ongoing surveys over time.

Survey researchers have developed and tested a number of tactics for reducing nonresponse, including the following:

- Repeated callbacks in face-to-face and phone interviews and repeated follow-ups in self-administered questionnaires (The Adult Education and Lifelong Learning [AELL] survey of the U.S. Department of Education, for example, used up to 20 call attempts to complete each interview in its 2001 survey.)

- Letters in advance of the interviewer contact

- Refusal conversion letters or phone calls, often from especially persuasive interviewers, to convert refusals into completed interviews

Methodological experiments using these techniques in AELL 2001 and a 2003 Pew Research Center Survey (both of which were telephone surveys) increased response rates from 34% to 43.4% and from 27.7% to 51.4%, respectively (Montaquila, Brick, Hagedorn, Kennedy, & Keeter, 2008, p. 576).

Whether low response rates cause a problem for the data analyst is predicated on the differences between respondents and nonrespondents. Do these two groups differ in their socio-demographic makeup, attitudes, or behavior? If they do, the analyst should be wary about drawing conclusions about the population from which the sample was drawn.

Interestingly, the AELL 2001 and 2003 Pew Research Center surveys noted above demonstrated few substantive differences between data sets based on minimal and extensive efforts to increase response rates.

It is often the case that we do not know about the attitudes and behaviors of a study's nonrespondents. It is more often the case, however, that we have independent data about the socio-demographic characteristics of the populations being sampled. The age, race, and gender distribution, say, of Orange County, Florida, residents are available from the U.S. Census Bureau and can be compared, for example, with the age, race, and gender distribution of any sample drawn from that population.

MULTIMETHOD DESIGNS AND • CONVERGENT RESULTS CAN OVERCOME THE LIMITATIONS OF ANY SINGLE RESEARCH DESIGN

Different research designs have different strengths and weaknesses. Some are better for answering some types of questions. The choice of the most appropriate research design depends on your questions, as well as the resources and capacities you (or others you hire) have to carry out the study. It should also be clear that research that combines several different designs is more likely to bear fruitful and insightful results and conclusions than research that relies on a single data collection strategy. The more viewpoints you bring to bear, the more likely you are to see the whole and rich complexity of the answers you seek. Even advocates of randomized control studies caution strongly against making generalizations to people or organizations beyond any particular experiment (Shadish & Cook, 1999, p. 299).[3]

The important point to repeat here is that the more the studies that address your questions, the more confident you can be in their answers and the decisions you base on them (assuming, of course, that the different studies arrive at the same conclusions). Such convergent results, for example, led C. Everett Koop as Surgeon General to conclude that cigarette smoking caused lung cancer despite the absence of RCTs (experiments) on that question. That is to say, people were not randomly assigned to smoke the equivalent of a pack a day for 20 years and compared with another group of people randomly prohibited from smoking or inhaling smoke from others. Yet the evidence from multiple studies and the size of the effect across many of these studies were collectively persuasive enough for most to draw the causal connection between smoking and lung cancer. Executives of some tobacco companies argued for years that the correlation found between cigarette smoking and cancer was the result of a hereditary condition that caused both cancer and a desire to smoke cigarettes. That is to say, they argued that the relationship between smoking and lung cancer was "spurious" and that extant studies (none of which were RCTs) had failed to rule out alternative causal explanations or the hereditary factors that were not measured in these studies. We will see later that this type of critique—"You didn't include a measure for a plausible alternative explanation in your study!"—is one that can be levied against nearly any nonexperimental study. Such a charge falls under the rubric of "failure to fully specify your model." It's a critique to anticipate and guard against in your own research (if possible).

● CONCLUSION

We turn in the next chapter to the concern of how best to ask questions, whatever the research design. Some of you may find it odd that I'm paying so much attention to matters of research design and question and question-naire construction in a textbook on statistics. To repeat a metaphor, statistics are tools with which to analyze data derived from one or more data collection methods, each with its own strengths and weaknesses. These designs can, however, produce seriously flawed data, inadequate to provide answers to the questions at hand. If so, no statistical technique—no matter how sophisticated—can save the study. No decisions can be confidently made with poor data, no building confidently constructed from faulty building materials and poor architectural plans. Or, as Light, Singer, and Willett write (1990), "You can't fix by analysis what you bungled by design" (p. v).

Richard Berk (2004, pp. 234–237) illustrates this point forcefully in describing the flaws in a study of racial profiling for the Los Angeles City Police Department (LAPD) in 2000–2001. The story begins with the mayor of Los Angeles signing a consent decree between the city and the U.S. Department of Justice in response to charges of corruption and misconduct. The decree required the Los Angeles police to provide quarterly "audits" of specific police activities to the local police commission and inspector general.

The audit reports were well staffed and funded. The LAPD hired a technical consultant to collect and organize the required data. The reports were also closely scrutinized by the mayor, the police commission, the city council, the police union, and the media.

The LAPD had been charged specifically with racial profiling of pedestrians and motorists. The consent decree sought to assess the veracity of this charge, which required the collection of information about the race and ethnicity of all people whom the police stopped and/or detained. Police officers were required to record on new forms the following information for each person stopped (Berk, 2004, p. 42):

1. Whether the individual was a pedestrian, a driver, or a passenger

2. Gender

3. Apparent descent (racial/ethnic background)

4. Apparent age

5. Incident number

6. The initial reason for being stopped

7. Whether the driver was required to exit the vehicle

8. Whether a patdown or frisk was required

9. Whether the detainee was asked to submit to a consensual search

10. If there was a warrantless search, the search authority

11. Whether a search was actually conducted

12. What was searched

13. What was discovered/seized

14. The action taken

15. Date

16. Time

17. Reporting district

18. Officer's serial number (for two officers if necessary)

19. Officer's police division number (for two officers if necessary)

20. Officer's name (for two officers if necessary)

Unfortunately, no information was collected about the location of the stop. No effort was made to collect baseline information with which to compare the data that were recorded on these new forms. Assuming that police officers could accurately observe and record race, ethnicity, and age, they were not asked to report the relative mix of motorists' or pedestrians' characteristics at the location where each stop occurred. Such data could have been collected through any number of means. Moreover, no outcome data were recorded. For example, what proportion of stops led to an arrest and conviction? Stops of minorities that led to no such outcomes could surely be suspected of racial profiling. And how do these outcome data compare with data from police departments in other cities?

Professor Berk (2004) concludes this story as follows:

> Clearly, important data are not being collected. And the data that ultimately will be available will have significant problems. One can predict, nevertheless, that there will be hundreds of pages of regression output addressing racial profiling. Reports from those analyses will be laden with p-values, hypothesis tests, and lots of causal talk. (p. 237)

You too will learn about p values, hypothesis tests, and more. You will even produce pages (not hundreds) of regression output if you complete the exercises that accompany most of the chapters of this book. I hope that you will do so with an understanding of the appropriate use of specific statistics under different conditions. But we must first understand what data to collect, what comparisons will help answer our questions, and what questions to ask and how.

● NOTES

1. Some of these experiments include the added feature of making assignments to treatment and control groups unknown and unknowable by the investigators as

well as study subjects, to eliminate any contamination of outcomes by the experimenter himself. These RCTs are called "double-blind" as a consequence.

2. For a state-by-state listing of academic and not-for-profit survey research organizations, see Bradburn, Sudman, and Wansink (2004, Appendix A).

3. Indeed, meta-analysis was developed about 20 years ago to systematically bring together multiple studies on the same question. This is a topic worthy of your attention but beyond the reach of this book. For those interested in exploring meta-analysis, consult Lipsey and Wilson (2001).

> No exercise here. One awaits the conclusion of the next chapter. Keep reading.

CHAPTER 3

MEASUREMENT

QUESTIONS AND CONSTRUCTS ●

You begin your research by asking what questions will help you or your client make more informed decisions and choices. No matter what the questions may be, however, you will have to decide what is of interest substantively. We often refer to these subjects of interest as "constructs" or "concepts." If you want to learn how better to reduce school violence in a public high school system, you need to be clear about what you mean by school violence. This isn't a simple matter. Are threats to be included? Is verbal abuse to be included or only physical harm? Do you include intent to harm or only efforts that succeed (e.g., a swing and a miss vs. a swing and a hit). This stage is referred to as designing "constructs."

Measuring them is the next stage. In other words, what questions will you ask to measure your constructs? How will you ask them and record the responses? And then, how will you check the data for data entry errors, perhaps looking for unusually large or small numbers, which are called **outliers**? The subject of how to ask questions will be addressed later in this chapter. We will provide tools for identifying outliers in Chapter 5 on descriptive statistics.

This chapter begins, however—as was recommended in the previous chapter on backward research designs—with where we want our measurements to end up: as valid and reliable indicators of the concepts we want to study. We turn later in this chapter to the techniques used, often in the context of small pilot studies or pretests, to increase the likelihood that our measures achieve the level of quality that makes us confident in the conclusions we draw from their analysis.

We will begin, however, with the techniques used for assessing the quality of measures already collected, often by someone else.

● RELIABILITY AND VALIDITY: THE BEDROCK OF QUALITY MEASURES

No Child Left Behind (NCLB) requires states to test students in public schools each year. These standardized tests are themselves required to produce indicators of how well students, schools, districts, and states are doing in helping students achieve proficiency in selected subjects such as mathematics and English. Some states have developed elaborate processes for trying to ensure that their tests are valid and reliable—the two bellwether terms for describing what any measure should be. But what do these terms mean, and how do we go about making sure that our measures are just that?

In many respects, the terms themselves are straightforward. A measure—whether the responses to a question on a telephone survey or a question on a standardized test—is said to be *reliable* if it generates *consistent* responses. If we test a fifth-grade student's mathematics proficiency with, say, the Texas Assessment of Knowledge and Skills (TAKS) today, will she score roughly the same on that test in a week (assuming that she hasn't participated in a crash study course during the intervening week)? A measure is said to be *valid* if it measures what it is *intended to measure*. Do the standardized tests spawned by NCLB really measure proficiency in mathematics or reading? Many argue that they may well measure how well or how poorly a student can take a test instead.

The **validity** and reliability of our measures are important for a number of reasons. Insofar as we fail to produce measures that are consistent and measure what we believe or want them to measure, we risk drawing incorrect conclusions when we analyze the data that they produce. If our measures are neither reliable nor valid, we may claim causal relations when none exist or fail to detect ones that do. We may conclude that things have changed (e.g., unemployment or inflation) when our measures are actually creating the appearance of change instead. We may fire high school principals for the failure of their schools' students to improve their understanding of mathematics, which is measured by instruments that assess something other than mathematical proficiency. Or we may hold back a student in the same grade for a year because of his performance on a test that didn't fully sample all the skills and knowledge that our curriculum expects him to learn. Improving the validity and reliability of many measures is indeed a high-stakes enterprise.

Unfortunately, these two concepts are challenging because they each take on a variety of meanings, are assessed in different ways, and are achieved through different measurement strategies and tactics.

Reliability

First, consider the various types of reliability. There are at least four types of a measure's consistency, which are defined by their consistency across or over one of four conditions:

- *Time:* This is called **test-retest reliability**. For example, we assess someone's skills today by using a particular test and then retest that same person, using the same or equivalent test, a week later to judge the reliability of the skills test. The length of time between the questions could be within the same survey (or test), within a day or two, or over much longer periods of time. The timing of the retest depends on whether the concept being measured is thought to change quickly over time. For example, the reliability of an attitude measure might be assessed over a relatively short period of time if changing contexts or events can alter that opinion easily. The reliability of personality traits might be assessed over longer periods of time if these characteristics are largely immutable to changing contexts and events. Test-retest reliability coefficients of .70 or above are marginally acceptable, but those above .80 are preferred (Salkind, 2006, p. 58). As we will see in a later chapter, correlations between measures with poor reliabilities will disguise (reduce) the estimate of their true relationship in the population from which we sample.

- *Items or questions in a survey or test:* This is called **internal reliability** and is easily confused with validity. Internal reliability—which we will see again when we learn how to use **Cronbach's alpha (α)** later in this book—is a measure of how well different items—say, in a questionnaire—"hang together." Insofar as they do, you can feel justified in combining the separate items into a single index or scale, an important type of data transformation to which we turn in Chapter 4.

- *Raters, coders, or evaluators:* This is called **interrater reliability**. This is an assessment of the extent to which, say, two coders who read the same person's response to an open-ended question agree that it falls in one of several response categories that the principal investigator and research assistants have agreed are legitimate responses to that question. Look for interrater reliability coefficients above .90 (Salkind, 2006, p. 58).

- *Forms:* This is called **parallel form reliability** and is used to assess the extent to which, say, two different tests or questionnaires measure the same thing.

Although validity and reliability are related, a reliable measure may not be a valid one. As Bob Schaeffer (cited in Strauss, 2007), director of public education at the National Center for Fair and Open Testing, stated,

If you got on a scale, and every time you got on, it said it was 237 pounds, it would be reliable, even if you weighed 120. You could rely on it to say 237 pounds. But it's not accurate or meaningful. (p. B2)

That is to say, it's not a valid measure of your weight.

Validity

Validity is a measure of the extent to which a measure actually measures what it is presumed to measure. For example, do questions about trust in government measure that concept, or do they provide an assessment of the current administration, confounded by respondents' partisanship? You guessed it, the latter (Bishop, 2004).

The validity of a measure also has different variants, each defined by the way in which we assess the extent to which a measure is more or less valid.

• *Criterion validity* is assessed through a measure's association or correlation with other things we know or believe it to be related to. This type of validity itself takes on two forms:

   o *Concurrent validity* is a measure of the extent to which your measure is correlated with, say, other items in the survey or questionnaire that you know or believe that it should be highly related to. Is your measure of personal income related to your measure of respondents' occupations, for example?

   o **Predictive validity** is a measure of the extent to which the responses predict what you presume such responses should predict. For example, do students' scores on the SAT (Scholastic Aptitude Test) as a senior predict grades in the first year of college? This apparently simple question is difficult to answer for a variety of reasons, but the generally accepted conclusion is that the SAT doesn't do a great job in predicting grades in the first year of college and declines in predictive ability as students move to higher grades (Bracey, 2006, p. 79).

• **Content validity** is achieved when a set of questions captures the full range of attributes thought to constitute what is being measured. A statistics test that only asks you to define the term **standard error** would hardly provide a valid measure of your statistical knowledge and skills.

• *Consensual validity* is established when some set of people agree that the measure is valid. Experts in question writing or subject matter may be the judges in such popularity contests.

- **Face validity** is the simplest, most folksy variety. That is to say, does the measure "on the face of it" make sense (one might say common sense)? "On what day and year were you born?" surely looks like a question that would produce a valid measure of one's age, as long as all respondents were using the Gregorian calendar to answer the question.

The Texas Department of Education, in seeking to produce valid test scores in TAKS, appointed advisory committees of educators at each grade and each subject on which students in Grades 3 to 11 are tested. These committees were joined by Department of Education staff and test development specialists to guide the development of the test instruments, including the review of results from field tests. Specific test items were drafted and tested with an eye toward what the statewide curricula were intended to teach and students were expected to learn. Educators across the state were provided opportunities to recommend changes to or the elimination of test questions.

In addition, scores from the 2004–2005 TAKS college readiness component were compared with two other sources: (1) a "contrasting group" of second semester college freshmen who took the same TAKS assessment and (2) correlations with scores on Texas Academic Skills Program, ACT (American College Test), and SAT I (Texas Education Agency, 2006, chap. 15, p. 144).

The technical report that describes efforts to ensure the validity of TAKS does not arrive at a firm conclusion about the tests' validity. The report, however, does note that Texas students judged to have "Met the Standard" in mathematics corresponded to a score of 20 on ACT, which 45% of a national study of 2002–2004 high school graduates achieved or exceeded. The corresponding figures for the comparison with the SAT I was 470 for mathematics, which 50% of the students in a national study of high school graduates achieved or exceeded. (Similar figures on English proficiency were reported as well, although they're not repeated here.) These percentages, however, are what this book will call "one-hand clapping" statistics. There's a key missing statistic (or hand): the percentage of students taking the TAKS college readiness component who were judged by the Texas Department of Education to have met or exceeded their standard. Was it between 45% and 50%? We're not told, although the *Time Magazine* report noted in Chapter 1 of this book ranked Texas in the middle of the pack of states in how closely state-run test results resemble the results of national tests such as the National Assessment of Educational Progress.

● THE ART AND SCIENCE OF ASKING QUESTIONS

Asking questions as part of a high-stakes standardized test is only one instance in which a question or response is being called for. No matter which research design (or combination) you select, it's very likely that you (or someone else) will have to ask people questions in order to collect the information you or your clients need. We all ask and answer questions all the time, so this shouldn't be difficult, right? Unfortunately, it's not as easy as it seems. Indeed, this chapter may make it appear to be a hopelessly difficult endeavor. Don't despair. It's not quite that bad. There are a number of challenges in asking (and answering) questions, however, that you should be aware of to construct better questions yourself and to evaluate others' questions.[1]

This section will also present some guidelines for detecting and correcting errors in this question-and-response process. The first (or last) such guideline, however, should be "Don't apply these guidelines blindly or mechanically. Use your judgment. One guideline will apply under one circumstance and not under another. The guidelines are not a cookbook."

With that caveat in mind, let's begin by thinking about the thinking process itself. Answering questions requires thinking, although some respondents may not be motivated or able to think very deeply before answering questions and may not think quite as elegantly or as linearly as the following discussion may imply.

Answering Questions Is a Cognitive Process

Asking and answering questions involves several cognitive processes:

1. *Encoding:* This is the process by which individuals move bits of information or experiences from short- to long-term memory, later to be called on by a question asked some time in the future. People can experience something without taking note of it, so not every experience is encoded. Asking respondents to report, say, what they ate last week may cause them to guess about what they probably ate because they took little note of what they ate. There's no "there there," you might say. (For one such study that showed the lack of correspondence between reports and detailed diary entries of eating, see Smith, 1991.)

2. *Comprehension:* The respondent listens to the question and interprets its meaning and intent, hopefully understanding the words in the question as intended by the person(s) who wrote the question. Meaning may be affected

not only from the question itself but from prior questions. In this latter regard, we will turn to the potential problem of "framing" in a subsequent section of this chapter.

3. *Retrieval:* The respondent may be required to recall information stored in her memory. The question may include retrieval cues (e.g., "Thinking about the past 6 months from [date] to today, . . ."). Clearly, some memories are easier to retrieve than others. Important, recent, and infrequent events, for example, are more likely to be recalled, although rich and specific retrieval cues and examples can help in this process.

4. *Judgment and estimation:* A question may require respondents to combine bits of information retrieved from memory or perform a mental calculation. It may be the case that you do not have an opinion about something until the very question asks you to report that opinion.

5. *Reporting:* Respondents formulate an answer and respond in their own words (as in answering an open-ended question that has no explicit possible responses) or select one or more of the alternative responses provided by the questioner (in what are called closed-ended questions). Responses to open-ended questions can be quite rich if the respondent is sufficiently motivated to take the time and energy to reply. They are also valuable when the questioner isn't confident that he knows the complete set of possible responses in advance and seeks to avoid the unfortunate (but not rare) situation of a large number of respondents selecting an "Other" response. Beware, however, that open-ended responses require one or more people to review all possible responses, develop numeric codes, and assign these codes to each response so that they may be subsequently analyzed (although increasingly sophisticated software is providing opportunities to reduce these costs). You will also want to assess the intercoder reliability of such classifications.

Some of these processes take time and energy on the part of respondents as well, which is not always forthcoming in an interview or when a respondent is completing a questionnaire. The difficulty of the task of answering questions may arise from the question or the mode of asking (e.g., Web vs. face-to-face). In such circumstances, respondents may engage in "satisficing" behavior (Krosnik, 1991; Simon, 1957), which has been shown to result in higher instances of "don't know" and item nonresponse and the selection of middle-response categories (Heerwegh & Loosveldt, 2008).

Questions (and their answers) are elicited in an incredibly diverse set of contexts. They can be gathered in a face-to-face encounter or by phone, mail, or computer. Questions can concern demographic characteristics of respondents (e.g., income, race, gender, age, nationality); attitudes, beliefs, feelings, and opinions; behavior, actions, and events; knowledge, aptitude, and skills; and more. Responses may be constrained to a yes/no reply, the selection of an offered set of optional responses, or open-ended.

The point here is that social scientists and survey methodologists have become increasingly aware of the complexity of the apparent simple process of asking and answering questions. They have also become increasingly aware of the many pitfalls of this process and look for a number of common and widely recognized mistakes in question and questionnaire construction that await the unwary.

Common Problems to Avoid

Misinterpretation

Who among us has misunderstood a question being asked of them? What's the most common source of such misunderstanding? It may very likely be the difference in meaning that you and your questioner attribute to one or more terms in the question itself. There's the classic example in Stanley Payne's 1951 book, *The Art of Asking Questions*, which describes a survey that sought to measure public opinion toward the regulation of corporate profits. The survey asked people across the country about their opinions on this topic. The researchers discovered during their analysis, however, that Southern black women reported an unexpected distaste for the regulation of profits. To better understand this result, interviewers were asked to return to the field and ask respondents the same question, but then to follow with the question, "And why is that?" They quickly discovered that many respondents thought that they were being asked about their attitudes toward regulating "prophets," not "profits." Being the good Southern Baptists that many of these women were, they quickly and emphatically replied that it was no business of government to mess with prophets like Abraham, Esther, Isaac, or Sarah.

Consider a mundane question that the National Center for Health Statistics might be interested in asking a sample of the American public (this example is taken from www.cdc.gov/nchs/ppt/duc2006/qbank_10.ppt): "In the last year, have you been bothered by pain in the abdomen?"

This seemingly simple question is pregnant with potential misunderstanding. What, for example, do people think of as their abdomen? There are at least two ways to resolve this possible source of misunderstanding. The first is to follow the question with another (e.g., "What, to you, is your abdomen?"), aided by a diagram of the upper torso as below:

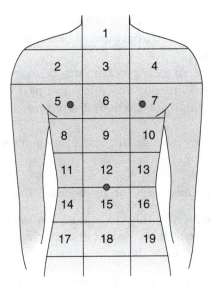

This solution, however, requires time-consuming and costly analysis. The other solution is to impose your own concept of the abdomen on the respondent by providing a picture of what you believe to be the region of the upper torso that you would define as the abdomen, as below:

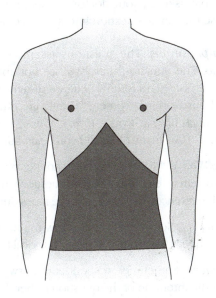

Of course, this might clear up only one of several sources of misunderstanding or lack of comprehension. What, for example, does "bothered" mean? Is it a minor ailment or the most excruciating pain a respondent has ever experienced? And what period of time is "last year"? Is it the prior 12 months working backward from the date of the interview? Or is it the last complete calendar year?

A possible solution to these problems may be to rewrite the question as follows: "In the past 12 months, have you had pain in the abdomen? By abdomen, we mean the shaded area in this picture [show respondent the above picture]."

What are the many possible sources of misinterpretation? Here's a list (Groves et al., 2004, p. 211):

- *Grammatical ambiguity:* This has been illustrated above.

- *Excessive complexity:* This can lead respondents to ignore or fail to recognize parts of the question. Fowler (1992) discusses the following question, asked in a study of methods for pretesting questions:

  > During the past 12 months, since January 1, 1987, how many times have you seen or talked to a doctor or assistant about your health? Do not count any time you might have seen a doctor while you were a patient in a hospital, but count all other times you actually saw or talked to a medical doctor of any kind. (p. 221)

Fowler concluded that asking about doctor's visits proved so complicated that he had to revise this single question into a series of four questions.

- *Faulty presuppositions:* The questions assume something that may not actually be true. The question thereby does not apply to the respondent or make sense to her. The following agree/disagree question harbors a presupposition about working women: "Family life often suffers because women spend too much time at work." Here's a more famous example of a faulty presupposition: "How many times did you beat your spouse last week?"

- *Vague terms:* What is "often" to you may not be "often" to me. It is possible to avoid this problem by embedding in the question what you believe to be "often" by an explicit reference—say, "five or more times during the past year."

- *Unfamiliar terms:* Not everyone will know the meaning of *rhetorical* in the agree/disagree question: "Statistics are a rhetorical tool for persuasion."

- *False inferences:* Sometimes respondents answer questions about what they believe is the intention of the question rather than its actual meaning. About a third of the American public answered "No" to the National Opinion Research Center's General Social Survey question "Are there any situations you can imagine in which you approve of a policeman striking an adult citizen?" The "No" respondents either have terribly weak imaginations or believed that they were answering a question about police violence.

- *Double-barreled questions:* These questions ask about two objects at once. Responses to the agree/disagree statement "Statistics is often boring and difficult to understand" cannot disentangle *boring* from *difficult*. (I threw in the vague term *often* for good measure.)

Memory Decay

Surveys are forever asking people to tell us about their past. These retrospective or memory-based questions provide an indispensable window to personal and collective experiences. Employment surveys, for example, ask respondents who are not employed to report whether they looked for work during the past 4 weeks in order to differentiate the unemployed from those officially designated as "not in the labor force." Respondents in crime surveys are asked whether they were robbed within the past 6 months. Health surveys ask people about the number of visits to the doctor's office during the past 12 months. And so on. Unfortunately for the questioner, people remember their pasts imperfectly. Indeed, there's considerable evidence to suggest that respondents *create* memories to conform to what they believe "must have" or "should have" happened in the past.

In general, there are four types of problems that affect our memories:

1. *Different encoding:* This problem arises when the terms we use in a question are not the same terms used to encode the event when it happened. For example, do we encode trips to the hardware store as "shopping"? If an investigator considers them shopping and asks you how many times you went shopping last week, you may report none because you don't think of, nor therefore remember, trips to the hardware store as "shopping." The solution to this problem is to incorporate such items into the question itself, at the potential price of increasing the question's complexity. As Groves et al. (2004) suggest, you may phrase such a question as follows: "On average, during the last 6 months, that is, since _____, how often have you gone shopping? For example, at drug, clothing, grocery, hardware and convenience stores" (p. 213).

2. *Embellishments to memory:* Your memory of a past event may unwittingly be augmented by additional information that you acquire after the event. Recollections of a high school graduation, for example, can be augmented by later perusal of the yearbook or photographs of the event.

3. *Retrieval failure:* The use of terms other than those in which the original event was encoded in memory, as above, is one source of retrieval failure. The passage of time itself can cause events to be lumped together or the time at which they occurred to be moved forward in time, a phenomenon referred to as "telescoping." And indeed, people "forget," although some cognitive psychologists suggest that the memories still exist but require stronger retrieval cues to bring forward into short-term memory for the purposes of answering a question. Figure 3.1 depicts the memory decay for several types of personal information (Tourangeau, Rips, & Rasinski, 2000). The solution to such problems is, first, to avoid the use of retrospective questions when possible. When not possible, provide

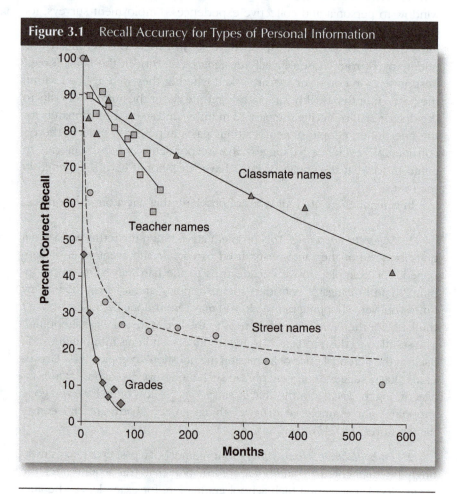

Figure 3.1 Recall Accuracy for Types of Personal Information

SOURCE: Groves et al. (2004, Figure 7.2). Used by permission. Copyright John Wiley & Sons.

"rich, relevant cues and give the respondent time and encouragement to think carefully" (Groves et al., 2004, p. 216).

4. *Theories about self and change:* Reconstructions of the past can be based on current states and "theories" about personal change or stability. Memory is often a construction in which images of the past and present are combined with inferences drawn from implicit theory about ourselves and society. Such processes can either exaggerate the consistency between the present and past or exaggerate the differences (Pearson, Ross, & Dawes, 1992).

In a study that examined an exaggeration of differences between past and present, for example, Conway and Ross (1984) studied students who wished to participate in a study skills improvement program. The first meeting of these students evaluated current study skills and then randomly assigned students either to the skills program or to a waiting list control group. After the program participants had attended three weekly skills sessions, they and the waiting-list subjects returned for a final meeting. Subjects were asked to evaluate their current study skills, recall their initial evaluation of their skills, and predict their grades at the end of the semester, which the researchers ultimately obtained.

At the second interview, the participants in the study skills improvement program recalled their original evaluations of their study skills as being worse than they had reported originally. As one such student may have reasoned, "Well, I took a study skills improvement program so I must have improved from what my current skills are." The respondents tended to evaluate current skills relatively accurately, so they had to remember their initial skills as worse than their current ones to produce the improvement in study skills that they reasoned must have taken place. In contrast, waiting-list subjects exhibited no systematic bias in recall.

In short, the program participants belittled their prior study skills, whereas waiting-list subjects did not. Although the program participants expected to achieve much higher grades than the control subjects, academic grades were not affected by the program. Interestingly, this did not prevent the program participants from subsequently recalling their performance as superior. When contacted 6 months later, the program participants thought they had better grades in their major than they had actually obtained. In contrast, waiting-list subjects did not exhibit a systematic bias in recall of their grades. This type of program evaluation is commonplace and, as we will see elsewhere in this text, subject to the same biases and distortions revealed in this experiment.

Surveys employ a variety of techniques for reducing the errors and biases associated with retrospective questions. They often try to make access to the event or attribute being recalled more directly by

- emphasizing to respondents through instruction and reinforcement the importance and need for accurate and precise answers;
- reinstating the context of the event or attribute being recalled;
- using "aided recall" methods, in which respondents are provided with lists related to the event being recalled and then asked to recognize them, as compared with the more difficult task of recalling them;
- keeping the reference period short (e.g., less than 6 months); and
- using landmark events as memory anchors (e.g., an earthquake, a holiday).

In panel studies (i.e., repeated interviews of the same respondents), one can "bound" the recall period by making explicit references to periods and information provided in previous interviews. Finally, survey researchers ask respondents to date events—if such dating is required—only after other questions about the events have provided contextual information to assist recall.

Judgment, Estimation, and Framing Effects

Many questions ask respondents to make judgments. How good a job is President Obama doing? Do you believe it was a mistake to invade Iraq? Some people carry firm beliefs or judgments about such matters and may be immune to different question wording or judgment requests. But those who don't can be strongly influenced by the particular wording of a question in formulating their judgment.

Elizabeth Loftus shows, for example, that judgments about the speed of a car viewed on a videotape will vary depending on whether a question about the tape asked how fast Car A was traveling when it "hit" Car B or how fast Car A was traveling when it "smashed into" Car B (Loftus & Palmer, 1974). Those who were asked about the "hit" provided substantially lower estimates of the speed of Car A than those who were asked the more dramatic "smashed into" version of the question.

You can also affect responses by altering the order in which items in a long list of responses are presented to the respondent, thus suggesting that respondents be randomly assigned questions that differ in the order of their responses. "Primacy effects" increase the chances that respondents will select the first item in a list. "Recency effects" increase the likelihood of selecting the last item in a list. Respondents to phone interviews are more likely the victims of recency effects. Respondents to mail questionnaires are more likely to succumb to primacy effects. In other words, try to have your named placed first on the ballot when running for election. It helps (Miller & Krosnick, 1998).

Finally, context matters because many judgments are made on the basis of comparison. Is the evaluation of President Obama's performance in office, for example, based on comparisons with President Clinton or President Bush?

Social Desirability Effects

Social desirability bias arises from the human desire to be seen, even by an interviewer, in a favorable light. This tendency results in people underreporting behaviors that are considered "bad" by society (e.g., illegal drug use) and overreporting behaviors that are considered socially desirable (e.g., voting).

Such effects may be subtle. For example, ask a mother whether she's satisfied with the quality of her child's day care. Such a question may be interpreted as asking how good a mother she is instead of the quality of child care. Why? What would an unfavorable response about your child's care say about you? What kind of a mother are you if your child is receiving poor care but you do nothing about it?

One possible solution to this bias is to ask sensitive questions via a self-administered medium rather than face-to-face (Tourangeau & Smith, 1996). Turner, Lessler, and Devore (1992), for example, found respondents 2.5 times more likely to report cocaine use in the past month when the questions were self-administered than when asked by an interviewer. Another solution is to ask questions about sensitive matters over a longer period of time than, say, the past month. This result is illustrated in the similarity of responses to the use of marijuana and cocaine during one's lifetime between self-administered and interviewer-administered questionnaires, as displayed in Figure 3.2 (Groves et al., 2004, p. 158).

A technique used to try to minimize overreporting of "good behaviors" such as voting in presidential elections is the attempt to use "forgiving" wording. Here's an example from the University of Michigan's National Election Survey:

> In talking to people about elections, we often find that a lot of people were not able to vote because they were not registered, they were sick, or they just didn't have the time. How about you—did you vote in the elections this November?

Unfortunately, studies indicate that this forgiving wording does not eliminate overreporting of voting (Groves et al., 2004, p. 225).

Guidelines for Writing Good Questions

Sudman and Bradburn (1982)—as modified by Groves et al. (2004, pp. 227–236)—offer guidelines for writing good questions, depending in part on whether the question asks about behaviors or attitudes and whether the question might be considered sensitive or not.

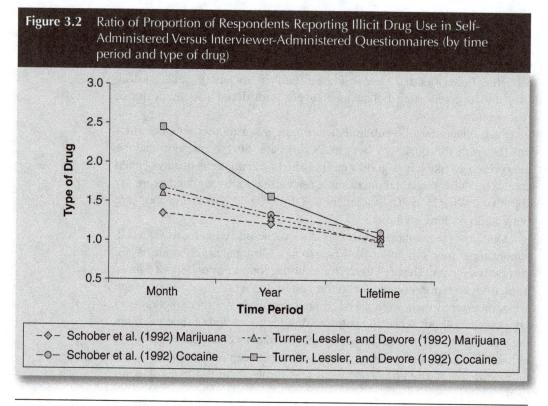

Figure 3.2 Ratio of Proportion of Respondents Reporting Illicit Drug Use in Self-Administered Versus Interviewer-Administered Questionnaires (by time period and type of drug)

SOURCE: Groves et al. (2004, Figure 5.4). Used by permission. Copyright John Wiley & Sons.

Some of these guidelines concern question wording. Others seek to reduce the impact of forgetting or memory decay.

● Include all reasonable response options in closed-ended questions. Respondents are reluctant to provide answers not offered to them.

● Make the questions as specific as possible, thereby reducing differences in interpretation.

● Make sure the object of your question is clearly understood. It is difficult to know what respondents' attitudes toward an object such as "enhanced interrogation methods" are unless the meaning of this is clear.

● Use words that nearly all respondents will understand. Similarly, use everyday terms instead of technical ones (e.g., "heart attacks" rather than "myocardial infarction"). Use explicit frequencies such as "every day" or "three or more times in the past week" instead of vague quantifiers such as "often."

● Avoid double-barreled questions, which ask about two matters at once. They are impossible to disentangle.

- Measure the strength of an attitude, the frequency of a behavior. If necessary, use separate items for this purpose. Typically, questions measure the strength of the attitude by asking whether respondents "strongly agree," "agree," "disagree," or "disagree strongly."

- Use opposite ends of an attitude in the question—for example, "Should the federal government provide health insurance to every citizen or should everyone be responsible for his or her own coverage?" Such bipolar choices discourage respondents from being too agreeable with the questioner.

- Consider whether to include "neither agree nor disagree," "no opinion," "haven't thought much about it," "couldn't vote," or "don't have enough information" alternatives in an attitude question. If you want to move people who are leaning one way or another on an item and who have an attitude, consider excluding these response categories (or following the question with another concerning which way the respondent is leaning). If you want to minimize the number of responses that may be uninformed, meaningless, or "nonattitudes," provide such options. Note, however, that many people who select the offered "no opinion" option do so because of poor motivation, interest, or fatigue. They actually may have the opinion that you seek to measure (Krosnik et al., 2002).

- In measuring change over time, ask the same question each time. Even minor changes in wording can change the meaning of a question. Changing the question will make it impossible to know whether attitudes or behaviors changed or were an artifact of the wording change.

- Ask general questions about a topic before more specific ones.

- Add memory cues and lengthen questions to improve recall. This guideline was illustrated above by listing the types of stores where someone might shop.

- Have respondents keep a diary when the events of interest are frequent but not very involving, such as the types of food eaten last week. Beware, however, that this can place a considerable burden on respondents and produce lower response rates.

- Use a life event calendar to improve reporting about long recall periods. Such a calendar identifies important events in a respondent's life, such as the dates of marriage, birth of a child, moving residence, and the beginning of a new job.

- Use bounded recall (e.g., reminding respondents what they had reported in a previous wave of a panel study) to reduce telescoping errors (i.e., remembering events as happening more recently than they did). Or ask respondents to consult household records (e.g., checkbook, payment receipts). Or do both.

- Consider whether proxies might be able to provide accurate information (e.g., asking parents to provide information about their young children) in order to lower research costs.

- Use long rather than short questions when asking retrospective questions. Longer questions may provide more retrieval cues and give the respondent more time to remember.

- Use open-ended rather than closed-ended questions to measure the frequency of sensitive behaviors. Closed ranges may convey to the respondent a false impression about the actual distribution of these behaviors in the population, which may encourage respondents to base their own reply on where they believe they lie on that distribution (e.g., more or less than average).

- Deliberately load a question that may be about sensitive behavior or induce social desirability effects, which the question above on voting illustrated as a "reasons-for-doing-it approach." There are several additional forms of this tactic (Groves et al., 2004, pp. 231–232):

  o "Everybody does it" (e.g., "Even the calmest parents get mad at their children sometimes. Did your children do anything during the past week to make you angry?")

  o "Assume the behavior" (e.g., "How many times during the past week did your children do something that made you angry?")

  o "Authorities recommend it" (e.g., "Many psychologists believe that it is important for parents to express their pent-up feelings. Did your children do anything in the past week to make you angry?")

- Ask about sensitive matters over long periods (such as one's entire lifetime) or periods from the distant past first. This guideline is illustrated above in the relatively similar rates of self-reported cocaine and marijuana use when asked about use over one's lifetime.

- Embed a sensitive question among other such items to make it stand out less. This tactic may make some behaviors appear less harmful by comparison.

- Use a self-administered format for sensitive questions or a random-response technique in which it is clear to the respondent that the interviewer does not know which of, say, two questions (one sensitive and one not) is being asked.[2]

- Collect validation data if possible (e.g., a urinalysis to verify responses about recent drug use).

- When asking multiple questions about a topic, start with the least popular one. Unpopular items are likely to seem even more so if followed by more favorable ones.

- Use 5- to 7-point response scales for attitude measures, and label points on that scale. Too few options lower the amount of information contained in responses. Too many options make it difficult for respondents to answer. Labels help respondents interpret the meaning of the responses similarly.

- Use analog devices (e.g., a thermometer) to collect detailed scale information.

- Ask respondents to rank items only if they can see all the alternatives. Otherwise, use paired comparisons.

- Ask for ratings of every item of interest. Do not use the "Check all that apply" response option.

I would also recommend that you consult previous surveys for the exact wording of questions. It would be especially useful if you can find questions that have undergone tests for reliability and validity. Ideally, the responses to these questions are also available, thus creating a readymade set of comparisons with your own results, depending, of course, on the sample or population from which the information was collected. (For a current effort to document such questions, see the National Center for Health Statistics' Q-Bank Tested-Question Database at www.cdc.gov/QBANK/QDRL.aspx.)

Guidelines for Questionnaire Design

There are three sets of people whose needs can be met through careful attention to the format of a questionnaire. They are (in declining order of priority) (1) respondents, (2) interviewers, and (3) data-processing staff (Bradburn, Sudman, & Wansink, 2004, chap. 10). Consider the following formatting characteristics of a questionnaire:

- *Font type and size:* Don't force eyestrain. Twelve-point fonts work well in most circumstances. Distinguish any interviewer instructions—placed in the questionnaire where they will be used—in a different font from the questions themselves.

- *Number questions:* This helps in following skip patterns (If "No," skip to Question 5."). It may also give interviewers a sense of progression through the questionnaire.

- *Precode closed-ended questions by assigning a number to every possible answer:* Include numeric codes for "don't know" or "no answer" if such possible responses are offered to the respondent, although do not provide these options on self-administered questionnaires. Give higher numeric codes to the response category that has the higher implicit value. It can be confusing to the data analyst to have the response of "High" designated as "1" and "Low" designated as "3."

Questionnaires take so many forms that it is difficult to offer anything but the most general guidelines for their overall structure or architecture. But these rules do appear to apply in most instances and parallel those found in nonsurvey settings such as focus groups.

- After explaining the purpose of the study, its auspices, and the approximate length of time it will take to answer the questions, begin with general, relatively easy questions that are clearly related to the purposes you've just described.

- Move from broad to narrow or more specific questions (called "funneling").

- Group similar content and format as groups or blocks of questions.

- Measure important concepts in multiple ways.

- End with personal characteristics (e.g., age, race, income). Don't begin with these questions because they can appear to the respondent as unrelated to the purposes of the survey and invasive, raising suspicions as to your true motives.

Ensuring Quality Questions: Tools for Spotting Problem Questions During Pilot Studies or Pretests

Suppose that you fully understand the cognitive processes underlying the asking and answering of questions, the common pitfalls in question construction, and the corresponding guidelines for assessing the validity and reliability of measures after they are collected. It is still the case that the questions you write may not "work." They may, for example, generate confusion on the part of interviewer or respondent. They may provide answers that mean entirely different things to different respondents. In other words, they may be inconsistent (i.e., not reliable) and may not measure what you think they measure (i.e., not valid). How can you seek to reduce such measurement problems in advance of fielding the study itself? The simplest answer is a single word: pretest.[3] But nothing, of course, is ever quite so simple.

In general, pretests (or pilot studies) involve the administration of the questions and/or questionnaire to some relatively small group of respondents who resemble the types of respondents to whom you will eventually administer your final questionnaire. The challenge is to conduct these pretests in ways that uncover difficulties with respect to specific items or the questionnaire itself. Fortunately, survey methodologists, psychometricians, and others have invented a number of tools to help in this task. Some date back as far as the founding of modern survey research in the 1930s. They are as follows:

- Interviewer debriefing
- Behavior coding
- Cognitive interviews
- Vignettes
- Response latencies
- Respondent debriefing
- Expert reviews
- Appraisal coding

Interviewer Debriefing

This technique is probably the earliest and most conventional form of pretesting. Experienced or "sensitive" interviewers are trained in the administration of a questionnaire, complete a handful of interviews, and then relate their experiences to the survey developers (Sudman & Bradburn, 1982, p. 49). What questions appeared difficult to answer? What skip patterns were difficult to follow? Which questions did the respondents ask for clarification or refuse to answer or say they "didn't know"? These problems are often revealed quickly in such pretests, which may have caused early practitioners to believe that it was sufficient to interview as few as a dozen pretest respondents in order to identify all the problem questions (Sheatsley, 1983, p. 226).

Stanley Presser and colleagues (Presser, Couper, et al., 2004; Presser, Rothgeb, et al., 2004), however, aren't convinced that these techniques are sufficient to uncover problems in question design. Such techniques don't actually ask the respondents about any difficulty they may have had in answering the questions. And respondents may themselves be unaware of a problem if a question made perfect sense to them, but in a different sense than was intended by the question writer. In short, interviewer debriefing is more likely to reveal the problems that interviewers experience than the problems faced by respondents. Of course, these are important problems to identify. You'll have to use additional techniques to identify a fuller set of difficulties in question construction, however.

Behavior Coding

Behavior coding can be used to evaluate both interviewer and question problems. As Presser, Couper, et al. (2004) write,

> Behavior coding involves monitoring or reviewing taped interviews (or transcripts) for a subset of the interviewer's and respondent's verbal behavior in the question asking and answering interaction. Questions marked by high frequencies of certain behaviors (e.g., the interviewer did not read the question verbatim or the respondent requested clarification) are seen as needing repair. (p. 116)

There are three elements of the behavior that can be examined for possible problems in the question: (1) Was the question read correctly by the interviewer? (2) Did the respondent choose one of the offered responses? (3) Did the interviewer code or record the answer correctly?

Cognitive Interviews

Cognitive interviews are intended to reveal the thought processes by which respondents interpret questions and arrive at answers. Cognitive interviews take one or both of two forms:

1. "Thinking-out-loud" protocols ask the respondent to verbalize her or his thought processes in answering a question. The interviewer may be instructed to ask, for example, "Tell me what you were thinking when you answered that question." Or pretest respondents may be invited early in the interview to report any thoughts or response strategies that they were aware of in answering any questions.

2. "Probes" involve more direct questions, such as "Can you tell me in your own words what that question was asking?" or "What does [a term] mean to you?"

Vignettes

Vignettes are hypothetical stories or situations that respondents are asked to evaluate. Their purpose is to explore how people think about concepts and to test how closely their meaning corresponds to the intended meaning.

Martin and Polivka (1995), for example, used vignettes to evaluate the meaning of "work" for respondents to the Current Population Survey, which provides national estimates of unemployment rates. Prior to 1994, the question used to determine a respondent's work status was "What were you doing most of last week—working, keeping house, going to school, or something else?" and, if the respondent was not working, "Did you do any work at all last week, not counting work around the house?" The second question was intended to catch people who thought that a few hours of paid work didn't constitute "work," although it certainly did to the Bureau of Labor Statistics (BLS), which is responsible for the survey.

Seven vignettes used in the study described different work situations and then asked respondents whether they considered these situations "work." An example of a vignette (and the percentage of respondents who answered "Yes," which BLS considers the correct answer) follows: Bill attended his college classes and got paid to tend bar for a fraternity party one night last week. Would you report him as working last week, not counting work around the house? (78%)

Response Latencies

This concept is a fancy way of asking, "How quickly did the respondent answer the question?" Such metrics are easy to collect when the questionnaire is administered via a computer or phone. The technique presumes that the length of time it takes to answer a question may be a consequence of several factors: uncertainty, inaccessibility, the weakness of one's attitude, the perceived lack of importance, and the degree of conflict with perceived majority opinions (Bassili, 2003). One study by Draisma and Dijkstra (2004) showed response latency and expressions of uncertainty to be associated with inaccurate responses. The length of time it takes to answer a question may also be an indication that the respondent is giving some thought to it, which could be a product of following some of the guidelines above about coaching respondents to answer questions carefully and thoughtfully.

Respondent Debriefing

Similar in some respects to cognitive interviews, respondent debriefings are typically unstructured and improvised questions asked by interviewers. They also explicitly enlist the help of the respondent in identifying problems in questions.

Expert Reviews

Having experts—both substantive and methodological ones—evaluate questions and questionnaires prior to administration is a variant of pretesting that is akin to the consensual validity that we discussed in the case of TAKS earlier in this chapter. The advantages of such reviews are clear. Such people bring a wealth of knowledge—both explicit and tacit—about the content of questions and the problems in, say, comprehension or judgment to which every question may fall victim. This form of pretesting may also be less expensive than conducting a pretest in the field.

Appraisal Coding

Appraisal coding entails one or more persons explicitly reviewing questions to identify features likely to affect comprehension, recall, judgment, and response accuracy. Such coders often use a checklist of concerns in evaluating questions. The process resembles the one in which we engaged in considering the problems with the question about pain in the abdomen. For example, were there any words that may cause problems of comprehension? (How about *abdomen, bothered by*, and *last year*?) Table 3.1 is an example of the type of checklist that can be used to evaluate questions (Forsyth, Rothgeb, & Willis, 2004, p. 530). (See Lessler & Forsyth, 1996, for a more detailed discussion of this technique.)

Unfortunately, Adequate Pretesting Doesn't Always Lead to Better Questions

This is quite an assortment of tools for evaluating questions. Unfortunately, we know little about which is best to use under which mode of administration (e.g., face-to-face, phone, computer assisted) or which cognitive process (e.g., comprehension or retrieval). More unsettling, however,

Table 3.1 Problem Classification Coding Scheme (CCS)

Comprehension and communication

Interviewer difficulties
    Inaccurate instructions
    Complicated instruction
    Difficult to administer

Question content
    Vague topic/item
    Complex topic
    Topic carried over from earlier question
    Undefined term(s)

Question structure
    Transition needed
    Unclear respondent instruction
    Question too long
    Complex, awkward syntax
    Erroneous assumption
    Several questions

Reference period
    Carried over from earlier question
    Undefined
    Unanchored or rolling

Memory retrieval

Shortage of cues
High detail required or information unavailable
Long recall period

Judgment and evaluation

Complex estimation
Potential sensitivity or desirability bias

(Continued)

Table 3.1 (Continued)
Response selection

Response terminology
  Undefined term(s)
  Vague term(s)

Response units
  Responses use wrong units
  Unclear what response options are

Response structure
  Overlapping categories
  Missing categories

Other

SOURCE: Presser, Rothgeb, et al. (2004, Table 25.1). Used by permission. Copyright John Wiley & Sons.

are the results of a study that explicitly addressed the question of whether pretesting leads to better measures.

Forsyth et al. (2004, cited in Presser, Rothgeb, et al., 2004) in Phase 1 of their study used three of these tools to identify question problems and to improve the quality of survey responses to 83 questionnaire items from three federal surveys. The tools were (1) expert review, (2) appraisal coding, and (3) cognitive interviews. Phase 2 of their study compared the results of responses with questions changed ("repaired") as a consequence of these pretesting techniques with "unrepaired" questions, each set asked of half of a random digit dial telephone survey.

Phase 1 identified 12 questions as being extremely problematic. Here's one:

Is local bus service available in your town or city? (Include only services that are available for use by the general public for local or commuter travel, including dial-a-bus and senior citizen bus service. Do not include long-distance buses or those chartered for specific trips.)

Revisions to the 12 problem-prone questions resulted in 26 new questions. The "quality" of the old versus new questions was based on three measures:

(1) item nonresponse and "Don't know" rates, (2) behavior coding results from an analysis of 98 audiotapes of the 1,862 completed interviews, and (3) interviewer ratings that came from interviewer debriefings after the administration of the "repaired" and "unrepaired" versions of the questionnaire.

The study drew several conclusions. First, the pretesting techniques consistently identified (predicted) the questions that were shown later in the Phase 2 surveys to be problematic (although more so for the respondents than for the interviewers). For example, if the pretest identified a question as highly problematic, 43% of the subsequent behavior-coded interviews identified one or more problems with those questions, in contrast to only 11% of the questions that the pretest judged to be unproblematic.

Second, the quality of the revised questions was not much better than that of the original questions. Item nonresponse rates declined for the new questions, but the differences were small (4.7% for new vs. 5.9% for old questions). Although not significantly different, the interviewers had slightly fewer problems with the old questions (6.9% for new vs. 4.4% for old), as did the respondents (25.9% for new vs. 23.6% for old), based on behavior coding. Interviewer debriefings gave the (statistically significant) edge to the old versions of questions in terms of the problems they had (24.8% vs. 11.0%), although the interviewers thought that the respondents had more trouble with the old version (45.3% vs. 55.3%).

The sobering conclusion of this study is that "we have better tools for diagnosing questionnaire problems than for fixing them" (Presser, Couper, et al., 2004, p. 124).

Although some solutions may introduce new problems, it is not always clear just how "bad" the problems are that pretests uncover. Floyd Fowler's previously cited work (1992) tested 60 questions then being used in health surveys in the United States. Phone interviews with 110 people were tape-recorded, and each question/response was then coded for whether respondents asked for clarification or provided an inadequate answer. When either of these behaviors occurred in at least 15% of the interviews, the question was considered problematic. Only 7 of the 60 items they tested were considered troublesome by these criteria. Not bad.

The Martin and Polivka (1995) study of work built on research in 1988 (Campanelli, Martin, & Creighton, 1989) that had demonstrated that the conventional question about whether respondents had worked in the previous week (noted above) led to

1. underreporting of activities related to setting up a business or working on a business at home, neither of which were for pay (BLS considers this "work" even though not paid);

2. underreporting of casual, although paid, labor for a few hours; and
3. overreporting of volunteer work.

Some examples of the vignettes used to evaluate these conditions follow:

Last week, Amy spent 20 hours at home doing the accounting for her husband's business. She did not receive a paycheck. Do you think she should be reporting as WORKING last week? (Only 50% of respondents considered this "work." BLS does.)

Sam spent 20 hours last week painting a friend's house and was given $20. (64% considered this "work." BLS does.)

Last week, Susan put in 20 hours of volunteer service at a local hospital. (38% considered this "work." BLS doesn't.)

The later work by Martin and Polivka (1995) compared the responses to vignettes using the conventional questions about work with those using revised questions. The newer version dropped the initial question, "What were you doing most of last week—working, going to school, keeping house, or something else?" New questions were added to pick up unpaid work in a home-based business or farm (which BLS considers work). And a new question was written to emphasize the importance of paid work, no matter how poorly paid or how few hours were worked: "Last week, did you do ANY work for (either) pay (or profit)?" Obviously, the question also defines work as related to pay or profit, even though BLS considers some nonpaid activities work.

Indeed, this latter change in the question resulted in fewer respondents considering Amy's nonpaid work for her husband at home as work (29% considered this "work" in response to the new question, "Would you report her as working for pay [or profit] last week?", in comparison with 46% of those who were asked the older, conventional questions). Similarly, substantially fewer thought of the following as work (61% for the new questions vs. 89% for the conventional ones): "Cathy works as a real estate agent for commissions. Last week she showed houses but didn't sign any contracts."

The new question did a better job of capturing the BLS meaning of work for four of the seven types of activities that were asked about. For example, Bill's bartending at the fraternity was considered work by 85% of the new-question respondents (vs. 78% who were asked the conventional questions).

These figures appear to represent large measurement errors irrespective of whether old or revised questions were used. There are two subtle but missing pieces of information about these figures, however. First, the vignettes were presented to all respondents, not just to those individuals who, say, worked 20 hours at home for their husbands without pay. These people might surely consider this "work." Second, just how many people in the United States actually spent 20 hours of unpaid accounting work for their husbands in the previous week? If the numbers of such people are tiny, the overall underreporting in the estimates of work will similarly be small, even if people tend not to share the same definition of what constitutes work with the BLS. Finally, it can be said that it's very difficult to write questions for a concept as befuddled as BLS appears to consider as work. Is it paid work? Well, not necessarily. The problem here lies perhaps as much with the concept as with the measures of it.

Your choice of diagnostic tools will, of course, be constrained by time and money. It is nonetheless important to know that these tools exist in order to select those that your judgment suggests are most appropriate and that your resources permit. It's also important to know whether other research you're evaluating uses them to help (but never guarantee that) the questions being asked and answered produce valid and reliable measures.

Levels of Measurement

We turn in the concluding section of this chapter to a set of measurement terms that will help you determine which statistical tool to turn to later in this book: levels of measurement. By measurement we mean here the assignment of a numeric value or label to a variable or outcome for each respondent, subject, or unit in your study. We may, for example, ask a respondent in a phone survey whether he agrees or disagrees (strongly or not) that the last contact he had with a county employee was conducted in a timely, respectful, or error-free manner.

Responses to these three questions by, say, a sample of adults in a particular county would create three variables. Some people will respond, "Agree" (which we might represent in an Excel spreadsheet as the number "3"), while others will respond, "Disagree strongly" (e.g., to which we might assign the number "1"). In this particular case, the variable by which we measure how respectful the county employee was to the respondent could take on values of 1, 2, 3, or 4.

There are four levels of measurement (although we'll collapse the final two into a single level for most of this book):

Nominal or categorical

Ordinal

Interval ⎫
⎬ Continuous
Ratio ⎭

Each level of measurement carries with it more or less information and acts more or less like an actual number in contrast to a quality to which we may assign a number in name only.

Nominal

Indeed, that's the first level of measurement: the nominal. We assign numbers to such response "in name only." Such measures or variables define the quality of some attribute. Let us say we are interested in understanding the possible influence of the region of the country in which one lives on, say, attitudes toward the regulation of hand guns. Region (a variable in our study that is assigned to each respondent) could have four values: Northeast, South, Midwest, and West. For ease of analysis, we may assign numeric values to each category such that respondents living in the Northeast are assigned a code or value of "4," people in the South, "3," and so on.

Think of each region as a bucket or bin into which we can sort and count respondents—first, to determine how many (or what proportion of our total sample) live in each region and, later, to test whether people in different regions tend, on average, to have different attitudes toward matters such as gun control.

Four Buckets

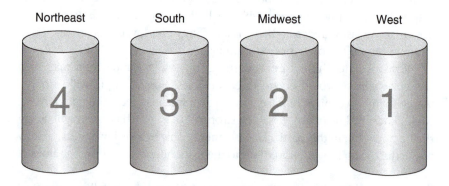

Northeast   South   Midwest   West

4   3   2   1

Note that respondents can be placed in one and only one category (bin). More important, the numbers to which we assign different categories do not, in the case of a **nominal variable** such as region, confer the qualities of numbers to them. Living in the Northeast is not somehow 33% more than living in the South. Living in the Northeast is not three more units than living in the West. It just doesn't make sense. The number here is simply a placeholder that gives comfort to statistical programs and heartache to many novice students of statistics. Stick with it. The importance of the levels of measurement will become clearer as we march through the book and its exercises. Suffice it here to illustrate this latter assertion by asking whether it makes sense to compute a mean score for region. It doesn't. Mode—the category with the most observations (e.g., people in this case)—would be quite appropriate, however. (You'll later learn which of these levels of measurement more sophisticated statistics require or assume in the variables being analyzed.)

Ordinal

The second level of measurement is the ordinal level. As suggested by its name, categories of such variables have an identifiable order of a more-or-less quality. But the distances between these categories are not necessarily numerically equal. We can agree that having a master's degree is "higher" or "more" education than having only a college degree, which is more than a high school degree alone, and so on. We may well assign a higher numeric code to a master's degree (say, "5"); a "4" to college graduates, a "3" to a respondent with some college, and so on. But the numeric distance between adjacent education levels is not really one, is it?

Likert scales are the most common of such measures for attitudes, especially as related to attitudes or opinions about levels or degrees of satisfaction, agreement, or perceived importance. These questions often offer from five to seven categories, as in

5 = *Very satisfied*

4 = *Somewhat satisfied*

3 = *Don't know/Can't say/Neither satisfied nor dissatisfied*

2 = *Somewhat dissatisfied*

1 = *Very dissatisfied*

Note that while these categories clearly have an order from more to less satisfied, the assignments of numeric values to each category is nonetheless arbitrary. We could just as easily have assigned the value of "5" to *Very dissatisfied*. More technically, the scale is based on another arbitrary assumption that the distance between adjoining categories is one unit. But is *Very satisfied* really only one unit more than *Satisfied*?

Measurement experts are more or less stringent about the way in which ordinal measures are treated. Some are "strict constructionists," who never depart from the dictum that order alone does not permit you to use statistics that assume that the distance between two adjacent categories is really one unit. Others pretend this to be close enough. Zumbo and Zimmerman (1983) have demonstrated through simulations that the distinction between ordinal and interval levels of measurement doesn't make much difference for many widely used statistics.

Interval and Ratio

In contrast, both interval and ratio measures have both an order and meaningful distances between their values. They are slightly different from each other, however: Ratio measures have a true zero (e.g., the number of children in a household), while interval measures do not (e.g., IQ scores do not have a true zero). The distinction, however, is unimportant for the work we will do in this text, and we will instead use the term *continuous* to refer to this level of measurement.

● CONCLUSION

Sound policy analysis depends on sound measures. Sophisticated statistical tools can no more compensate for bad measures than they can for poor research designs. Indeed, statistics will render false evidence if your measures are neither the valid nor reliable indicators that good evidence and analysis require. The challenges we face as data collectors and analysts are made all the more difficult by the complexity of human communication that lie at the heart of most measurements. The tasks here are formidable, but we have tools to help in achieving our objectives or in assessing how close we come to our desired ends of reliable and valid measures. We can use all these tools to help make decisions on sound evidence and to spot the weaknesses, limitations, and distortions that others make in order to advance a position on grounds other than principled evidence. *Caveat emptor.*

● NOTES

1. This section draws heavily from Groves et al. (2004), which should be consulted for a more detailed discussion of the issues raised here.

2. A random response technique can offer two questions to a respondent, one a harmless, nonthreatening question, such as "Were you born in December?", and the other a sensitive question of interest, such as "Did you smoke marijuana within the past 30 days?" The choice of which of these two questions is used is based on the toss of a

coin or some other random choice device. The interviewer does not know which of the two questions the respondent is answering. Given the known probabilities of landing a head and being born in December, the incidence of the behavior in question can be estimated, reducing some (although not all) of the downward bias in answering such a sensitive question.

3. Obviously, methodological studies to assess the effects of question wording or order can be embedded within a nationally representative sample and have been. The emphasis of this section is on using techniques to judge the quality of measures and taking steps to improve that quality before engaging in the greater expense of a full-blown study.

> To practice and reinforce the lessons of the first three chapters of this book, turn to Exercise 2 in the *Student Workbook* (available at http://www.sagepub.com/pearsonsp/).

DATA EDITING, TRANSFORMATION, INDEX CONSTRUCTION, AND WEIGHTS

We have yet to raise a statistical finger in the text as we turn the page to Chapter 4. We will begin to do so here, but the emphasis of this chapter is in the preparation of data for analysis and presentation. Editing, in particular, is akin to cleaning the surface of a wall before painting it, lest the grease and dirt on the surface cause problems with the adhesion of the paint. And we clearly want our statistics to "stick."

EDITING ERRANT DATA BY DECLARING MISSING VALUES

There are a variety of reasons for editing data prior to analyzing them, but the most typical situation is that the data are "dirty," with stray or inappropriate codes or values that need to be corralled in some way. This situation arises from a number of sources: an incorrect entry by a respondent in a computer-assisted self-interview or an errant keystroke by an interviewer in a computer-assisted telephone interview. You may be entering value codes from a survey you administered yourself and hit the key "8" instead of "5" as you create an Excel spreadsheet at 2:00 a.m.

We often edit errant values by dumping them (figuratively) into a bin that we label as "missing" or "nonvalid." Telling SPSS, for example, that anyone with the value, say, of "8" or "9" in response to Question X is to be considered missing is the same as telling SPSS to exclude any such case from the statistics we request SPSS to compute. If we want to calculate the mean household income for every respondent in our survey and code anyone who failed to answer that question as, say, "–9," we surely don't want these values distorting the real mean of those respondents with legitimate responses.

You can often observe whether the data set has already coded these values as missing by examining the data themselves and, in SPSS, looking for the declaration that certain values are already user designated as missing. In the Missing column in the Variable View screen of SPSS for the Orange County, Florida, public perception data set, for example, we see that the value of "3" for the variable named LAWENF will be considered missing in any calculation you request on this variable.

Another key to identifying errant values is to observe the statistics that fall outside the range you expect. If, for example, we code *female* as "1" and *male* as "2" but discover that the mean for gender in our survey is "3.4," it's very likely that we have some folks who were coded "8" or "9" for gender because they refused to answer that question, say, in a self-administered mail questionnaire. But someone also failed to let SPSS know that values of "8" and "9" should be considered missing.

Such missing values can arise from data entry mistakes or from the fact that people fail to answer a question. They may fail to do so because they're not asked the question (a previous response asks them to skip a question), they fail to understand the intent of the question, they can't retrieve the memory of a past event, or the respondent believes that the question is inappropriate (e.g., a question about family income). People may also give responses such as "Don't know" or "Can't say," which we may want to exclude from our analysis.

We will exclude cases that are considered missing from any analysis in this book, although we will have choices later between whether we exclude missing observations on a listwise or pairwise basis, which we'll discuss later. Interestingly (surprisingly?), entire books have been written about missing values (see, e.g., Allison, 2001), and analysts have devised ways of imputing values that are missing. We won't.

Let's jump right into one example of editing by turning to the Orange County public perception data set, using SPSS.

Step 1: Open the Public_Perceptions_Orange_Cnty.sav in SPSS (Version 18.0 is being used below).

Step 2: In either the Variable or Data View screen (the Variable View is shown below), click at the top of your screen on Analyze/Descriptive Statistics/Frequencies:

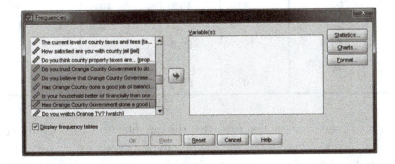

Step 3: In the resulting dialog box, highlight the five variables beginning with the variable TRUST ("Do you trust Orange County employees to do what is right most of the time?"), and click the arrow button to move these variables into the Variables box.[1]

Step 4: Click the Statistics button and select "Minimum" and "Maximum" in the box for Dispersion. We're checking for values outside of those we expect. Click Continue and then OK, which should produce a chart like the following, plus the first two (of five) frequency tables.

Statistics

		Do you trust Orange County Government to do what is right most of the time?	Do you believe that Orange County Government works efficiently?	Has Orange County done a good job of balancing growth against environmental concerns?	Is your household better of financially than one year ago?	Has Orange County Government done a good job of managing growth?
N	Valid	991	1031	1032	1024	1028
	Missing	43	3	2	10	6
Minimum		1	1	1	1	1
Maximum		2	3	3	3	3

Do you trust Orange County Government to do what is right most of the time?

		Frequency	Percent	Valid Percent	Cumulative Percent
Valid	Yes	708	68.5	71.4	71.4
	No	283	27.4	28.6	100.0
	Total	991	95.8	100.0	
Missing	Can't Say	42	4.1		
	System	1	.1		
	Total	43	4.2		
Total		1034	100.0		

Do you believe that Orange County Government works efficiently?

		Frequency	Percent	Valid Percent	Cumulative Percent
Valid	Yes	524	50.7	50.8	50.8
	No	419	40.5	40.6	91.5
	Can't Say	88	8.5	8.5	100.0
	Total	1031	99.7	100.0	
Missing	System	3	.3		
Total		1034	100.0		

You can see from the first table that the variable TRUST has a minimum value of "1" and a maximum of "2," while the other, similar variables have minimum and maximum values of "1" and "3," respectively. If you return to the Variable View screen, you'll see that someone has coded the value "3" for TRUST as missing. You'll also see in the detailed frequency tables that SPSS reports "Missing System" observations. In these two tables, you see 43 missing observations for TRUST and 3 for WORKS. Some of the missing values for TRUST were assigned by the user (e.g., by you or by someone who gave you the file). SPSS assigns "System-missing" values when a blank is encountered or when an illegitimate value is detected, such as an alphabetical character for a variable that has been defined as numeric, or when a variable transformation creates an illegal calculation, such as division by 0.

We want to assign the value "3" as missing in the four variables that have not yet declared a missing value. That is to say, I don't want to include respondents who answered "Can't say" to any of these questions.

Step 5: In the Variable View screen, move your cursor to the box defined by the intersection of the Missing column and the variable row for WORKS. Click on the box in the right side of that cell, select the radio button for "Discrete missing values" and enter "3" (without quotation marks) into one of the three empty boxes, as shown below. Then click OK.

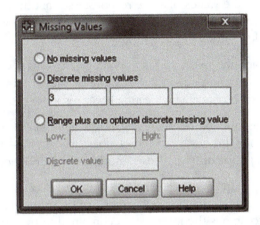

Step 6: Move your cursor to the box that now shows "3" as a user-supplied missing value for WORKS. Right click and select Copy.

Step 7: Highlight the missing-value boxes for the three remaining variables, right click, and select Paste. You have now told SPSS that anyone with a "3" code for any of these five variables (the "Can't say" respondents) is to be excluded from any subsequent statistical analysis. (If you save the file at this point, these missing values will remain in future analysis sessions.)

There are a variety of ways in which you can edit data. Declaring a particular value or range of values as missing is only one. You can, for example, achieve a similar result by recoding one or more values into a bin that has already been designated as missing. If you have access to the questionnaires themselves, you could identify the cases with stray codes and see if the error was at the data entry stage. If so, you could enter the correct response for the one now considered missing. We will return throughout the text to other ways of editing data, which is in some respects one of many types of data transformation.

● DATA TRANSFORMATION

The novice analyst will be surprised at how frequently she must transform data in some way. There are actually a wide variety of reasons for doing so, beyond moving errant values into missing-value categories:

• To reorder the values of some responses so that they align from low to high in the same direction as other variables, which you will combine in an index or scale

• To combine the respondents in two or more bins if we discover too few observations of a particular value or range of values or if we want to simplify the presentation of data by creating fewer response categories

• To change a variable by, say, taking its square root or log in order to create a distribution of this newly created variable that conforms more closely to the **normal distribution** (you'll learn more about distributions later)

• To create an index or scale from a combination of variables (we dedicate a separate section to this topic below) in order to create a summary measure that combines the information contained in two or more related variables, perhaps because you believe that the responses to a set of similar questions are tapping into the same underlying concept, which you can better capture through a combination of these variables

• To select only a subset of respondents or to give greater weight to the responses of some people than of others

Index Construction

Combining Two or More Related Items Into a Single Scale

Index construction is a special case of data transformation. Rather than transforming a single variable, however, creating an index or scale requires the analyst to combine the responses to two or more variables.

Suppose that the Orange County mayor is interested in understanding how the citizens of his county evaluate the quality of their contacts with county employees. He commissions a local university to conduct a random digit dial telephone survey of about 1,000 people and wants to know how satisfied citizens are with matters such as the timeliness of the county employees' responses, their friendliness, and whether responses are error-free. The survey is conducted, and results are at hand from questions that evaluate six different qualities of contact with county employees. The mayor's chief data analyst recommends that an index of satisfaction be created from the responses to questions about the quality of those contacts. Indeed, this clever analyst will rescale the index so that it will have a possible top value of 100, a perfect score. The analyst wants to transform the responses into a scale because he believes that such transformed data can be more easily communicated to the mayor and the broader public. In this case, the analyst believes that nearly everyone will understand results that describe the proportion of citizens' contacts on this summary scale, which can be graded as A (90–100), B (80–89), and so on.

The first task in any analysis or transformation of data is to request descriptive statistics on the variables of interest. We're examining a limited number of such statistics at this point only for the purpose of making sure there's nothing strange about the data, which is a part of the data-editing process. We will turn to a more detailed discussion of descriptive statistics in the next chapter. Let's examine the following five variables: HELPFUL, RESPECT, FRIENDLY, NOMISTAK, and TIMELY.

Note: Variable labels such as TIMELY are mnemonics—that is, a pattern of letters or a word that assists you in remembering the meaning of the variable. I'll be using these labels throughout the text. It makes analysis easier, and these shorthand tags save time and space. Avoid using them in communicating with others, however. This type of "geek speak" is an easy trap to fall prey to but gets in the way of communicating outside the confines of a statistics book.

(In looking at the questionnaire that was used in this study, you may have raised some questions about EXCEED, the question that asked whether the service exceeded the respondents' expectations. Answers to this question are difficult to interpret because we have no knowledge of whether the respondent's expectations were high or low. Exceeding low expectations may not be worthy of praise, while falling somewhat short of unreasonably high expectations may not be too bad. In other words, we will drop EXCEED from our analysis in this example because of its questionable face validity.)

Step 1: Open the Public_Perceptions_Orange_Cnty.sav SPSS file, if you haven't already done so.

Step 2: In either the Variable or the Data View screen, click at the top of your screen on Analyze/Descriptive Statistics/Frequencies (as shown in the previous example).

Step 3: Move the five variables (HELPFUL, RESPECT, FRIENDLY, NOMISTAK, and TIMELY) into the Variable(s) list box.

Step 4: Click on Statistics and select "Minimum" and "Maximum."

Step 5: Click Continue and then Charts. Select Bar Charts in the Chart Types and Percentages in the Chart Values boxes. Click Continue.

Step 6: Click OK.

You will see that these variables are relatively well behaved: no values beyond what we expect from the Codebook (i.e., ranges of 1–4) and a substantial number of "valid" observations for each of the variables except TIMELY. We'll return to TIMELY later. It is also the case (from a quick scan of the bar charts, which are not displayed here) that most people respond with "Agree" to the various statements about the quality of service they received from county employees.

Let's use these five variables about the quality of contacts to create an index that will look and feel like an **interval variable**, although composed of variables that are measured at the ordinal level. We should begin, however, with an examination of how these five variables "hang together." In other words, do they appear to be measuring the same underlying construct such that the newly created index variable (or scale) is internally consistent? There is a widely used tool for making this assessment: the Cronbach's alpha (α) coefficient.

Step 1: From the menu at the top of your SPSS screen, click on Analyze/Scale/Reliability Analysis.

Step 2: Move the five variables (i.e., HELPFUL, RESPECT, FRIENDLY, NOMISTAK, and TIMELY) into the box marked Items.

Step 3: In the Model section, select Alpha.

Step 4: Click on the Statistics button. In the "Descriptives for" section, click on "Item," "Scale," and "Scale if item deleted." Click on "Correlations" in the Inter-Item section, as in the following screen:

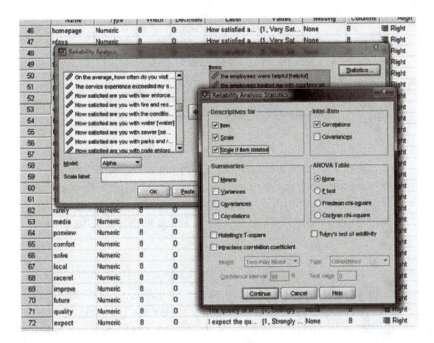

Step 5: Click Continue and then OK.

The output from this analysis should look like the following:

Case Processing Summary

		N	%
Cases	Valid	628	60.7
	Excluded[a]	406	39.3
	Total	1034	100.0

a. Listwise deletion based on all variables in the procedure.

Hmmm, SPSS excludes over a third of the cases from the analysis. What might be going on here? Note that the footnote indicates "Listwise deletion." This means that SPSS assigns a missing value for the index to any respondent who had a missing value for *any* variable in the list of five.

Reliability Statistics

Cronbach's Alpha	Cronbach's Alpha Based on Standardized Items	N of Items
.877	.881	5

As a rule of thumb, Cronbach's alpha should be above .70 for you to be confident that the items that you will combine into a single index or scale are related enough to warrant their combination into a single scale. An alpha of .88 is quite good. Pat yourself on the back. These items hang together.

Note: Cronbach's alpha is sensitive to the number of items in the scale and will tend to produce numbers below .70 when 10 or fewer items are being assessed, as is the case here. That's why we requested the interitem correlation for these five variables because we could have used the mean of these correlations in judging the appropriateness of their combination into a single scale. Briggs and Cheek (1986) suggest that interitem correlations of .2 to .4 justify the combination of items into a scale of fewer than 10 items. (We will return in more detail to correlation coefficients in Chapter 10.) As it turns out from the following output, the mean interitem correlation of these five variables is .60 (calculation not shown), surpassing even Briggs and Cheek's rule of thumb.

Inter-Item Correlation Matrix

	the employees were helpful	the employees treated me with courtesy and respect	The employees were friendly	The service was provided without mistakes	The service was provided in a timely manner
the employees were helpful	1.000	.720	.693	.580	.586
the employees treated me with courtesy and respect	.720	1.000	.746	.484	.528
The employees were friendly	.693	.746	1.000	.522	.549
The service was provided without mistakes	.580	.484	.522	1.000	.564
The service was provided in a timely manner	.586	.528	.549	.564	1.000

Item-Total Statistics

	Scale Mean if Item Deleted	Scale Variance if Item Deleted	Corrected Item-Total Correlation	Squared Multiple Correlation	Cronbach's Alpha if Item Deleted
the employees were helpful	8.34	4.314	.781	.630	.834
the employees treated me with courtesy and respect	8.36	4.421	.739	.638	.844
The employees were friendly	8.31	4.472	.754	.625	.842
The service was provided without mistakes	8.22	4.487	.634	.423	.869
The service was provided in a timely manner	8.14	4.228	.659	.444	.866

Finally, the Item-Total Statistics table above provides some potentially useful diagnostic tools for assessing the extent to which any one of the items in the scale doesn't fit. This table shows you how the scale would differ if any one of the items was deleted (Columns 1 and 2). Not much action here, as you would expect given the high alpha. Column 3 shows you the degree to which each item is correlated with the scale. Correlations of less than .30 should flag an item for removal from the index scale. We're okay here too.

This type of analysis would be included as part of a technical appendix in which you could write something like the following:

> The Satisfaction With Contacts With County Employees Scale has good internal consistency, with a Cronbach's alpha coefficient of .87, which exceeds the generally accepted minimal standard of .70.

Let's proceed to create an index variable from the sum of these five variables (with an added twist of changing its maximum possible value to 100). To help us interpret and communicate the meaning of this new index variable, let's first recode the five variables so that "high" numeric values (in each instance, the value of 4) indicate a strongly positive evaluation. People have a general tendency to think of more as better, so let's go with that flow. As you can see, we need to transform variables all the time to make them bend to our purposes, which may not have been those of the person(s) who designed the original study, collected the data, and—in this instance—provided codes that ranged from "1" for *strongly agree* to "4" for *strongly disagree*, which we are now going to recode.

If a respondent strongly agrees that his most recent contact with a county employee was helpful, then that respondent will have a value of

"4" on our newly recoded variable, to which we'll give the variable name HELPFUL_RECODE. If a respondent strongly agrees that employees treated her with courtesy and respect, RESPECT_RECODE will take on the value of "4," and so on. We'll recode the *agree* responses as "3." Similarly, we'll flip the values of the *disagree* responses, *strongly disagree* responses taking on the new value of "1" and *disagree* responses taking on the value of "2."

To perform these recode transformations, the following steps should be taken:

Step 1: Return to the Public_Perceptions SPSS file.

Step 2: From the menu at the top of the screen, click on Transform/ Recode Into Different Variables.

Step 3: Move the variable HELPFUL into the variable box.

Step 4: A dialog box will appear into which you'll enter the new variable name and label (see the Output Variable box on the right side of the open dialog box).

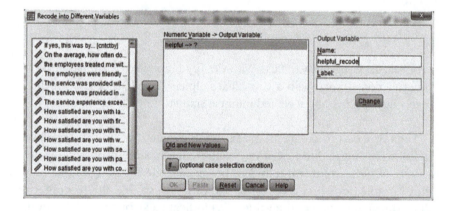

Step 5: Click on the button Old and New Values. Enter the value of the old variable (e.g., 1) and its new value or bin number (e.g., 4). Click the Add button for each recode you'll be making. The screen below shows my last step in recoding HELPFUL.

Step 6: Click on Add and then Continue, following the same procedure for each of the remaining variables.

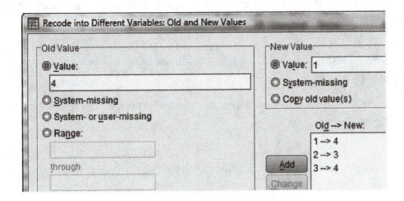

Step 7: Don't forget to change the labels associated with each of the numeric categories of these recoded variables (i.e., value labels). Even though we'll be creating a transformed variable with these five variables shortly, it's always good practice to make these labeling changes at the time you transform the variables, lest you forget how you recoded them. How? Here's one of several ways:

a. In the Variable View screen of the Public_Perceptions SPSS file, scroll down to the bottom, where you will find your five newly recoded variables. Click on the cell in the column Values for the first of your recoded variables. This cell will become highlighted, and a gray box with three dots will appear in that cell.

b. Click on the gray box, and relabel the category values:

1. Assign "1" the value label *strongly disagree*. (Don't use quotes.) Click Add.
2. "2" is *disagree*. Click Add.
3. "3" is *agree*. Click add.
4. "4" is *strongly agree*. Click Add and OK.

Step 8: After changing the labels for one variable, you can Copy and Paste these value labels to the remaining four variables by right clicking in the Values box of the first variable (in the Variable View mode of SPSS) for which you've provided new labels. Select Copy. Click and drag on the Values cells of the four other variables for which you would like to copy the same labels. Click the right button, and select Paste.

Now, create an index variable to which you will give the label SATIS-FAC_INDEX1 by following these steps:

Step 1: From the menu at the top of the screen, click on Transform/Compute.

Step 2: Enter your new variable name (SATISFAC_INDEX1) into the Target Variable box.

Step 3: Enter your formula for the new variable, the sum of the five variables multiplied by 5, thereby creating an index with a possible highest score of 100.

Your screen should look something like this:

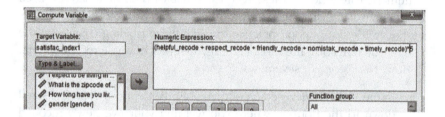

Step 4: Click OK toward the bottom of the Compute Variable box. You've got a new variable.

Step 5: Run descriptive statistics on this new variable to make sure everything works properly. Request the statistics reported below. You should produce output something like the following:

Statistics

satisfac_indiex1

N	Valid	628.00
	Missing	406.00
	Mean	73.29
	Median	75.00
	Mode	75.00
	Minimum	25.00
	Maximum	100.00

satisfac_indiex1

		Frequency	Percent	Valid Percent	Cumulative Percent
Valid	25	8	.8	1.3	1.3
	30	1	.1	.2	1.4
	35	4	.4	.6	2.1
	40	4	.4	.6	2.7
	45	6	.6	1.0	3.7
	50	9	.9	1.4	5.1
	55	23	2.2	3.7	8.8
	60	30	2.9	4.8	13.5
	65	56	5.4	8.9	22.5
	70	80	7.7	12.7	35.2
	75	282	27.3	44.9	80.1
	80	31	3.0	4.9	85.0
	85	20	1.9	3.2	88.2
	90	16	1.5	2.5	90.8
	95	20	1.9	3.2	93.9
	100	38	3.7	6.1	100.0
	Total	628	60.7	100.0	
Missing	System	406	39.3		
Total		1034	100.0		

These statistics show that about a third (35.2% in the Cumulative Percent column) of our respondents gave their county contacts a score of 70 or less out of 100. About two thirds gave 75 or more points. Indeed, 75 was the most common score (the mode), suggesting that the respondents tended to answer "Agree" across the five evaluative questions. If we interpret these scores as grades on an exam, we could conclude that about a quarter of our citizens give their contacts a failing grade (i.e., 65 or less), while county employees get an A in about 12% of the contacts. Would you conclude from these results that the county has some room for improvement in the delivery of its services?

So what really should we say about these numbers? Not much. The number of valid and missing values is still unsettling. If you return to the questionnaire from which these data were collected, you will note that a prior question asked whether the respondent had contacted a county employee within the past 12 months. This question appears to have been used by some interviewers as a filter for the subsequent questions that are of interest to us here. Some respondents who answered "No" to having contacted a county employee during the past 12 months appear not to have been asked the subsequent questions that evaluate those contacts.

If you ran descriptive statistics on the responses to this question, which is labeled "CONTACT," you will observe that only 520 people said that they had contacted a county employee within the past 12 months. Yet the statistics above show 628 "valid" responses (a term that SPSS uses to indicate "nonmissing"). The questionnaire, I would argue, led some telephone interviewers astray. Our five questions were asked of many respondents who did not contact an Orange County employee during the past 12 months. The CONTACT question was also not asked of many who did *not* contact a county employee in the past 12 months. If you believe (like many interviewers) that the respondents should not have been asked questions about contacts older than 12 months ago, there are many respondents with scores on our index variable who should be assigned (by you, the analyst) as missing in action. Conversely, we want to select only the 520 respondents who contacted a county employee during the past 12 months in our analysis.

This is a matter of selecting cases for whom we have recorded the number 1 for the variable CONTACT, derived from a question that precedes the battery of evaluative questions—HELPFUL, RESPECT, and so on.

See if you can figure out how to select just these people. (*Hint:* Data/ Select Cases/If)

Or ask SPSS for help in selecting cases.

Ask for frequencies on the new index variable after selecting for just those respondents who contacted a county employee during the past 12 months. You will discover that about a third of the 520 contact cases are missing in our index variable. That's a little disturbing too. As you know, SPSS will consider any case missing if the value for any one of the five component elements of the index is missing.

If you run descriptive statistics on the five recoded variables after selecting for only those with a contact, you'll see that about 30% of the data for the variable TIMELY are missing. For some reason, quite a few people who should have answered this question didn't do so. Given the question's location at the bottom of the page, it may not have been printed on a number of questionnaires. For whatever reason, this is an intolerable level of missing data, which damages the integrity of our summary index. At this point in the analysis of these data, I would recalculate a satisfaction index to exclude the variable TIMELY, describing my reasons for doing so in a technical appendix or footnote in any report or memorandum I might write to the county mayor. The exercise for this chapter provides you with the opportunity to do just that.

But before turning to that exercise, let's consider two common and important additional transformations that adjust for changes in the value of money and changes in population size.

Indexes That Adjust for Changes in the Value of Money: The Constant Dollar

As we will see in Chapter 6, "Charts and Graphs," numerous examples exist of the display of financial or budget data over time that express each month's or each year's data in what are called "current" dollars. For example, consider the U.S. national debt, the data for which you can access as an Excel file at the Congressional Budget Office's Web site at www.cbo.gov/budget/historical.shtml.

The national debt represents the amount of money the federal government has spent in excess of the revenues it has collected. It's a cumulative figure, representing all the debt accumulated since the founding of the Union. It's a big number, which if reported in current dollars would appear to show an astronomical increase in the latter part of the 20th century, as displayed in the SPSS chart in Figure 4.1.[2] (The graphical qualities of this chart can be improved considerably, a task to which we turn in Chapter 6.)

The national debt was $290 billion in current dollars in 1968 (as represented in the first circle in the graph above). It grew to $5.04 trillion in 2007 (the last circle). Wow! That's a 1,638% increase ((5,040 − 290)/290). What kind of a bill are we passing on to our children and their children, and how many government bonds are we selling to China to finance that debt?

We all know, of course, that money changes value over time, typically declining in value with price inflation. Displaying current dollars will distort real change by conflating changes in the value of money with changes in revenues or expenses over time. (This is a favored tactic of those who wish to demonstrate dramatic growth, say, in the size of government or expenditures on any program, be it defense or welfare spending.) If you ever see a chart expressed in current dollars over time, you should smell a rat.

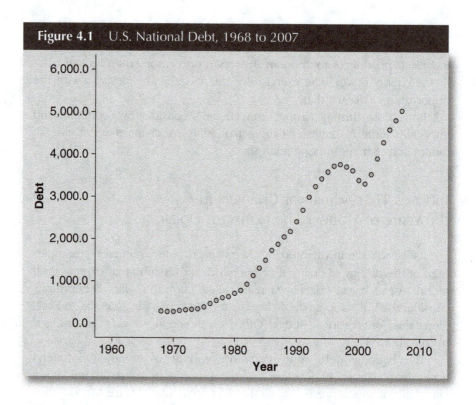

Figure 4.1 U.S. National Debt, 1968 to 2007

To adjust for changes in the value of money (and provide a less deceptive portrait of change) requires the analyst to transform dollar figures into what are called "constant" dollars. That is to say, an analyst transforms the data to express the national debt in 1968 according to the relative value of the dollar in, say, 2007. (One can also reverse this process and express the national debt in 2007 in 1968 constant dollars.)

Obviously, "current" dollars don't take into account the changing (declining) value of the dollar. In other words, a buck in 2007 can't buy what it did in 1968. To take the changing value of the dollar into account requires that we have a measure of the value of the dollar. There are many, but we will use for our purposes the one produced by the U.S. Department of Labor's Bureau of Labor Statistics—the Consumer Price Index (CPI). The CPI records monthly changes in the prices paid by urban consumers for a representative basket of goods and services.

Using the CPI to calculate constant dollars is simple, though it is laborious for a large set of numbers.

Step 1: Open the Department of Labor's Web site at www.bls.gov/cpi/.

Step 2: Go to Calculators, and select the Inflation Calculator.

Step 3: To express $290 billion in 1968 in constant 2007 dollars, enter the appropriate numbers, as I have done below. Click on Calculate.

The following screen should appear:

That measly $290 billion in 1968 was worth about $1,728 billion in 2007. Don't get me wrong; that's still a substantial increase in the national debt over those 39 years. But it's a 192% increase ((5,040 − 1,728)/1728), not 1,640%!

Indexes That Adjust for Population Growth or Decline: The Per Capita

Another sleight of hand arises in reporting data over time that do not adjust for population growth (or decline). A time series of this kind is deceptive in at least two ways and fails to communicate meaningful numbers in yet another way. First, it takes no account of the fact that the number of people in a geographic area like the United States increases with time. Second, it fails to account for the changing value of money, as we demonstrated above. And finally, figures such as $5 trillion (the national debt in 2007) are simply so large that it's difficult for most of us to get our arms or brains around it. (If you laid that many dollar bills end to end, they would make 96,928 round trips between New York City and Los Angeles. (That's actually true if my arithmetic is correct, but not much of an improvement in communicating the point, is it?)

One solution to this problem is to divide the debt by the size of the population each year, thus creating a per capita (per person) index. U.S. population figures can be found on the Web site of the U.S. Bureau of the Census at www.census.gov/popest.

Expressed in these terms, the national debt in 1968 was $1,442 per capita for per every person (man, woman, and child) in the United States. It has grown to $16,720 per capita in 2007. But this calculation uses current dollars, which exaggerate the differences. Per capita national debt in 1968, when expressed in constant 2007 dollars, was $8,609. Again, the growth has been dramatic, but it is much less so when the changing value of the dollar is taken into account or, one might say, held constant. The 2007 per capita debt is nearly equal to the entire yearly earnings of a three-person household considered to be in poverty ($17,600 in 2006). The per capita debt of 1968 would have been the equivalent of half of such a family yearly earnings (in constant 2007 dollars).

● WEIGHTS: COUNTING SOME PEOPLES' ANSWERS MORE THAN OTHERS'

We saw in Chapter 2 that not everyone asked to participate in a study agrees to do so. Or the mode by which you collect data—for example, a telephone survey—may systematically exclude members of your population who do not have access to a phone. The general term for the exclusion of members of your sample frame from the survey is nonresponse. Nonresponse can produce biased results if the people who do not (or cannot) respond are unlike those who do. We will later, in Chapter 9, examine statistical tests for determining whether sample respondents differ from the population from which they were drawn. But we will leapfrog to one of the possible solutions to this problem (if your tests show it to be so)—that is, giving greater weight to the types of respondents who are underrepresented in your study (for a more detailed discussion of **weights**, see Dorofeev & Grant, 2006; Lee & Forthofer, 2005).

Consider, for example, the fact that the Orange County survey includes 453 (43.8%) men and 580 (56.1%) women, yet you can discover from the U.S. Bureau of the Census that women made up only 51% of the county's residents in 2000. Women were either more willing to participate in the survey than men or more accessible via phone. Whatever the source, there are more women in the sample than in the population from which the sample was drawn (and vice versa for men). Insofar as gender is associated with something we want to estimate from the survey, our results could well be biased by this oversampling of women. One way to adjust for this discrepancy is to give greater weight to men's responses (and less to women's). We can do so by "weighting" the data.

In effect, weighting data can be used to simulate a data set with 51% females and 49% males, even though the data include 56.1% female and 43.8% male respondents. We need to create yet another new variable that we will call a *weight variable*. How can we accomplish that? Well, one way is to give each man's responses a simulated "boost" of 49/43.8, or by a factor of 1.12. Similarly, women's responses are adjusted by 51/56.1 or counted at a rate of 0.91. Another way of expressing these weights is like this: Desired proportion/Observed proportion.

You can accomplish this feat in SPSS by creating the weight variable through the following steps:

Step 1: (Using the Orange County data) Click on Transform/Recode Into New Variable.

Step 2: Select Gender as the old variable to be recoded, and name and label your new variable WEIGHT, as shown in the dialog box to the left below.

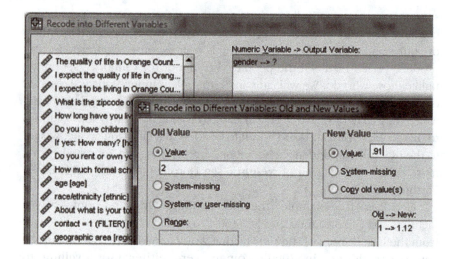

Step 3: Click on the Old and New Values button, and recode the value "1" (*males*) to 1.12 and "2" (*females*) to 0.91. The second of these two recodes is shown above in the right dialog box. Click on the Add button after each recode. Click on Continue after you've made these two recodes.

Step 4: Click the Change button. Click OK.

If you return to the Variable View screen of SPSS, you'll see that a new variable, WEIGHT, has been added at the bottom of the list of variables. It is always a good idea to run a simple set of descriptive statistics (as we have done earlier in this chapter) to make sure you executed the recode transformations properly. (The first time I tried to create this particular weight variable, I forgot to hit the Add button after the second recode and thus created a variable that had only one value, 1.12. SPSS recoded all the women as "System-missing.") You should get a table that looks something like the following, indicating that the recodes were (this time) properly executed.

Gender weights

		Frequency	Percent	Valid Percent	Cumulative Percent
Valid	.91	580	56.1	56.1	56.1
	1.12	453	43.8	43.9	100.0
	Total	1033	99.9	100.0	
Missing	System	1	.1		
Total		1034	100.0		

Now, you've created a weight variable, but you haven't applied it to the data yet. This requires you to "turn on" the weight variable. This you do in the following step:

Step 5: Click on Data/Weight Cases.

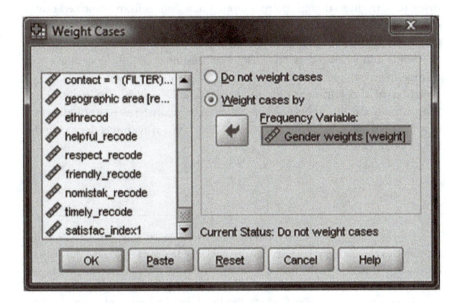

Step 6: Select the radio button for "Weight cases by," and move WEIGHT into the Frequency Variable box from its location at the end of the list of variables on the left of the dialog box. Click OK.

SPSS will now give more weight to male responses and less to female responses in such a way as to retain the overall sample size. If men and women differ in their responses to some questions, the descriptive statistics for these variables will differ between the weighted and unweighted files. (Obviously, you can turn off the weights by returning to Data/Weight Cases and selecting "Do not weight cases.")

CONCLUSION ●

Preparing data for analysis requires you to run some simple descriptive statistics and graphs of the variables you will be studying. Your objective is to identify any problems with the data, for which there are many possible sources. This exploration and editing process begins to get you acquainted with the data, including their foibles and faults. Many of these faults can be treated, either in data editing or in transforming variables to better conform to the assumptions that some statistics make of the data or to your analytic or communication needs. Data transformations will be required of any analysis you do, again for many reasons. In so doing, you're sculpting new figures from unformed clay. It can be fun, and your creative talents can shine (especially if bolstered by a high Cronbach's alpha).

Some transformations are absolutely essential for understanding real change from change that is an artifact of population growth or inflation or deflation of the currency. But tools are readily available to make these transformations. Be especially aware, however, of analyses presented to you that fail to make these transformations. They are (un)wittingly deceiving the unwary reader.

● NOTES

1. SPSS's dialog boxes are often rather narrow, which makes it difficult in the Frequencies box above to read very much of a variable's label. You can rectify this by clicking and dragging on the right and/or left borders of the dialog box and dragging your cursor right or left. This will expand the box as shown above.

2. After creating an SPSS file from the Excel data for years and national debt, I created the chart shown in Figure 4.1 through the following steps:

Step 1: Click on Graphs/Legacy Dialog/ScatterDot.
Step 2: Select the Simple Scatter box and click on the Define box.
Step 3: Move "Year" into the box for the *X*-axis and "Debt" into the box for the *Y*-axis, and click OK.

Excel can create a similar chart through the procedures Tools/Data Analysis/Regression.

To practice and reinforce the lessons of this chapter of the book, turn to Exercise 3 in the *Student Workbook* (available at http://www.sagepub.com/pearsonsp/).

CHAPTER 5

STATISTICS AS DESCRIPTION

DESCRIPTIVE STATISTICS ARE THE ● FOUNDATION FOR INTERPRETATION AND ANALYSIS

You have already encountered descriptive statistics in the previous chapter as tools to use in detecting errant codes and in checking data transformations. We performed these procedures to get a feel for the data. Were there values that were outside the range of valid codes? Were there errors in coding that needed to be corrected or observations that we needed to declare as "missing"? We did not examine the properties of these statistics in any detail, however. Nor did we use these statistics to draw any substantive conclusions that the data were collected to answer.

We will call on descriptive statistics in this chapter to explore the data for patterns or to describe a condition by summarizing the data in one or more ways. There are three principal types of statistics (called "summary" or "descriptive" statistics) that are helpful in this regard:

1. *Central tendency:* What is in the center of a variable's distribution?
2. *Dispersion or spread:* How much do our observations vary from each other?
3. *Shape:* Is there a particular form or shape that the distribution of observations takes on?

These statistics are the foundation for all subsequent statistics and can tell you a great deal about the data at hand and the populations they seek to describe. Indeed, one should not attempt to conduct more sophisticated statistical tests without thoroughly grounding that analysis in an understanding of the basic descriptive statistics of the data. And one shouldn't ignore these statistics even after moving on to more complex statistics. They help us make sense of and provide context for our interpretation of more advanced tools such as regression, as we will see in Chapters 11 to 13. This chapter will help you explore these descriptive statistics, the conditions under which they're most appropriate to calculate and report, and their interpretation.

● THE CENTER OR "AVERAGE"

Good things come in threes. This book will argue, for example, that there are only three kinds of statistics: (1) descriptive, (2) group differences, and (3) relational. And just as there are three types of descriptive statistics, there are three measures of the first of these statistics, central tendency: *mean*, *median*, and *mode*. Formally speaking, each is an "average." Do not necessarily assume that someone is referring to the mean when she talks about "the average tax savings from this legislation." She could well mean the median. This is a common mistake. Usage of the term *average* usually refers to the arithmetic mean, but statisticians haven't yet conceded that ground, even though programs such as Excel designate mean as the function AVERAGE.

- *Mean:* The arithmetic average, this measure of central tendency is calculated by summing the values of all observations (e.g., the heights of everyone in the class) and then dividing that sum by the total number of observations on which the sum is based (often designated "n"). The mean income of the richest 5% of households in the United States in 2005 was $281,155, according to the Current Population Survey (CPS).

- *Median:* This measure of central tendency is the value for the observation that falls exactly in the center of a set of observations. A total of 50% of the observations are above the median, and 50% are below the median. The median household income in the United States in 2005 was $46,326 according to the CPS. Half of the households had income greater than that amount; half had less. Another way of expressing the median is to say that it is the number that defines the 50th percentile, a concept to which we will return in Chapter 7.

- *Mode:* The mode is the single value among your observations that occurs most frequently. Not the most useful measure of "average," it is rarely reported. Clearly, it doesn't make much sense to report the mode of household income in the United States. The Census Bureau certainly doesn't bother to.

The Mean

Let's say we wanted to know the mean number of people on welfare after the enactment of welfare reform legislation in 1996. Such data through 2006 are available below—imported from the U.S. Census Bureau Web site—thus providing 10 years of data pertinent to the question at hand. The steps for calculating the mean in Excel are displayed below. (Remember, we can access this function from the drop-down box next to "Σ" on the toolbar.) These data are included in a file available to you that also includes a number of measures of economic conditions during the period 1960 to 2006 (the file name is "welfare and economics").

Clicking on Average above would produce in Cell C49 (note that I highlighted the empty cell below the range of values for which I wanted to calculate the mean, which I also highlighted.) the mean number of people on welfare during this 10-year span (1997–2006): 6,012,120.

	A	B	C
28	1986	3,763,252	11,037,797
29	1987	3,775,573	11,026,664
30	1988	3,748,580	10,914,679
31	1989	3,798,348	10,992,248
32	1990	4,056,584	11,694,712
33	1991	4,497,186	12,930,472
34	1992	4,829,094	13,773,319
35	1993	5,011,827	14,205,484
36	1994	5,032,632	14,160,920
37	1995	4,790,749	13,418,386
38	1996	4,434,160	12,320,970
39	1997	3,740,179	10,855,284
40	1998	3,050,335	8,347,136
41	1999	2,581,270	6,874,471
42	2000	2,214,800	5,776,849
43	2001	2,102,996	5,362,700
44	2002	2,048,204	5,069,010
45	2003	2,023,778	4,928,878
46	2004	1,978,616	4,748,115
47	2005	1,894,515	4,471,393
48	2006	1,781,411	4,166,659
49			6,060,050
50			

The cell reference shows C39 with formula =MEDIAN(C2:C3

The Excel function AVERAGE did the following calculation without us seeing it perform this feat:

$$(10,375,993 + 8,347,136 + 6,874,471 + 5,776,849 + 5,362,700 + 5,069,010 + 4,928,878 + 4,748,115 + 4,471,393 + 4,166,659)/10 = 6,012,120.$$

As a formula, the mean can be expressed as the sum of these observations divided by the number of observations:

$$\bar{X} = \Sigma \frac{X_i}{n}$$

Many statistics use the mean in their formulas, which has an important consequence to which we will frequently return in the pages ahead.

While means are used frequently in everyday discourse, they have one property that should give us pause: They are heavily influenced by extreme values (often called "outliers"). (This is also the case, by the way, for the more complex statistics such as regression and correlation, which we'll see later.) Data that include outliers will distort the mean's ability to accurately represent the central tendency or center of a distribution. Household income is one such variable with extreme values that pull the mean in an upward direction and give the false impression that American families are richer than they actually are.

It is no accident that George W. Bush's administration was fond of reporting the tax savings of its 2001, 2002, and 2003 tax cuts as means. Likewise, those groups that opposed these cuts used the median to describe the "typical" amount of tax savings the "average" American received as a consequence of this legislation. According to a report published on the Web site of the liberal Center on Budget and Policy Priorities (Friedman & Shapiro, 2004),

> The Administration has consistently employed "averages" in a manner that falls far short of a reasonable use of statistics and overstates the benefits of the tax cuts to middle-income households. The Administration's average tax-cut figures are skewed upward by the very large tax cuts that go to a small number of very high-income taxpayers. The large majority of U.S. households will receive less than the average tax cut the Administration cites. In fact, the typical (or median) household will receive less than half the amount the Administration describes as being the "average" tax cut.

A single simple statistic such as the mean can produce dramatic responses or insights, especially when it runs counter to our prior beliefs or expectations, the schemas that cognitive psychologists say we carry around in our heads to explain reality and to guess what's likely to happen in a particular circumstance. A corollary of this observation is that powerful stories can be constructed about some status, such as being a welfare recipient, college graduate, or embezzler, by reporting what our data show people in these categories *not* to be or how poor a set of conditions are in explaining how someone came to be a welfare recipient, white collar criminal, or star athlete.

The Median

The median has a straightforward and intuitive meaning. Its calculation can be somewhat less so. Although programs such as Excel and SPSS will crunch the number for you painlessly, it is useful to understand how such a number is actually calculated because it will help us better understand some later graphical ways of displaying the dispersion of a measure (especially when we turn later in a subsequent chapter to the **boxplot**, also known as the box and whiskers graph).

Medians are derived, first, by sorting the measure in question from the lowest value to the highest value and then identifying the value exactly in the middle of that distribution. So the median height of a basketball team of five players would be determined by ordering the heights from low to high, as in the following (in inches):

72, 73, 80, 81, and 84,

and then observing that exactly half of the players are above 80 and half below 80 inches (not including our 80-inch-tall ballplayer).

But what if you have an even number of observations as in the case of the 10 years of welfare under TANF (Temporary Assistance for Needy Families) that we saw in the example for calculating the mean above? No problem. We simply calculate the mean of the middle 2 observations that have been rearranged from the lowest to the highest. The median number of people receiving TANF between 1997 and 2004 can be shown to be the average of the two values in the bracket below (reported in 1,000s here):

$10{,}375 + 8{,}347 + 6{,}874 + 5{,}776 + \underbrace{5{,}362 + 5{,}069} + 4{,}928 + 4{,}748 + 4{,}471 + 4{,}166$

$(5{,}362 + 5{,}069)/2 = 5{,}216.$

If you were using Excel to calculate the median of these numbers from the "welfare and economics" spreadsheet on the course Web site, you would do the following:

Step 1: Highlight a blank cell somewhere in the table (e.g., D49).

Step 2: Use the drop-down box next to "Σ" to select More Functions and find MEDIAN in the set of functions available in the Statistics menu. Double click on MEDIAN.

Step 3: Enter "C39:C48" for the range of values for which you want Excel to calculate the median, or click and drag on that range, which will appear in the Number 1 box of the Function Arguments window.

Your screen at this point should look something like the following:

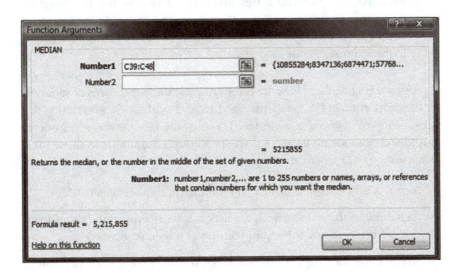

The result of this calculation appears in the dialog box (where the arrow is pointing).

Step 4: Click OK, and the number 5,215,855 will appear in Cell D49.

MEASURES OF DISPERSION: MEASURES ● OF CENTRAL TENDENCY TELL ONLY PART OF THE STORY ABOUT OUR POPULATION

It is easy and commonplace to calculate a statistic like the mean. Add up (i.e., sum) the values of all our observations on a variable (e.g., height), and divide that number by the total number of observations (e.g., the number of people who responded to our question, "How tall are you?"). You've even seen *only* this statistic reported to characterize a population: "The average grade on the last assignment was 91," a professor might report to her class.

A lonely mean can be a useful descriptive statistic but not as informative as we should demand. Why? Because it doesn't tell us how many of our subjects differ from that general characteristic and by how much. This is the job of our tools for measuring variation, variability, or dispersion. These statistics are

- minimum, maximum, and range (the difference between maximum and minimum);
- **variance** and **standard deviation** (we'll discuss the meanings of these after determining their values through Excel and SPSS); and
- **interquartile range**, which we will defer examining until Chapter 6 in the context of boxplots.

Using the same Excel file above, let's request these measures of variation for the proportion of U.S. residents, aged 16 years and above, who during the period 1960 to 2006 were considered "out of the labor force" (i.e., unemployed and not looking for work). The procedures are similar to those used in calculating the median above.

Step 1: Activate a cell in which you want Excel to place a statistic.

Step 2: Select the statistic from the lists available to you in the drop-down box next to "Σ" near the top of your Excel screen (e.g., Max).

Step 3: Enter the range of cells for which you want the statistic calculated, and click OK.

Step 4: Repeat this for all the statistics above (you can simply subtract minimum from maximum to determine the range).

The keyword for variance in Excel's Insert Functions (Statistics) dialog box is VAR. The keyword for standard deviation is STDEV.

The results from these repeated steps are as follows:

A	B
% out of lab force 16plus	
Standard Deviation	3.04279423
Sample Variance	9.25859674
Range	8.41799794
Minimum	32.9025811
Maximum	41.320579

As with most statistics, SPSS provides an easier way of requesting these statistics.

Open the SPSS version of the "welfare and economics" data set.

Step 1: Click Analyze/Descriptive Statistics/Frequencies, as shown in the following screen shot:

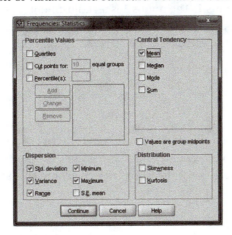

Step 2: Move "%_out_of_lab_force_16plus" into the Variables box:

Step 3: Click the Statistics button on the same dialog box, and select in the Dispersion box "Std. deviation," "Variance," "Range," "Minimum," and "Maximum."

Also, select "Mean" in the Central Tendency box. We'll use it to illustrate the calculation of variance and standard deviation below:

Step 4: Click Continue and OK, which will produce a table that should resemble the one here:

Statistics

%_out_of_lab_force_16plus

N	Valid	47
	Missing	0
Mean		36.453
Std. Deviation		3.0428
Variance		9.259
Range		8.4
Minimum		32.9
Maximum		41.3

But what are variance and standard deviation, beyond two types of dispersion? One geeky answer is that standard deviation is the square root of variance. It's actually used more frequently than variance for reasons I will reveal shortly. Okay, then. What's variance?

Variance is a summary statistic of how far, on average, each observation on a variable departs from the mean of that variable. Because some observations are above and some below the mean, the formula for variance employs a clever little trick of squaring those differences. Negative values disappear as a consequence of the fact that a negative multiplied by a negative is positive. Taking absolute values (another way of calculating an average dispersion) is more cumbersome arithmetically. The variance sums all these squared differences from the mean and then divides by the number of observations minus 1. The minus 1 is an adjustment for calculations based on samples, but we need not bother with the justification for the $n - 1$.

As a formula, the variance can be written as follows:

$$\Sigma \frac{(X_i - \bar{X})^2}{(n-1)}.$$

Take the square root of this formula, and you've got your standard deviation. In the example above, the first four values for percentage of the U.S. population who were out of the labor force (beginning in 1960) are as follows:

40.6

40.7

41.2

41.3

Knowing that the mean of this variable is 36.5 from our results above, we can calculate the first four squared differences as $(40.6 - 36.5)^2 + (40.7 - 36.5)^2 + (41.2 - 36.5)^2 + (41.3 - 36.5)^2$. We would do this for the remaining values and divide the sum of these squared differences by 46, which will equal 9.26. Taking the square root of that number gives us a standard deviation of 3.04.

We will turn shortly to an examination of the shape of the distribution of the observations around their mean and discover (or be reminded) that standard deviation, mean, and median have some interesting properties if the distribution is what statisticians call "normal," one of many terms whose meaning in statistics is slightly askew from its meaning in everyday conversation.

CHARACTERISTICS OF ●
DISTRIBUTIONS: HOW'S MY SHAPE?

The Normal Distribution

The distribution of any measure (e.g., height, attitudes toward a particular candidate for office) can take on a particular shape that has important and meaningful mathematical properties that analysts can take advantage of. To know, for example, that a distribution is "normal" tells you that the mean and median are approximately the same; that observations fall symmetrically around, and peak at, the mean; and that about two thirds of the observations fall within ±1 standard deviation of the mean. A normal distribution also has the handy property of about 95% of all its observations falling within about ±2 standard deviations of the mean. We will see in later chapters that some statistics assume that the variables in their calculations are normally distributed. Violations of that assumption can lead to errors in the conclusions you draw about the strength of relationships or the differences between groups.

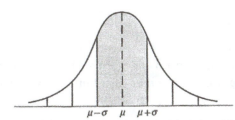

68.26% of all values lie within one standard deviation of the mean

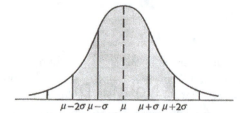

95.44% of all values lie within two standard deviations of the mean

Interestingly, there's nothing "normal" about the normal distribution if we mean regular, average, common, typical, frequent, or expected, as we often mean in *normal* conversation. In statistics, normal refers to a distribution with a specific mathematical formula, which looks pretty scary (this will not be on the test):

$$\frac{1}{\sigma\sqrt{2\pi}}e^{\frac{1}{2}\left(\frac{X-\mu}{\sigma}\right)^2}.$$

The formula includes two famous irrational numbers: π (3.1416 . . .) and e (2.7182 . . .). We'll run into e again when we talk about transforming variables by taking their natural log. The two unknowns in this equation are mu (μ) and sigma (σ), which are symbols for the population mean and standard deviation. We estimate both of these numbers from our study's mean and standard deviation. But the magic of the normal distribution arises from the facts with which I began this section. If a distribution is normal, you also know that the mean and median are approximately the same; that observations fall symmetrically around, and peak at, the mean; and that about two thirds of the observations fall within ±1 standard deviation of the mean and about 95% of all observations fall within ±2 standard deviations of the mean. (These facts may very well be on the test.) These characteristics will be especially handy when we turn in Chapter 8 to sampling and consider a measure of the standard deviation of the means of many samples drawn from a population, the standard error.

Other Distributions

We focus in this section on the normal distribution, but it may be useful to note in passing that other distributions exist that can also be defined mathematically. The *Poisson distribution*, for example, is a distribution that is skewed right (a term we will examine shortly). Most observations in such a distribution cluster at the low end of a range of values, and a few cases can be found at the very high end of this distribution. Each value or category of a *uniform distribution* has an equal (or constant) probability of occurring—for example, the percentage of times a fair die would result in a 1, 2, 3, 4, 5, or 6 with repeated throws. A *binomial distribution* describes the possible number of times (or percentage of times) that a particular event with only one of two outcomes will occur in a sequence of observations or trials. The event is binary in that it may or may not occur—for example, if you succeed or fail. The classic illustration of a binomial distribution comes from tossing a coin. The likelihood of obtaining a head on any one toss of the coin is half. But the likelihood of obtaining 0, 1, 2, 3, or 4 heads with four sequential tosses of a coin is 1/16, 4/16, 6/16, 4/16, and 1/16, respectively. When the number of observations is 5 or greater, the binomial distribution approaches that of a normal distribution.

How to Know if a Distribution Is Normal

Does It Quack Like One?

Knowing that a distribution is normal gives us some important information about that distribution. It is also the case, as we will see later in this book, that many measures of group differences or relationships between/among two or more variables assume that the variables are normally distributed. It's important and useful, therefore, to know whether a variable is actually normally distributed, and there are several tips and tests that will tell us that. To help in that regard, we can take any number of the following steps:

1. Check to see whether the *mean* and *median* are relatively close together. They are the same in a perfectly normal distribution. Substantial differences would suggest possible departures from normality.

2. Examine the statistics for **skewness** (a measure of whether a distribution is "lopsided," with a relatively small number of extremely low or extremely high values in a distribution) and **kurtosis** (a measure of how sharp or steep the peak of the distribution is or, conversely, how fat the tails of the distribution are).

Skewness can be either positive or negative. It is positive when the peak is "off" to the left and the tail is long to the right (i.e., positive side). It is negative when the peak is "off" to the right and tail is long left. Is skewness positive or negative in Figure 5.1? (Answer: Positive)

Kurtosis measures the extent to which data are concentrated in the peak or tails (its "peakedness") and also takes on positive or negative values. It is positive when data are concentrated in the peak of the distribution. It is negative when the data are spread widely, creating "fat tails," as is illustrated in Figure 5.2.

In using kurtosis and skewness to assess whether a distribution is normal, look not only at their size and sign but, more important, whether the absolute values of skewness and kurtosis are less than two times greater than their respective standard errors.

3. Request a histogram of the distribution, which is a graphical representation of the distribution. SPSS will create a graph in which each bar of the histogram (what SPSS and Excel call a "bin") has an equal range of values and the height of each bar represents the number of observations that fall in that bin. You can even ask SPSS to superimpose a normal or bell-shaped curve on your distribution, which you can eyeball to assess how close or distant your distribution is to (or from) a normal distribution.

Let's check out these three guidelines for our measure of the percentage of the U.S. population who were out of the labor force between 1960 and 2006. We'll turn to SPSS for this.

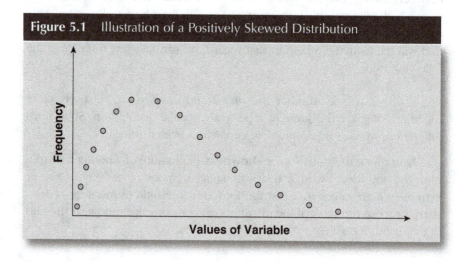

Figure 5.1 Illustration of a Positively Skewed Distribution

Figure 5.2 Illustration of Positive (solid line) and Negative (broken line) Kurtosis

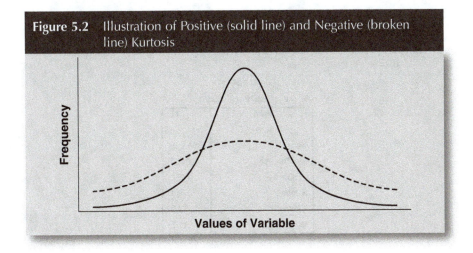

Step 1: Open the "welfare and economics" data set in SPSS, and click Analyze/Descriptive Statistics/Frequencies

Step 2: Move the variable for percentage out of the labor force into the Variable(s) box.

Step 3: Click on the Statistics button, and check the boxes as shown on the following screen capture:

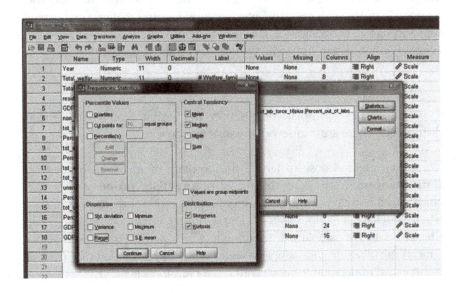

Step 4: Click Continue, and click on the Charts button. Select Histogram, and check the box for "With normal curve." Click Continue and OK, which should produce output that includes the following table and histogram:

Statistics

%_out_of_lab_force_16plus

N	Valid	47
	Missing	0
Mean		36.453
Std. Deviation		3.0428
Variance		9.259
Range		8.4
Minimum		32.9
Maximum		41.3

The mean and median are fairly close together and the ratio of skewness to its standard error is well within the guideline of 2:1. Kurtosis falls slightly outside that guideline, but not badly.

The graph Figure 5.3 (with edits that we will cover in Chapter 6) tells quite a different story.

The histogram displays combinations of bimodal and uniform distributions with a spike of observations between 33% and 34%. It certainly doesn't look normal in comparison with the normal distribution line that SPSS has superimposed on the distribution. Geez, what's a guy to do? There's one more test we can conduct, the One-Sample Kolmogorov-Smirnov Test. Unfortunately, the interpretation requires that you understand topics in statistical significance, *p* values, and null hypotheses, which are not covered until Chapter 7. We will return to this test in Chapter 12.

What Is to Be Done if Distributions Are Not Normal?

What should you do if you discover your variables are not normally distributed? There are a variety of possible responses:

● You might choose to ignore the problem by invoking the **central limit theorem**, which states that the **sampling distribution** of these variables will be normally distributed even when the variables themselves are not when you have a sample larger than 50 observations. As you will see in Chapter 7, it's the sampling distribution to which we turn to assess whether a mean calculated from a sample is an accurate representation of the actual mean in the population from which the sample was drawn.

● You might also transform the variable(s) by, say, taking its log (which will dampen down extreme values that often cause variables' distributions to depart from normality). Some of these transformations, however, make the results more difficult to interpret and communicate.

● You could conduct two parallel lines of analysis, one with transformed (normally distributed) variables and the other with untransformed variables. You can then see if your substantive conclusions differ as a consequence of these transformations. If not, report the untransformed variables, noting the transformations you made and the parallel analysis you performed in a technical appendix or footnote.

● You could also use **nonparametric statistics**, again comparing them with the results of transformed and untransformed variables, using parametric statistical tests. We will discuss the meaning of parametric and nonparametric statistics in Chapter 9.

● With any of these steps, it's a good idea to examine a graphical display of the data if you can.

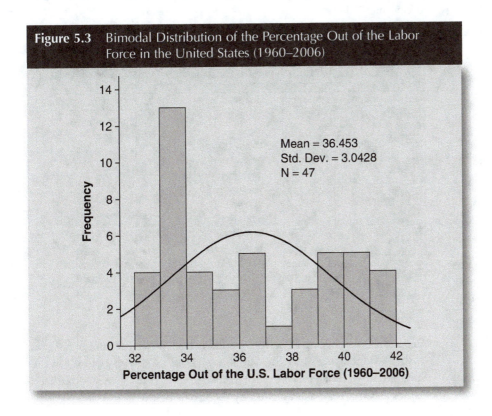

Figure 5.3 Bimodal Distribution of the Percentage Out of the Labor Force in the United States (1960–2006)

● TRANSFORMATION REDUX: STANDARDIZATION AND z SCORES

There was at least one general type of data transformation that we did not introduce in the previous chapter because it requires that you be armed with an understanding of the mean and standard deviation, which we covered in this chapter. **Standardization** (or what one accomplishes in creating what statisticians call **z scores** or **standard scores** of variables) helps solve the proverbial problem of comparing apples with oranges. It does so by making all such transformed variables have a mean of 0 and a standard deviation of 1. What? Sounds like an unnatural act, doesn't it? We'll encounter far more strange statistical animals than this one.

As with nearly all statistical procedures, creating standardized scores of variables can be achieved by several techniques. One of these ways is through the Descriptive Statistics function in SPSS.

Step 1: Click on Descriptive Statistic/Descriptives in the "welfare and economics" file.

Step 2: In the resulting Descriptives dialog box, move the variable(s) you wish to standardize into the Variable(s) box, as shown below for the variable, %_out_of_lab_force_16Plus. Check the box "Save standardized values as variables," as indicated by the arrow below.

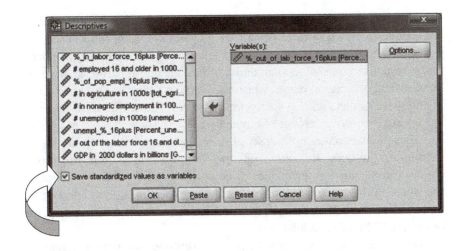

SPSS will create a new variable by assigning the prefix "Zscore" to the variable's name. It calculates this new variable from the old by subtracting the mean of that variable from every observation in our file and dividing by the variable's standard deviation, thus creating a variable with mean of 0 and standard deviation of 1. If you don't believe that, check out the mean and standard deviation in the descriptive statistics table below.

Statistics

Zscore: %_out_of_lab_force_16plus

N	Valid	47
	Missing	0
Mean		.0000000
Std. Deviation		1.00000000
Skewness		.363
Std. Error of Skewness		.347
Kurtosis		-1.512
Std. Error of Kurtosis		.681

CONCLUSION •

Statistics tend to come in three's, including the number of general characteristics by which we can describe a variable: (1) its central tendency, (2) the extent of its variability, and (3) the shape of the variable's distribution. Each of these three descriptive statistics includes different tools to capture different elements of each variable's character. As you have seen, and will see frequently in the pages to come, some of these statistics are more appropriate under certain circumstances than under others. Means, in particular, have an Achilles heel of extreme values, which will lead us to later use tools for identifying these outliers and, in some circumstances, taking the drastic step of kicking such observations out of our analysis.

These somewhat simple descriptive statistics are extremely useful in helping us understand our data and lay the foundation for more sophisticated statistical techniques to be taken up later. Beware, of course, that some of them can be used to slant the story to one side or another, as in the difference between mean and median tax breaks from the early years of George W. Bush's administration.

Some descriptive statistics help us determine whether a variable's distribution is "normal." Many statistics rely on this famous bell-shaped curve, with its several (magical?) mathematical properties (e.g., two thirds of all observations fall within ±1 standard deviation of the mean). Assessments of normal distributions are both somewhat informal (e.g., eyeballing a variable's histogram relative to a normal distribution superimposed on it by SPSS, at our request) or more formal, as in a test developed by a couple of Russians in the past century that we will examine later in the book.

One measure of central tendency (mean) and dispersion (standard deviation) can be used to transform variables so as to permit comparisons of otherwise apples and oranges by creating the sleepy transformation of z scores of variables that have means of 0 and standard deviations of 1. This is one of many data transformations that an analyst will return to his toolbox to use, as are the charts and tables to which we turn in the next chapter.

To practice and reinforce the lessons of this chapter of the book, turn to Exercise 4 in the *Student Workbook* (available at http://www.sagepub.com/pearsonsp/).

CHAPTER 6

CHARTS AND GRAPHS

THE CAPACITIES AND ●
FUNCTIONS OF CHARTS AND GRAPHS

While a "picture may be worth a thousand words," graphs and charts rarely speak entirely for themselves. When joined by statistics and text, however, graphs and charts can help produce principled and persuasive argument, strengthen storytelling, and aid in pattern recognition. Graphs, of course, can also mislead, and we will display several examples in this chapter where graphs either wittingly or unwittingly do just that.

As we look at examples of good and bad graphical display in this chapter, we will also provide guidelines, based on good practice and research on perception and cognition, on which we should base the production of graphs and by which we can evaluate the quality of others' graphs. Aspects of graphs (and tables as well) can be chosen in ways that highlight what's important in the story we seek to tell. Conversely, violations of these principles obscure important points, highlight sideshows, confuse readers, and even misinform.

As you will see in the exercises you complete, statistical software programs such as SPSS and Excel easily produce graphs and charts. Unfortunately, the "default" graphs they produce invariably violate the principles of good graphical display. Fortunately, these software packages also provide editing tools for you to bring their graphs, charts, and tables into closer compliance with the guidelines for effective graphical display that this chapter will provide. These software packages also entice the user with numerous graphic bells and whistles, many of which get in the way of effective communication. You will discover in the pages that follow that there are plenty of defaults to derail and options to avoid in producing good graphs and charts.

Graphs Complement Statistics, Detecting Patterns Where Statistics Alone Fail

Consider Anscombe's Quartet, named after its inventor, F. J. Anscombe (1973). He begins with four sets of data (displayed in Tufte, 2001, pp. 13–14), as shown in Table 6.1.

Clearly, it's difficult to deduce much from this assortment of numbers by simply eyeballing them. What's interesting about them is that they produce the same results if each is entered into a regression equation. We'll turn to regression analysis in Chapter 11, so don't worry about the meaning of particular numbers below except to note that these statistics are the same for each set of paired numbers in Table 6.1.

Number of observations (n) = 11
Mean of the xs ($\bar{x}$) = 9.0
Mean of the ys ($\bar{y}$) = 7.5
Regression coefficient (b_1) of y on x = .5
Equation of regression line: $y = 3 + .5x$
Sum of squares of $x - \bar{x}$ = 110.0
Regression sum of squares = 27.50 (1 df)
Residential sum of squares of y = 13.75 (9 df)
Estimated standard error of b_1 = 0.118
Multiple R^2 = .667

Table 6.1   Anscombe's Quartet Design

I		II		III		IV	
X	Y	X	Y	X	Y	X	Y
10.0	8.04	10.0	9.14	10.0	7.46	8.0	6.58
8.0	6.95	8.0	8.14	8.0	6.77	8.0	5.76
13.0	7.58	13.0	8.74	13.0	12.74	8.0	7.71
9.0	8.81	9.0	8.77	9.0	7.11	8.0	8.84
11.0	8.33	11.0	9.26	11.0	7.81	8.0	8.47
14.0	9.96	14.0	8.10	14.0	8.84	8.0	7.04
6.0	7.24	6.0	6.13	6.0	6.08	8.0	5.25
4.0	4.26	4.0	3.10	4.0	5.39	19.0	12.50
12.0	10.84	12.0	9.13	12.0	8.15	8.0	5.56
7.0	4.82	7.0	7.26	7.0	6.42	8.0	7.91
5.0	5.68	5.0	4.74	5.0	5.73	8.0	6.89

SOURCE: Tufte (2001, pp. 13–14). Used by permission from Graphics Press.

Note too, however, what happens when we produce a graph of each set of paired numbers. We see that these four sets of numbers, although characterized exactly the same by a number of descriptive and regression statistics, reveal quite different patterns and thus tell quite different stories in Figure 6.1 (Tufte, 2001, p. 14).

Figure 6.1   The Graphical Display of Anscombe's Quartet

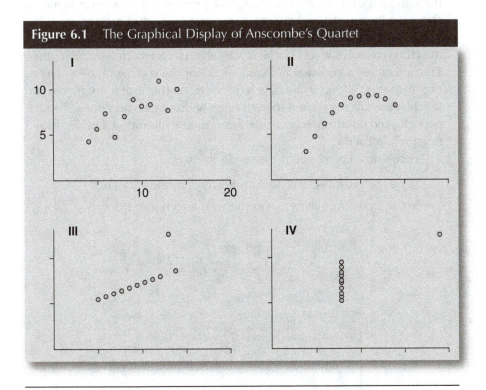

SOURCE: Tufte (2001, p. 14). Used by permission from Graphics Press.

The point of these four graphs is to show that statistics alone do not always adequately describe the patterns that we look for in the data. The story is in the picture *and* the statistics. Don't tell only part of a story by relying on statistics (or graphs) alone.

Graphs Can Help Diagnose Problems in the Data

I ask students in my statistics class to complete the survey found in Appendix C at the beginning of each semester. The purpose of this exercise is to illustrate some of the problems and pitfalls that face those who write questions and design questionnaires. But one pair of questions is intended to demonstrate that all measurement errors aren't as bad as one might believe from the discussion of the complexities of asking and answering questions. In this latter regard, I ask two versions of the same question about the height of each student. One is self-reported; the other is an "objective" measure of height taken by a fellow student. This latter measure is arrived at by using tape measures that I tape to the wall at four different locations throughout the classroom. I position the tape measures to begin at 36 inches above the floor, which will factor into the story's conclusion below.

To demonstrate to myself and to the students in my class one year that these two measures would not be exactly alike but pretty close to each other, I ran a regression equation in Excel, asking for the correlation between the two measures. (A correlation is a measure of the extent to which two variables are linearly related to each other and can take on values of +1.0 if perfectly, and positively, related; .0 if not related at all; and −1 if perfectly, and negatively, related.)

Here's how I produced these results in Excel[1]:

Step 1: Select Tools/Data Analysis/Regression, and click OK.

Step 2: Enter the values as shown in the screen shot below.

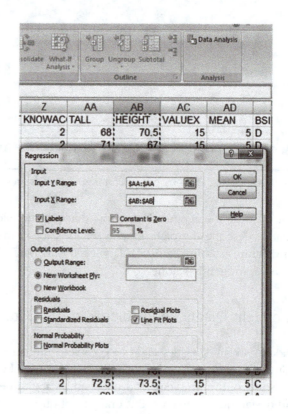

I was shocked to discover that the correlation between height as measured in these two ways was only .30, far less than I had expected. I then turned to the scattergram that accompanies the regression analysis (because I specified "Line Fit Plots" in the dialog box above). The resulting default graph (Figure 6.2) is quite uninformative and directs attention to the regression line or predicted values of measured height, given the measures of self-reported height.

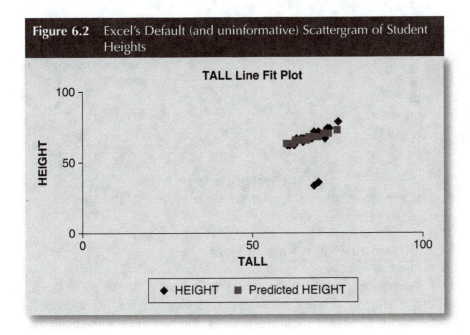

Figure 6.2 Excel's Default (and uninformative) Scattergram of Student Heights

This graph violates nearly every principle of graphical design that we'll examine later in this chapter. Here's what the graph should look like (Figure 6.3) after overriding the defaults and applying several principles of graphical design.

It is fairly clear from this picture that two students reported their measured height without adding the 36 inches that the tape measure was hung above the floor. The graph enabled me to spot the problem quickly. (By the way, these 2 observations represent what we'll later call **bivariate** (i.e., two-variable) **outliers**. These stray observations can be easily corrected in the spreadsheet and the above analysis rerun, which would show a correlation of .94 instead of .30. I was right after all, but I could only demonstrate this with clean data.

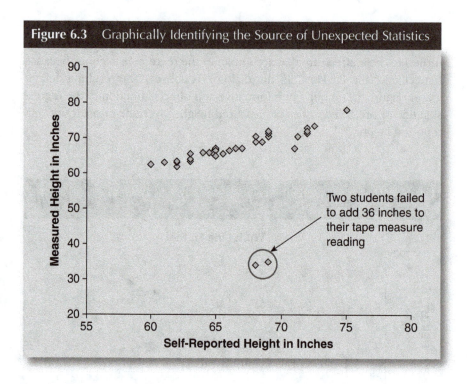

Figure 6.3   Graphically Identifying the Source of Unexpected Statistics

Graphs Can Display Tons of Data

The power of graphs lies in part in their ability to display a lot of data. Tufte (2001, p. 30) demonstrates this point with a graph of New York City's weather for 1980 (see Figure 6.4). The graph displays the temperature, precipitation, and relative humidity for every day of that year. It displays 1,888 different numbers. Can you imagine what the tables with these numbers would look like? Surely, we could more precisely identify specific values in such tables but not their patterns as easily as the graph enables. Indeed, a table is more appropriate than a graph if your purpose or need is to find and compare precise values. Graphs are better at identifying patterns and irregular observations.

It is also the case that graphs can often convey information more efficiently than text can. Here again is another example to illustrate that point from Tufte (2001, p. 37). Figure 6.5 displays counts of the outgoing mail from the U.S. Congress, arrayed in a time series for the years 1967 through 1972. The peaks occur in October of even-number years. Why might that be? You guessed it. The peaks are the months prior to congressional elections.

Figure 6.4 Graphical Display of 1,888 Different Numbers to Reveal Patterns

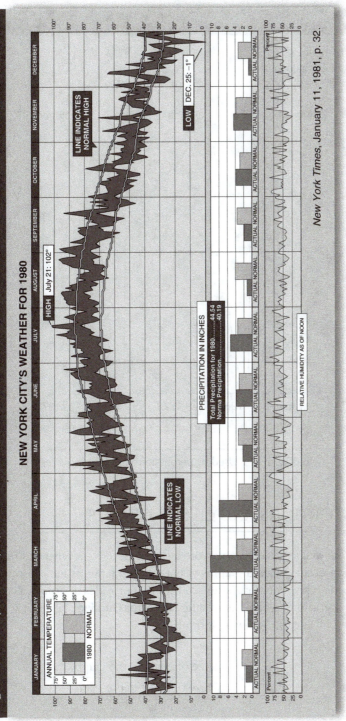

NEW YORK CITY'S WEATHER FOR 1980

SOURCE: Tufte (2001, p. 30). Used by permission from Graphics Press.

New York Times, January 11, 1981, p. 32.

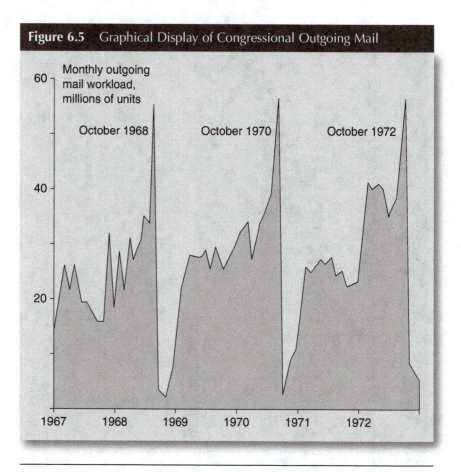

Figure 6.5 Graphical Display of Congressional Outgoing Mail

SOURCE: Tufte (2001, p. 37). Used by permission from Graphics Press.

● SPOTTING DISTORTIONS AND LIES IN GRAPHS

Graphs, as well as statistics and words, can be used to deceive and mislead. Distortion occurs when a graph's visual representation is inconsistent with its numeric representation. Tufte (2001, p. 57) provides a formal calculation of such distortions, which he calls the **Lie Factor Quotient**. He calculates this number by using the following formula:

$$\text{Lie Factor} = \frac{\text{Size of effect in the graph}}{\text{Size of effect in the data}}.$$

Distortion quotients less than 0.95 and greater than 1.05 constitute substantial distortion in Tufte's view. Let's examine an illustration and calculate the Lie Factor for it.

Consider the graphical depiction (Figure 6.6) of fuel economy standards for new automobiles set by the U.S. Congress in 1978 (reproduced in Tufte, 2001, p. 57, from *New York Times*, August 9, 1978, p. D-2.)

Fuel standards for new cars were to increase from 18 miles/gallon in 1978 to 27.5 by 1985, an increase of 53% ((27.5 − 18.0)/18.0). The graph as originally displayed, however, represented 18 miles/gallon by a line 0.6 inches long. It represented the 27.5 mile/gallon target in 1985 with a line 5.3 inches long. This graphical increase was 783% ((5.3 − 0.6)/0.6). The Lie Factor was therefore

$$\frac{783}{53} = 14.8.$$

Figure 6.6   Graphical Distortions of Fuel Economy Standards for Automobiles

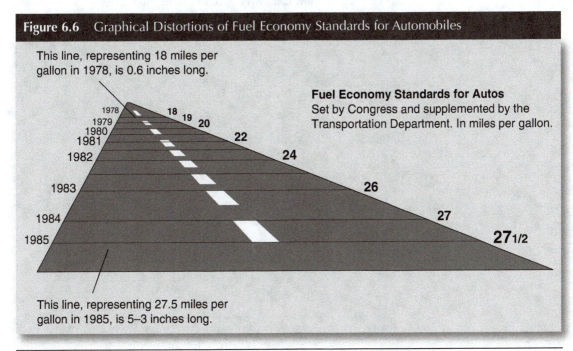

SOURCE: Tufte (2001, p. 57). Used by permission from Graphics Press.

It's a creative graph, but one that leaves an impression substantially at variance with the facts. Tufte provides a simpler and more honest presentation of the same data (with the added and useful figures for the expected average fuel economy for all automobiles in 1978 and 1985). It's not as artistic but certainly more truthful (see Figure 6.7).

Another example of graphical distortion is provided by the National Science Foundation (NSF), the agency charged with supporting basic research in the United States. NSF issues biennial chartbooks of statistics about science and technology. But it also must go before Congress each year and request and typically justify larger requests for funds. The temptation is to massage the data in ways that make a more compelling case for increased funds. Would a precipitous drop in the number of Nobel Prizes for science awarded to U.S. scientists help? Someone must have thought so, because the 1974 *Science*

Figure 6.7 Honest Graphical Depiction of Fuel Economy Standards

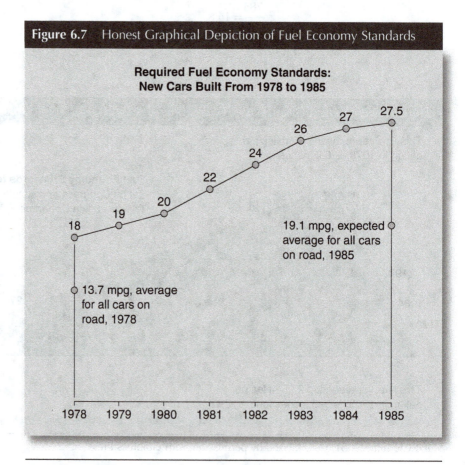

SOURCE: Tufte (2001). Used by permission from Graphics Press.

Indicators chartbook included a graph of Nobel prizes in science awarded to the citizens of selected countries (reproduced in Tufte, 2001; see Figure 6.8).

Wow, U.S. science looked like it was in trouble, didn't it? Can you spot the sleight of hand in this chart? The graph changes the total number of years in the final data point. While all others represent a 10-year period, the last on

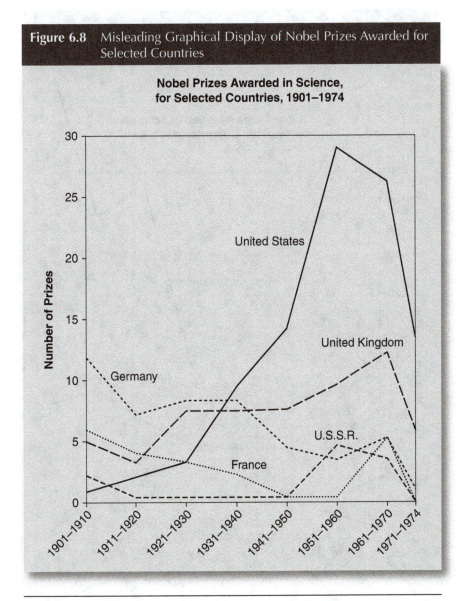

Figure 6.8 Misleading Graphical Display of Nobel Prizes Awarded for Selected Countries

this chart includes the number of Nobel prizes in science awarded during a 4-year period. Of course, there will be fewer of them during this truncated period, as is the case with every country represented here.

What do the data show when the remaining 6 years of awards are included? Tufte (2001, p. 60) cleverly displays the results in a graph (see Figure 6.9).

Figure 6.9 Honest Graphical Display of Nobel Prizes for Selected Countries

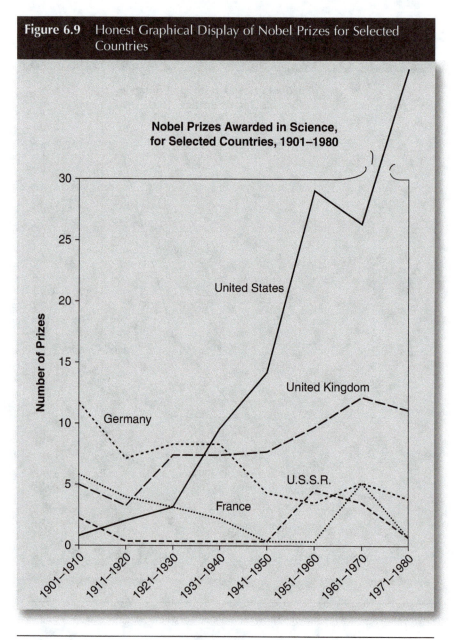

SOURCE: Tufte (2001, p. 60). Used by permission from Graphics Press.

Our third example (Figure 6.10) is a chart of the aid to localities provided by the state of New York during the 11-year period from 1966–1967 to 1976–1977 (Tufte, 2001, p. 61).

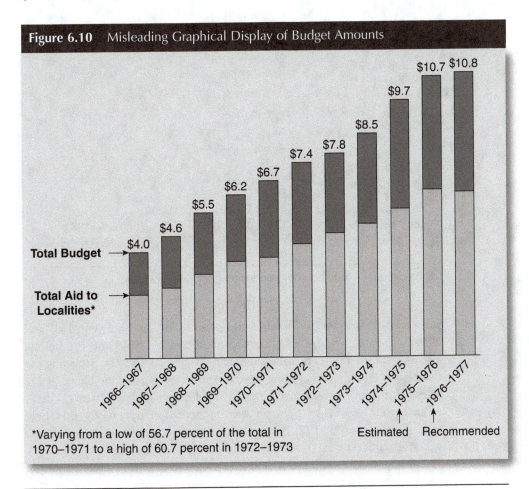

Figure 6.10 Misleading Graphical Display of Budget Amounts

*Varying from a low of 56.7 percent of the total in 1970–1971 to a high of 60.7 percent in 1972–1973

SOURCE: Tufte (2001, p. 61). Used by permission from Graphics Press.

Another example of out-of-control government spending, isn't it? That's certainly the impression I get. But which two factors may be causing much of this apparent increase in aid to localities? Remember from Chapter 4's presentation of index construction that time-series financial data should always be adjusted for changes in the value of money and population size. Not doing so conflates real change with the change brought about, in this case, by inflation and population growth. How do you, therefore, correct the distortions contained in Figure 6.10? (The steps for doing this can be found in Chapter 4.) Figure 6.11 (Tufte, 2001, p. 68) provides a more truthful story by transforming the data into per capita, constant budget expenditures. The

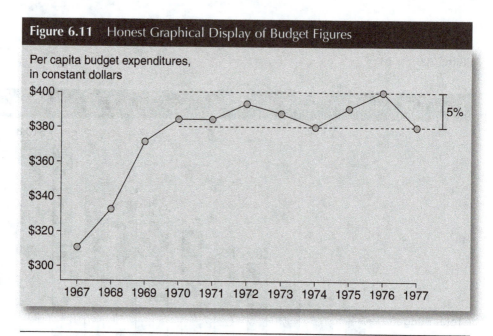

Figure 6.11   Honest Graphical Display of Budget Figures

Per capita budget expenditures,
in constant dollars

SOURCE: Tufte (2001, p. 68). Used by permission from Graphics Press.

story is one of substantial growth in revenues to localities between 1967 and 1970 but relatively stable revenue streams thereafter. Note also the helpful visual cues Tufte (2001) provides in telling this graph's story by providing the two dotted lines and translating this range into the percentage figure of 5%. These attributes satisfy two of the graphic guidelines we'll see later: (1) don't require your viewer to perform the mathematical operations that help interpret the chart and (2) direct the observer's attention to the point you want the data to reveal by enclosing the data in some fashion.

Finally, imagine yourself a staunch supporter of stricter enforcement of highway speed limits because you believe, as did Governor Abraham Ribicoff of Connecticut in the mid-1950s, that such a crackdown would result in fewer traffic fatalities. You'd be rather pleased to share the graph shown in Figure 6.12 with those who would look and listen (Tufte 2001, p. 74, as originally presented in Campbell & Ross, 1968).

You'd also be engaged in a form of graphical tomfoolery. Why? There are at least four reasons:

1. The scale on the vertical *Y*-axis (i.e., the number of traffic fatalities) is severely truncated, exaggerating the 1-year change.

Figure 6.12 Misleading Graphical Display of Traffic Deaths in Connecticut

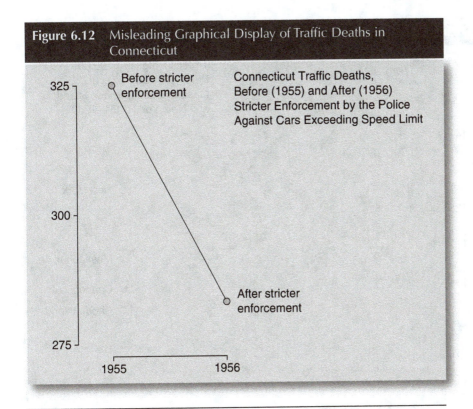

SOURCE: Campbell and Ross (1968, Figure d, p. 38). Used by permission. Copyright John Wiley & Sons.

2. The graph includes only two data points yet wants to argue that this is a trend caused by stricter enforcement. Chance or random fluctuation is inherent in nearly every human phenomenon. Two successive observations of anything are likely to vary. Two observations do not make a trend.

3. The graph lacks context both in terms of a longer series of observations for Connecticut traffic fatalities and in comparisons with other states that, during this period, did not crack down on speeding.

4. The graph doesn't take population size into account. The more the people, the more the drivers, the more the miles driven, and the more likely you'll have traffic fatalities. Increases in fatalities may be an artifact of such increases. Decreases may be an artifact of population decline and/or fewer miles driven.

Figure 6.13 corrects for these possible distortions (Tufte, 2001, p. 75).

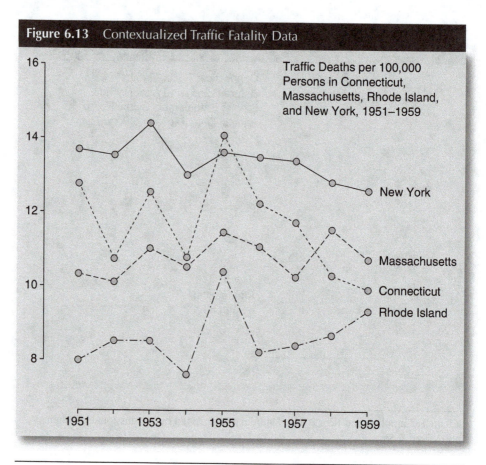

Figure 6.13 Contextualized Traffic Fatality Data

SOURCE: Tufte (2001, p. 75). Used by permission from Graphics Press.

You can note several features of this more useful graph that might shake your faith in stricter enforcement, although we would need to know much more about this time period than this graph alone provides. Assuming that the other three Northeastern states displayed here did not crack down on speeding in 1955, we see that all states experienced reductions in traffic fatalities. What might have caused this? Bad weather, a sharp rise in gasoline prices, or any number of things that might have reduced traffic overall, which could have led to declines in traffic fatalities. If Connecticut continued its stricter enforcement, however, the graph displays a continuing decline in fatalities, which the other states did not experience, so your faith in stricter enforcement may not be quite so shaken.

This graph illustrates another point to which we will return later in this book. To make a convincing case (e.g., stricter enforcement of speeding laws produces fewer traffic fatalities) requires that you rule out other possible causes for the patterns you observe (e.g., weather, increasing gasoline prices). Physicians might call this "diagnosis through exclusion." You do so in a statistical sense by "controlling for" these other factors, to which we will turn in the chapters ahead. Of course, you can't control for other possible causes unless you measure them. Statisticians give this the fancy name of **full model specification**, a concept to which we will return in later chapters.

Having viewed some bad and misleading graphs, let's consider next how our understanding of perception, cognition, and memory helps us design better graphs, charts, and tables.

PERCEPTION, COGNITION, AND MEMORY ● INFLUENCE THE INTERPRETATION OF GRAPHS

Applied policy research like the kind that this book examines is predicated, first, on asking what we need to know to help make better decisions. This will invariably involve a search for answers in the existing literature. Although research on the questions you're asking may be extensive, it will often come up short of answering the question in the specific context you face. In such cases, additional research may be needed, often involving the collection of data from which the statistics in this text help you extract the answers or tell a story. The narrative of such a story should arise from the data and your analysis of them. But there are at least three challenges facing you after the data have revealed their story:

1. Your primary audiences are likely to be very busy people with limited knowledge of statistics. This requires you to determine what the story line is, that is, what are the important points that come from your data and analysis. A memorandum and PowerPoint presentations are likely to be the forms of such communication. (This communication might also be a 30-second elevator speech, but we won't address that type of communication in this text.)

2. Your secondary audiences are other data analysts, who will look carefully at your methodology to make sure that your arguments are based on principled statistical analysis. This is especially likely to be the case if the

questions you're answering are important ones with powerful stakeholders, some of whom may not benefit from your conclusions. A technical appendix is the likely form for such communication.

3. In both instances, you have to determine which point(s) you should make, how to direct or draw the reader (or listener) to those points, and how to make them stick.

Graphs and charts can help accomplish these objectives, especially if you understand what grabs peoples' attention and helps them cognitively process (i.e., understand, remember, and retrieve) the points you're trying to make. Research on perception and cognition provides some helpful clues here that will inform the guidelines for effective graphical display. Of course, there's a flip side to this coin. To wit: How do you reduce or eliminate things that get in the way of achieving these objectives? We'll provide some "don'ts" as well as "dos" in the guidelines you'll find below.

As with asking and answering questions, presenting and understanding a written argument depends on recognizing or paying attention to the message and processing that information in ways that aid understanding, memory, judgment, and retrieval. Graphs are a visual means of communication and are subject to the mechanisms and processes of sight. It is useful, therefore, to understand how those mechanisms and processes work.

The process begins with sensation; that is, we sense some kind of stimuli, whether words on a written page, the voice of a colleague down the hall, or a graph in a memorandum we're reading to help determine how to reduce teenage pregnancy or increase high school completion rates. When we focus on a page, our eyes can distinguish as many as 625 separate points in a square inch (Tufte 2001, p. 161). But that focus is fleeting, fixing on a particular spot for less than half a second before jumping to another. While our eyes are receiving millions of bits of information, our attention and perception attend to a limited amount of that information (Few, 2004, p. 95).

The brain processes the stimuli first in iconic or sensory memory, analogous in a computer to a keyboard buffer that serves as a (very) temporary waiting room. The electrical signals may then pass into short-term memory, analogous to a computer's working memory. Stimuli are translated here into meaningful terms to interpret and respond to the stimuli. Under certain conditions (e.g., rehearsal or repetition), these stimuli may be stored in what is called long-term memory, to be retrieved (with the right cues) at a later time.

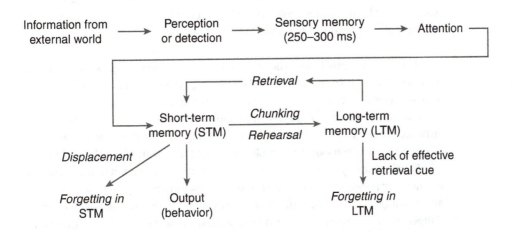

Sensory memory is automatic and unconscious and, for these reasons, is considered as pre-attentive processing, attention, or recognition. We'll later see that there are aspects of graphs that are more (or less) likely to "grab your attention" through, say, the location of an item or the color of an object on a page. For example, recall how your attention was drawn in Figure 6.3 to the two errant height measurements because I enclosed them in a circle and pointed an arrow at them.

Short-term memory has two attributes that affect the principles of graphical display. Short-term memory is both (1) temporary and (2) limited in storage capacity.

The second of these is perhaps the more important consideration for graphical design. Many believe that people can store only seven plus or minus two items in short-term memory at any one time (Miller, 1956). (This conclusion may more precisely be the case for the short-term memory of college students recalling lists of digits, but we don't need to bother ourselves with such details or with such debates in cognitive psychology about whether short-term and long-term memory are really two different structures.) If your short-term memory register is full, moving a new item into it requires that an item already there be moved to long-term memory or forgotten. There are at least two implications of this fact for graphical design:

1. A legend with 10 or more colors or shapes for different categories will tax the reader to continually return to the legend.

2. Combining information into coherent patterns may help combine multiple bits of data into a single "chunk," thus saving space in short-term memory. You may recall that remembering the names of the Great Lakes is made easier by the mnemonic "HOMES," a chunk representing the first letters of Huron, Ontario, Michigan, Erie, and Superior.

Although we saw in our measurement chapter the implications that long-term memory harbors for asking and answering questions (e.g., use of language in which prior events were encoded and retrieval cues to help recall), it does not inform the design of graphs and tables as much as do pre-attentive visual attributes and short-term memory characteristics. Let's turn to these two forms of memory and flesh out their implications for the design of graphs and tables.

Recall (have you stored this in long-term memory yet?) that sensory memory or pre-attentive processing is unconscious and automatic. It may be an evolutionary relic of our distant ancestors' need to quickly recognize danger in their environment and take flight or fight. We may be hardwired to have our eyes move toward those stimuli that are different or that take on certain attributes. We modify below Colin Ware's (2000) and Stephen Few's (2004) specification of categories and attributes that have lessons for the design of tables and graphs.

Category	Attribute
Form	Orientation
	Line length
	Line width
	Size
	Shape
	Curvature
	Added marks
	Enclosure
Color	Hue
	Saturation
	Lightness
Spatial position	Two-dimensional positioning
	Proximity
Context	Contrast

Attributes of Form

Differences in each of the attributes of form are illustrated below. Note how your eye is drawn to those attributes that differ from those with which they are enclosed (Few, 2004, p. 99).

Attributes of Form

Attribute	Illustration	Attribute	Illustration
Orientation		Shape	
Line Length		Curvature	
Line Width		Added Marks	
Size		Enclosure	

SOURCE: Few (2004, p. 99).

Attributes of Color

Color is actually composed of three different attributes: hue, saturation, and lightness. (It's threes again.) We usually think of hue as color (e.g., red, green, blue), but we'll call it hue because of the different pre-attentive properties of saturation and lightness. Saturation is the degree to which a hue displays its quality (Few, 2004, p. 101).

Lightness is the degree to which a color is characterized by being fully black or white.

Consider the difference between hue and, say, line length as they relate to graphical design. We naturally ascribe greater value to longer line lengths than to shorter ones. In other words, line length attributes are encoded quantitatively. But is that the case with hue? Is green perceived to be larger than red? No. Different hues are perceived as different categorically but not quantitatively. Different hues, therefore, are of little assistance if we mean to represent quantitative differences. Saturation and lightness, however, can be perceived quantitatively and used as an aid in our graphs in expressing differences of degree. Therefore, use hues in your graphs to demark different categories or draw attention to objects or numbers, not to suggest differences in quantity. Also, remember that colors are more expensive to print and don't necessarily photocopy well (unless using a color copier). In other words, stick with shades of gray to convey quantitative differences in graphs, a guideline to which we'll return below.

Attributes of Spatial Position

Two-dimensional (2-D) spatial positioning on a page can be illustrated by the following box. Here, the eye gravitates toward the one object that differs in position from the others.

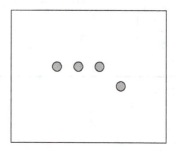

The eye's attention will also be drawn to the grouping of objects in proximity to each other. We perceive the 10 objects in the following box, for example, as belonging to three groups because of their spatial proximity.

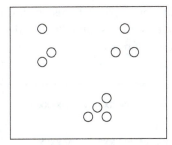

This *principle of proximity* (Few, 2004) is based on work by the Gestalt School of Psychology in the early 20th century, as are the other principles noted in this section. We can use these principles, for example, to subtly instruct a reader's eyes to scan the rows or columns of a table by grouping the observations more closely in a row or in a column, as the following figure demonstrates. Your strong visual inclination is to read the left box as rows and the right box as columns as a consequence of the principle of proximity.

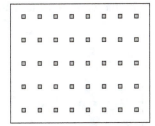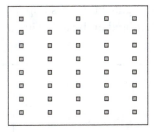

We also perceive objects that are similar in size, color, shape, and orientation as belonging to the same group. This is referred to as the *similarity principle*. This principle or effect is illustrated in the figure below. The gray circles are visually recorded as members of the same group because of their similarity of color, no matter what their proximity is.

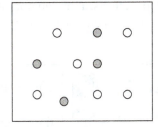

We can again use this principle (e.g., using similarity of both color and shape) to guide the reader's eye, as the following figure does in causing the eye to see columns instead of rows.

xxxx yyyy **xxxx** yyyy **xxxx** yyyy

xxxx yyyy **xxxx** yyyy **xxxx** yyyy

xxxx yyyy **xxxx** yyyy **xxxx** yyyy

The *principle of enclosure* achieves a similar result. It uses visual borders to set off elements in the enclosure from those outside it, again suggesting group membership. It also achieves the effect of drawing your eye first to those elements inside the enclosure, which in graphs and tables can be used to highlight what is important or what you want the reader to view first, as illustrated in the following figures:

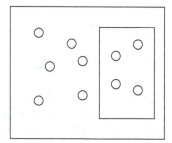 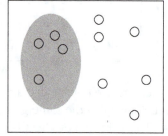

The *principle of connection* argues that objects that are connected by a line are conceived of as part of the same group. Indeed, this effect trumps the proximity and similarity effects, although not the enclosure effect, as you can see in the following figure (Few 2004, p. 114).

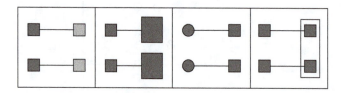

SOURCE: Few (2004, p. 114).

Points on a graph that are not connected by lines are difficult for us to connect without their aid. They reveal the shape of the data as well as link the objects. They are commonplace (essential) in graphs of time-series data.

Attributes of Context and Contrast

Every attribute of visual perception is influenced by its context. Objects can seem to be brighter when lit in a dark room than in one flush with sunlight. Hues can be made to appear lighter or darker depending on the saturation of the surrounding colors. In the context of a table or graph, for example, it is easier to read black text on a white background.

Our visual senses evolved in ways that cause us to be particularly aware of differences, which are themselves defined by the contrast of an object to its context. Our brain is not only drawn to these differences but also tries to make some sense of them. Contrast is especially effective if one item in a group of others has a distinguishing attribute in contrast to all others. The more items with that attribute, however, the less any one of them will stand out.

Don't make your reader work at the comparisons by requiring additional calculations to make the point you want the reader to come away with. If you want the reader, for example, to focus on the rates of child mortality in the United States in contrast with selected developed countries, as shown in Figure 6.14, you could do so by expressing other countries' rates as a percentage of the U.S. rate.

Tables and graphs should provide the reader with "affordances," that is, characteristics that reveal their purpose and use. A handle on a door tells you implicitly to pull; a plate, to push. Coloring Finland dark gray in the child mortality graph (Figure 6.14) signals to the reader that I'm going to devote particular attention in the text to that country in trying to explain why its child mortality rate is half that of the United States.

Limits to the Perception of Attributes

There are, of course, limits to our abilities to perceive attributes. Ware (2000), for example, reports that people can distinguish no more than about eight different hues in a graph, about four different orientations, and about four different sizes. Few (2004, p. 106) suggests that, with the exception of hue and shape, it's best to limit the number of different attributes to no more than four. In addition, pre-attentive processing tends to be limited to one attribute at a time. That is to say, it's okay to vary lightness (especially if, say,

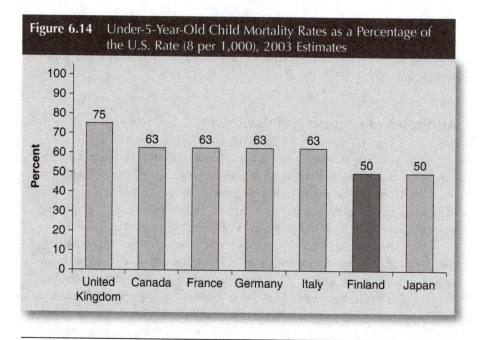

Figure 6.14 Under-5-Year-Old Child Mortality Rates as a Percentage of the U.S. Rate (8 per 1,000), 2003 Estimates

SOURCE: World Health Organization, www.who.int/healthinfo/statistics/mortchildmortality/en/index.html, accessed June 18, 2008. The chart was constructed using Excel.

the four variations of gray are quite distinct) but not to add differences in shape at the same time.

Tufte (1990, p. 90) recommends the use of hues that are found in nature, especially the lighter shades of gray, yellow, green, and blue, which are easy on the eye. This is particularly useful if you don't want to draw attention to numbers or objects. Conversely, objects painted in deeply saturated versions of any hue will draw the eye toward those items.

● GUIDELINES FOR CREATING EFFECTIVE GRAPHS

We have already provided a few guidelines for graphical display above in the context of aspects of visual perception. We'll repeat them here and add more that are consistent with our understanding of sensory and short-term memory and that also build on experience and good practice. You might even use these dos and don'ts as a checklist in creating graphs and tables.

Don'ts

- Do not use three dimensions to represent one. A third dimension, say, in a 3-D bar chart will exaggerate visual differences because you're now comparing volumes instead of line lengths or areas. Three-dimensional graphs also make actual values of lines or bars difficult to compare with grid values. In short, don't use 3-D graphs.

- Do not use severely truncated ranges on your vertical axis. This causes the visual impression to depart substantially from what the data say. So too does fake perspective. Don't use either.

- Do not select arbitrary starting points or change the scale within a graph.

- Do not enclose an entire graph by using a box or color because it causes the reader to attend to those elements in contrast to the data (Few 2004, p. 113).

- Do not use vivid line fill patterns in bar graphs (e.g., cross-hatching) because they can cause a dizzying visual effect called "moiré vibration" (Few 2004, p. 64).

- Do not introduce elements in a graph that puzzle the reader (e.g., unusual interval values on the *Y*- or *X*-axis). This may inspire mystery but lead the reader to look for clues to solve the mystery rather than understand what the data say.

- Do not lead a reader to focus on an element by contrasting it with others in size, shape, orientation, and so on, unless you want the reader to attend to those objects or numbers.

- Do not make your reader work by requiring additional calculations to make the point you want the reader to come away with.

- Do not manipulate the aspect ratio of your graph (i.e., the ratio of height to width) to exaggerate or minimize the pattern or slope of the data.

- Do not design graphs for the purpose of showing off your technical proficiency. If your graphs cause the reader to think, "Gee, I wonder how she did that," you've led the reader off the point. Graphs should help tell the story, not *be* the story.

Dos

- Devote most of the graph's ink to the data instead of the supporting components, such as grids (Tufte, 2001). Many nondata elements are unnecessary to the meaning or impact you want the graph to have and can get in the way of that message by moving the eye away from the data. Delete or mute the nondata elements.

• Avoid clutter; it taxes our sensory and cognitive capacities. For example, use no more than five different distributions in a line graph. Use multiple box-plots when displaying more than five distributions.

• Label in plain English, not with mnemonics or abbreviations (ditto for tables and explanations in text).

• Use black on white for text.

• Label data elements directly on the graph itself. Minimize the use of legends whenever possible. Legends require storing the meaning of each line or bar in short-term memory, which is limited in time and space.

• Because our eyes are practiced in detecting deviations from the horizon, graphics should tend toward the horizontal, where "cause" is displayed on the horizontal (X) axis and effect, vertically (on the Y-axis). In general, make your graphs wider than they are tall.

• Use different hues in your graphs to demark different categories or draw attention to objects or numbers, not to suggest differences in quantity.

• The width of bars in a bar chart should be approximately equal to the white space between them. (There's no scientific evidence to support this prescription that I know of. I just think it looks clean and clearly displays each bar.)

• Provide enough context to accurately present the data (e.g., more than two time points, comparisons with similar units).

• Tables and graphs should provide the reader with "affordances," that is, characteristics that reveal their purpose and use.

• Rotate bar charts so that categorical labels and bars run horizontally from high to low if your purpose is to make such comparisons and to emphasize those categories that are at the top and the bottom of such rankings.

• Adjust for inflation in graphs that include time-series financial data. Adjust for population change in data that can be reasonably supposed to be influenced by population size.

• Sort, group, organize, sequence (e.g., top to bottom, left to right), and prioritize the data (through the use of contrasting visual attributes such as more saturated hues) in ways that serve the graph's purpose.

● The top and left positions of a graph in Western cultures tend to be considered the beginning. Place the categories you want to receive the greatest emphasis in those positions.

● Use simple geometric forms, such as straight lines, circles, and squares.

● Locate explanatory text as close as possible to the data to which it refers.

● Add good titles that clearly tell the reader what the graph's story line is.

● Annotate extensively, including the sources of data.

● Colors do not have a natural visual hierarchy; varying shades of gray show quantities better and are more likely to photocopy accurately.

● When creating a related series of graphs, use the same characteristics in each (e.g., scale, aspect ratios, colors, shapes, fonts).

● Editing and revision are as essential in producing good graphs and tables as they are in good writing.

● Always think about the "yo' momma" rule: Would your mother understand what you are trying to communicate in this graph?

● Finally, apply none of these principles rigidly. Use good judgment. Think about the purpose of your graph and how the elements work to achieve that purpose.

THE TOOLS OF GRAPHICAL DISPLAY ●

Histograms

Histograms display the distribution of continuous variables. Histograms are, therefore, useful for at least three different purposes:

1. To visually display the extent to which the distribution can be characterized as "normal," which is a characteristic that many statistics assume variables have

2. To draw substantive conclusions about the overall pattern of the distribution or individual observations within that distribution (e.g., half of the cities in your study have child mortality rates of less than 4 in every 1,000 births; a particular city falls within the upper half of the set of similar cities in terms of its per capita homicide rate)

3. To visually identify unusual observations or outliers

Let us create a histogram of the frequency or number of violent crimes in the largest cities in the United States in 2004.

Step 1: Open the Community Indicators data set in SPSS.

Step 2: Click on Graphs/Legacy Dialogs/Histogram, as shown on the screen save below:

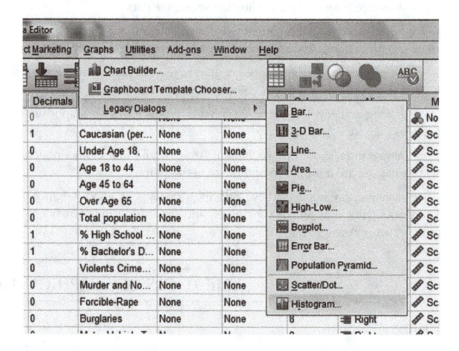

Step 3: Move VIOLENTCRIME (Violent Crimes – Total) into the variable box, and hit OK.

The histogram that SPSS produces has a range for each bar that SPSS defines for you. These are not always helpful or informative. Fortunately, we can change them, as we can nearly all the attributes of a graph produced by SPSS. We may not need to do so in a preliminary analysis of the data, but we almost always have to do so before presenting the charts to a target audience. The default features of these charts invariably violate our guidelines for graphical display.

Here's what your histogram for the number of violent crimes in 95 of these 98 cities will look like:

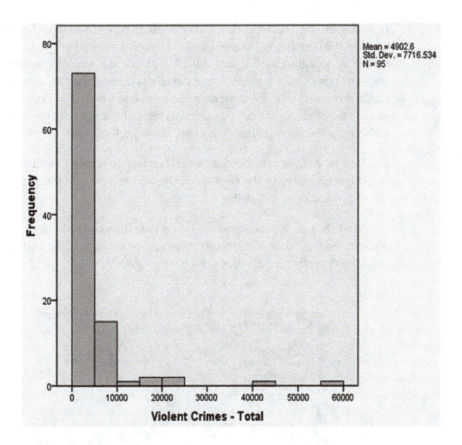

How might this graph be improved? You probably shouldn't bother. It's a fatally flawed graph because it doesn't take into account the population size of each city, thus violating an important graphic design guideline.

We should transform the variable before asking for its histogram. One of the more easily interpretable and communicable transformations is to create a variation of per capita for total violent crimes. We don't, however, merely want to divide, say, the total number of violent crimes by the total population of each city. We would find, for example, that there were 0.007 violent crimes per each resident of New York City in 2004 (55,688/8,008,278) and 0.008 violent crimes per each resident of St. Paul, Minnesota (2,408/287,151).

These per capita numbers, however, are difficult to communicate in a way that audiences can "get their arms and brains around." And who wants to keep track of decimal places?

Per 100,000 is a potential candidate for the type of transformation we want to perform, and you can help your audience grasp the resulting number by an explicit reference to the number of people watching a college football game on a Saturday in the fall in Pasadena, California (University of Southern California), or in Ann Arbor, Michigan (University of Michigan). It may also be easier to imagine 100 people (e.g., two bus loads of people) or 1,000 (e.g., a small movie theater in a multiplex). But let's use 100,000. (By the way, the number we're about to compute is a yearly figure per 100,000 residents. We could further divide this number by 365 if we wanted, say, to know how many violent crimes would take place on any day (on average) throughout the year, thus creating a daily rate, which may be easier to grasp, although likely to be very small.)

Step 4: A new variable for violent crimes is created by dividing the original variable by the population size for each city and then multiplying that number by 100,000.

In SPSS, this is accomplished by clicking Transform/Compute Variable and entering the following information in the Target Variable and Numeric Expression boxes (as below). Click OK.

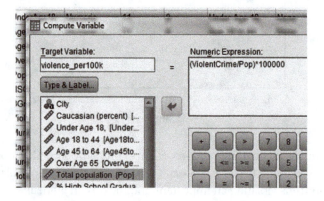

Step 5: After creating this new variable, run summary statistics to make sure the data transformation appears to have executed properly.

Your summary statistics table should look like the following:

Statistics

violence_per100k

N	Valid	95
	Missing	3
Mean		875.7300
Median		776.7507
Std. Deviation		420.70371
Minimum		151.12
Maximum		2044.80

This transformation may have created not only numbers that are more communicable but also variables that are better "behaved" versions of violent crimes. If we had run descriptive statistics on the old variable, we would have noticed that the means and medians of the newly transformed variables are closer together and the ratios of kurtosis and skewness to their respective standard errors are close to or better than our guideline ratio of 2:1.

The histogram for our transformed violent crime data is presented below. (*Note:* we could skip the step of Graph/Legacy Dialogs/Histogram by asking for this chart within the descriptive statistics command we used to produce the table above. There's a "Charts" button in the Frequencies dialog box that we could have clicked to request a histogram.)

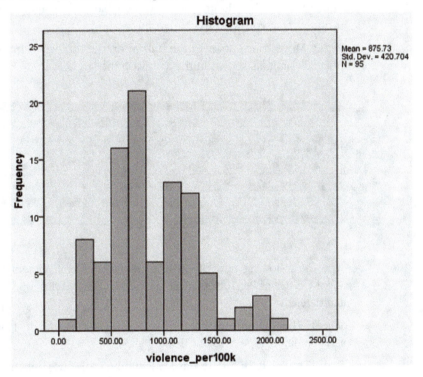

How might this chart be improved?

To illustrate how to change nearly any attribute of a default graph in SPSS, consider the following changes:

1. Add an informative title.

2. Rename the horizontal and vertical titles, repositioning the vertical title to run horizontally.

3. Create narrower ranges for each of the "bins" or what appear here as bar

4. Remove decimal places from the horizontal scale, and increase t' font size.

5. Increase the size, and move the summary statistics inside the chart area.

6. Make the background white (color ink cartridges are expensive, and the background baby blue adds nothing to the story).

7. Change the color of the bars to gray, which they are not in the original printout.

8. Eliminate the top and right borders.

How would you do all this?

Step 1: Move your cursor to somewhere in this histogram in your output file, right click, and select Edit Content/In Separate Window. This will launch SPSS's Chart Editor, which will enable you to change any of the attributes that you want to change above.

Step 2: Move your cursor to the button on the toolbar to Insert a Title, and click on it, as shown in the arrow on the left below.

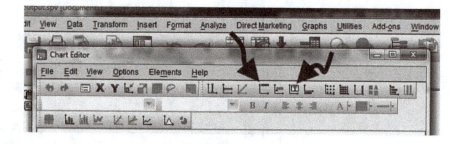

Type the following new title in the highlighted box: Violent Crimes in Major U.S. Cities Per 100,000 Residents, 2004. Double click on "Histogram" and delete.

Step 3: Highlight the bottom title on the X-axis, and instead of the variable name, type "Violent Crime Rates."

Step 4: Double click on the Y-axis title. In the Properties box that appears, change the Preferred size to 12 points. Hit Apply. Open the tab Text Layout and turn on the radial button for horizontal. Hit apply. Left click on the Y axis and replace "Frequency" with "Number of Cities." If you want to have the Y axis title appear on two lines, move your cursor before "Cities" and hit Shift/Enter.

Step 5: Double click anywhere inside one of the bars. Click on the Fill & Border tab, and highlight one of the gray boxes in the color palette. Click Apply.

Step 6: In the Binning tab, X axis box, activate the Custom radial button Interval width and enter 50. Hit apply. Double click on one of the numbers of the horizontal scale.

- In the Text Style tab, change Preferred Size to "12." Click Apply.
- In the Scale tab, change maximum to "2200." Click Apply.
- In the Number Format tab, insert "0" (i.e., zero) into the Decimal Places box. Click Apply and Close.

Do the same thing for the numbers on the vertical axis.

Step 7: Double click on Mean or Std. Dev to the right of the chart.

Move your cursor to the border of the box in which these statistics reside until your cursor changes to a figure that looks like the four arrows of a compass, and drag that box into the upper right corner of the chart. Change minimum size to 12 in the Text Style tab. Expand the box (if needed) so that each of these three statistics is on only one line. Click Close.

Step 8: Double click on the blue background.

- In the Fill & Border tab, click on the Fill Box, and click on the white box in the color palette.
- In the Border box within the same tab, select the white or transparent palette. Click Apply and Close.

Step 9: Click on Edit at the top of your screen, and select Copy Chart, which you can paste into an MS-Word document to be submitted to whomever you'd like.

Your chart should look something like this:

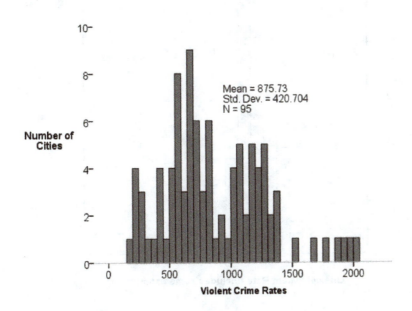

Violent Crimes in Major U.S. Cities Per 100,000 Residents, 2004

Mean = 875.73
Std. Dev. = 420.704
N = 95

Number of Cities (vertical axis)

Violent Crime Rates (horizontal axis)

Scatterplots

Scatterplots or scattergrams enable the user to display the patterned relationship between two continuous variables. We have already seen this graphical tool in the graph of self-reported student height with measured height.

Let's illustrate how to produce a scattergram by examining the relationship between violent crime and cities' unemployment rates. We would, of course, first examine the summary statistics for the second variable, as we did for violent crime rates to make sure there weren't any stray or inexplicable observations. Here's what the summary statistics and histogram (unedited) for unemployment rates look like:

Statistics

Unemployement Rate (incudes some estimates of counties)

N	Valid	90
	Missing	8
Mean		8.634
Median		8.300
Std. Deviation		2.8369
Range		14.8
Minimum		4.1
Maximum		18.9

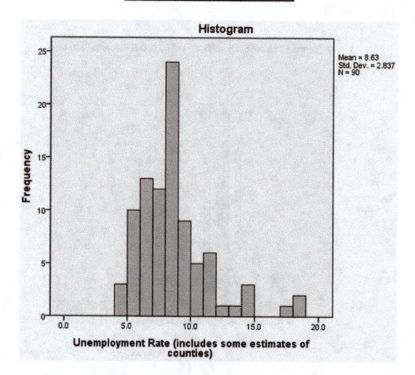

Some of the rates are high but believable. So we'll move ahead with a request for a scattergram of the unemployment and violent crime rates across the cities for which we have nonmissing values on these two variables.

Step 1: Create dichotomous versions of the % of population under 18 and the cities' unemployment rates.

Step 2: Click on Graph/Legacy Dialogs/Scatter/Dot.

Step 3: Select Simple Scatter, and click on the Define button.

Step 4: Move "Crime per 100,000 Residents" into the *Y* and "Unemployment Rate" into the *X*-axis variable boxes. Click OK.

These steps should produce (after some editing) something like the following scattergram:

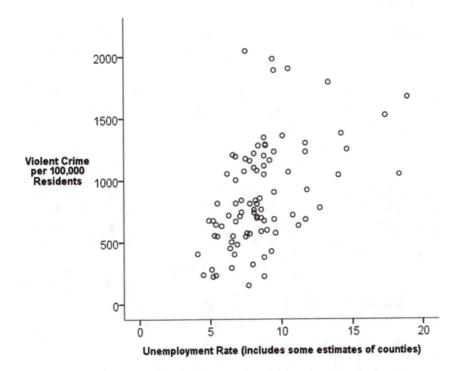

It would be useful, of course, to augment this graph with statistics that provide summary measures of the degree to which these two variables are related (e.g., an increase of 1 percentage point in unemployment is associated with an average rise of *X* number of violent crimes per every 100,000

residents in a city). But our purpose here is to demonstrate how to produce a scattergram. Its interpretation would be aided by the addition of correlation and regression statistics (as well as descriptive statistics).

Bar Charts

Bar charts display the frequency or percentage of one or more continuous variables by one or more **categorical variables**. Let's examine the violent crime rate (a continuous variable) by two **dichotomous variables** that roughly divide the 98 cities in the community data set in half according to (1) the percentage of their residents under 18 years of age and (2) the city's unemployment rate. We'll first look just at violent crime rate per 100,000 by whether a city has a low or high proportion of residents under 18 years of age and then create a bar chart that looks simultaneously at both dichotomous variables.

Step 1: Click on Graphs/Legacy Dialogs/Bar. Select Simple, and click on the Define button.

Step 2: In the Bars Represent box, click on "Other statistic" (e.g., mean), and move the variable for violent crime per 100,000 residents into the variable box.

Step 3: Move the dichotomous variable for the proportion of residents under age 18 into the Category Axis box, as indicated in the following screen capture. Click OK.

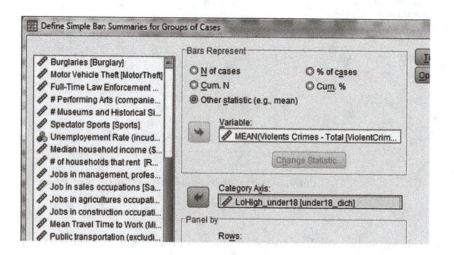

These commands produce the unedited bar chart below:

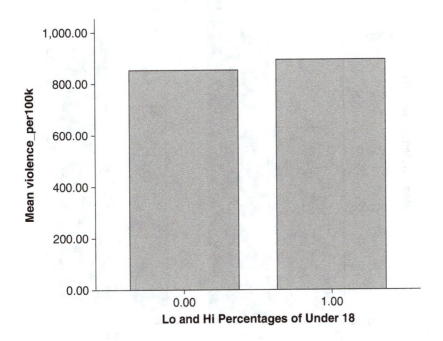

Rates of violent crime appear unaffected by the proportion of a city's residents who are under 18 years of age. We typically wouldn't continue to use this variable in analyzing violent crime rates via bar charts, but let's illustrate how we could display two categorical variables in the same bar chart.

Step 1: Click on Graphs/Legacy Dialogs/Bar. Select Clustered, and click on the Define button.

Step 2: In the Bars Represent box, click on "Other statistic" (e.g., mean), and move the variable for violent crime per 100,000 residents into the variable box.

Step 3: Move the dichotomous variable for the proportion of residents under age 18 into the Category Axis box and the dichotomous variable for unemployment rates into the Define Clusters By box. Click OK.

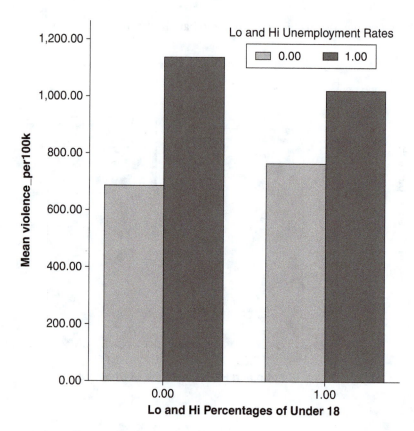

The unedited bar chart above shows rather pronounced differences in violent crime rates in cities that vary in their unemployment rates, as we had seen earlier in the scattergram of the two continuous versions of these variables.

Bar Charts and Rankings:
Vertical Versus Horizontal Display

Consider the 27 items included in the first question asked in the Orange County Public Perception Survey. The respondents were asked how important each of a number of issues is "for you." The response categories included Very Important, Important, Somewhat Important, and Unimportant. You can easily request summary statistics and bar graphs for all 27 of these variables, but how would you present their complete results, say, in a single graph or table?

A typical solution to this problem, and one with some justification in both design and information processing, is to order them from most to least important. Listing them alphabetically requires a reader to scan the list and try to remember the order of the 27 items, a cognitive task that far surpasses our short-term memory capacities.

Interestingly, we have 27 different variables in this instance, not a single variable with 27 different categories. You will have to do a "two step" in order to display all the information contained in responses to these 27 questions. First, calculate, say, the percentage of respondents who judged each item to be "Very Important."

In tabular form, such a table might look like Table 6.2.

Table 6.2 Rank of Issues Considered "Very Important" by Citizens of Orange County, Florida, 2000	
Issue	Percentage (Number) of Citizens Selecting This Response
1. Fighting illegal drug use	70 (722)
2. Helping public schools	67 (682)
3. Addressing the problem of gangs	65 (669)
4. Protecting sensitive lands	57 (585)
5. Reducing I-4 congestion	57 (584)
6. Reducing discrimination	53 (543)
7. Youth improvement programs	53 (540)
8. Controlling government spending	49 (501)
9. Public safety	46 (468)
10. Increasing the level of wages	45 (463)
11. Condition of roadway system	44 (449)
12. Senior citizens' needs	43 (446)
13. Water quality of lakes	43 (437)
14. Controlling development and growth	40 (411)
15. Better job training	39 (402)
16. Welfare-to-work programs	38 (391)
17. Cutting property taxes	36 (363)
18. Code enforcement	34 (350)
19. Promoting high-tech jobs	32 (329)
20. Mass transit	31 (314)
21. Helping neighborhoods	30 (307)
22. Storm water drainage	27 (275)
23. Promoting the arts	23 (241)
24. Improving parks	22 (230)
25. Appearance of roadways	21 (214)
26. Addressing business needs	17 (168)
27. Building a light rail	15 (154)

Although not shown here, the top three issues differ in their ranking depending on whether we use just "Very Important" or combine this category with "Important." These differences (or, conversely, the failure to find convergent results from different methods) lead us to be conservative in our declarations. We should not say that the single most pressing issue for the citizens of Orange County is "Fighting illegal drug use" or "Helping public schools," because this ranking depends on a rather arbitrary choice of combining or not combining response categories. In such a circumstance, it would be more prudent for us to report that the top three issues facing respondents were fighting drugs, helping public schools, and addressing gang violence.

Unfortunately, you cannot move from this manually constructed table to a graph easily. Indeed, the information in Table 6.2 must be entered into SPSS or Excel before creating a graph that displays these results.

In Excel, the spreadsheet would look like the following:

	A	B	C	D
	Issue	Percent Very Important	Number of respondents	
1				
2	Government Spending	49	501	
3	Property Taxes	36	363	
4	I-4 Congestion	57	584	
5	Mass Transit	31	314	
6	Light Rail	15	154	
7	Roadway System	44	449	
8	Roadway Appearance	21	214	
9	Development & Growth	40	411	
10	Sensitive Ecologies	57	585	
11	Illegal Drug Use	70	722	
12	Gangs	65	669	
13	Code Enforcement	34	350	
14	Public Schools	67	682	
15	Youth Programs	53	540	
16	Job Training	39	402	
17	Public Safety	46	468	
18	Storm Drainage	27	275	
19	Lakes	43	437	
20	Welfare-to-Work	38	391	
21	High Tech Jobs	32	329	
22	Discrimination	53	543	
23	Arts	23	241	
24	Business Needs	17	168	
25	Senior Citizens	43	446	
26	Neighborhoods	30	307	
27	Parks	22	230	
28	Wages	45	463	
29				

To sort these from the most to the least important, we would have to

- highlight the contents of the file (A2:C28),
- click on Data/Sort,
- select "Descending" in the dialog box that appears, and
- click on OK.

To add a number for the rank order of each issue,

- insert a column to the left of A,
- type the number 1 in cell A2 and the number 2 in cell A3,
- highlight these two cells, and
- grab the box in the lower right corner of these two highlighted cells and drag your cursor downward until you reach the number 27.

To quickly create a chart in Excel,

- highlight Columns B and C and
- click F11.

You should see the following chart appear in a chart sheet (named Chart 1):

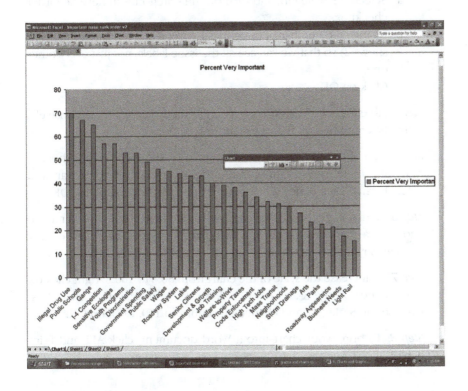

Not bad for one keystroke. But you can improve upon this chart by following some of the basic principles of graphical display that we've discussed above.

You may alter elements of this table by right clicking on the element or by using the chart toolbar, which is displayed here. Let's go through a number of steps in Excel to clean up this quick and dirty chart in order to convey our results better to the Orange County mayor, who commissioned this study.

Step 1: Delete the legend by right clicking on Legend and selecting Clear. A legend is usually superfluous if you properly label the chart or table.

Step 2: Flip the chart so that the issue categories are on the left axis, which makes these labels easier to read by right clicking on any bar in the chart to select Chart Type.

Select the Standard Types tab. Click on the horizontal bar chart icon and then on OK to choose the highlighted chart subtype in the upper left corner.

Step 3: Reverse the order from the least important issue at the top of the chart to the most frequently cited issue at the top by right clicking on one of the issue labels and selecting Format Axis.

  a. Select the Scale tab, and turn on the Categories in Reverse Order checkbox.
  b. Change the number of categories between tick mark label to 1 (if it shows 2) so that we can see all the issue labels, not just every other one.
  c. Click on OK.

Step 4: To eliminate the gray background (ink cartridges are expensive!), right click anywhere in that area, and select Clear.

Step 5: To show the actual percentage of respondents who chose a particular issue as "Very Important," right click on any blue bar, and select Format Data Series. Click in the Value box, and then click OK.

Step 6: To eliminate the vertical bars, which are unnecessary insofar as we show the actual percentages that each bar represents, right click on any vertical bar, and select Clear.

Step 7: To increase the scale of the chart from 80% to 100%, right click on any number on the X-axis (0, 10, 20, 30, etc.), and select Format Axis. Choose the Scale tab, and change Maximum to 100. Click on OK.

Step 8: To bring your chart into a Word document, click ALT and Print Screen (assuming the chart is staring you in the face).

Open your Word document to the place where you want to place your graph. Right click on Paste. On the Picture toolbar, click on the Text Wrapping icon (which looks like a dog on a background of horizontal gridlines), and select Behind Text, which permits you to move the chart anywhere in the document you like.

Step 9: To add the actual number of respondents who said "Very Important" to each item, return to the Excel spreadsheet, center the numbers in the column, highlight the column, right click, and copy and paste it into an empty Word document. Then click on Select Table/Delete Gridlines, right click and copy this table, move back to the Word document into which you've pasted your graph, click on Edit/Special Paste/Word Object, and move it to the right of your original chart.

Percentage (and Number) of Orange County Residents Who Reported That an Issue Is Very Important to Them

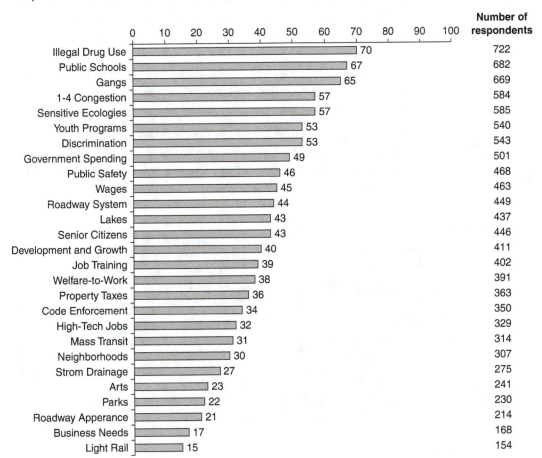

Issue	Percentage	Number of respondents
Illegal Drug Use	70	722
Public Schools	67	682
Gangs	65	669
1-4 Congestion	57	584
Sensitive Ecologies	57	585
Youth Programs	53	540
Discrimination	53	543
Government Spending	49	501
Public Safety	46	468
Wages	45	463
Roadway System	44	449
Lakes	43	437
Senior Citizens	43	446
Development and Growth	40	411
Job Training	39	402
Welfare-to-Work	38	391
Property Taxes	36	363
Code Enforcement	34	350
High-Tech Jobs	32	329
Mass Transit	31	314
Neighborhoods	30	307
Strom Drainage	27	275
Arts	23	241
Parks	22	230
Roadway Apperance	21	214
Business Needs	17	168
Light Rail	15	154

Boxplots and Outliers

Boxplots provide a visual display of the distributions of variables. Boxplots serve purposes similar to that of a histogram, except that they can do so for multiple variables in the same graph. They also differ from histograms in their attention to displaying certain percentiles in the distribution and identifying specific observations that these charts consider as "outliers" and "extreme points."

Let's use a boxplot to display the distribution of two variables that we may be considering for a later analysis but whose distribution we want to examine at this point in order to see if we might consider any cities in the Community Indicators data set as outliers in terms of these two variables:

- Violent crimes per 100,000 residents
- Full-time law enforcement officers per 100,000 residents (a new variable constructed as we did the violent crimes per 100,000 residents variable)

Step 1: Run a boxplot for these variables by clicking on Graphs/Boxplots. From the dialog box that appears, select Simple and Summaries of Separate Variables, and then click on Define.

Move the two variables into the Boxes Represent box, and move the variable CITY into the Label Cases by box, which will identify by name the cities that may be considered **univariate outliers** on the distribution of these two variables. Click OK.

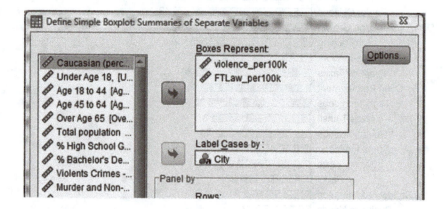

The resulting output should look like the following (to which I have added descriptions of the boxplots' elements):

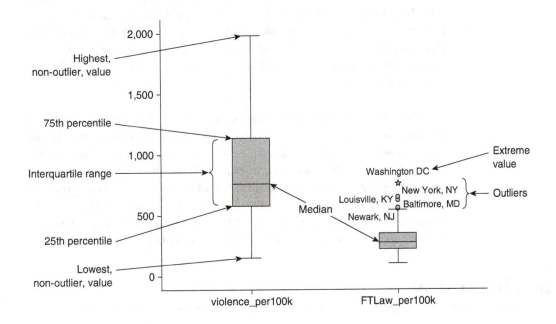

Case Processing Summary

	Cases					
	Valid		Missing		Total	
	N	Percent	N	Percent	N	Percent
violence_per100k	79	80.6%	19	19.4%	98	100.0%
FTLaw_per100k	79	80.6%	19	19.4%	98	100.0%

How do we interpret these boxplots?

• The dark horizontal line inside each of the boxes is the median value for each variable. Half of all observations fall above that line and half below it.

• The top of each box is the "third quartile," which marks the 75th percentile in the distribution. The bottom of each box is the second quartile and marks the 25th percentile.

• The difference between these two quartiles (i.e., the height of the boxes themselves) is called the interquartile range (IQR). The middle 50% percent of all cases falls within the IQR.

- The stems or "whiskers" that extend from the boxes represent the lowest and highest values that are not considered outliers by SPSS. Boxplots define an observation as being an outlier if it lies more than 1.5 times the IQR above or below the box itself. Any case identified by an open circle is an outlier (e.g., New York, Louisville, Baltimore, and Newark in terms of full-time law officers per 100,000 residents). Any case identified by an asterisk is considered an "extreme" case, falling more than three times the IQR above or below the box.

The case-processing summary indicates that only 79 cities provided valid or nonmissing values for both variables. The default processing rule is list-wise deletion of missing values, thus reducing the number of observations on which these distributions are displayed. This can be changed. It's your choice whether you want to exclude about a fourth of all the observations in your data set because of this default rule for missing values. I wouldn't. We're throwing out too much information. Check out what's behind the Options button on the boxplot dialog box to change this default.

● CONCLUSION

Graphs can enlighten or mislead. You now have the tools and insights to produce enlightened graphs that build on an understanding of perception, cognition, and memory. You now know many of the signs of graphical tomfoolery and can formally express graphical distortions of what the data say through calculation of the Lie Factor Quotient. And you can produce histograms, scattergrams, bar charts, and boxplots and can edit them according to the principles of good (and bad) graphical design. Go forth, and with that knowledge, make fishers of men (and women).

To practice and reinforce the lessons of this chapter of the book, turn to Exercise 5 in the *Student Workbook* (available at http://www.sagepub .com/pearsonsp/).

● NOTE

1. If your version of Excel does not include an Analysis ToolPak, you can add it through the following steps:

Step 1: Click the **Microsoft Office Button** ⊕, the click **Excel Options.**

Step 2: Click **Add-Ins,** and then in the **Manage** box, **select Excel Add-ins.**

Step 3: Click **Go.**

Step 4: In the **Add-Ins available** box, select the **Analysis ToolPak** check box, and the click **OK.**

> If **Analysis ToolPak** is not listed in the **Add-Ins available** box, click **Browse** to locate it.

> If you get prompted that the Analysis ToolPak is not currently installed on your computer, click **Yes** to install it.

Step 5: After you load the Analysis ToolPak, the **Data Analysis** command is available in the **Analysis** group on the **Data** tab.

CHAPTER 7

PERCENTAGES AND CONTINGENCY TABLES

The word *percent* has become far too familiar. We rarely think about it as the world's most frequently used data transformation. Nor do we think about its meaning. To wit,

per, as in "for every"

and cent, as in (you've guessed it) "one hundred."

Consider, for example, the percentage (or proportion, a kissing cousin to *percentage*) of welfare recipients in Washington State who admitted in a phone interview from a contract research organization in 1999 that they had used crack or cocaine one or more times between July 1998 and March 1999.[1] Surely, no one would admit that to a stranger on the other end of a telephone connection, would they?

It turns out that 700 of 3,043 welfare recipients in the Washington State 1999 sample survey admitted to having used crack or cocaine some time during the year prior to their phone interview. That is,

$$\frac{700}{3043} = .23, \text{ or } 23\%.$$

Here's another way of arriving at that percentage, which uses the cross product ratio formula you learned some time ago:

$$\frac{700}{3043} = \frac{x}{100}.$$

The cross product ratio can be read in the following way: 700 is to 3,043 as x (our unknown) is to 100—that is to say, per cent. The cross products are $700 \times 100 = 3{,}043x$. Dividing each side of the equation by 3,043, we arrive at 23%. Fascinating, isn't it? (By the way, only 2% of the general population of Washington admitted to having used crack or cocaine during a similar time period. As we will note below, single percentages without comparison with meaningful other groups can be misleading.)

Percentages are ubiquitous and, as such, are readily communicated to wide audiences who have not read this book. Percentages are also the bedrock of what statisticians call **contingency tables** or **crosstabs**. They are the statistical tool we turn to next.

● CONTINGENCY TABLES

Percentage Differences Between Two or More Groups

The logic of causal relationships (that is to say, claiming that your data are consistent with the belief that X causes Y) is to compare the characteristics of a group of interest with the characteristics of people unlike them. Any characteristic that distinguishes or differentiates one group from another may be "causing" that result. You can uncover these differences through the use of percentage differences.

Let's say that your theory predicts that young women in high school who give birth are considerably more likely to drop out of school than those who do not. The test of the relationship between childbearing and dropping out is conducted by comparing the dropout rates of young women who gave birth during high school with young women who did not give birth during high school. (*Note:* You can also calculate the proportion of these two groups who complete high school, but this information is entirely redundant in this case.) Such a table would look like Table 7.1, which is based on data from California (Berglas, Brindis, & Cohen, 2003, p. 24). I've included the redundant, unnecessary column to demonstrate an important point about whether rows or columns should sum to 100%. Presenting a table in which

Table 7.1 High School Dropout Rates of Childbearing Teenagers and Women Who Delay Parenthood in California

	Percentage Who Drop Out of High School	*Percentage Who Complete High School*
Teen mothers	70%	30%
Women who delay parenthood until 21 or older	24%	76%

SOURCE: Adapted from Berglas et al. (2003, p. 24).

the dependent-variable categories sum to 100% is a common mistake found in many research reports and articles. It matters. Do it right.[2]

Note that the categories of the **independent variable** (whether a girl became a teenage mother or delayed parenthood until 21 or older) sum to 100%. This is required of tables in which one variable (the independent variable) is believed to cause another (the **dependent variable**). As we will see in Chapter 10, there are a number of measures of association, including the percentage difference, that are called **asymmetric** in that they presume that one variable is causing the other (i.e., "*X* causes *Y*"). It may well be that "*Y* causes *X*," however, and the percentage difference will likely vary depending on whether you specify one or the other variable as independent or dependent. Just burn into your brain the fact that categories of the independent variable in a table should sum to 100%, as can be demonstrated when you include the redundant column as I have done above. Or, if it helps, remember, "Percentage across, compare down." Note that the column percentages do not sum to 100%. We examine the differences in percentages for evidence of an independent variable influencing a dependent variable (here, 54%). The larger the percentage difference, the more the data are consistent with the conclusion that the independent variable has a large effect.

This type of analysis requires you to collect information from both groups in order to determine whether the characteristic that distinguishes them (birth/no birth) is associated with the condition in which you're interested (dropping out of school). A study of just high school dropouts would not provide adequate data for exploring or testing causal arguments about what may cause dropping out. In addition, one must measure the other factors that your theory believes are the cause of high school completion and other characteristics that competing theories believe are at work (for you to show that these theories or hypotheses are wrong or only partially correct and do not account for or explain the relationship in which you may be interested). Recall from Chapter 6 that a compelling explanation "rules out," "excludes," or "controls for" other plausible explanations for the results you find. (We'll return to this latter point under the topic of full model specification in Chapter 8.)

Here's another example. Suppose you want to know if men are promoted more quickly than women in your organization and, if so, why. You have to measure the same criteria for both men and women that your theory believes can explain the differences in promotion rates (productivity, ambition, etc.). If you happen to find that men and women who are promoted at different rates have the same levels of productivity, for example, you can probably rule out differences in productivity as an explanation of the differences in promotion rates that your data reveal. If you don't measure and rule out these alternative explanations, someone will invariably come along and discredit your conclusion because you failed to account for plausible alternative explanations.

Let's turn to an example to demonstrate how a contingency table can be produced from categorical variables in the Texas Academic Excellence Indicator file.

Step 1: Open the Texas Academic Excellence sample file in SPSS.

We will *assume* that test scores are our outcome or "dependent" variable and that the other ("independent" or "explanatory") variables in this exercise are influencing or "causing" the different levels of academic performance.

Step 2: From the toolbar at the top of your screen, click Analyze/Descriptive Statistics/Crosstabs.

Step 3: Let's treat three variables that are recoded from interval- to categorical-level variables as independent variables that one might believe have an effect on test performance. All these variables have been recoded into three, roughly equal size categories.

The three independent variables are

- the size of the school district (n_of_students_thirds),
- teaching experience (teach_w_11to20_thirds), and
- the economic status of the school districts' students (econ_disadvs_ thirds).

The dependent variable in this example has also been recoded to contain three categories (test_passed_percent).

One way to ensure that your independent variable categories sum to 100% is to move the independent variables into the Row(s): box and the one dependent variable into the Column(s): box and to ask for row percentages, *not* column percentages.

> *Note:* It's generally not a good idea to recode continuous variables into categorical or ordinal ones, as I've done in this example, because you lose analytical oomph. You are in effect reducing the variance of each variable by recoding it this way and, as we will see later, reducing the size of the effect as calculated by some measures of association, several of which we will examine in Chapter 10 and beyond. However, what you lose in statistical prowess by recoding continuous variables into categorical ones may be offset by gains in your ability to present your results to nonstatistical audiences. That trade-off may be worth it in some circumstances.
>
> Unless there's a good reason for doing otherwise, recode continuous variables into groups of approximately equal size. Some statistics are more robust to assumption violations if the groups have approximately equal numbers of observations.

Step 4: Click Cells, and then turn on the Observed box, Row Percentages, Total Percentages, and No Adjustments. Click Continue.

We'll consider the statistics you can request through this procedure in the next chapter.

Step 5: Click Format, and select "Descending Row Order" (e.g., placing most experienced teacher districts [recoded to have a numeric value of "3"] at the top of the tables, with the other categories, "2" and "1," following). Click Continue. Click OK.

Your output will include four tables. The crosstab of teacher experience with test performance should look something like the following:

Teachers w 11-20 years exp in thirds * Percent of students passing tests Crosstabulation

			Percent of students passing tests			Total
			Lowest third	Middle third	Highest third	
Teachers w 11-20 years exp in thirds	Most experienced teachers	Count	19	51	65	135
		% within Teachers w 11-20 years exp in thirds	14.1%	37.8%	48.1%	100.0%
		% of Total	4.6%	12.5%	15.9%	33.0%
	2.00	Count	34	49	53	136
		% within Teachers w 11-20 years exp in thirds	25.0%	36.0%	39.0%	100.0%
		% of Total	8.3%	12.0%	13.0%	33.3%
	Fewest experienced teachers	Count	85	23	30	138
		% within Teachers w 11-20 years exp in thirds	61.6%	16.7%	21.7%	100.0%
		% of Total	20.8%	5.6%	7.3%	33.7%
Total		Count	138	123	148	409
		% within Teachers w 11-20 years exp in thirds	33.7%	30.1%	36.2%	100.0%
		% of Total	33.7%	30.1%	36.2%	100.0%

This table displays a **positive relationship** in that high values of test performance (highest third among districts) tend to be associated with high levels of teacher experience (high proportions of teachers with 11–20 years of experience in a school district). Similarly, low levels of test performance tend to cluster in districts with the lowest proportion of experienced teachers. This relationship is also suggested in the preponderance of observations that fall in the "diagonal," which is noted by the oval above.

Even though we requested a minimum number of numbers, the table nonetheless includes a lot of stuff—indeed, too much to foist on our audience (i.e., a special assistant to the Governor or the Secretary of the Department of Education). This numeric "overkill" is the case with nearly every statistical procedure we request in SPSS or in any other statistical software package, which doesn't know your exact needs and, therefore, tries to satisfy many at once.

The most parsimonious, yet complete, presentation of these percentage differences is to report a single set of row percentages (and the number of cases associated with each percentage). Let's look on the bright side and report the percentages of high-performing school districts (those school districts whose students' test performance place them in the top third of districts in our sample) by each category of teacher experience. Because I want to emphasize the importance of teacher experience (which is the story of this table), I place the highest level of experience at the top of the table. In so doing, the table conforms to one of the guidelines for graphical display, which we saw in Chapter 6. Table 7.2 was manually created in Word.

Do you see where these numbers come from in the table from the output displayed in the SPSS table? Note that Table 7.2 is constructed to highlight differences in percentages, which play the lead role. The frequency counts associated with each of these percentages play only a supporting role

Table 7.2	Teachers' Experience Matters
	Percentage$_{(Number)}$ of Districts in the Top Third of Test Performance on TAKS[a]
Districts with the highest proportion of teachers with 11–20 years' experience	48.1$_{(65)}$
Districts with the second most experienced teaching faculty	39.0$_{(53)}$
Districts with the least experienced teachers	21.7$_{(30)}$

SOURCE: A simple random sample of one third of the school districts and selected variables included in the 2006 Texas Academic Excellence Indicator System, www.tea. state.tx.us/perfreport/aeis/.

NOTES: a. Total number of school districts = 409. TAKS, Texas Assessment of Knowledge and Skills.

in the story by showing the reader that there are enough observations on which to feel confident about the results.

School districts with a high proportion of experienced teachers are more than twice as likely as districts with the least experienced teachers to do well on the 2006 Texas Assessment of Knowledge and Skills tests in Grades 3 through 11. The percentage point difference of about 26 points is moderately strong. Obviously, teacher experience doesn't account for all the difference across districts in student performance on standardized tests, but it appears at first blush to tell a substantial part of the story.

If you examined the last of the tables in the output from our crosstab procedure, you would have seen that the economic status of the districts' students is even more strongly related to performance than teachers' experience.

Indeed, it may well be the case that the wealth (or poverty) of the districts' students (or their parents) not only explains some of the differences across districts in test performance but may also explain the relationship we observe between teaching experience and student test performance. This would happen if relatively wealthy school districts are able to recruit and retain more experienced teachers. It could also be the case that experienced teachers tend to gravitate toward wealthier school districts that pay more (a hypothesis that these data can test). If so, the relationship between teacher experience and performance is spurious (or "explained" by the joint relationship that district economic conditions have with each of these two variables). An arrow diagram of such a relationship would look like the following:

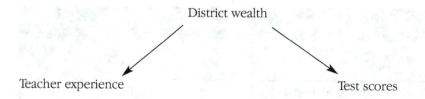

We can assess whether something like this might be taking place by "controlling for" districts' economic status.

We can use our indicator of the economy of the districts' students by entering what SPSS calls a "layer."

Step 1: Click on Analyze/Descriptive Statistics/Crosstabs

Step 2: Enter TEACH_W_11TO20_THIRDS into the row box (our independent variable).

- Enter TEST_PASSED_PERCENT into the column box (our dependent variable).
- Enter ECON_DISADVS_THIRDS into the layer box (our **control variable**).

The cell parameters will still be active from your entries in the first set of tables above (if not, repeat those in the initial set of steps).

Click OK. All these numbers (there are a total of 96 numbers in the resulting table) can be reduced to Table 7.3 (manually created in Word).

Table 7.3 Teachers' Experience and District Wealth Matter			
	Percentage$_{(Number)}$ of Districts in the Top Test-Performing Districts		
	Economically Disadvantaged Districts	Middling Districts	Economically Advantaged Districts
Districts with the highest proportion of teachers with 11–20 years' experience	17.4$_{(4)}$	33.3$_{(16)}$	74.1$_{(43)}$
Districts with the second most experienced teaching faculty	8.3$_{(3)}$	36.4$_{(20)}$	67.4$_{(29)}$
Districts with the least experienced teachers	10.3$_{(7)}$	20.5$_{(8)}$	48.4$_{(15)}$

SOURCE: A simple random sample of one third of the school districts and selected variables included in the 2006 Texas Academic Excellence Indicator System, www.tea.state.tx.us/perfreport/aeis/.

NOTE: Total number of school districts = 401.

There's quite a bit to conclude from this table. For example, economically advantaged districts are four to eight times more likely to be among the top-performing school districts no matter what level of teacher experience they have. Teacher experience is associated with higher test performance across different levels of economic advantage, but not as dramatically as the economic conditions of a district's students.

Did your eye, however, catch the fact that there are seven school districts in this sample of Texas school districts that have inexperienced teachers with poor kids that nonetheless do well on test scores? Maybe the Department of Education should look more closely at these districts to determine if there's anything wrong here (i.e., cheating on tests) or, conversely, if there is something worth trying to bottle and give to similar kinds of districts. (Although not shown here, you can see in your output that there are four school districts that are relatively wealthy and have more experienced teachers but nonetheless perform in the bottom third of all districts. Should the state also send someone there to investigate why?)

Percentage comparisons are both simple to calculate and easy to communicate. The lessons to be drawn from the examples above, however, are several fold:

• Compare the row percentages of independent variable categories (and likewise, enter these variables into the Row(s): box and request Row Percentages in the Cells dialog box of SPSS).

• Do not report all the numbers that these procedures produce. Think about the guidelines for graphic display. Many of them apply to crosstab presentations as well. For example, think about the position or sequence of your categories (good or important categories might be presented at the top because of the importance such a position holds in Western cultures).

• Emphasize the importance of the percentage comparisons by, say, making them larger than the frequency counts, but provide these latter numbers as well, so that the reader can view the number of cases on which the percentages are based.

• Provide an informative title that helps tell the story.

• Annotate the table with information about the source of data and any other information that may be useful to the reader.

- Beware that crosstabs quickly become difficult to read when displaying more than two independent variables. **Expected cell frequencies** are also quickly depleted in such large tables and generate individual percentages that are, therefore, unreliable because they are based on so few cases.

The Limits of Contingency Tables and Percentages

Beware of the Sound of One-Hand Clapping

The murder trial of former NFL (National Football League) player O. J. Simpson included testimony that Mr. Simpson had beaten his wife, Nicole Brown Simpson, on several occasions before her murder. Defense attorney Johnnie Cochrane sought to deflect this fact by reciting the following statistic: Only 1 in 1,000 men who beat their wives end up killing them. (It is sadly true that this happens and that we have statistics about it.) Although expressed as a ratio, this number could also have been expressed as a percentage: Only –1/10 of 1% of men who beat their wives kill them. Cochrane, thereby, argued that the likelihood that Simpson killed his wife was only 1/10 of 1%. A clever statistic, but misleading. The causal relationship between spousal abuse and murder requires a comparison of the percentage of those who have beaten their wives and also kill them versus those who have not previously beaten their wives but kill them.

The rate of murder among the second group is considerably lower than in the case of wife-beaters. The comparison and evidence strongly suggest that beating your wife increases the likelihood of murdering her. Mr. Cochrane's statistic was true but lacked a proper comparison.

Another percentage was also missing here: What percentage of women who are killed by their husbands had previously been beaten by them? The answer: about 90% (Goleman, 1995, p. 22). In many regards, however, these statistics are not especially helpful, either for the trial or for policy in general. While a history of abuse typifies men who kill their wives (the 90% figure), such hindsight provides little capacity to predict which abusers will commit such homicide in the future. As the *New York Times* article about this reports, Professor Richard Gelles also examined nine additional characteristics of such men (e.g., poor economic status, age 18 to 30, illicit drug use, high school dropout) to achieve a 70% correct prediction rate. But note that such a predictive model would be wrong 30% of the time. Applying it to the approximately 2 million men who abuse their wives in the United States would falsely identify 600,000 men as prospective murderers. This presents another (statistical) problem, to which we turn next.

Beware of Claims Using Percentages Without a Base

Here's an example of a common, but misleading, claim using percentage differences: People who consume a particular food are 40% more likely to develop a particular disease than those who don't. But what if these figures are based on the following facts: 1.4 in 10,000,000 who eat food X develop a disease, in contrast to 1.0 in 10,000,000 who don't eat food X? The percentage increase in risk is properly reported but unimportant. A drug ad that claims that it reduces bad cholesterol by 40% may be employing the same card trick, especially if the manufacturer fails to report the base rates on which the percentage increases or decreases are based (quite independent of the incidence of side effects). Such statistics may be even more misleading if the studies on which they are based use samples of individuals with, say, high risk factors for heart attacks yet are prescribed to populations without these factors (a problem that a statistician would refer to as having questionable **external validity**).

A commonplace example of statistics without a comparative base is the oft-reported fact that most automobile accidents occur within x miles of home. Okay, but doesn't most driving occur within x miles of home as well (Hooke, 1983)?

A variation on this theme introduces the possibility of measurement error in similar instances of rare events. Suppose that a hypothetical (and large) company employs 100,000 employees and is intent on administering a drug test to all its employees in order to identify those using illicit drugs. The company wants to fire these folks and/or provide drug counseling. Let's say that 0.25% (one fourth of 1%) of these employees consume such drugs—that is to say, 250 of the 100,000. Suppose that the best available drug tests are "95% accurate." That is to say, 95% of the 250 (i.e., 238) would be identified as illegal drug users. Furthermore, suppose that the test produces false positives in 1% of the cases. That is to say, the test will identify 1,000 employees as using illicit drugs when in fact they are not. The total number of employees whom the test will identify as using drugs is 1,238 (238 + 1,000). The probability that a positive test result is accurate is, therefore, 238/1,238, or 19%. Would it be a sound decision to fire or counsel 1,238 employees? Of course not. The point here is to beware of the dangers of using percentages and percentage changes in basing decisions on rare events, especially in the presence of measurement error.

● PIVOT TABLES

Pivot tables, unlike the contingency tables we've examined above, are useful in instances in which your dependent variables are continuous and your independent variable(s) is(are) categorical. In the example above of the relationship between, say, teacher experience and districtwide test performance, we could use pivot tables if we did not want to lose the information contained in the untransformed district scores (i.e., percentage of kids in Grades 3–11 in each district who pass the state's test). Let's redo the prior analysis through pivot tables, using interval-level measures for the dependent variable, the original variable for the proportion of district students passing the state-level achievement tests ("Grades 3–11 All Tests Taken").

Step 1: At the top of your Data or Variable View screen, click on Analyze/ Compare Means/Means

Step 2: Move the dependent variable (the unrecoded percentage of students in a district passing all tests) into the Dependent List: box and the three-category version of teaching experience into the Independent List: box. Note that this box is headed by the title "Layer 1 of 1." This is the first independent variable for which we'll calculate proportions of passing.

Within the "Layer 1 of 1" box click Next to enter your first control variable (in this case, the economic status of the districts), as indicated by the arrow below.

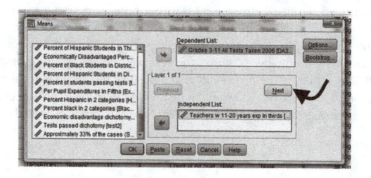

Step 3: Enter the control variable, ECON_DISADVS_THIRDS into the Independent List in the box that is now labeled "Layer 2 of 2." Click OK.

The resulting output should include something like the following:

Report

Grades 3-11 All Tests Taken 2006

Teachers w 11-20 year...	Economically ...	Mean	N	Std. Deviation
Fewest experienced teachers	Poorest third 63.1 to 100 percent	48.03	68	18.386
	Middle third	52.97	39	22.404
	Well off third 0 to 47 percent	64.39	31	19.375
	Total	53.10	138	20.696
2.00	Poorest third 63.1 to 100 percent	55.56	36	8.361
	Middle third	67.22	55	9.225
	Well off third 0 to 47 percent	73.00	43	10.670
	Total	65.94	134	11.614
Most experienced teachers	Poorest third 63.1 to 100 percent	62.13	23	10.755
	Middle third	66.31	48	10.521
	Well off third 0 to 47 percent	76.14	58	9.867
	Total	69.98	129	11.712
Total	Poorest third 63.1 to 100 percent	52.72	127	15.802
	Middle third	63.00	142	15.596
	Well off third 0 to 47 percent	72.36	132	13.650
	Total	62.82	401	16.966

Step 4: This isn't quite as easy to read as the last crosstab. It might be if we flipped the layers, which you can do easily by evoking the Pivot Trays dialog.

In the SPSS Viewer screen, highlight a cell in the table, and right click in that cell. Select Edit Content/in Viewer. Right click on: Teachers w 11–29 year . . ." Select Pivoting Trays. This will produce the Pivoting Trays screen.

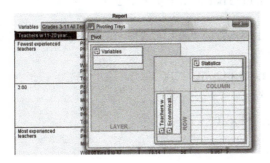

Step 5: You can change the variable being displayed in the rows by left clicking on one of the two independent variables and dragging it above (or below) the other variable. You'll see the table change before your eyes.

● PERCENTAGE CHANGE

Homicides in Philadelphia fell from 406 in 2006 to 392 in 2007. What percentage decline is that?

The question here is how much smaller the 2007 amount is than the 2006. The 2006 number is our anchor, the initial condition from which we want to know how much decline in homicides the city experienced in 2007. I emphasize this to make the point that this anchor becomes our denominator in the quotient that will answer our question. Another way of saying this is to subtract the ending value from the beginning value and then divide by the beginning value.

$$\frac{406 - 392}{406} = 3.4\%.$$

Remember that *denominator* begins with the letter *d*, which is also the first letter of the word *down*. It's the number on the bottom (i.e., downside) of our fraction, Up/Down.

Here's another example, with a twist: In 1993, 14,142,710 people received welfare benefits under the AFDC (Aid to Families With Dependent Children) program. The total U.S. population was estimated to be 258,137,000 that year; the percentage of the total population receiving welfare was, therefore, 5.5% (14,142,710/258,137,000).

In 2000, 5,776,849 people received welfare benefits under the TANF (Temporary Assistance for Needy Families) program, which was enacted by the U.S. Congress and signed by President Clinton in 1996. This was 2.1% of the total population. Which of the following numbers is the correct expression of change between 1993 and 2000?

a. $14{,}142{,}710 - 5{,}776{,}849/14{,}142{,}710 \times 100 = 8{,}365{,}861/14{,}142{,}710 \times 100 = 59\%.$

b. $5{,}776{,}849/14{,}142{,}710 \times 100 = 41\%.$

c. $5.5\% - 2.1\% = 3.4\%.$

d. $5.5 - 2.1/5.5 \times 100 = 62\%.$

In some respect, they are all "correct." Each, however, has a somewhat different interpretation.

The first of the answers (a) is, like the previous homicide rate example, a percentage decline in the number of people receiving cash assistance, a decline of 59%. It is calculated by subtracting the 2000 number from the 1993 number (initial condition) and dividing by the initial condition. This is a fair and accurate description of the change.

The second kind of change (b) is an end state expressed as a percentage of the beginning state. The number of welfare recipients in 2000 was only 41% of what it had been in 1993. Again, fair and accurate, but obviously different from 59%.

The third figure (c) is also correct but quite a bit different from the first two calculations of change. This version of change is often employed by those who want to suggest that the change is small. But they mislead unless they explicitly report a 3.4 percentage *point* difference. This is the absolute difference in the percentage of people on welfare between these 2 years. Given that the percentage was relatively low to begin with, a change in such a percentage—expressed in this fashion—will tend to appear small as well.

Finally, the fourth figure (d) is in some respects the "trickiest" of them all because it requires the reader to understand that it's a percentage change of two percentages. It's again calculated as the difference between the initial and end states divided by the initial condition. It more closely resembles the first two estimates but is not always as easy for readers to understand as is the simpler percentage change expressed in (a). The point here, as throughout the text, is to beware of the variety of different, and correct, ways to calculate change. Some of these are easier to communicate, and one will invariably express an apparently small amount of change, the percentage point difference.

CONCLUSION ●

Percentages are the most common statistic likely to be found (along with simple frequency counts) in everyday discourse. They are perhaps also the most common data transformation. Given their simplicity and ubiquity, they are also a good statistic to report to nontechnical audiences. And percentage differences contain the epistemological essence of causal arguments in that differences in the percentages of some outcome (e.g., high school completion) across different groups, categories, or conditions (e.g., giving birth [or not] while a high school student) may suggest the conditions that "cause" such an outcome.

We display percentage differences through the device of a contingency table, also known as a crosstab. We can do so correctly by calling on a software program such as SPSS to calculate these differences such that the categories of the independent variable(s) sum to 100%. Deciding how many of these percentages to display (because some will be redundant) presents a trade-off between parsimony and clarity about which variables are being considered as independent.

There are, as with most statistics, limitations to contingency tables. This chapter displayed a table of one dependent and two independent variables. The table was rather complex, with just three variables. Tables with more than three variables become increasingly hard to interpret and, even with samples of 1,000 respondents, can quickly "run out of" expected cell frequencies.

It is also important to understand the logic of comparisons and, conversely, to be aware of arguments that report a single percentage without a proper comparison. Avoid generating or believing such "one-hand-clapping" statistics. Also beware of percentages that are not accompanied by a base number or frequency, especially when the percentages are relatively small or rare.

Finally, expressing change in terms of percentages requires careful scrutiny because of the variety of legitimate, but different, ways in which those percentage changes can be expressed. Such differences can be used to distort as well as enlighten. Have I said that too frequently already?

● NOTES

1. Data are from Washington State's WorkFirst Study. The sample was drawn from the statewide list of adults receiving welfare assistance in March 1999 (1999 cohort) and October 2000 (2000 cohort). The 1999 cohort respondents were interviewed in 2000 and again in early 2001. The 2000 cohort respondents were interviewed in early 2001. This report uses survey data from 3,037 interviews in the first year, the 1,955 reinterviews with the 1999 cohort, and the 1,334 interviews with the 2000 cohort. See www.workfirst.wa.gov/research/3000/study2000demo.pdf

2. I am being dogmatic about displaying the dependent variable as the variable displayed in columns. It need not be. If you have a preference for showing independent variables in columns, remember a different rule for display: "Percentage down, compare across."

To practice and reinforce the lessons of this chapter of the book, turn to Exercise 6 in the *Student Workbook* (available at http://www.sagepub .com/pearsonsp/), but only after you've read and committed to long-term memory the lessons of Chapter 9 as well.

CHAPTER 8

SAMPLES AND STATISTICAL INFERENCE

The chapters ahead examine an array of statistical tools that have been developed to help analysts identify meaningful patterns and relationships in data. In many instances, these tools were designed to be used hand in glove with data collected from samples. But before turning to these statistical tools and tests, you need to know something about samples.

Clearly, samples are as ubiquitous as the percentages we examined in the prior chapter. Whether assessing the quality of the beer brewing in a vat or the nation's unemployment rate, samples are used to draw conclusions about a population based on an often very small part of that population. The reason for sampling's popularity is obvious. It's simply a lot cheaper, say, to question 1,000 people than 300 million. Less obvious is the fact that samples can, if properly executed and coupled with appropriate statistical tools, accurately and efficiently describe a population. Samples may even do a better job than a full census of the population because of potentially higher nonresponse biases (e.g., the poor, those difficult to reach, and transient members of populations are invariably undercounted in a census). That samples do a good job of providing accurate information about the population from which they are drawn is so in part because every population's diversity (or variety) is finite and estimable.

Consider the simple illustration of a jar of beans, all of which are white. How many beans would you need to sample in order to estimate the color of all the beans in the jar? One, because they are all alike. That is to say, the population doesn't vary in color. Clearly, populations such as all adults in the United States will vary more than white beans in a jar. But it can be shown that, for many purposes, all we need to sample is about 1,000 adults in order to draw conclusions about the averages of millions of adults who live in the United States. To draw conclusions about a population (whether people or manufactured automobile parts) on the basis of a sample of that population is called statistical inference. We infer the characteristics of a population on the basis of a sample. You may consider this a rare instance of the language of statistics being clear and simple.

Inference is important because we are rarely interested in the characteristics of a sample alone. We take a sample because it's more efficient or less costly than a census, but we do so with the hope of being able to describe the population from which it is drawn.

Statisticians have developed a number of ways to help us judge how good the inferences are that we draw from samples, to move across the bridge of inference from the sample to the population. Among the elements of this bridge are the standard error, **confidence intervals (CIs)**, statistical significance, and p values. These components of our statistical infrastructure are fundamental to our ability to make sense of the world from samples of it. This chapter will explain each of these terms and their use, noting some of their more confusing properties and how they can be used to deceive the unwary reader. But before doing so, let us briefly examine the theory and practice of sampling, especially as it applies to human populations.

● SAMPLING

What is the key to being able to make an inference about a population on the basis of a sample? Surprisingly enough, it's chance. *Chance* has a specific meaning in this context, however. It means random and known probabilities of selection. In selecting respondents on the basis of randomness, we remove all human influences, both unknown and known, from the selection process.

Why is that important? First, in doing so we avoid selecting respondents, wittingly or not, in ways that confirm our predispositions or biases. Second, random selection enables us to use theories of mathematical probabilities to calculate how close our estimates are to the "true" values (the population "parameters") and how confident in those judgments we can be.

To read in a newspaper that President Obama's job approval rating is 52% ± 4% is a statement about how close we believe our sample estimate to be to the true percentage of people in the population who approve of the way in which he's performing his job. Such a statement, however, fails to let the reader know how confident he should be with that estimate. When this is unstated (which it often is in journalistic reports of voting intentions or approval ratings), the author is implying that the true population parameter would fall within ±4 percentage points of 52% (i.e., between 48% and 56%) in about 95 out of 100 similar samples drawn from the same population. The range of 48% to 56% is a "confidence interval."

The third reason why random selection into a sample is important is that the alternatives—purposeful, convenience, haphazard (which should not be confused with random), and self-selected samples—provide no means of establishing either the closeness or the confidence of our estimates. Worse still, nonrandom selection mechanisms can produce wrong or biased estimates about the populations we are interested in understanding.

The 1936 *Literary Digest* survey of voters' intentions in that year's presidential election offers one of the more famous illustrations of the difference between random and nonrandom sample selection. The *Literary Digest*, first published in 1890, was a popular magazine in its time. Its presidential straw polls were widely anticipated and reported in the early part of the 20th century in the United States. These polls had considerable credibility, having correctly predicted the winning presidential candidates in all contests from its first poll in 1916 up to the election of 1936.

In seeking to forecast the upcoming election of 1936, the *Digest* mailed 10 million surveys to people across the United States. The questionnaire asked which presidential candidate the recipient planned to vote for: the Republican challenger, Alfred M. Landon, or the Democratic incumbent, Franklin Delano Roosevelt (FDR). About 2.4 million replies poured into the *Digest's* offices in the weeks preceding the report of the results in their October 31, 1936, issue. That issue reported that Landon would defeat FDR, receiving 52% of the popular vote and 370 to 161 electoral votes for FDR. The report was careful to state that "we make no claim to infallibility" and disavowed credit for the claim of "uncanny accuracy" that others had bestowed on its previous polls. With an apparent gleam in their eyes, the editors of the magazine went on to write,

We never make any claims before election but we respectfully refer you to the opinion of one of the most quoted citizens today, the Hon. James A. Farley, Chairman of the Democratic National Committee. This is what Mr. Farley said October 14, 1932:

"Any sane person cannot escape the implication of such a gigantic sampling of popular opinion as is embraced in *The Literary Digest* straw vote. I consider this conclusive evidence as to the desire of the people of this country for a change in the National Government. *The Literary Digest* poll is an achievement of no little magnitude. It is a Poll fairly and correctly conducted." (http://historymatters.gmu.edu/d/5168/, accessed July 8, 2008)

The actual results in 1936: FDR won 61% of the popular vote and 523 electoral votes to Landon's 8.

What went wrong here? There are at least two plausible explanations. One is nonresponse bias. It could be that the 24% who returned the questionnaire differed from the 76% who did not. It is easy to imagine that those angry with FDR's first term in office (and there were many such people) would have been more motivated to respond to the survey than those who were pleased with FDR's administration, many of whom undoubtedly planned to vote for him. We can assume that anger would be a more powerful motivator than satisfaction in voluntarily responding to a questionnaire about voting intentions.

Another likely explanation concerns a different kind of bias: sampling bias. The 10 million people to whom the survey was mailed were drawn from three sources:

1. Subscribers to the *Literary Digest*

2. Car registration records

3. Telephone owners

People who fell into any of these three lists in 1936 were hardly representative of the American public in the midst of the Great Depression. The probability of poorer folks being in the sample was thus much less than the probability of wealthy people being included, and socioeconomic class was related to voting behavior in the election of 1936.

Luck would have it that the same election was predicted correctly by the 35-year-old statistician George Gallup, who randomly selected 50,000 people for interviews. The moral of this story is punctuated by the fact that *The Literary Digest* went out of business within 2 years of its calamitous prediction, while Gallup's survey business prospered for decades to come.

We will return later in this chapter to determining the proper sample size. We need a few more tools in our kit before we can do so, especially the concept of the standard error, to which we turn next. Suffice it here to say that it is not the sheer number of responses that matter in a sample. Surely the *Literary Digest*'s 2.4 million respondents were a lot of people. Nor is it the proportion of a population that matters. A sample of about 1,000 is needed as much to make inferences about the citizens of Milwaukee as it is to make inferences about all adults in the United States.

● THE STANDARD ERROR AND CONFIDENCE INTERVALS

Like many other statistical terms, the etiology of "standard error" is difficult to divine. It is "standard" only if you mean that it takes on the shape of a normal distribution when your sample is sufficiently large. It's an error only in the sense that it provides a measure of how far your estimate is likely to be from the actual population parameter. This begins to get a little ethereal. Let's try to understand it via an example.

Let's say that we have a jar of 720 beans, half of which are white and the other half, red. But let's assume that we do not know the distribution of white and red beans but instead want to estimate, say, the number or average of red beans in the entire jar (i.e., the population) on the basis of a sample drawn from it. Let's draw a random sample of 20 beans. If "1" represents a red bean, you may get the following result of 9 red beans from a single sample of 20 beans.

$$0, 1, 1, 1, 0, 1, 0, 0, 1, 1, 1, 0, 0, 0, 0, 1, 1, 0, 0, 0$$

Asking Excel for summary descriptive statistics on this sample produces something like the following table:

Descriptive statistics from one sample of beans	
Mean	0.45
Standard Error	0.114132887
Median	0
Standard Deviation	0.510417786
Count	20
Confidence Level (95.0%)	0.238882876

The mean in this table is the proportion (otherwise stated as 45%) of red beans or, in this instance, the mean of red beans. Excel also gives us statistics for standard error and standard deviation, carried out to the ninth decimal place, surely a prize winner for false precision. We have seen the standard deviation in Chapter 5. It is one of the tools we have to measure how dispersed or varied the distribution of our observations is.

The standard error (*SE*) is derived mathematically from the sample standard deviation (*s*) and square root of the sample size (*n*) in the following relationship:

$$SE = \frac{s}{\sqrt{n}}.$$

In this case, the standard error equals $0.51/4.48 = 0.11$. In every case, the standard error will always be smaller than the standard deviation of a single sample. The standard error of a sample of 100, for example, will be 1/10 as large as the standard deviation of any mean calculated from that sample. Okay, but what is the standard error, and what is it used for?

Here's where it gets a little tricky. The standard error is a measure of the dispersion of the "sampling distribution." You could call a standard error the standard deviation of the sampling distribution. The sampling distribution in the case at hand is the distribution of means derived from many replications of the sample. In most instances, this is somewhat of a "virtual" distribution because you will be very unlikely to field tens or hundreds of samples of the same size and design from the same population. These distributions can, however, be simulated, as we will do below in drawing 38 samples from our jar of red and white beans. In a more general sense, we could create a population with a known percentage of red beans or a known percentage of people with blue eyes and repeatedly draw samples from that population, calculating the mean of all replicated samples from this sampling distribution and plotting these in a histogram.

Happily for us, statistical theory (and the central limit theorem in particular) proves (trust me) that the sampling distribution will take on the properties of a normal distribution when the sample size of a single survey used to estimate the standard error is large (say, 50 or more observations). You will hopefully recall some of the properties of a normal distribution. The most important one for us here is that 95% of all the observations in the sampling distribution will fall within about ±2 standard errors of the sample mean. This range on the sampling distribution provides the "confidence limits" of any given estimate or statistic. (We are considering estimates of counts, percentages, or means here, but standard errors can be calculated for more sophisticated statistics such as correlation or regression coefficients, which we will see later in the text.)

Confidence limits or intervals are used for telling the reader how confident he can be in an estimate derived from a single sample. In the case of our single sample of beans above, we can be confident that the "true" mean of red beans in the jar of beans is $0.45 \pm (2.09 \times 0.11)$ (i.e., ±0.24)[1] in 95 out of every 100 hypothetical samples of the same size and design (i.e., a random sample of 20 beans). That is to say, we can be confident (statistically speaking) that the true percentage of red beans in the jar will fall between 21% and 69% in approximately 95 out of every 100 samples of equal size and design. The range is fairly broad here because the sample size is small ($n = 20$).

Ninety-five percent certainty or confidence is a common benchmark in statistics. It's arbitrary but a standard frequently used as a threshold for how confident you should strive to be about an estimate. We'll see it repeated throughout the remainder of this text. If you'd like to be more confident about your estimates, by all means feel free to use, say, a 99% confidence interval. Your confidence intervals, however, will be larger because you'll be multiplying your standard error by ±2.575 (instead of ±1.96 in samples larger than 50).

Now, let's actually draw repeated samples of 20 beans and count the number (or percentage) of red beans in each sample. It's important that you realize that your sample of 20 beans may yield 11 red beans or 7 or 14. Occasionally, you will draw 10 red beans out of 20, hitting the population parameter in this example (50%) on the head.

Figure 8.1 displays the results of 38 such samples that I drew one year for students in my statistics class. I placed each random sample of 20 beans in a cup and asked students to count and report the number of red beans in each of their samples. The frequency of red beans from 38 different samples is displayed in the edited Excel histogram. The histogram you see is a distribution of the number of red beans found in 38 samples drawn from a jar of beans with equal numbers of red and white beans.

In this particular case (other replications in different classes have yielded more normal distributions), eight students counted 8 red beans in their cups, seven counted 9 red beans, six counted 10 red beans, and so on. One student reported 20 red beans, a very unlikely event. (Indeed, the student later confessed

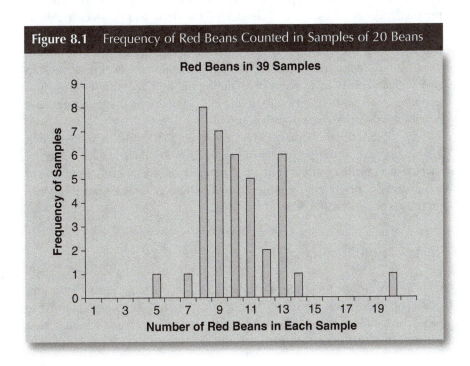

Figure 8.1 Frequency of Red Beans Counted in Samples of 20 Beans

that she thought the task was to count all the beans in her cup, not just the red ones. Is there no haven from measurement error? Don't count on it.)

The larger a sample is, the more normal the sampling distribution will become and the more clustered the observations will become around the population mean of 10 red beans. You might even say (if sufficiently old and humorously juvenile),

Beans, beans. They're good for your head. The more you sample, the lesser the spread. So sample those beans.

● STATISTICAL SIGNIFICANCE, THE NULL HYPOTHESIS, AND *p* VALUES

Nearly every statistical textbook includes a chapter on significance testing, the null hypothesis, and p values. Understanding these terms will help you interpret the output from future exercises in SPSS and interpret the research results that others present. Briefly stated, a significance test assesses the likelihood that a statistic generated from a sample is the result of the random selection process by which the data were generated. Recall above that not every random sample will precisely produce the actual population parameter that it seeks to estimate. The luck of the draw will produce different results, but repeated draws will produce a range of estimates that tend to cluster around the true value of the population parameter.

The null hypothesis is a proposition that your statistical tests seek to reject. Statisticians love rejection. Often, the null hypothesis is a "nil" hypothesis because it seeks to reject the hypothesis that a value or a relationship is zero in the population.

A p value is the probability of rejecting the null hypothesis as false when it is in fact true in the population from which you draw a sample. Each of these concepts arises in the context of samples and the inferences you want to make about population parameters on the basis of sample statistics. More on these concepts will follow.

Tests of Significance

One metaphor for understanding significance testing is that of a jury trial. The accused is presumed innocent (the null hypothesis) and the prosecutor's (analyst's) job is to assemble enough evidence to make that probability of innocence appear very unlikely:

Do you really believe Mr. Doe is innocent in light of the following facts: Five eyewitnesses have testified under oath that they witnessed Mr. Doe shoot Mr. Smith, DNA evidence has placed Mr. Doe at the scene of the crime, the registration of the murder weapon is in Mr. Doe's name, and his fingerprints (and only his fingerprints) were found on the murder weapon. I call upon you, the jury, to return a verdict of guilty (by rejecting the null hypothesis that he's innocent).

Get it?

A more statistical explanation goes as follows. What is the probability of observing a mean of 3.52 from a random sample if the true value in the population from which your sample was drawn is actually zero? Similarly, what are the chances that the observed value of 3.52 is the result of the luck of the draw, realizing that a random sample always has some chance of producing such a number even when the true value is zero? Tests of statistical significance determine, say, whether the differences or relationships one observes are "real" or simply an artifact of the random sampling process from which the data were derived.

Unfortunately, far too much weight is given to statistical significance in the analysis of sample data. R. A. Fisher, who invented the term, may well have selected the word *significance* because the term in the early 20th century in Great Britain meant that something mattered or signified something. It has since come to mean "important" in everyday discourse. This difference between common usage and statistical meaning is not unique to this term. But it doesn't help for a concept that is widely misunderstood and frequently misapplied.

Tests of statistical significance tend to direct students' and readers' attention away from a concern for the size of a relationship or the magnitude of differences between two or more groups of observations. Instead, it conveys a sense of authority or importance on any sample statistic that wears its badge. Beware that such an honor is as much a function of the size of the sample as it is of the magnitude of the differences or the strength of the relationships being estimated. Large sample sizes of, say, 10,000 respondents are not uncommon in government surveys that need to calculate accurate statistics for small subgroups within the population. But nearly every statistic that such surveys produce will be "significant," no matter how small the actual effect. Remember that statistical significance simply tells you whether the results you obtain from a single sample are likely to have arisen from the luck of the draw. The larger the sample, the less likely that chance is producing the results. Or, in statistical speak, the larger the sample, the smaller will be your standard error, the measure of the dispersion of your sampling distribution.

Let us not, however, throw the baby out with the bathwater. While it is important to always consider the size of an estimated effect quite apart from its statistical significance, a small effect can nonetheless be important for policy purposes if it can be changed relatively easily and inexpensively in comparison, say, with other effects that may be larger but cannot be easily changed (see Abelson, 1995).

Also be aware of the possible misinterpretation of the absence of statistical significance. While large samples will invariably produce "significant" results, small samples will invariably be hard-pressed to do so. Small samples may lack what statisticians call **power**, that is, the ability to detect real differences or relationships that in fact exist in the population from which a sample is drawn. Sampling statisticians are looking for a Goldilocks solution to sample size: not too big and not too small but just right, a topic to which we will turn later in this chapter.

If misery loves company, you may be happy to know that there's quite a lengthy and distinguished line of scholars who have criticized the preoccupation with statistical significance, including Yates (1951), Rozeboom (1960), Bakan (1966), Meehl (1967), Lykken (1968), Morrison and Henkel (1970), Carver (1978), Guttman (1985), Oakes (1986), Loftus (1991, 1994), Cohen (1994), Schmidt (1996), and Ziliak and McCloskey (2008).

Regrettably, significance tests and their associated p values are here to stay. Students should become familiar with their generation and interpretation, although it is good practice to generate and report confidence intervals as well as the level of statistical significance. (I also recommend reporting effect sizes, but we'll turn to that topic in Chapter 10). Grin and bear it.

The Null Hypothesis

The null hypothesis has come to take up a position of honor in statistical inference. But it's an odd creature to be sure. The null hypothesis is more often than not a conjecture that an analyst hopes to reject. It is often stated as a hypothesis that a relationship between two variables or the difference in the means of two groups is zero. It need not be nil, however. You can hypothesize that the average recidivism rate for prisoners convicted of armed robbery is 30% within 6 months of release from jail and conduct a random sample to determine whether the evidence enables you to reject this null hypothesis.

Consider the following research on a program intended to deter delinquent juveniles from further wrongdoing. At least nine randomized control trials (aka experiments), including nearly 1,000 juveniles or young adults in all, have sought to test whether participation in programs such as

Scared Straight successfully redirects adolescent offenders (or those at risk of becoming adult offenders) away from "a path of crime." Inmates serving life sentences in a New Jersey prison in the 1970s were the first to design the Scared Straight program, although a similar program in California (San Quentin Utilization of Inmate Resources, Experience and Studies [SQUIRES]) began in 1964. New Jersey inmates invited delinquents to prison, where they were given graphic depictions of the brutality of prison life, including exaggerated stories of rape and murder. A television documentary of the New Jersey program in 1979 claimed that 16 of the 17 delinquents whom it interviewed had remained out of trouble during the 3 months after their visit to the prison (a 94% success rate). The program received wide recognition, and it, or some variation of it, spread to at least 30 other jurisdictions nationwide and to jurisdictions in Australia, the United Kingdom, Norway, Germany, and Canada (see Petrosino, Turpin-Petrosino, & Buehler, 2003).

One of the nine randomized control trials of these programs was conducted in New Jersey in 1982 (Finckenauer, 1982). The null hypothesis of this experiment was that there was no difference in criminal behavior between the delinquent juveniles who were randomly assigned to participate in Scared Straight and a randomly assigned group of delinquent juveniles who received no such "treatment." Those who believed in the program's efficacy were undoubtedly expecting the treatment group to have gotten in trouble with the law far fewer times than the control group in the months after the program. These program advocates wanted or expected the differences in crime rates between these two groups to be statistically significant—that is to say, not the result of the differences likely to be produced as a result of random selection into a control or treatment group as part of an experiment. In other words, they wanted to reject the null hypothesis of no effect.

Contrary to many program supporters' hopes and expectations, the randomly assigned adolescents who were "scared straight" were subsequently five times more likely to commit new offenses than the randomly assigned adolescents who did not participate in the program. (The confidence interval of this odds ratio estimate is 1.65–18.02, the large width of this interval being a function of the fact that only 46 youth were assigned to the treatment group and only 35 to the control group.) Seven of the other eight experiments showed similar negative results (only one experiment demonstrated positive results, but these were not statistically significant). The null hypotheses were rejected in many instances, contrary to many people's expectations.

Interestingly, one study in Illinois also found that the program had no effect on attitudes toward crime or toward the program. In contrast, interviews and mail surveys of participants, parents, and teachers registered unanimous support for the program. Inmates were positive and enthusiastic about their efforts.

The authors of a review (Petrosino et al., 2003) of the nine randomized control trials of Scared Straight and similar programs note a final irony in their study. Despite the evidence to the contrary, such programs continue to be in use.

> As Finckenauer and Gavin (1999) noted, when the negative results from the California SQUIRES study came out, the response was to end evaluation— not the program. Today the SQUIRES program continues, evaluated by the testimonials of prisoners and participants alike. (p. 59)

This is a weak reed on which to base the continuation of a program that may actually harm the participants.

p Values

A *p* value is the probability of rejecting the null hypothesis when you shouldn't. Customarily, we hope that this number, which SPSS reports to you under the pseudonym "Sig.," is less than .05. The *p* value is a numeric estimate of the probability that the evidence you have at hand (whether a mean or a correlation coefficient) is sufficiently different from your null hypothesis to matter. Another way of defining a *p* value is to say that it is an estimate of the probabilities that the facts you have at hand are the result of the "luck" of a random draw from a population. Whereas we are led to believe that big is good and bigger is better, the statistical analyst in you should want to discover very small *p* values. When it comes to *p* values, small is beautiful. Commit that mantra to memory (although also be prepared to think otherwise in a small number of statistical tests we will see later that posit null hypotheses that we hope not to reject).

In sum, the prosecuting attorney (statistical analyst) in you wants to convict (reject) the presumption of innocence (null hypothesis) in the accused by providing so much evidence that the odds of falsely convicting an innocent man are small (a *p* value of less than 5 in a 100).

Power

To extend our jury metaphor, it is also the case that weak evidence (e.g., evidence with insufficient "power") can lead a jury to let a guilty man go free. Statistically speaking, you can fail to reject the null hypothesis (innocence) when it is actually false (guilty). The likely cause of this is too small a sample for the size of the effect in the population. We will not tarry long with the concept of statistical power. There are several aspects of "power," however, to commit to memory:

- Worry whether a sample has sufficient power if small. You don't want to let a lot of guilty people go free because the district attorney only interviewed one witness who had poor eyesight.

- In general, strive for a sample size that produces at least a power of .80. Even then, you'll let a guilty man go free in 20% of such circumstances, but you'll be less likely to exceed your budget.

- To calculate power, consult a Web site such as www.danielsoper.com/statcalc/calc09.aspx.

- The sample size required to detect an effect in the population will vary by the size of that effect and the type of test you plan to conduct (to achieve a power of .80), as illustrated in Figure 8.2 (we will turn to eta-square and rho-square in a subsequent chapter).

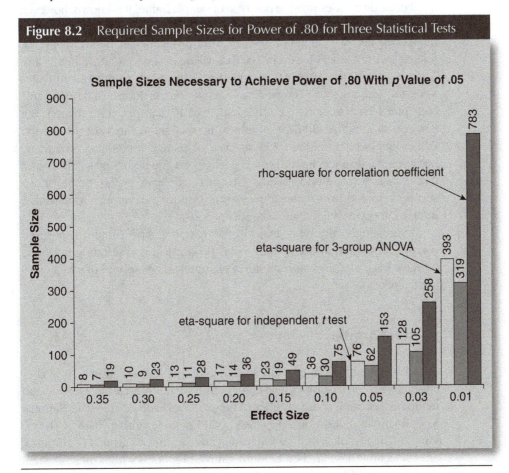

Figure 8.2 Required Sample Sizes for Power of .80 for Three Statistical Tests

SOURCE: Field (2005).

● SAMPLE DESIGNS

Simple Random Samples (SRS)

Calculations of sample variance for various statistics typically assume that the data come from simple random samples in which every member of the population has a known and equal probability of selection. Such sample designs require that you have a list of all members of the population to be sampled (otherwise known as a sample frame). Each element (person) in the frame can be assigned a unique number, and a computer program can generate random numbers equal to the size of the sample you wish to conduct (more on sample size in a moment).

Phone directories provide one type of sample frame. It is known, however, that about 15% of the entries in residential portions of national telephone directories are no longer in service. This problem can be overcome by selecting 118 numbers for every 100 that will be in service (118 × 15% = 18). A random digit dialing (RDD) survey of all households in the United States faces an additional challenge. One such frame includes all known area code/prefix combinations (i.e., the first six of 10-digit phone numbers). But 85% of all possible 10-digit numbers in this frame are not in service. Discovering which of these 85% are out of service (or out of your frame because it's a business instead of a residence or a line dedicated solely to a fax machine) is a costly undertaking (Groves et al., 2004, p. 74). Some phone surveys combine RDD with samples from telephone directories to maximize sample coverage while minimizing survey costs.

Interestingly, the vast majority of national, government-sponsored surveys conducted in the United States do not use simple random sample designs. Instead, they use some form of stratification, several of which we'll briefly mention here.

Cluster Samples

Cluster samples are taken by selecting groups of population members or clusters (e.g., a city block), listing all the elements in each cluster, and randomly selecting some number of people from each cluster. The National Assessment of Educational Progress (NAEP), for example, uses a cluster sample. The sample's first set of clusters are counties or groups of counties. After selecting these areas, a random sample of schools within these clusters is selected. Within each selected school, a random sample of students in Grades 4, 8, and 12 is chosen to take NAEP tests.

Stratified Samples

Stratified samples are similar to cluster samples in that they group elements in the sampling frame into mutually exclusive strata. Population elements might be grouped by gender or race, for example, assuming that you have this type of information as part of your sampling frame. Stratified samples are taken by randomly selecting separate samples from each group. In so doing, stratified samples avoid the possibility of, say, randomly selecting elements from a list in such a way that only men end up in the sample. One can sample with proportional or disproportional rates within each stratum.

Systematic Selection

Systematic selection again begins with a list of population members. After determining the ratio of the population to your desired sample size (e.g., you want to sample 1 of every 100 members of the population), you randomly select a member within the first 100 on your list and then select every 100th person thereafter.

DETERMINING THE SAMPLE SIZE ●

In theory, determining how large a sample to draw is a function of only three conditions:

1. How wide a range of error you can tolerate in your estimate (e.g., ±3 percentage points in estimating a mean)

2. How confident you want your estimates to be (e.g., the true population parameter will be found within that margin of error in about 95 of 100 samples of similar design and size)

3. The variability of your estimate in the population (i.e., the standard deviation)

Let us say that we want to determine how large a sample to take in order to estimate the mean level of recidivism among convicted drug users who participate in a court-ordered cognitive behavioral therapy program. All you need to do is determine how close and confident you want your estimate to be (1 and 2) and estimate or guess the standard deviation for the average level (or rate) of recidivism.

The more precise formula for determining sample size (n) is

$$n = \left(\frac{z \times s}{E}\right)^2,$$

where z is the number of standard deviations from the mean of a normal distribution in which you'll find the desired confidence limit (e.g., 1.96 for 95%), s is the estimated standard deviation, and E is the amount of error you can tolerate on either side of your estimate (e.g., .03). If we guess that the standard deviation for the recidivism rate is .20 (the rate can theoretically vary from 0 to 1.0) or determine this from a previous study, and plug in our old friends, we would strive to achieve a sample size of 179:

$$\left(\frac{1.96 \times .20}{.03}\right)^2.$$

Let's examine one more example. Suppose we wanted to estimate the proportion of adults in Philadelphia who are morbidly obese but we have no knowledge of the standard deviation of adult obesity in Philadelphia. The most conservative strategy in such a situation is to assume that the standard deviation of the proportion of obese people in the population is as high as it can get. When is that? When half are obese and half are not. In general, the standard deviation of a proportion is the product of the proportion of a population with the condition and the proportion without. Its maximum value in this example, therefore, is the square root of .50 × .50, which magically turns out to be .50. If we wanted to be within .03 of the actual percentage of people in Philadelphia who are morbidly obese and if we wanted to be 95% confident about our estimate, we would seek a sample size of 1,065.

$$\left(\frac{1.96 \times .50}{.03}\right)^2.$$

All this is to demonstrate that samples of 1,000 to 1,500 are good for estimating means with an accuracy of about ±3% in 95 out of 100 samples of the same size.[2]

But wait a minute. We have been determining sample sizes as if the purpose of our sample was only to measure a single statistic—for example, the proportion of our population who are morbidly obese or the rate of recidivism among ex-drug offenders. Surely, most sample surveys have more than these modest purposes. Indeed, determining the sample size to estimate a regression coefficient will depend on

- how close and how confident you want your estimate to be to the "true" population parameter (as above),
- the size of the effect in the population (the smaller the actual effect, the larger the sample must be to detect it),
- the number of independent variables you are examining, and
- the power of the test (.80 or above).

Andy Field (2005, p. 173), drawing on Miles and Shevlin (2001) and using a power of .80, calculated the sample size required for analysis when varying the number of independent variables and the size of the effects in the population, as shown in Figure 8.3.

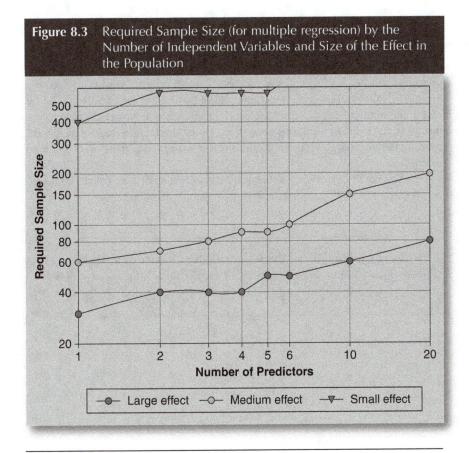

Figure 8.3 Required Sample Size (for multiple regression) by the Number of Independent Variables and Size of the Effect in the Population

SOURCE: Field (2005).

Again, don't worry about the details here. Many textbook formulas for determining sample size are meant only to illustrate how to think about sample size. Given the multiple objectives of any single sample and the typical departures from the simple random sample selection procedures, these formulas should not be strictly applied in an actual study.

Indeed, it is often the case that the resources available trump sampling theory in determining sample size. The question then becomes "How large a sample can I afford?" The analyst then seeks to estimate the possible standard error, given guesses about what the actual standard deviation of the statistic might be. This is a good place to consult an expert sampling statistician if the answers to your questions are important and the resources issue serious. Knowing when to ask for help is a good thing to learn. Designing and executing a sample is one such instance. Analyzing the results is easier, as we will begin to see in the next chapter.

● NOTES

1. The 2.09 figure uses the *t* distribution instead of the normal probability distribution for which a 95% confidence interval is ±1.96 standard deviations from the mean. The *t* distribution is used with samples of 30 or fewer observations, as is the case in this example. Excel and SPSS select this distribution for you in calculating confidence limits. Don't fret with this detail. It can be left unexamined "under the hood," recalling the metaphorical objective of this text to make you better drivers, not auto mechanics.

2. This result applies when sampling from a population of more than 20,000 members because of something called the finite population correction factor. Don't ask.

To practice and reinforce the lessons of this chapter of the book, turn to Exercise 5 in the *Student Workbook* (available at http://www.sagepub.com/pearsonsp/).

CHAPTER 9

STATISTICS AS GROUP DIFFERENCES

A s noted earlier (but worth repeating), there are three genres of statistics. One (Chapter 5) describes relatively simple, but important, characteristics of data by answering three questions:

1. Where is the center of a variable's distribution? (e.g., What is its mean, median, and/or mode?)

2. How diverse or varied are its observations or values? (e.g., What is its range, minimum, maximum, and/or standard deviation?)

3. What's the shape of its distribution? (e.g., Is the distribution normal, skewed, or kurtotic?)

A second class of statistics seeks to answer the question whether two or more groups differ from one another on some characteristic. Do men differ from women in their child-rearing practices? Are taller people promoted more quickly than shorter people? Is the crime rate higher in the summer than in other seasons? Do countries with national health insurance provide better-quality health care than countries that principally offer health insurance through private markets?

The third set of statistics (e.g., measures of association, correlation, and regression) assesses the extent and ways in which two or more conditions are related to one another. Is a person's years of education related to his or her annual salary? Is gender related to the rate at which someone is promoted at work? Do murder rates vary with the time of year?

Of course, these latter two genres of statistics are actually different sides of the same coin. To ask if men and women differ in their child-rearing practices is the flip side of the coin that asks if there is a relationship between gender and child-rearing practices. To ask if the average annual salary of college graduates is higher than for those who did not complete college is the opposite side of a coin that asks if there is a relationship between education and income. These are simply two different ways of framing your analytical question.

Whether you ask the question one way or another is in part a function of your analytical style, the way in which your data were collected, the prevailing conventions in your academic discipline or work environment, and the choice of which of the two questions is more easily understood and communicated to your intended audiences. Neither side of this coin is superior to the other in most instances. It is, however, the case that each of these two perspectives evokes a different set of statistical procedures (although their basic algorithms are often similar and many of their assumptions the same).

This chapter turns to that set of analytic tools intended to ask the group difference question. There are a number of such tools. We'll discuss a limited, but useful, set of them, including the following:

- *t tests* to assess differences between *only two groups* (There are five varieties of these tests.)
- **Analysis of variance (ANOVA)**, to test for differences between *three or more groups* on a continuous dependent variable
  - *Between-groups or independent-sample* ANOVA, when subjects or respondents in each group are different people whose responses are independent of other respondents in the sample
  - *Repeated-measures or paired-sample* ANOVA, to test for differences at two different times on the same people or on pairs of people who were selected because they are alike except on one or more characteristics
- **Analysis of covariance (ANCOVA)**, which is akin to ANOVA but throws in a continuous independent variable among the categorical ones

It is the case that the percentage differences that are produced by cross-tabulations or contingency tables and pivot tables are part of this genre of statistics, but we've chosen in this book to separate them from *t* tests and ANOVA because of their differences in procedure and interpretation from the statistics that are the subject of this chapter.

All the following tests of group differences in this chapter have two things in common: (1) the dependent variable is continuous and (2) one or more of the independent variable(s) is (are) categorical. Indeed, the categories define what we mean by "group." The tests vary by the number of independent variables they include, the number of categories (or groups) each independent variable may have, whether the data are parametric or not (e.g., Is the dependent variable continuous and normally distributed?), and whether the observations or samples are independent or dependent. (We will define and illustrate these terms later in the chapter.) Let's start with the simplest of these tests of group differences and move to more complex ones. The following sections first describe the purpose of each statistic and then illustrate how you request the statistic from SPSS and interpret its output.

ONE-SAMPLE *t* TEST ●

Purpose: To test whether the mean of a variable in your file differs from a number that you provide. This test is useful, for example, in testing whether your sample's characteristics differ from those of the population from which you drew the sample (assuming you have independent and credible data about the "true" value of those characteristics in the population).

Step 1: Open the Public Perceptions data set.

Click on Analyze/Compare Means/One-Sample T Test, and move Gender (assuming the variable is coded 0 = *male* and 1 = *female*) into the variable box. Enter .51 into the Test Value: box as shown below. (.51 is the proportion, expressed as a decimal, of women in Orange County, a fact that the U.S. Census Bureau provides.)

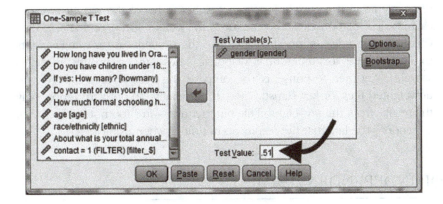

Step 2: Click on OK, which will produce the following tables:

One-Sample Statistics

	N	Mean	Std. Deviation	Std. Error Mean
gender	1033	.56	.496	.015

One-Sample Test

	Test Value = .51				95% Confidence Interval of the Difference	
	t	df	Sig. (2-tailed)	Mean Difference	Lower	Upper
gender	3.332	1032	.001	.051	.02	.08

By God, these tables include the statistics we talked about in the previous chapter: standard error (in this case, of the mean), Sig. (otherwise known as a p value), and a 95% confidence interval (in this case, of the difference between the percentage of women in the sample and in the population of Orange County, Florida). The column "t" represents what's called a critical value, which, in combination with **degrees of freedom (*df*),** is used to calculate the level of statistical significance represented by p (which SPSS calls "Sig."). The implicit null hypothesis (which hardly seems worth stating) is that there is no difference between the percentage of women in the sample and the percentage in the population.

These tables provide sufficient evidence to reject that null hypothesis. The Public Perception survey has a statistically significant higher proportion of women in the sample (an estimate of 5 percentage points more, although we'd be real confident in believing that the sample had between 2 and 8 percentage points more women than actually live in Orange County). Do you remember how to interpret the p value or Sig? If not, you're in trouble. Do not proceed. Return to Chapter 8, or ask for help.

One possible response to the disproportionate number of women respondents in the sample is to use weights to boost the weight given to each male's responses and/or reduce the weight given to females (see Chapter 4 for a discussion of weights and the procedures for using weights to compensate for differential response rates among groups in one's sample). Another response is to compare the results of weighted and unweighted files for key statistics and, if the results do not vary, report only the results from the unweighted file but mention—in a footnote or technical appendix—the fact that the results do not differ when using weights.

● *t* TEST FOR INDEPENDENT SAMPLES

Purpose: To test whether the means of two groups differ significantly on a continuously measured dependent variable.

Independent samples is an unfortunate term. It only means two different groups of people (e.g., men and women) whose selection into a sample was independent of each other. Another way of saying this is that the selection of one male in the sample was not dependent on the selection of another man (or woman). The data are likely derived from a single data collection effort, not two different samples.

Step 1: Let's see whether the respondents' assessment of Orange County government services differs between those who had contact with the county in the past year and those who did not. (Recall that many people were asked to assess the timeliness, helpfulness, etc. of government employees even when they had not had such contact within the past 12 months. This might be considered a subtle check on the validity of the responses to these questions if the responses don't differ. Such an outcome might demonstrate that actual contacts aren't being recalled in these questions—unless perhaps a memorable negative or very positive encounter. No differences in the evaluation of services between those with and without such a contact in the past 12 months just might indicate that we've got a measure of the sense of how much or little a respondent likes county government instead of the specific character of the services themselves, e.g., timely, mistake-free.)

Click on Analyze/Compare Means/Independent-Samples T Test

Step 2: Enter the satisfaction index that you created in Chapter 4 and contact variables into their appropriate variable boxes, as follows:

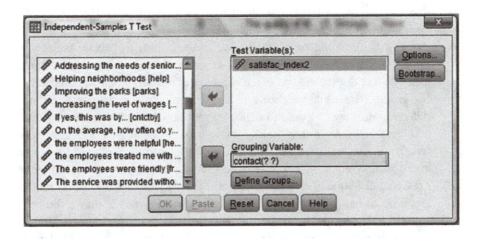

Note that I can't click on OK here and proceed. I haven't specified the values of the grouping variable. Click on Define Groups button.

After defining groups corresponding to the valid values of 1 and 2 for CONTACT (as they are coded in this file), click on OK to produce the following two tables:

Group Statistics

	Have you had any contact with any Orange county...	N	Mean	Std. Deviation	Std. Error Mean
satisfac_index2	Yes	481	73.7786	14.56182	.66396
	No	351	74.1987	12.33476	.65838

Independent Samples Test

		Levene's Test for Equality of Variances		t-test for Equality of Means						
									95% Confidence Interval of the Difference	
		F	Sig.	t	df	Sig. (2-tailed)	Mean Difference	Std. Error Difference	Lower	Upper
satisfac_index2	Equal variances assumed	7.617	.006	-.438	830	.662	-.42013	.95942	-2.30331	1.46305
	Equal variances not assumed			-.449	811.727	.653	-.42013	.93505	-2.25862	1.41528

The overall level of satisfaction differs by less than 1 point on a scale that ranges from 25 to 100. Those who contacted the county government had no statistically different assessment of those services than those who did not have any contact within the past year. The *p* value is .66.

Note too that the second table has a box for **Levene's test** for the equality of variances. This test is among a handful of such tests in this book that flip a null hypothesis on its head. That is to say, its null hypothesis is that the variances of the two groups are equal, which you'd prefer not to reject because the independent-samples *t* test is based on a formula that assumes that they are. You would, therefore, hope to find a *p* value (Sig.) that is higher than our customary level of .05, instead of smaller. It is .006. The variances in each group appear not to be equal.

This is not a big problem. As you can see from the above table, SPSS provides (without even asking) a test of group differences (using a different formula) that doesn't rely on equal variances of the dependent variable for the two groups. The results are the same: The two group means are not significantly different. Moreover, violation of the assumption of equal variances—and the additional assumption that the distributions of the variable in both groups are "normal"—are not damaging with relatively large samples and groups that have approximately equal numbers of observations. Simple life forms such as the *t* test and **chi-square (χ^2)** are fairly robust. That is to say, they don't tend to break down easily when assumptions are violated, which is unlike the more sophisticated species of statistical animal to which we turn in later chapters.

A hardnosed, conservative data analyst might, however, be troubled by any violation in the assumptions, no matter how robust the statistic. Fortunately, she can call on a nonparametric test that makes no such assumptions, the *Mann-Whitney U test*, whose procedures are outlined in the following box.

Nonparametric Test of Two Independent Sample Means: Mann-Whitney *U*

Note that there exist several tests for the differences in the means of two groups when parametric assumptions are not met. That is to say, the dependent variable is measured at the ordinal rather than the continuous level, the two group variances are unequal, or the dependent variable is not normally distributed. The one statistic that we can use here is the Mann-Whitney *U*.

By the way, nonparametric test statistics are less likely to find statistically significant relationships than are parametric tests such as the Student *t* test above. So the example below is unnecessary, except to illustrate the steps used in SPSS to generate this nonparametric test.

Step 1: Click on Analyze/Nonparametric/Legacy Dialogs/2 Independent Samples

Step 2: Move the dependent variable into the box for Test Variables: (satisfac_index2) and the independent variable into the Grouping Variables: box (CONTACT). Define Groups as you did before (1, 2), select Mann-Whitney, and click OK, which will produce the following tables:

Ranks

	Have you had any cont...	N	Mean Rank	Sum of Ranks
satisfac_index2	Yes	481	411.62	197987.50
	No	351	423.19	148540.50
	Total	832		

Test Statistics[a]

	satisfac_index2
Mann-Whitney U	82066.500
Wilcoxon W	197987.500
Z	-.728
Asymp. Sig. (2-tailed)	.467

a. Grouping Variable: Have you had any contact with any Orange county employees during the past 12 months

(Continued)

> (Continued)
>
> Each two-tailed significance value estimates the probability of obtaining a z statistic as large as or more extreme (in absolute value) than the one displayed, if there truly is no effect of the treatment.
>
> The p value of .467 indicates that the differences are not statistically significant (i.e., you cannot reject the null hypothesis of no difference).

● PAIRED-SAMPLES t TEST (OR REPEATED-MEASURES TEST)

> *Purpose:* To test whether the means of the same set of subjects or respondents have changed over time.

Note: The Public Perception survey does not question the same individuals at two points in time to see if their evaluation of county government workers changes, say, after the county inaugurated a new customer service training program for employees. To conduct an analysis appropriate for repeated measures would require you to, say, conduct another in-class survey that will include repeated responses to some of the original questions that were asked on the first day of class. This might be of interest if you wanted to determine whether the course reduced anxiety about statistics or increased one's knowledge and skills. The following steps assume that this second survey has been conducted and the data added to the first with a new set of variables that have a "2" suffix to denote being measured at, say, the middle or end of the semester.

Step 1: We will see whether your index of being primed to do well in the class has increased with time. We, therefore, must first create a new variable from the sum of responses to LOOKING2, READY2, and CHALLENGE2. Do this (*Hint:* Transform/Compute). Remember to rescale this index such that the highest value could be 100. Label this new variable PRIMED2.

Step 2: Run Descriptive Statistics on PRIMED2 to make sure it's well behaved.

Step 3: Now for the paired-samples *t* test.

Click Analyze/Compare Means/Paired Samples T Test. Move PRIMED and PRIMED2 into the Paired Variables: box. Click OK.

Read the resulting tables much as you would the others we've seen up to this point. Are students any more primed now than they were at the beginning of the semester?

Nonparametric Tests for Paired Samples: Wilcoxon Signed Rank Test

Like the *t* test for independent samples, a test statistic is available if our parametric assumptions are seriously violated. It is the Wilcoxon Signed Rank Test.

Let's assume for illustrative purposes that our measures of PRIMED AND PRIMED2 aren't as well behaved as we would hope (or there's some suspicions that we can allay by resorting to this more robust, but conservative, test of the differences of the same subjects at two points in time).

Step 1: Click on Analyze/Nonparametric Tests/2 Related Samples
Step 2: Select Wilcoxon in the Test Type box, and Click OK.
Step 3: Interpret the asymmetric significance test as a *p* value to judge whether to reject the null hypothesis that the means for subjects at Time 1 are no different than at Time 2.

ONE-WAY ANALYSIS OF VARIANCE ●

Purpose: To assess the mean differences on a continuous variable across three or more groups (which SPSS calls "factors"). The test also compares the variability (i.e., variance) of the dependent variable between groups (which is attributed to the independent variable) with the variability within groups (which is believed to be due to chance or error).

Like the *t* tests for independent samples and paired samples, one-way ANOVA is appropriate under two conditions: (1) when you have different subjects or cases (called between-groups ANOVA) and (2) when you are measuring the same subjects under different conditions or at different points in time (called within-subjects or repeated-measures ANOVA). In both instances, we will use the more conservative post hoc tests rather than planned comparisons because we are not absolutely sure about the direction of the relationship in the population.

Between-Groups ANOVA

Let's return to the Texas Education Indicator data set to learn whether there is a difference in test performance across districts that are distinguished by their per pupil expenditures (in this case, a variable recoded into five groups with roughly equal numbers of school districts: Expend_Per_Fifths).

Step 1: Open this data set, and click at the top of the screen on Analyze/Compare Means/One-Way ANOVA.

Step 2: Move the dependent variable ("Grades 3–11 All Tests Taken") into the Dependent List: box and the independent variable (Expend_Per_Fifths) into the box labeled "Factor."

Step 3: Click the Options button, and enable "Descriptive Statistics," "Homogeneity of variance test," "Brown-Forsythe," "Welsh," and "Mean Plots." Make sure that "Missing Values" exclude cases analysis by analysis.

Step 4: Click on the button marked Post Hoc. Click on Tukey. Click Continue and then OK.

Your output should look something like the following:

Descriptives

Grades 3-11 All Tests Taken 2006

	N	Mean	Std. Deviation	Std. Error	95% Confidence Interval for Mean		Minimum	Maximum
					Lower Bound	Upper Bound		
Lowest fifth 3364 to 7684	83	58.18	23.676	2.599	53.01	63.35	5	91
Second fifth 7585 to 8515	83	63.52	15.343	1.684	60.17	66.87	15	88
Middle fifth 8516 to 9459	76	62.99	14.181	1.827	59.75	66.23	8	94
Fourth fifth 9460 to 10950	88	64.02	13.335	1.421	61.20	66.85	35	92
Highest fift 10951 to 31016	68	67.59	12.003	1.456	64.68	70.49	45	95
Total	398	63.11	16.566	.830	61.48	64.74	5	95

Here again, you can learn a lot from the simplest of statistics, which fore-shadow what we will find in subsequent ANOVA results in this example. The mean of tests passed does not vary dramatically across different expenditure levels (although the groups themselves vary considerably in per pupil expen-ditures by as much as 10:1). The districts in the lowest fifth do fare worse than the others, but there's considerable variation in that group, which might give hope to policy wonks that poor districts can match wealthy dis-tricts in test performance despite meager resources.

Test of Homogeneity of Variances

Grades 3-11 All Tests Taken 2006

Levene Statistic	df1	df2	Sig.
15.615	4	393	.000

Again, Levene's test for the homogeneity of variances presents an instance in which the null hypothesis is that the variances are equal. The p value of .000 in this table says that the variances are not equal (probably the lowest-expenditure group is causing this result).

The Welsh and Brown-Forsythe tests for homogeneity of variances show the same results, which suggests that we may want to turn to the nonparametric ANOVA test in this instance through the Kruskal-Wallis Test (more on this below).

The ANOVA table should look something like the following:

ANOVA

Grades 3-11 All Tests Taken 2006

	Sum of Squares	df	Mean Square	F	Sig.
Between Groups	3468.712	4	867.178	3.231	.013
Within Groups	105474.424	393	268.383		
Total	108943.136	397			

The Sig. of .013 means that there is a significant difference somewhere among the mean test scores of districts that are grouped by per pupil expen-ditures. But it does not tell you which one(s) is (are) different, although you should have a good hunch from having inspected the Descriptive Statistics table above. The post hoc results will confirm (or overthrow) our hunches about which group means are different.

Post Hoc Tests

Multiple Comparisons

Grades 3-11 All Tests Taken 2006
Tukey HSD

(I) Per Pupil Expenditures in Fifths	(J) Per Pupil Expenditures in Fifths	Mean Difference (I-J)	Std. Error	Sig.	95% Confidence Interval	
					Lower Bound	Upper Bound
Lowest fifth 3364 to 7684	Second fifth 7585 to 8515	-5.337	2.543	.223	-12.31	1.63
	Middle fifth 8516 to 9459	-4.806	2.601	.348	-11.93	2.32
	Fourth fifth 9460 to 10950	-5.842	2.507	.137	-12.71	1.03
	Highest fift 10951 to 31016	-9.408*	2.680	.005	-16.75	-2.06
Second fifth 7585 to 8515	Lowest fifth 3364 to 7684	5.337	2.543	.223	-1.63	12.31
	Middle fifth 8516 to 9459	.531	2.601	1.000	-6.60	7.66
	Fourth fifth 9460 to 10950	-.505	2.507	1.000	-7.37	6.36
	Highest fift 10951 to 31016	-4.070	2.680	.551	-11.41	3.27
Middle fifth 8516 to 9459	Lowest fifth 3364 to 7684	4.806	2.601	.348	-2.32	11.93
	Second fifth 7585 to 8515	-.531	2.601	1.000	-7.66	6.60
	Fourth fifth 9460 to 10950	-1.036	2.585	.994	-8.07	5.99
	Highest fift 10951 to 31016	-4.601	2.735	.446	-12.10	2.89
Fourth fifth 9460 to 10950	Lowest fifth 3364 to 7684	5.842	2.507	.137	-1.03	12.71
	Second fifth 7585 to 8515	.505	2.507	1.000	-6.36	7.37
	Middle fifth 8516 to 9459	1.036	2.585	.994	-5.99	8.07
	Highest fift 10951 to 31016	-3.566	2.845	.861	-10.81	3.68
Highest fift 10951 to 31016	Lowest fifth 3364 to 7684	9.408*	2.680	.005	2.06	16.75
	Second fifth 7585 to 8515	4.070	2.680	.551	-3.27	11.41
	Middle fifth 8516 to 9459	4.601	2.735	.446	-2.89	12.10
	Fourth fifth 9460 to 10950	3.566	2.845	.861	-3.68	10.81

*. The mean difference is significant at the 0.05 level.

The above Multiple Comparisons tells you that the bottom fifth of districts (in terms of per pupil expenditures) are statistically different from the districts that spend the highest amount (as reflected in p value of .005). Secondly, districts in the second to highest group of districts do not differ from each other.

The Mean Plots chart shows these differences but distorts the differences by severely truncating the Y-axis range. The impression the chart conveys is rather misleading.

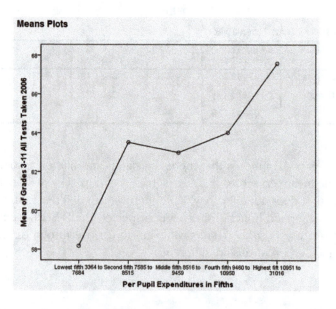

Means Plots

To compensate for the graph's distortion, you can calculate (by returning to Analyze/Descriptive Statistics/Crosstab) **eta**, which when **squared (η^2)** gives you an estimate of the variance in test performance that is explained in this case by per pupil expenditures. Or you can calculate this statistic rather easily by hand, using the following formula:

$$\eta^2 = \frac{\text{Sum of squares between groups}}{\text{Total sum of squares}}.$$

In this case, $\eta^2 = 0.03$. In other words, about 3% of the variation in test scores is explained by district finances (when the latter is a categorical variable divided into five roughly equal groups).

Note: We may not want to dismiss this finding because of a low percentage of explained variance. If money really matters, you could reallocate $1 billion of the total of $40.5 billion that Texas spends on education (these 2005 expenditure data are not shown here) from those districts in the top 80% of the funding distribution and give it to the poorest fifth. If the relationship we observe here holds, this Robin Hood strategy would raise the poorest districts' tests scores as high as 65.2% passing (in contrast to 57.6%). This represents an increase of 13% ((65.2 − 57.6)/57.6) in the percentage of students from poor districts who would pass the state exam. I'm sure the voters in the top 80% of school districts wouldn't mind spending $1 billion less on their schools.

A Nonparametric Alternative for One-Way ANOVA: The Kruskal-Wallis Test

Let's say that we were disturbed by the unequal variances that we observed in this example and wanted to be especially conservative in our statistical analysis, even if we end up burying the results in a technical appendix because we obtain the same results as when using the parametric tests in the one-way ANOVA above.

Like many nonparametric statistics, the Kruskal-Wallis procedure transforms the data out of our sight by sorting in rank order all the observations. In our case, it ranks districts from the highest to the lowest percentage of students passing the TAKS (Texas Assessment of

(Continued)

(Continued)

Knowledge and Skills) tests. It then calculates the average rank for each of the independent-variable categories (e.g., the five different expenditure groupings in this example). SPSS reports the average rank for each group in the Ranks table below.

Step 1: Click Analyze/Nonparametric Tests/Legacy Dialogs/K Independent Samples.

Step 2: Move the dependent variable ("Grades 3–11 All Tests Taken 2006") into the Test Variable box and the five-category recode of district expenditures into the Grouping Variable box (Expend_Per_Fifths).

Step 3: Select Define Range, and enter "1" into "minimum" and "5" into "maximum" (without the quotes). This is the range of the independent variable. Click Continue.

Step 4: Click Options, and select "Descriptive Statistics." Click Continue. Click OK.

Your results should look something like the following:

Ranks

	Per Pupil Expenditures ...	N	Mean Rank
Grades 3-11 All Tests Taken 2006	Lowest fifth 3364 to 7684	83	190.66
	Second fifth 7585 to 8515	83	202.02
	Middle fifth 8516 to 9459	76	187.44
	Fourth fifth 9460 to 10950	88	196.58
	Highest fift 10951 to 31016	68	224.47
	Total	398	

Test Statistics[a],[b]

	Grades 3-11 All Tests Taken 2006
Chi-square	4.629
df	4
Asymp. Sig.	.328

a. Kruskal Wallis Test

b. Grouping Variable: Per Pupil Expenditures in Fifths

The most important number to look at is the Asymp. Sig., which in this case is .328. Because this value is greater than .05, we cannot conclude that the data are consistent with the argument that district finances significantly affect the proportion of students passing the state's academic tests. It also doesn't tell us where any differences may lie, although the descriptive figures above give us an interesting clue that the poorest districts perform poorly, the richest perform well (no surprise here), but the second poorest districts outperform even the richest (who would have thought so?). Post hoc tests for group differences exist but are beyond the scope of this book. If you are interested in learning more about these tests, consult Field (2005, pp. 550–557).

Graphically, you can get a better sense of where the differences lie by asking for boxplots of test performance within each level of expenditure. This may also help you determine whether any of the descriptive results above might be influenced by outliers within any category of finance.

To request such a set of boxplots, complete the following steps:

Step 1: Click Graphs/Legacy Dialogs/Boxplot. Select sample, Groups of Cases, and Summaries. Click Define.

Step 2: Move the test score variable into the Variable: box. Move the five-category expenditure variable into the Category axis: box. Move the District Number variable into the Label Cases by: box (this last step will help you pinpoint which districts, if any, are identified as outliers). Click OK.

Your output should look something like the following:

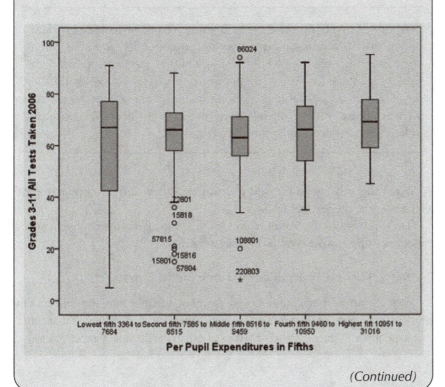

(Continued)

(Continued)

If anything, the mystery of the performance of the second poorest set of districts thickens. A number of outliers in this group of districts are far below the median for such districts. Removing these outliers, if substantively justified, would increase the "average" performance levels of the districts in this expenditure category.

Before moving on to the extension of one-way between-groups ANOVA, it is also possible to conduct one-way repeated-measures ANOVA. The purpose of such a test is much like the between-groups analysis, except that we're measuring a concept repeatedly for the same individuals, say, prior to and after a program intervention. For more information on these procedures, see Pallant (2005, pp. 223–228).

● TWO-WAY BETWEEN-GROUPS ANOVA

Purpose: To test the separate and joint effects of *two* categorical independent variables on one continuous dependent variable. Such a procedure permits us to determine whether the two independent variables interact, that is, an effect of one variable depends on the level of a second variable. Is it the case, for example, that the effects of teacher experience on test performance vary according to how relatively poor or wealthy the districts are?

You will probably be pleased to learn that there are no nonparametric alternatives to the test below.

Let's return to an examination of just those comparisons: teacher experience and district wealth on test performance.

Step 1: Click on Analyze/General Linear Model/Univariate

Step 2: Move your continuous dependent variable into the Dependent variable: box, and move your two categorical variables for teacher experience ("Teachers w 11–20 years of exp in thirds") and district economic (dis)advantage ("Economically disadvantage percent in thirds") into the Fixed Factors: box. (SPSS calls these independent variables "factors" to distinguish these categorical variables from continuous independent variables, which are called "covariates.")

Step 3: Click on the Options button, and select "Descriptive Statistics," "Estimates of Effect Size," "Residual Plot," and "Homogeneity Tests." Click Continue.

Step 4: Click the Post Hoc button. Highlight the two independent variables in the left box, and move them into the right box. Select Bonferroni and Tukey. Click Continue.

Step 5: Click on the Plots button. Move the independent variable with the most categories into the Horizontal box. (Both variables in this example have an equal number of categories, three, so pick one.) Move the other independent variable into the Separate Lines box. Click Add. Click Continue. Click OK.

The Descriptive Statistics table is the same as the one we produced in the Pivot Tables example of Chapter 7.

Levene's test (shown below) tells you that the variances of the errors in predicting your dependent variable from knowledge of your independent variables are not equal across all the categories (groups) of those independent variables. (We will return to the concept of errors or residuals in regression analysis. Don't be bothered if you don't quite understand the first sentence of this paragraph.)

Levene's Test of Equality of Error Variances[a]

Dependent Variable:Grades 3-11 All Tests Taken 2006

F	df1	df2	Sig.
9.559	8	392	.000

Tests the null hypothesis that the error variance of the dependent variable is equal across groups.

a. Design: Intercept +
teach_w_11to20_thirds +
econ_disadvs_thirds +
teach_w_11to20_thirds *
econ_disadvs_thirds

Because the variances are not equal, we should set a more stringent significance level (e.g., .01) for our evaluation of the two-way ANOVA results that follow.

Examine the Tests of Between-Subjects Effects table, which should look something like the following:

Tests of Between-Subjects Effects

Dependent Variable:Grades 3-11 All Tests Taken 2006

Source	Type III Sum of Squares	df	Mean Square	F	Sig.	Partial Eta Squared
Corrected Model	37036.070[a]	8	4629.509	23.236	.000	.322
Intercept	1432883.238	1	1432883.238	7191.719	.000	.948
teach_w_11to20_thirds	11284.234	2	5642.117	28.318	.000	.126
econ_disadvs_thirds	14651.836	2	7325.918	36.769	.000	.158
teach_w_11to20_thirds * econ_disadvs_thirds	779.772	4	194.943	.978	.419	.010
Error	78102.359	392	199.241			
Total	1697774.000	401				
Corrected Total	115138.429	400				

a. R Squared = .322 (Adjusted R Squared = .308)

One way of cutting through these numbers is as follows:

• Look first for the presence of an **interaction effect** (Does the effect of one independent variable depend on the level of the other?). If you find such an effect, your interpretation of main effects becomes a little more complicated.

• To find this effect, look at the line in which the variable names of the two independent variables are joined by an "*" or multiplication symbol. It's the fifth line down on the table. Check the Sig. column. Is it less than .01? No. Move on. If it had been, you would have concluded that an interaction effect exists; that is, the effect of a district's teacher experience varies depending on how relatively poor or wealthy the district is.

• Check out the main effects on the third and fourth lines, and again, read the number in the Sig. column. Both are statistically significant.

• Okay, they're statistically significant, but how large are their effects? According to Cohen (1988), η^2 can be interpreted as follows:

0.01 to 0.05 = *small effect.*

0.06 to 0.13 = *moderate effect.*

0.14 or above = *large effect.*

Our partial eta-square (partial because it takes into account the other independent variable) is large for economic (dis)advantage (0.16) and moderate for teacher experience (0.13).

● But where do the greatest differences between groups occur? Look at the two Multiple Comparisons tables (not shown here), one for teacher experience and the other for students' economic status.

Both Tukey and Bonferroni tell the same story (it's not uncommon for them to agree): Every level of the districts' teacher experience is significantly different from the others and the more this is so, the better for district test performance.

ANALYSIS OF COVARIANCE ●

Purpose: To assess the influence of one or more categorical independent variables on one continuous dependent variable after controlling for the effects of one or more other continuous variables, which are called "covariates." Let us say we want to assess the influence of teacher experience (when districts are divided into three roughly equal sets of groups in this regard) with test scores, after controlling for the percentage of students in districts who are economically disadvantaged, which might be a useful analysis if we don't believe that the state can afford (financially and/or politically) or knows how to increase the economic conditions of its poorest parents and their children. (You should have noticed that this is a variation on the exercise that we've seen in the cross-tabulation, pivot table, and two-way between-groups ANOVA above.)

There is an additional set of assumptions required of ANCOVA, more about which you can learn in Pallant (2005, pp. 263–267). From the analysis not shown here, these variables satisfy several of these additional assumptions, including linearity and homogeneity of regression slopes.

Step 1: Click Analyze/General Linear Model/Univariate.

Step 2: Move the continuous version of the test performance into the Dependent Variables: box.

Move your independent, categorical, grouping variable ("Teachers w 11–20 years of experience in thirds") into the Fixed Factor: box.

Move the percentage of districts' students who are economically (dis)advantaged (i.e., its continuous variant) into the Covariate: box.

Step 3: Click on the Model button, and select Full Factorial in the Specify Model section. Click Continue.

Step 4: Click on the Options button.

Move your independent, categorical variable into the Display Means: box.

Select "Descriptive Statistics," "Estimates of effect size," and "Homogeneity tests." Click Continue and OK.

The main results are displayed in the Test of Between-Subjects Effects, which should look something like the following:

Tests of Between-Subjects Effects

Dependent Variable:Grades 3-11 All Tests Taken 2006

Source	Type III Sum of Squares	df	Mean Square	F	Sig.	Partial Eta Squared
Corrected Model	38157.716[a]	3	12719.239	66.468	.000	.330
Intercept	323301.730	1	323301.730	1689.517	.000	.807
DPETECOP	16835.590	1	16835.590	87.980	.000	.178
teach_w_11to20_thirds	10204.907	2	5102.453	26.665	.000	.116
Error	77499.805	405	191.358			
Total	1737215.000	409				
Corrected Total	115657.521	408				

a. R Squared = .330 (Adjusted R Squared = .325)

Your interest lies in interpreting the fourth row, which (seeing a Sig. of .000) indicates that different levels of teaching experience are significantly related to test scores even after controlling for the proportion of students in districts who are economically (dis)advantaged. According to Cohen's (1988) guidelines, teaching experience is "moderately" related to test performance when controlling for the proportion of students in districts who are economically (dis)advantaged (the partial eta-square suggests that 12% of the variation in district tests scores can be attributed to teachers' experience after controlling for students' economic status in a district).

The estimated marginal means (below) show the mean level of test performance after controlling for percentage of economically (dis)advantaged. The numbers in the mean column can be compared with 53.10, 66.0, and 69.97, respectively, which was the percentage of passing before we controlled for percentage of districts' students who are economically disadvantaged.

Teachers w 11-20 years exp in thirds

Dependent Variable:Grades 3-11 All Tests Taken 2006

Teachers w 11-20 years exp in thirds	Mean	Std. Error	95% Confidence Interval	
			Lower Bound	Upper Bound
Fewest experienced teachers	55.737[a]	1.211	53.357	58.117
2.00	65.618[a]	1.187	63.285	67.952
Most experienced teachers	67.683[a]	1.215	65.294	70.072

a. Covariates appearing in the model are evaluated at the following values: Economically Disadvantaged Studetns, Percent = 54.076.

It is also the case that the covariate (economic [dis]advantage) is significantly related to test scores when holding teaching experience constant (Sig. < .000), and the effect is "strong" ($\eta^2 = 0.18$).

CONCLUSION ●

Your statistical tool box now includes a set of procedures for assessing the differences between or among groups (or variable categories). This chapter includes such procedures, ranging from the simplest comparison of two group means to multiple group means. You also have a tool that controls for the effects of continuously measured independent variables. (There's also a procedure, not discussed here, where these same procedures are applied to multiple dependent variables—MANOVA. For a discussion of this procedure, see Warner, 2008, chap. 17). These procedures report which groups differ from others in terms of statistical significance (p values) and in terms of effect size (η^2). The multiple-independent-variable versions in SPSS automatically check for the presence of interaction effects. That is to say, they judge whether the effects of one independent variable is a function of (or contingent on) the levels of another independent variable. (Although interaction effects can also be examined in **multiple regression (R)**, SPSS does not check for them automatically.)

As with nearly all statistics, these group-difference procedures make certain assumptions about the data. They assume that the dependent variable is continuous and normally distributed, although the latter assumption is important only for small samples with, say, fewer than 50 observations (although there are no hard and fast standards for "small" and "large" samples here). The assumption of linearity, which is so prevalent in the measures of association to which we next turn, is more easily relaxed and detectible through these procedures.

Violations of assumptions about normal distributions, equal variances, and large (enough) samples may be overcome by one of several tactics:

- Transform the variables (e.g., take their log or remove outliers).
- Use nonparametric, and somewhat more statistically conservative, procedures.
- Do all the above, and see how sensitive the final substantive conclusions are to any adjustment, reporting the original data if they are not.
- Ignore the violations (e.g., for nonnormal distributions if sample sizes are greater than 50 and for unequal group variances if the sizes of groups are similar).

Beware, of course, of analysis that ignores assumption violations. It may be trying to hide something or be unaware of the need to attend to these matters.

● NOTE

1. I believe you can lead a happy life without worrying about degrees of freedom, at least as long as you report the number of observations on which any statistic is based. In this example, $n = 1,033$. Degrees of freedom takes into account the fact that, in this case, only $n - 1$ values of our variable are free to vary because the sum of differences between all observations and the mean will equal zero. It's as if we knew eight of the numbers in a row or column of Sudoku. We would then know the ninth number. Only eight numbers in a row or column are free to vary. Once we know eight of them, we have exhausted out degrees of freedom in knowing all the numbers in that row or column. We'll see in regression that degrees of freedom is also affected by the number of independent variables we have in our regression equation, but this hardly matters. Report n and p (as well as other stats) and df.

> To practice and reinforce the lessons of this chapter of the book, turn to Exercise 6 in the *Student Workbook* (available at http://www.sagepub .com/pearsonsp/). You've read Chapter 7 too, right?

CHAPTER 10

STATISTICS AS RELATIONSHIPS

MEASURES OF ASSOCIATION ●

Cross-tabulations, and the percentage differences they display, provide simple, but often effective, ways of communicating differences across groups or categories of nominal or ordinal variables. Their cousin, the pivot table, can display differences in means, medians, or totals from a continuous variable, broken down by the categories of nominal or ordinal independent variable(s). Neither, however, provides summary estimates of the strength of the relationship or tells you whether the results you obtain from a sample allow you to confidently assert that your results characterize the population from which your sample was drawn (i.e., are statistically significant).

Statisticians have worked hard over the past century to provide you with a wide variety of measures of association that do just that. These measures are often used in combination with crosstabs or pivot tables to convey a fuller sense of the size and direction of the relationship than tables or graphs alone can provide.

The challenge for the analyst is to determine which one or more of these measures of association are appropriate in assessing a particular relationship between two or more variables. The selection of the most appropriate of such test(s) depends on a number of characteristics of the variables you are analyzing. These include (roughly in declining order of importance) whether

1. the variables are parametric (i.e., normally distributed, a mean that is a valid measure of central tendency, and equally spaced interval scores);
2. the level of measurement of the variables in the relationship is nominal, ordinal, or continuous;
3. observations are independent (e.g., my selection into the study has nothing to do with your selection into the study) or dependent

(e.g., before and after scores of the same respondents, respondents who are selected to be in a study because they match other respondents in the study on certain characteristics, and ratings of different people by the same evaluators);

4. you assume causation or merely argue that the variables move together without a change in one *causing* a change in another (i.e., Is the relationship "asymmetric"? or "symmetric," to use more technical jargon);

5. relationships are linear or nonlinear;

6. sample size is small (under 50) or not;

7. the contingency table is square or rectangular (i.e., the numbers of rows and columns differ); and

8. you have one or more predictor(s) and/or outcome variable(s).

Moreover, different measures of association look at relationships through different lenses:

1. Some focus on how strong a relationship is and its direction. Many such measures range from −1.0 to +1.0, where these extremes represent a relationship between, say, two variables that are perfectly and precisely aligned with each other. Such variables are said to covary perfectly. Zero means no relationship. Negative numbers mean the relationship is negative (i.e., high numeric values of one variable tend to be paired with low values of the other). Positive numbers signify positive relationships (i.e., high values of one variable tend to be paired with high values of the other).

2. Other measures of association assess how much of the variation of a dependent variable is "explained by" one or more independent variables. Obviously, such a number can range from 0% to 100%.

3. And still others estimate how much better your prediction of one variable is, given knowledge of the level or score of another. Such measures of association are known as **proportional reduction in error (PRE)** measures.

Believe it or not, some stats look at relationships from more than one of these vantage points.

Note: The assignment of a numeric value (i.e., a number) to categories of nominal or ordinal variables is arbitrary. I can code *males* as "1" and *females* as "2" or vice versa. Statistical software programs don't know or care whether the "1" is actually half of "2" or, instead, a numeric placeholder that allows you to analyze males and females (or gender) in your study. Nor do these programs care if you assign "4" to a response of *strongly agree* or to *strongly disagree*. To label any relationship composed of nominal or ordinal variables as negative or positive is okay, but it is entirely a function of to which categories you assign higher or lower numbers. To say, for example, that gender is positively related to an attitude makes sense only if you know how these variables are coded in your data set.

Indeed, I recommend that you discard positive and **negative relationship**-speak from your statistical rhetoric when analyzing nominal and ordinal variables (continuous variables are a different story because their numeric values have real meaning). It is preferable to report something like "Women are more likely than men to oppose capital punishment" than to say "There is a positive relationship between gender and attitudes toward capital punishment," which requires you to know and report how these two variables are coded.

Many of you at this point will feel hopelessly at a loss, and with some reason. If you multiplied the eight conditions above by the three perspectives, you'd find yourself asking whether you have to examine 24 different possibilities before selecting the most appropriate measure of association. Fortunately, SPSS simplifies the selection process for you by grouping different measures of association into sets, depending on the most important characteristics above. It is also the case that many of these statistics, although based on different algorithms or interpretations, tell essentially the same story about the strength, direction, and statistical significance of a relationship. If you are totally confused by the bewildering array of tools from which to choose, you can always try several, then step back and see if they produce similar results. This is what we might call internal convergence. That is to say, the conclusions from a single analysis are not an artifact of the particular statistical tools selected to draw those conclusions.

Let's work through some of these measures by asking SPSS to calculate them.

NONPARAMETRIC MEASURES OF ASSOCIATION ●

By definition, measures of association for nominal and categorical variables are nonparametric. Dichotomous, "dummy" variables that are coded "0" and "1" are not normally distributed, but they come closest to approximating a normal distribution when the two groups have about the same number of cases. (We will return to this special case later).[1] Because the numeric distances between categories of categorical variables are arbitrary (see also Note 1), the mean of such numbers is not a valid measure of the variables' centers. Nor are such variables normally distributed.

This is not at all a problem because of the variety of measures of association that are available for assessing the strength of those relationships that do not assume that the variables are continuous and normally distributed. There are even measures of association that are suitable for mixed combinations of nominal, ordinal, and continuous variables.

Let's return, first, to the Public Perceptions data set to illustrate some of these measures, beginning first with nonparametric measures of association under the condition that the observations are "independent," which is clearly the case with this survey. (Again, note that we are using the term *independent* as it modifies *observations*, which is a tip-off that its meaning is not that of *independent variable*.) Let's focus first on measures of association for nominal variables.

Nominal (and Thus Nonparametric) Variables of Independent Observations

Let's examine the relationships between HELPFUL, FRIENDLY, and WORKS. (Ignore for the moment that these variables are actually "ordinal." We will shortly transform them into nominal variables in this example.)

Step 1: Open the Public Perceptions data set in SPSS.

Step 2: Click Analyze/Descriptive Statistics/Crosstabs.

Step 3: Move HELPFUL into the Row(s): box and FRIENDLY into the Column(s): box. We are not assuming that one of these variables causes the other, so it doesn't matter which is entered as a row variable and which is entered as a column variable.

Step 4: Click Statistics, and select "Chi-square,", "Phi and Cramer's V," "Uncertainty Coefficient," "Lamda." Click Continue.

Step 5: Click Cells, and activate "Expected" and "Observed" in the Counts box and "No adjustments" in the Noninteger Weights box. Select Row%. Click Continue.

Step 6: Click Format, and select "Descending." I like the highest numeric values at the top of the table. Click Continue and OK.

The differences between the observed and expected counts are used to calculate chi-square. Observed counts are the number of cases that fall in each cell of the crosstab. Expected counts indicate the number of observations you would expect to find in a cell *if there was no relationship* between the variables (mathematically, this number is the product of the row and column marginal frequencies for a cell divided by the total number of cases in the entire table, which explains why many of the expected observations have a decimal place).

Chi-square makes very few assumptions. It's kind of like the sledge hammer of statistics. But one of those assumptions is that no cell in the table has an expected value less than 5. You can see from the crosstab generated from the above procedure (a table not displayed here) that there are a number of cells in which this is the case. Indeed, it's important enough that SPSS even tells us in a footnote to the chi-square table (shown below) that we've violated this assumption five times.

Chi-Square Tests

	Value	df	Asymp. Sig. (2-sided)
Pearson Chi-Square	1075.478[a]	9	.000
Likelihood Ratio	599.839	9	.000
Linear-by-Linear Association	407.741	1	.000
N of Valid Cases	845		

a. 5 cells (31.3%) have expected count less than 5. The minimum expected count is .76.

As a possible solution to this violation of one of chi-square's assumptions, let's create new variables of these two that have only two values:

0 = *disagree* and *strongly disagree*.

1 = *agree* and *strongly agree*.

Name these variables HELPFUL2 and FRIENDLY2. This recoding creates two of the infamous "dummy" variables about which you'll read more in the chapter on regression. Among their several interesting properties, the mean of such variables tells you what percentage of your cases are designated as "1" (in this case, *agree* or *strongly agree*). (If you need to refresh your memory for transforming variables via the recode command, return to Chapter 4 or click on Tranform/Recode Into Different Variables and follow your instincts, as well as the logic of SPSS's dialog boxes. You won't break anything. Give it a go.)

After creating these two variables, rerun the steps above. The resulting chi-square table should look something like the following:

Chi-Square Tests

	Value	df	Asymp. Sig. (2-sided)	Exact Sig. (2-sided)	Exact Sig. (1-sided)
Pearson Chi-Square	234.772[a]	1	.000		
Continuity Correction[b]	230.621	1	.000		
Likelihood Ratio	176.213	1	.000		
Fisher's Exact Test				.000	.000
Linear-by-Linear Association	234.494	1	.000		
N of Valid Cases	845				

a. 0 cells (.0%) have expected count less than 5. The minimum expected count is 18.69.

b. Computed only for a 2x2 table

We're good on expected cell frequencies.

The size of chi-square, however, is partly a function of the number of cells and observations (n), so it doesn't have a handy interpretation other than to say whether its Sig. value is statistically significant. In other words, chi-square provides no sense of how large or small the relationship is or its direction (e.g., positive or negative). It only tells you whether the relationship is statistically significant (i.e., What are the probabilities that our results are the "luck of the draw"? Can we be confident in rejecting the null hypothesis of, in this particular instance, no relationship between the two variables in the analysis?).

The *continuity correction* corrects for the fact that chi-squares are a little too generous in their estimates in a 2 × 2 table like the one here. **Fisher's exact test** is typically calculated only on a 2 × 2 table and can be used when you have expected cell frequencies of 5 or fewer observations (which is likely to happen when you have fewer than 50 observations in your study). Fisher's exact test is itself a p value. Values less than .05 can be interpreted as statistically significant, using our conventional **confidence level**. Ignore the other stats in this table. If you're really curious about them, use the Help function in SPSS to tell you more.

We can also ignore, in this example, the table of directional measures because we are making no assumption that one of these variables "causes" the other. We will invoke this assumption below in seeing whether respondents' evaluation of the service results in a more trusting attitude that the county government will do what is right most of the time (TRUST).

Symmetric Measures

		Value	Approx. Sig.
Nominal by Nominal	Phi	.527	.000
	Cramer's V	.527	.000
	Contingency Coefficient	.466	.000
N of Valid Cases		845	

Phi (φ) falls between 0 and 1 only in a 2 × 2 table. Beyond these dimensions, it has no upper bound and, therefore, suffers from the same limitations as chi-square.

The *contingency coefficient* has a PRE interpretation (i.e., a value of .47 indicates that knowledge of one variable reduces error in predicting values of the other variable by 47%). Its algorithm, however, makes it very difficult ever to reach a value of 1.0.

Cramer's V varies between 0 and 1, irrespective of the dimensions of the crosstab (i.e., the number or rows and columns). And it is equivalent, as above, to phi in a 2 × 2 table. It seems to me that Cramer's V trumps these other measures, so let's just request it and chi-square in future analyses of nominal variables. (Include chi-square because of its familiarity and the fact that Cramer's V is derived from it, adjusting for sample size and the number of rows and columns in a table). That simplifies matters, doesn't it? Report chi-square, its degrees of freedom, and the Sig. level, as well as Cramer's V value and Sig.

Is a Cramer's V of .53 small, moderate, or strong, however? Such judgments help in a narrative report of the findings. But they are somewhat arbitrary, and authors will differ somewhat on the ranges they assign to these adjectives. Here's one such designation for values of Cramer's V:

.00 to .20	Weak
.21 to .40	Moderate
.41 to .60	Strong
.61 to 1.00	Very strong

So "Having a friendly encounter with a county employee is strongly related to having a helpful one as well," your memo to the county mayor might read.

Assuming Causation Leads to a Different Choice of Statistics

If we assume that one nominal variable is the outcome of another, we'll select a different set of statistics that are designated as "directional" or "asymmetric."

We can repeat many of the same steps above, except assume that respondents' evaluation of the helpfulness of county employees leads them to be more trusting of the county government to "do what is right most of the time." As a result, we'll also ask for row percentages in Cells. Be sure, as we did in the Crosstab exercise, to place the dependent variable (TRUST) in the Column: box and the independent variable (HELPFUL2) in the Row: box and ask for row percentages, not column percentages.

The chi-square of 40.16 with 1 *df* is statistically significant. So too are some of the directional measures of association, as shown in the table below:

Directional Measures

			Value	Asymp. Std. Error[a]	Approx. T[b]	Approx. Sig.
Nominal by Nominal	Lambda	Symmetric	.024	.030	.770	.441
		Dichot of Helpful Dependent	.000	.000	.[c]	.[c]
		Do you trust Orange County Government to do what is right most of the time? Dependent	.035	.044	.770	.441
	Goodman and Kruskal tau	Dichot of Helpful Dependent	.049	.017		.000[d]
		Do you trust Orange County Government to do what is right most of the time? Dependent	.049	.017		.000[d]
	Uncertainty Coefficient	Symmetric	.045	.015	2.927	.000[e]
		Dichot of Helpful Dependent	.057	.019	2.927	.000[e]
		Do you trust Orange County Government to do what is right most of the time? Dependent	.038	.013	2.927	.000[e]

a. Not assuming the null hypothesis.

b. Using the asymptotic standard error assuming the null hypothesis.

c. Cannot be computed because the asymptotic standard error equals zero.

d. Based on chi-square approximation

e. Likelihood ratio chi-square probability.

SPSS doesn't know which variable your theory or model is assuming to be the independent or dependent variable, so it calculates it both ways for you to choose. Lambda and the uncertainty coefficient also present symmetric versions that don't assume a causal relationship.

Lambda (λ) is a PRE measure and, therefore, ranges between 0 and 1. In this example, a helpful encounter with a county employee improves our prediction of how trusting citizens are of the government by about 4%, although this result may have arisen from chance.

Goodman and Kruskal tau is a variation of lambda. Instead of determining how much better your prediction would be in comparison with the category with the largest number of observations (as lambda does), tau uses the proportion of observations within each category to calculate its improvement in prediction.

The *uncertainty coefficient* (*U*) also has a PRE interpretation (i.e., a value of .04 indicates that knowledge of one's assessment of the helpfulness of an encounter with a county employee reduces error in predicting the value of trust in the county government by 4%). In this particular instance, the relationship is statistically significant, while it is not so in lambda. Don't sweat the small stuff. Lambda is simply calculated in ways that will not detect a relationship in this instance. Your report might read,

> While Goodman and Kruskal's tau and the uncertainty coefficient are statistically significant and lambda is not, the important point to make is that the relationship is negligible. The results are inconsistent with the belief that providing helpful service to citizens will improve the trust they have in the county government to do what is right most of the time.

Measures of Association When the Variables Are Ordinal (and the Observations Are Still Independent and the Variables Are Not Assumed to Be Causally Related)

The tools at our disposal under these circumstances (nonparametric, independent, ordinal, and nondirectional) are

tau-*b*,

tau-*c*, and

gamma (γ).

Let's illustrate the use and interpretation of these statistics by examining the relationship between satisfaction with schools and satisfaction with county taxes and fees (both of these variables are ordered from *Very Satisfied* to *Very Dissatisfied*; I recoded the "Don't know" responses as Missing). Note that a positive relationship between these two attitudes may be caused by order effects or priming in this questionnaire. Insofar as county taxes support schools, saying that I'm satisfied with the county schools may incline me to respond to the very next question in the survey that I'm satisfied with the county taxes.

Step 1: Click Analyze/Descriptive Statistics/Crosstabs.

Step 2: Move one of the variables into the Row(s): box and the other into the Column(s): box. Because we're not arguing that one variable is causing the other, it doesn't matter which is moved to which box.

Step 3: Click Statistics, and select "Tau-b," "Tau-c," and "gamma." (We'll reserve **Somer's *d*** for the next section because it assumes a causal relationship between the two variables.) Click Continue.

Step 4: Click Cells, and activate "Expected" and "Observed" in the Counts box and "No adjustments" in the Noninteger Weights box. Click Continue.

Step 5: Click Format, and select "Descending." Click Continue and OK.

Your measures of association (appropriate if we assume no causal relationship between these variables) are reported below:

Symmetric Measures

		Value	Asymp. Std. Error[a]	Approx. T[b]	Approx. Sig.
Ordinal by Ordinal	Kendall's tau-b	.158	.033	4.681	.000
	Kendall's tau-c	.123	.026	4.681	.000
	Gamma	.265	.054	4.681	.000
N of Valid Cases		781			

a. Not assuming the null hypothesis.

b. Using the asymptotic standard error assuming the null hypothesis.

These three measures of association are based in whole or in part on calculations that contrast the number of observations that are alike (e.g., have a value of "4" on both variables) and unlike (e.g., have a value of "4" on one variable and a value of "1" on the other).[2]

Gamma invariably produces a higher value than either tau-*b* or tau-*c*, as is the case in this example. It is, therefore, sometimes chosen when the investigator wants ever so much to argue that his variables are related to each other. Buyer beware!

Kendall's tau-*b* (τ-*b*), unlike gamma, also takes into account pairs of observations that are "tied."[3] It can achieve the values of −1.0 or +1.0 only when the table on which it is based has the same number of rows and columns (i.e., it's square), and it therefore, has that one small drawback, although it remains a commonly used measure of association.

Kendall's tau-*c* (τ-*c*) is designed to take the number of rows and columns into account, as well as the number of observations. It may be used with square or rectangular tables.

There is one other measure of association that can be used with ordinal variables: **Spearman's rank order correlation (*r*)**. This measure is nonparametric and is used with observations that are independent. It is often employed when your variables have a large number of categories. The question this test answers is whether the rank orders of two variables are related. That is to say, does an observation that ranks highly on one variable also rank highly on another? Spearman's rho, as it is also called, presumes no causal order and can be used when variables are not related in a linear way, as perhaps revealed by a scattergram. Rho may also be your tool of choice when you have two continuous variables that are not normally distributed.

You follow a slightly different procedure to use this tool, which we illustrate in the following example.

Step 1: In the Public Perceptions data set, click Analyze/Correlate/Bivariate.

Step 2: In the Correlation Coefficients box, select Spearman and Kendall's tau-*b* (for comparison). Move EDUC (how much schooling) and INCOME (total annual household income) into the Variables: box. Click OK to produce the following table:

Correlations

			How much formal schooling have you had?	About what is your total annual household income?
Kendall's tau_b	How much formal schooling have you had?	Correlation Coefficient	1.000	.353**
		Sig. (2-tailed)	.	.000
		N	1021	833
	About what is your total annual household income?	Correlation Coefficient	.353**	1.000
		Sig. (2-tailed)	.000	.
		N	833	839
Spearman's rho	How much formal schooling have you had?	Correlation Coefficient	1.000	.420**
		Sig. (2-tailed)	.	.000
		N	1021	833
	About what is your total annual household income?	Correlation Coefficient	.420**	1.000
		Sig. (2-tailed)	.000	.
		N	833	839

**. Correlation is significant at the 0.01 level (2-tailed).

As with a great deal of output from statistical software programs, there's a lot of redundancy in this table. Every number is repeated, and you shouldn't be shocked to find that schooling is perfectly related to itself (as is income). Education and income (at least in Orange County, Florida) are moderately related to one another and statistically significant whether you look at Kendall's or Spearman's statistic.

An Ordinal Measure of Association, Assuming Causation: Somer's *d*

Hopefully, you've got the gist of calling for such measures by now and don't require instructions.

Other Nonparametric Measures of Association

- *Cochran's Q:* For dichotomous dummy variables (coded "0" and "1") (*Note:* It has a chi-square distribution and is sensitive to samples of less than 20.)
- *Friedman test:* Used in a repeated-measures ANOVA design, without the assumption of normal distribution
- *Mantel-Haenszel test:* Used to assess the relationship between two dichotomous variables when controlling for one or more continuous variables (called "layers" by SPSS; the statistic is computed for all layers at the same time, not separately or one at a time)

● PARAMETRIC MEASURES OF ASSOCIATION FOR CONTINUOUS VARIABLES

There are two sets of statistics that can be used when your observations are independent and your variables continuous and normally distributed: (1) Pearson correlation coefficient (and partial and **part correlation** coefficients) and (2) regression. We'll turn to regression in the next chapter.

Both sets of statistics are calculated to determine the strength and direction of linear relations. If two variables are closely related but not in a linear fashion, the statistics generated in correlation and regression will appear as if there is no relationship, when it is more proper to note that the variables are not related *linearly*. (Nonlinear bivariate relationships can sometimes be detected by examining a scatterplot of two such variables.) The Pearson correlation coefficient does not assume a causal relationship, whereas regression analysis does. (Note that the square of r, which is called the coefficient of determination, is interpreted as the proportion of variation in one variable explained by another, but it can be either one or the other.)

One formula for the calculation of Pearson's r is

$$\sum \frac{z_x \times z_y}{n-1}.$$

The zs are the standardized scores we first encountered in Chapter 5. That is to say, the X and Y variables are transformed by subtracting the observations from their means and then dividing by each variable's standard deviation. As noted previously, this transformation (automatically performed by SPSS when you ask for correlations) "standardizes" each variable (X and Y) to have a mean of 0 and a standard deviation of 1. As a consequence, the value of *r* (which can theoretically range from −1.0 to + 1.0) is not affected by the units in which the variables were originally collected. In other words, whether you express height in inches or centimeters and weight in pounds or kilograms will not influence the calculation or interpretation of the correlation between height and weight. (This is not the case for regression coefficients, for which the unit of measurement is important in both its calculation and its interpretation, a point to which we will return in the next chapter.)

Returning to the equation above, you can see that a high positive value for *r* will arise when highly positive scores on *Y* are paired with highly positive scores on *X* and when highly negative scores (remember that standardized scores have a mean of 0, and some cases will therefore have negative values) on each are paired with each other (insofar as the product of two negative numbers is positive). Such observations are called concordant. But this label means less than the influence of such pairs on the size of the correlation.

It is also important to note that the size of *r* is influenced by several other characteristics: outliers, restricted ranges, nonnormal distributions, and low measurement reliability. A more subtle influence arises from a shotgun approach to the selection of variables to calculate correlations between. Some of these characteristics are subject to manipulation by the analyst and, therefore, can be used (un)wittingly to bolster or reduce the size of the coefficients in order to conform better to a fabricated (and false) story about the population from which the sample is drawn. Let's examine several of these possibilities (see Warner, 2008, pp. 277–292, for a more detailed exposition).

Outliers and the "Kitchen Sink" Approach to the Selection of Variables

Step 1: Open the Texas education data set. Let's be a little statistically mischievous and request a Pearson correlation matrix of a half-dozen or so variables. Click on Analyze/Correlate/Bivariate.

Step 2: Select Pearson in the Correlation Coefficient box, and move the following variables into the Variable box, then click OK.

- Total enrollment count
- Economically disadvantaged students, percent
- Students in gifted programs, percent
- Hispanic students, percent
- District 2005 instructional expenditures per pupil
- Average years of teachers' experience
- Teacher turnover rate
- Test scores for Grades 3 to 11

		Total Enrollment Count	Economically Disadvantaged Studetns, Percent	Students in Gifted Programs, Percent	Hispanic Students, Percent
Total Enrollment Count	Pearson Correlation	1	.077	.171**	.157**
	Sig. (2-tailed)		.118	.001	.001
	N	411	411	411	411
Economically Disadvantaged Studetns, Percent	Pearson Correlation	.077	1	-.222**	.589**
	Sig. (2-tailed)	.118		.000	.000
	N	411	411	411	411
Students in Gifted Programs, Percent	Pearson Correlation	.171**	-.222**	1	-.067
	Sig. (2-tailed)	.001	.000		.174
	N	411	411	411	411
Hispanic Students, Percent	Pearson Correlation	.157**	.589**	-.067	1
	Sig. (2-tailed)	.001	.000	.174	
	N	411	411	411	411
District 2005 Expend on Instruction Per Pupil	Pearson Correlation	-.071	.106*	.149**	.047
	Sig. (2-tailed)	.152	.033	.002	.339
	N	408	408	408	408
Aver Yrs Experience of Teachers	Pearson Correlation	.017	-.255**	.432**	-.193**
	Sig. (2-tailed)	.737	.000	.000	.000
	N	411	411	411	411
Teacher Turnover Rate	Pearson Correlation	-.120*	.308**	-.456**	.221**
	Sig. (2-tailed)	.016	.000	.000	.000
	N	408	408	408	408
Grades 3-11 All Tests Taken 2006	Pearson Correlation	.009	-.492**	.384**	-.334**
	Sig. (2-tailed)	.856	.000	.000	.000
	N	410	410	410	410

**. Correlation is significant at the 0.01 level (2-tailed).

Reading the last column of this correlation matrix (only half of which is shown above), we can see that higher district test performance appears to be related to the proportion of districts' students who are (in descending size of coefficient)

- taught by a low percentage of new teachers (turnover),
- less economically disadvantaged (the negative sign means that the more poor kids in a district, the lower the percentage of students passing the state's standardized tests),
- taught by experienced teachers,
- enrolled in gifted programs,
- not Hispanic, and
- taught in districts with higher per pupil expenditures (although this last statistically significant variable is only weakly associated with test scores).

The size of the school district is not related to test performance (or to anything else in a substantial way).

Why is what I did possibly mischievous (and perhaps even wrong)?

1. Even a set of random numbers will generate some statistically significant relationships, so recklessly aiming your statistical shotgun is likely to hit something, no matter how inaccurate your aim. One way to ask for multiple comparisons of this kind is to apply the **Bonferroni correction**. This correction is achieved by dividing your previously accepted level for p values (e.g., .05) by the number of independent variables. We have eight in this example, so we would accept a relationship as being statistically significant, using the very conservative Bonferroni correction, if the p values were less than or equal to .007 (.05/7). But

this is overkill. I didn't randomly select the variables in this matrix. I had some reason to suspect that they were related. Although I have no hard evidence, I suspect that investigators do this type of analysis all the time and don't fess up or call for help from Bonferroni.

2. I may have been wrong in applying this tool because I didn't inspect each of these variables' distributions to assess whether they were normally distributed. If they were not, I could have called for help from Spearman's rho or transformed the variables by, say, taking their log, square root, or square and then checking whether these transformed variables were normally distributed. These variables may have been more strongly related in a nonlinear fashion, which Pearson's r would not have detected but which an examination of a scatterplot may have.

Correlations of the kind displayed above can also be displayed graphically. This is a good idea, if for no other reason than to determine (via eyeballing the graph) whether the relationship is linear.

Step 1: Click Graphs/Legacy Dialog/Scatter/Dot.

Step 2: Select Simple Scatter, and click on Define.

Step 3: Move the test score variable into the *Y*-axis box and the per pupil instructional expenditure into the *X*-axis box, and click OK.

Your unedited scatterplot should look something like the following:

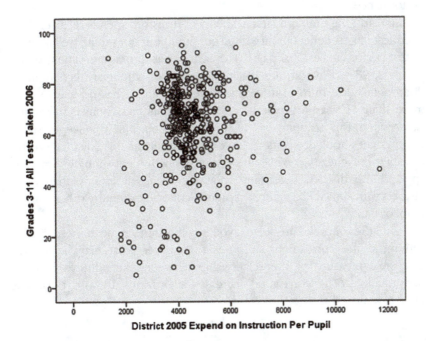

Step 4: Request a Pearson correlation coefficient by clicking on Analyze/Correlate/Linear, and move the same two variables above into the variables box. The r for the graph above is .16 ($p = .002$, $n = 407$).

The scatterplot, however, reveals things that the correlation statistics alone disguise. One school district spends about $12,000 per pupil on instruction but doesn't appear to be getting the same bang for the buck that other districts do. It may well be that this district has a high percentage of children with special (and relatively costly) needs that are related to lower academic performance on standardized tests. An analyst would want to identify which districts these are and seek explanations for this apparent anomaly. (We will see how to do this later through the Case Summaries procedure in SPSS.)

The district with the highest per pupil expenditure is Boys Ranch Independent School District in Oldham County, Texas. It has a total enrollment of 340 students, 77% of whom are economically disadvantaged, 14% are Hispanic, and 9% are black. Eight percent of their teachers are new. Little seems out of the ordinary at first blush except that class size is about 5.5 students per teacher, which is far lower than the mean for all school districts. This latter statistic may be an indication that the students have special needs that are related to lower performance on standardized tests. If true, you would be substantively justified in removing such an outlier from the file and recalculating the relationship between expenditures and performance.

Similarly, the Children First Academy of Houston[4] spends relatively little to educate its students (about $1,400 per pupil) but does quite well in terms of test performance (90% pass). This school has a total enrollment of 434 students, 97% of whom are black and 100% of whom are economically disadvantaged. A third of its teachers are new, and it has no teacher with more than 11 years of experience in any of its classrooms. An average classroom in this Academy has 24 students per teacher. The skeptic sitting on my right shoulder wants to look more closely at this "district" for the possibility of cheating, while the optimist on my left shoulder wants to applaud the district, determine what it's doing differently than other districts with similar characteristics, and encourage or require other districts to follow suit.

Until these puzzles are solved, you might want to remove these districts and rerun the correlations in order to uncover what may be a more defensible measure of the relationship between expenditures and test performance. (The correlation increases slightly to .19 with these two outliers removed.)

Restricted Ranges and Extreme Values

The range of scores on your *X* and *Y* variables can also influence the size of the sample correlation. Ideally, you want a random sample that includes observations that represent the full range, variance, and distribution values in the population. You do not, for example, want to estimate the correlation between GPA (grade point average) and SAT (Scholastic Aptitude Test) scores on the basis of a sample of honors students. The distribution or range of both GPA and SAT scores will be restricted to the upper ends of these distributions, and the resulting correlation will be suppressed as a consequence.

Consider, for example, the consequences of examining the correlation between violent crime and unemployment rates in just those cities in the top quartile of each of these variables (i.e., 9.5% or above unemployment rate and 1,174 or more violent crimes per 100,000 residents). Figure 10.1 displays the scattergram. The top quartile of these cities are identified in the box.

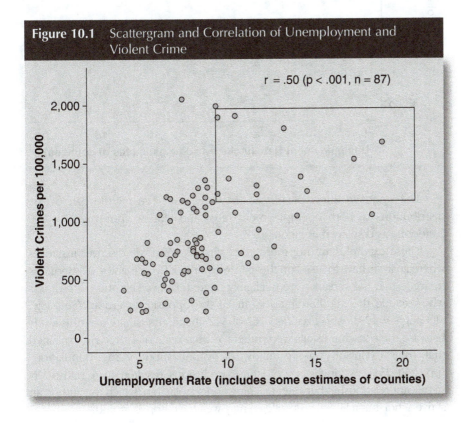

Figure 10.1 Scattergram and Correlation of Unemployment and Violent Crime

You can see in Figure 10.2 that the graph includes just those extreme cases in the top quartile of each variable's distribution. The **Pearson r** changes from .50 for the full range of values on both variables to .03 when examining just the top quartile on both variables.

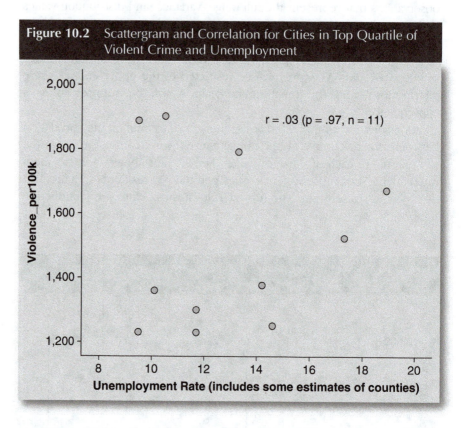

Figure 10.2 Scattergram and Correlation for Cities in Top Quartile of Violent Crime and Unemployment

The opposite effect occurs when we remove the middle half of the distributions of both unemployment rates and violent crime per 100,000 residents, as displayed in Figure 10.3.

These examples are not mere idle "what ifs." You will discover instances where analysts have focused on the extreme parts of two variables' distributions to argue that the variables are negligibly related. Conversely, there are others who exclude the middle ranges to make the opposite assertion. (See, e.g., McCaughey, 1993, who excluded 167 of 512 liberal arts faculty from his study because their teaching skills were rated "3" on a scale of 1 to 5. He explained that their exclusion was to "allow dichotomization of the population" [pp. 250–251]. Wittingly or not, these exclusions resulted in a statistically significant relationship between teaching and scholarship, which the author, an active scholar at a liberal arts college, may well have hoped to find.)

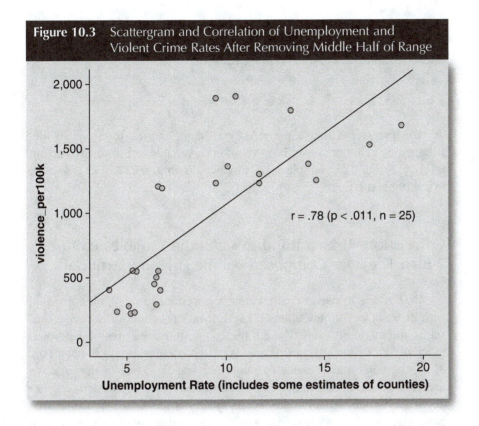

Figure 10.3 Scattergram and Correlation of Unemployment and Violent Crime Rates After Removing Middle Half of Range

The point here is to be wary of any conclusions about a population that exclude a substantial part of the sample used to estimate the relationships. Such exclusions, either purposeful or accidental, will likely either exaggerate or attenuate the estimate of the correlation. Insofar as such exclusions are readily available to any analyst through the data selection functions of statistical software, beware of any such selections made prior to calculating an estimate such as Pearson r (and the regression analyses we will turn to in the next three chapters).

Unreliable Measures Reduce Correlations Too

Variables with low test-retest reliabilities will result in estimates of sample correlations that are less than their real correlation in the population from which they are drawn. (Given the poor or unknown reliabilities of many measures in policy analysis, it may not come as a surprise to find few large correlations in the analysis of survey-based data.) Indeed, the observed correlation between X and Y in a sample is equal to the "true" correlation in the population (ρ, or rho) times the square root of the two variables' test-retest reliabilities, as in the following equation:

$$r_{XY} = \rho_{YY} \overline{)r_{XY} \times r_{YY}}.$$

You may recall that a preferred coefficient for test-retest reliabilities (Chapter 3) is .80 or above. But even if both variables are measured at this level of reliability, our sample correlation would only be 80% of its true value in the population.

Correlations Between Indexes and the Variables From Which They Are Composed Will Be High but Artificial

Do not be surprised to read that people's education is highly correlated with their socioeconomic status (SES). Education (along with occupational status and income) is one of the three component measures of the typical index of SES. Insofar as any variable is perfectly correlated with itself (i.e., +1.0), the correlation between an index or scale and one of the variables used to create the scale will be high but artificially so. Don't work up a lather about such coefficients but suspect as much if you find a high correlation between a poorly described scale and a measure that might be a part of that scale.

The Partial Correlation Coefficient

We may want to examine the degree to which two variables are linearly related to each other while controlling for one or more other variables. We do so by requesting **partial correlation** coefficients.

There is a bit of statistical nomenclature associated with partial correlations. A correlation is said to be a *zero-order correlation* if it controls for no other (zero) variables. Such a relationship is denoted by r_{y1} if it is the bivariate correlation between Y and X_1, for example.

A *first-order partial correlation* is the relationship between two variables when controlling for a third. The designation of $r_{y1.2}$ signifies a first-order correlation between Y and X_1 when controlling for X_2.

A *second-order partial correlation* is the relationship between two variables when controlling for two others. The symbol $r_{y1.23}$, for example, is the second-order partial correlation between Y and X_1 when controlling for X_2 and X_3. And so on.

You can examine the influence of a third categorical variable on the relationship between two other continuous variables by running the correlation for each category of the control variable by asking for the bivariate correlations after telling SPSS to split the file into each categorical part (using the Data/Split File command). You could also calculate the partial r between X_1 and Y when controlling for X_2 by hand if you know r_{Y1}, r_{Y2}, and r_{12}. (This might be useful if you only have available to you a correlation matrix from a published journal article.) The formula (which will not be on the test) for this partial correlation is

$$r_{Y1.2} \frac{r_{1Y} - (r_{12} \times r_{2Y})}{\sqrt{1 - r_{12}^2}\ \sqrt{1 - r_{2Y}^2}}.$$

But the easiest way, of course, is to ask SPSS to perform the calculations for us.

Let us say we want to examine the partial relationship between the proportion of a school district's students who are Hispanic and test performance when controlling for the extent to which the district is economically disadvantaged in the Texas education file.

Click on Analyze/Correlate/Partial, move the variables into the Variables: and Controlling for: boxes as shown below, and click OK.

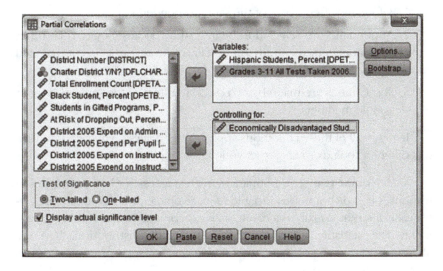

The output would look something like the following:

Correlations

Control Variables			Hispanic Students, Percent	Grades 3-11 All Tests Taken 2006
Economically Disadvantaged Studetns, Percent	Hispanic Students, Percent	Correlation	1.000	-.062
		Significance (2-tailed)	.	.210
		df	0	407
	Grades 3-11 All Tests Taken 2006	Correlation	-.062	1.000
		Significance (2-tailed)	.210	.
		df	407	0

Recall that the zero-order correlation between the proportion of district students who are Hispanic and test scores in the previous correlation matrix was $-.33$ ($p < .001$, $n = 410$). In other words, about 9% of the variation in test scores across sample districts is "explained" by the proportion of students in a school district who are Hispanic. This correlation, however, declines to $-.06$ when controlling for the economic resources of the district students and their parents. We can no longer be confident that this relationship is not zero (i.e., it is no longer statistically significant). It is clearly negligible when controlling for economic (dis)advantages.

Measures of Association for Dependent Samples or Dependent Observations

As we have noted before, there are three conditions under which the observations in a data set are said to be dependent:

1. Before and after scores of the same respondents

2. Respondents are selected to be in a study because they match other respondents in the study on certain characteristics (i.e., a matched comparison study)

3. Observations are made by two or more raters of the same objects or sample members

If any or all of these conditions apply in your analysis, you've got to turn to a different toolbox to construct your story.

● **McNemar test:** This nonparametric test assesses whether changes in responses to a dichotomous variable (e.g., favorable or unfavorable) are statistically different, usually as a result of an experimental intervention or treatment. The statistic is based on the chi-square distribution. Use the McNemar-Bowker test of symmetry for changes in responses measured with more than two categories.

- *Cohen's kappa (κ):* This measure assesses the level of agreement between two raters of the same objects. A value of 1 indicates perfect agreement. A value of 0 indicates that agreement is not better than chance. Kappa is available for tables in which both raters use the same category values (i.e., 1, 2, or 3) to rate objects.

CONCLUSION ●

A large variety of measures of association assess the strength, direction, and statistical significance of relationships between two or more variables. These measures may or may not be used in conjunction with contingency tables to summarize these aspects of the relationship among variables. Their choice depends on many conditions, ranging from the presumption of causal influence to whether the variables are parametric, which itself is an often loosely defined set of conditions in which variables are normally distributed and continuous and the variances of group scores are relatively equal. The analyst faces several choices when faced with departures from these conditions: (a) use nonparametric statistics (some of which convert the observations to ranks), (b) transform variables to come more closely in conformance with assumptions, or (c) ignore the departures because the results of both parametric and nonparametric statistics often tell the same story.

Many measures of association focus on the strength (often from −1.0 to +1.0) and direction (negative or positive) of relationships, while others may be used to characterize the proportion of variation in a dependent variable that can be "explained" by one or more independent variables. Measures of association can assess the strength of a relationship when "controlling for" or "holding constant" the influence of other variables. These relationships can indicate whether the data are consistent with a model or theory of the pattern of relationships among a set of variables or can be used to isolate the unique influence of one or more variables on an outcome.

Unlike the group-difference statistics we saw in the previous chapter, the measures of association we considered in this chapter do not as easily detect nonlinear relationships (without the aid of graphical procedures such as scattergrams), nor do their multivariate versions check automatically for interaction effects, although they can detect these with a little more work on your part.

Beware that the size of the coefficients that are calculated by these procedures can be influenced by a number of factors beyond the true size of the effect or relationship in the population from which your sample is drawn. Examining nonlinear relationships will be poorly served by these measures of association.

Basing a correlation on restricted ranges of the distribution of the variables will likely suppress the size of these effects. Conversely, removing the great unwashed middle parts of the distributions of variables will likely cause the relationship to be exaggerated. Low test-retest reliabilities will suppress effect sizes, and part-whole correlations—correlations between an index or scale and one of its components parts—will be artificially high.

To help select the most appropriate measure of association, given the diverse conditions that apply to these measures, you may want to consult Appendix B.

● NOTES

1. As we saw in the data transformation chapter, categorical variables can be transformed in ways that make them behave as if they are parametric. This is the idea behind log-linear models that transform categorical variables into logarithms and analyze them using the parametric statistical procedure of regression, to which we'll turn in a subsequent chapter. Log-linear analysis, however, is beyond the scope of this book. For more information about this technique, see Field (2005, pp. 695–718).

2. The more formal designation of these conditions is "concordant" and "discordant."

3. "Tied pairs" are the same as concordant pairs—that is, observations that have the same values on both variables.

4. Anomalies in data sets are commonplace and require careful attention on the part of the analyst. Here's an example of a fairly striking anomaly in this file. While the file is ostensibly about public school districts in Texas, charter schools are treated as if they are districts, instead of a single school within a district. About 16% of all "districts" in this file are single charter schools. An analyst may be well served in analyzing these districts separately. They can be identified through the variable DFLCHART.

> To practice and reinforce the lessons of this chapter of the book, turn to Exercise 7 in the *Student Workbook* (available at http://www.sagepub.com/pearsonsp/).

CHAPTER 11

REGRESSION ANALYSIS

Regression is an elegant statistical tool. It explores the relationship between one or more independent or predictor variables and a continuous dependent or outcome variable. (We will consider the case of a dichotomous dependent variable when we turn to **logistic regression** at the conclusion of this chapter.) Regression analysis is widely used and analytically powerful but—like sophisticated audio equipment—is a more complicated statistical tool than some others. It has many features and quite a few diagnostic gauges that you should become familiar with to make sure you're not violating any speed limits.

Among the three major classes of statistics, regression falls into the "statistics-as-relationship" genre. Its strength lies in part in its ability to provide estimates of relationships or effects between two variables when "controlling for" or "holding constant" the effects of other variables on that relationship. For example, do we still find the empirical relationship between teachers' experience and students' test scores in school districts when holding constant the proportion of district students who are poor or Hispanic?

Regression can also be used to estimate the simultaneous effects of a number of independent variables on a dependent variable. You may call the theorized set of relationships among independent and dependent variables a *model*, a concept to which we will return in Chapter 12. Regression analysis, in this regard, can tell you the extent to which public expenditures on schools, turnover rates among teachers, and the level of new teachers' salaries each vary with the proportion of students in districts who pass state-mandated tests, controlling for their shared effects on test scores.

Regression can also estimate the relative impact of different conditions on an outcome. For example, is teacher experience more important in predicting test performance than the socioeconomic status of a district's students and their parents?

Regression analysis can be used to identify particular units, cases, or respondents that perform exceptionally well or poorly, relative to what one would have predicted if the model were an accurate reflection of these relationships in the population from which they were sampled. For example, regression can identify which school districts in poor areas with inexperienced teachers score higher than would be expected on test scores, given these two characteristics.

Finally, regression analysis can be used as a forecasting or prediction tool and as a means for evaluating the short- and long-term effects of programs, topics to which we will turn in Chapter 13.

Regression's analytic capabilities come at a price, however. Regression—like many of the measures of association we examined in the previous chapter—rests on a number of assumptions or conditions that the analyst and the consumer of such analysis need to examine—for example, conditions such as linearity, normal distributions, and similar variances on the dependent variable throughout the full range of values on the independent variable(s). It requires corrective steps in response to violations of some of these assumptions (we'll turn in the next chapter to diagnostic tools and correction procedures). And its veracity depends in part on whether the results come from multiple analyses that converge on the same substantive conclusions, although this holds true of all analyses on which important decisions are to be made.

> The word *assumption* here can be a little misleading. A regression analysis won't choke, break down, or blow up if your data violate one of these assumptions. Regression assumes, for example, that the relationships you're estimating are linear. If not, the regression results are likely to indicate that there is no relationship between, say, an independent and a dependent variation when there is. It's simply not linear.

Regression comes in two varieties. The first, *simple regression*, is a tool for assessing the linear relationship between two continuous variables (leaving aside, again, dichotomous dummy variables). In other words, simple regression is a tool used to assess the strength, direction, and statistical significance of a bivariate relationship when both variables are continuous and one is assumed to cause the other. In this regard, it is very much a friend of the Pearson correlation coefficient (r). Indeed, correlation coefficients are among the ingredients used to calculate the regression coefficient in one set of equations (along with the standard deviations of both variables). The interpretation of the regression coefficient (*b*), however, differs from that of the correlation coefficient. The correlation coefficient assumes no causal direction and is a measure of the extent to which observations can be defined by a straight line. A regression coefficient tells you how many units of a dependent variable increase or decrease with a unit increase or decrease in an independent variable. The latter, therefore, is sensitive to the units by which the variables are measured, whereas the correlation coefficient is not.

There is a subtle epistemological trap that is easy to fall into here. It is easy to be persuaded that your regression analysis proves (or disproves) the causal relationships that you posit. Instead, the results tell you the magnitude and significance of the relationships if your model happens to be right about the causal mechanisms that you stipulate when identifying variables as independent or dependent. Your results may be "consistent with" your model or theory, but they don't prove or confirm your theory. It's best to write about your results in this way.

You may find some solace in the statistician George Box's counsel: "All models are wrong, but some are more useful than others" (Julien & Hanley, 2008, p. 112).

The second variety of this technique is multiple regression, which gets its name from assessing the relationship between two or more independent variables on an outcome, all the variables being measured at a continuous or dummy dichotomous level of measurement.

SIMPLE REGRESSION ●

You may recall from your high school algebra class a formula that defines the position and slope of a line:

$$Y = a + bX,$$

where Y is a measure on the vertical axis, X are those values found on the horizontal axis, a is the point at which the line intercepts or crosses the Y-axis, and b is the slope of the line (i.e., for every unit increase in X, the number of units of Y increases). Such a formula creates the following graph:

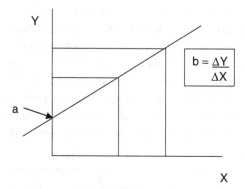

Regression analysis is the kissing cousin of this algebraic expression because it uses observed values of some *Y* (e.g., respondents' annual income) and some (or many) *X*(s) (e.g., years of schooling) to calculate *a* and *b*. Because the relationship between income and education is unlikely to perfectly define a line, regression equations add another term (*e*) to represent how our real observations depart from that perfect linear fit. (Statisticians chose the term *error* [yet another type] to designate these departures.) Our regression equation can, therefore, be written as

$$Y = a + bX + e.$$

Graphing a regression equation might look something like the following, where each of the small circles represents the values of, say, a city's crime rate (*Y*) and unemployment rate (*X*), as we first saw in the form of a scattergram in Chapter 6.

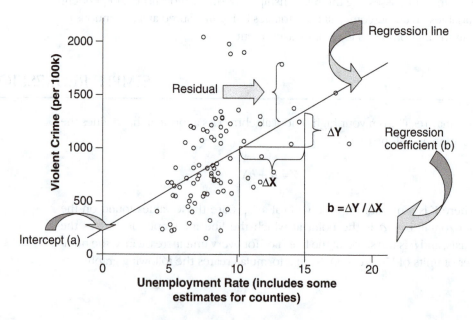

We see in this particular example that there's a positive linear relationship between violent crime and unemployment among major U.S. cities. The regression line is calculated by SPSS in this illustration so as to minimize— brace yourself—the squared differences between the line and each circle (as measured on the Y-axis). This type of regression has the unsurprising name of "least squares regression."

> Squaring a number is used frequently in statistics because this operation has the useful property of eliminating negative values and avoiding the use of absolute values. We'll later see the term *sum of squares,* which is an essential component of the equations on which are based many of the statistics we'll see in regression analysis.

The graph above identifies the following:

- **Intercept** *(a)*, the value of Y when X is 0
- *Regression line*, the line that minimizes the sum of squared differences between itself and the actual observations
- Residual, the difference between the predicted value of Y for each value of X
- *Regression coefficient (b)*, which is the expected unit change (Δ) in Y for each unit change (Δ) in X

Running a regression of the dependent variable, violent crime, *on* (this preposition is part of statistics speak) the independent variable, unemployment rates, produces the following regression equation:

$$\hat{Y} = 235 + 75X.$$
$$(P < .001)$$

$\hat{Y}$ (or Y-hat) is the predicted value of violent crimes. The intercept does not always make sense and often is not reported in an analysis. Its value of 235 here is the number of violent crimes per 100,000 residents that you would predict in a city with a zero unemployment rate. You'll never see a zero unemployment rate, thus the reason for moving right along.

The regression coefficient *(b)* tells us that an increase of 1% in unemployment (the "unit" of our independent variable) is empirically associated with an increase of 75 violent crimes per 100,000 residents (the "units" of our dependent variable). The number within the parentheses below the regression coefficient can be the standard error of the coefficient, a *t* value, or the p value. I prefer the p value (which is reported here). Reporting standard errors and t values requires the reader to turn to an appendix of critical values in order to translate these numbers into a p value, so make it easy on the reader by taking that extra step for her. (Although we will return to matters of presentation in Chapter 14, report a p value that SPSS reports as a Sig. of .000 as <.001. It's not likely to be exactly 0, as .000 implies.)

Let's flesh out a more thorough simple regression analysis of our sample of public school districts in Texas. Let's start by examining the relationship between two variables, the percentage of a school district's students who passed the Texas Academic Knowledge and Skills (TAKS) test, our dependent variable Y ("Grades 3–11 All Tests Taken"), and total instructional expenditures per pupil, our independent variable X ("District 2005 Expend on Instruction Per Pupil"). Those who advocate greater per pupil expenditures for students living in poorer districts typically believe that there is a strong relationship between the amount of money spent on educating students and their academic achievement. It's obviously not quite so simple and direct. Let's see what the nature of this relationship is in Texas, using SPSS.

(By the way, you should always start with descriptive summaries of all the variables you will use in a regression analysis to make sure that they behave properly—i.e., no unreasonable outliers, no marked departures from normal distributions if the sample has fewer than 50 cases, etc. We'll pass those steps here.)

Step 1: From the menu at the top of your SPSS data file (I'll start with the Variable View), click Analyze/Regression/Linear, as in the following screen:

Step 2: Populate the resulting boxes as follows:

- Move "Grades 3–11 All Tests Taken 2006" into the Dependent box.
- Move "District 2005 Expenditures on Instruction Per Pupil" into the Independent box. (Beware, there are a number of different expenditure variables in this file.)
- Make sure that Enter is showing in the Method box. This provides you a standard regression equation in which all independent variables are entered at the same time.
- Click on the Statistics button.
  - o Check the boxes marked "Estimates," "Confidence Intervals," "Model fit," and "Descriptives." We will discuss these in the context of the results of this example when we examine the output of our analysis below.
  - o Click Continue.
- Click Options, and check "Exclude cases pairwise." Click Continue.
- Click OK for some of the following results.

Correlations

		Grades 3-11 All Tests Taken 2006	District 2005 Expend on Instruction Per Pupil
Pearson Correlation	Grades 3-11 All Tests Taken 2006	1.000	.155
	District 2005 Expend on Instruction Per Pupil	.155	1.000
Sig. (1-tailed)	Grades 3-11 All Tests Taken 2006	.	.001
	District 2005 Expend on Instruction Per Pupil	.001	.
N	Grades 3-11 All Tests Taken 2006	410	407
	District 2005 Expend on Instruction Per Pupil	407	408

Well, life doesn't always generate the expected results. Per pupil expenditures on instruction in school districts appear to have only a small linear relationship with test performance among Texas public school districts. The Pearson correlation coefficient is an anemic .16. This measure of association, as you may recall from Chapter 10, is intended for use when the variables are continuous and normally distributed and the relationship is assumed to be linear. The coefficient varies between −1.0 and +1.0, where 0 signifies no relationship.

We can also see that a *p* value (Sig.) of .001 falls below our standard threshold of .05. Formally speaking, we would expect to find a correlation of .16 in our sample by chance if the true relationship between revenue and test scores was 0 in about 1 in 1,000 samples of equal size and design. The effect is "statistically significant" but substantively small.

Remember the analysis of variance (ANOVA) of a similar set of comparisons in the percentage of students passing tests in districts that had been sorted into five different categories of instructional expenditures? That analysis showed that the lowest spending fifth of all school districts had meaningfully lower performance outcomes. This is another way of saying that the relationship between instructional expenditures and test performance may be nonlinear. Nonlinear relationships cannot be detected in the regression statistics that we've examined above.

Having found a small relationship, much of the remaining statistical output from our request will tell the same story, but let's walk through these tables for practice. We'll return to some more meaningful results shortly.

Descriptive Statistics

	Mean	Std. Deviation	N
Grades 3-11 All Tests Taken 2006	62.95	16.818	410
District 2005 Expend on Instruction Per Pupil	4518.83	1194.619	408

A smart analyst would have begun by looking at the simple descriptive statistics for these two variables. There's often a story to be found there. The descriptive statistics generated within regression are not as detailed as those you would find by requesting them via Analyze/Descriptive Statistics/Frequencies. We can, nonetheless, deduce from the numbers above that between 47% and 79% ((63% ± .96) × 16.81) of the students pass this particular skills test in about two thirds of all school districts in Texas. (Recall that about two thirds of all observations of a normally distributed variable can be found within about ±1 standard deviation of the mean of the distribution.) Similarly, about two thirds of our sample of Texas school districts had per pupil total instructional expenditures between $3,371 and $5,665. (These are rough approximations because the distributions of these variables are not perfectly normal.)

Model Summary

Model	R	R Square	Adjusted R Square	Std. Error of the Estimate
1	.155[a]	.024	.022	16.835

a. Predictors: (Constant), District 2005 Expend on Instruction Per Pupil

We see from the Model Summary the Pearson correlation coefficient again (.16) and its square, which is interpreted as the percentage of variation in our dependent variable that is explained by our independent variable.

Coefficients[a]

Model		Unstandardized Coefficients		Standardized Coefficients	t	Sig.	95.0% Confidence Interval for B	
		B	Std. Error	Beta			Lower Bound	Upper Bound
1	(Constant)	53.079	3.230		16.434	.000	46.730	59.429
	District 2005 Expend on Instruction Per Pupil	.002	.001	.155	3.162	.002	.001	.004

a. Dependent Variable: Grades 3-11 All Tests Taken 2006

The Coefficients table above provides statistics to express the relationship as the following regression equation:

$$\hat{Y} = 53 + .002X.$$
$$(P < .001)$$

Does this look odd to you? We've got a statistically significant linear relationship between expenditures and performance ($p < .001$), but the size of the regression coefficient is tiny (.002). How can this be?

This is not a case of a large sample causing a very small coefficient to be statistically significant, as many of you might think. The conundrum here is explained by the scale in which the independent variable is being measured: per pupil expenditures in dollars. Think about what that ".002" means. It means that for every additional dollar per pupil spent on instruction (yes, only one measly dollar), you can expect an increase of 0.002 percentage point of students passing TAKS in a district. No one expects one buck per pupil to make much of a difference in test scores. This is a case where knowing how the dependent and independent variables are being measured is critical. It is also a case where knowing the range of the variables is important for interpreting the results. It also reinforces the point that regression coefficients such as *b* are sensitive to the units in which the variables are measured.

It may be reasonable from a policy perspective to ask what difference in test scores we would predict if we spent as much on the schools at the point that demarks the bottom third of our expenditure distribution (the 33rd percentile) as we do on those districts at about the 66th percentile. As we saw above, this average difference is roughly between $3,000 and $6,000.

Given the regression equation above, we would conclude that test scores in districts around the 33rd percentile in instructional expenditures would increase by 0.6 percentage point if $3,000 more per pupil were spent on instruction. These modest results suggest that we need to look elsewhere for policy levers to improve performance (assuming, of course, that improving standardized performance is our goal).

Let's jump ship here and backtrack, to mix two metaphors. Again, a picture might be as valuable, if not more so, as these numbers. Let's ask for a scatterplot of per pupil instructional expenditures and test scores. Remember that regression (like the means on which its calculations are based) is sensitive to extreme values and to the nature of the relationship. Strong relationships that happen to be nonlinear will show up as small or negligible relationships in the statistics we've generated above. Maybe one or the other of these conditions (outliers and nonlinear relationships) is leading us to the conclusion of no relationship.

You may recall that to generate a scatterplot of these two variables in SPSS, you would enter the following commands:

Step 1: Select from the top of your screen Graphs/Legacy Dialogs/ Scatter/Dot. Select Sample Scatter and click on Define.

Step 2: Move the dependent variable, average district test scores for Grades 3 to 11 in 2005, in its proper box. Ditto for the independent variable, per pupil instructional expenditures.

Step 3: You may add chart titles if you wish.

Step 4: Click on OK to generate a scatterplot that looks something like Figure 11.1 (after some editing).

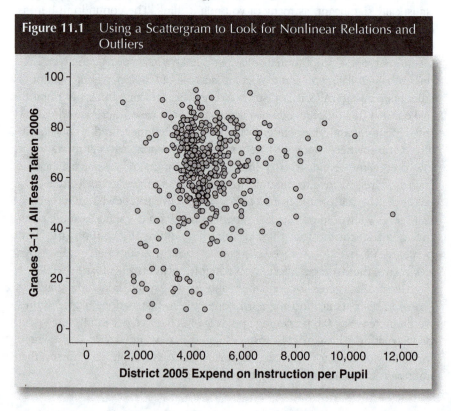

Figure 11.1 Using a Scattergram to Look for Nonlinear Relations and Outliers

It can be difficult to read scatterplots with as many as 400 observations, but we can draw a couple of conclusions from this chart, which may be easier than from the regression coefficients and tests above. First, the middle two thirds of school districts in Texas with instructional expenditures between \$3,300 and \$5,600 vary considerably in test performance. In addition, there are several apparent bivariate outliers—that is, some districts that spend relatively high amounts on instruction with only average test performance and a few districts that spend relatively little but perform with the best of them. One might consider eliminating these districts and rerunning the analysis because they may be so unlike all the other districts as to distort the fundamental relationships in which we are interested.

Another tactic is to examine districts at the top and bottom of the performance distribution in greater detail. That is to say, do the top-performing districts differ from the bottom-performing districts? And might these differences provide clues to understanding how a state legislature or local school board member could direct resources and attention to factors that have a chance of improving test performance? (I am not suggesting that you throw out the middle observations and rerun the regression analysis. As we saw in the previous chapter, doing so may well increase the size of the regression coefficients but at the expense of telling an accurate story. The purpose here is exploratory. I'm not going to make an argument about the size and direction of the relationship in the population.)

How would you identify and examine the cases at the top and/or bottom of this bivariate relationship? We can see, simply by eyeballing the scatterplot, that there are about 6 districts whose mean test scores are about 90% or above. We could select these school districts and compare them on various measures with the 10 or so school districts that fall below 18% on mean test scores. How would you do this? There are, of course, several ways. You could sort all the cases by mean test score and copy the top 6 and bottom 10 to a new SPSS or Excel file. Or you could select cases that fall above 90% or below 18%. You could also use the Case Summaries facility of SPSS, which will be demonstrated later.

MULTIPLE REGRESSION ●

There are essentially three basic types of multiple regression:

1. *Standard or simultaneous regression:* Standard regression is the most commonly used version and typically the default procedure of any statistical software package. It tests for the effect of independent variables as a block on an outcome or dependent variable as well as the effect of each independent variable when controlling for the other independent variables. In this latter

regard, standard regression tells you the effect of one independent variable, net of the effect of other independent variables that are entered into the regression equation simultaneously.

2. *Hierarchical or sequential regression:* As suggested by its title, this version of multiple regression permits the analyst to enter independent variables into the equation in the order he desires. The order should, of course, be grounded in some substantive theory. The technique, in effect, assesses the predictive power of one or more variables after other variables have been controlled for as a block. The output from this procedure also tells you how well all the variables, and each block, predict the outcome or dependent variable.

3. *Statistical multiple regression:* This version of multiple regression enters or removes variables from the equation on the basis of the magnitude of the relationship found in the data. There is some controversy about this technique as it often increases the risk of rejecting the null hypothesis when it is true. In excluding variables from a regression equation because they fall below some threshold of a relationship, you also throw out potentially useful information about what is *not* related to your dependent variable. We will not call on this technique in this text.

Let's illustrate the standard and hierarchical multiple regression analysis models by returning to the Texas Education Indicators data set.

Standard or Simultaneous Multiple Regression

Let's examine first a set of conditions that the state and school districts may be able to change in order to boost districts' test score performance. Another way of framing that task is to ask which variables might predict district test score performance and how well. From those available in this particular data set, I postulate that the following simple causal relationships are at work (you may not agree with any of these "theories" or may have better ones):

Graphically, this "theory" or "model" can be represented in the arrow diagram of Figure 11.2. The positive or negative sign indicates the direction of the relationship (e.g., higher per pupil expenditures on athletic programs are theorized to be associated with higher test scores).

The verbal description of these hypotheses can be described as follows:

1. Large school districts (in terms of student enrollment) will perform more poorly than small schools on test performance because they are more impersonal.

2. Districts that devote resources to athletics fuel a healthy relationship between mind and body and will outperform districts that spend less per pupil on these activities.

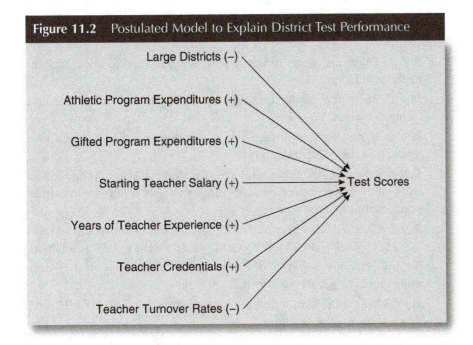

Figure 11.2 Postulated Model to Explain District Test Performance

3. Districts that devote resources for gifted students will outperform those that do not because such programs signal to all students that the district is committed to academic excellence.

4. The higher the average salary for new teachers, the higher a district's test scores will be because better teachers will seek higher-paying districts.

5. The higher the average years of experience that districts' teachers have, the higher too will be districts' test scores because experienced teachers are better teachers, poorer teachers self-selecting out of the profession with time.

6. Similarly, more highly educated teaching staffs (as measured by the proportion of teachers with master's degrees) will produce better-performing students. The more you know, the more you have to teach.

7. Higher teacher turnover rates damage the ability of students to take standardized tests because it's harder to stay the curricular course with different captains at the helm during the school year.

This model is a fairly simple—even naive—rendering of the ways in which different conditions may affect district test scores. Such models, however, are commonplace. Simplicity has some value, and testing this model may provide a sense of the relative influence of different factors on test performance when controlling for other variables.

Let's see if the data are consistent with our hunches, hypotheses, theories, or mode by putting them to a test in SPSS.

Step 1: Open the Texas Indicator System data set, and click Analyze/ Regression/Linear.

Step 2: Move the continuous version of district test scores into the Dependent: box.

Step 3: Move the seven independent variables specified in the above model into the Independent: box.

Step 4: Make sure that Enter is selected for Method. This calls on SPSS to enter all the independent variables simultaneously, otherwise known as standard multiple regression.

Step 5: Click on Statistics, and select "Estimates," "Confidence Intervals," "Model fit," "Descriptives," and "Part and Partial correlations." Click Continue.

We will examine some of the assumption diagnostics in the next assignment but ignore them here.

Step 6: Click on Options, and select "Exclude cases pairwise" in the Missing Values section. Click Continue.

Your output should look something like the following (we have truncated the display of the full table):

Correlations

		Grades 3-11 All Tests Taken 2006	Total Enrollment Count	District 2005 Expend on Athletics Per Pupil	Distrrict 2005 Expend on Gifted Per Pupil
Pearson Correlation	Grades 3-11 All Tests Taken 2006	1.000	.009	.246	.274
	Total Enrollment Count	.009	1.000	-.159	.132
	District 2005 Expend on Athletics Per Pupil	.246	-.159	1.000	.148
	Distrrict 2005 Expend on Gifted Per Pupil	.274	.132	.148	1.000
	Aver Salary for New Teachers	.052	.310	-.216	.177
	Aver Yrs Experience of Teachers	.410	.017	.455	.244
	Percent of Teachers w Masters Degree	.062	.203	-.114	.144
	Teacher Turnover Rate	-.509	-.120	-.363	-.271
Sig. (1-tailed)	Grades 3-11 All Tests Taken 2006	.	.428	.000	.000
	Total Enrollment Count	.428	.	.001	.004
	District 2005 Expend on Athletics Per Pupil	.000	.001	.	.001
	District 2005 Expend on Gifted Per Pupil	.000	.004	.001	.
	Aver Salary for New Teachers	.168	.000	.000	.000
	Aver Yrs Experience of Teachers	.000	.368	.000	.000
	Percent of Teachers w Masters Degree	.105	.000	.011	.002
	Teacher Turnover Rate	.000	.008	.000	.000

We have seen a correlation matrix before. Although half of the matrix is redundant, it displays the bivariate correlations among all the variables in the model, including the size of each correlation, its direction (negative or positive), the level of statistical significance, and the number of cases on which the correlations are calculated (i.e., the nonmissing pairs of variables).

What substantially might you conclude from this matrix? Which, if any, of the independent variables is linearly related with test scores, at least moderately so (i.e., above or below ±.30)?

You will see in the next chapter that this table can also provide clues as to whether your mode faces the problem of **multicollinearity**. Any bivariate correlation above |.70| may cause the algorithms underlying the statistics to produce wacky regression coefficients. But we'll address that issue later.

The first column of the correlation table above provides the bivariate correlation coefficients between each of the independent variables and the dependent variable, percentage of tests passed in a district. Nearly all these variables have a nonnegligible relation with test scores. The exceptions are the total enrollment count, percentage of a district's faculty with master's degrees, and new teachers' salary levels. These "nonfindings" are potentially important from a policy perspective, and I would likely include a discussion of these findings in the policy memorandum. If we can inform the state that these three variables don't seem to pay dividends in terms of tests scores, there may be ways for the state to allocate its resources in more fruitful ways. (We will also examine their multivariate relationships with test scores when controlling for all other variables in the equation to make sure that there aren't any relations that are suppressing these zero-order correlations.)

There is, of course, always the possibility that "nonfindings" are the product of nonlinear relationships. You will recall that regression analysis (as well as many other statistical techniques) are tests of the *linear* relationship between two or more variables. The easiest, although not statistically elegant, way of examining relationships for nonlinearity is to plot each of these variables against the dependent variable (via a scatterplot).

Neither of these two scattergrams indicates nonlinear relations, a fact to be included in a technical appendix but not noteworthy enough to bother the special assistant to the governor. Figure 11.3 is the unedited scattergram of the percentage of district teachers with master's degrees and test scores.

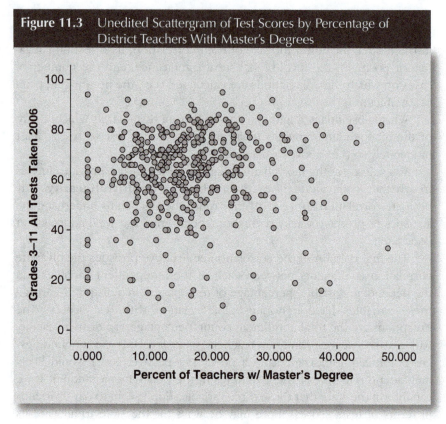

Figure 11.3   Unedited Scattergram of Test Scores by Percentage of District Teachers With Master's Degrees

Let's return to the regression results.

Model Summary

Model	R	R Square	Adjusted R Square	Std. Error of the Estimate
1	.546[a]	.298	.284	14.231

a. Predictors: (Constant), Teacher Turnover Rate, Aver Salary for New Teachers, Percent of Teachers w Masters Degree, District 2005 Expend on Gifted Per Pupil, Total Enrollment Count, District 2005 Expend on Athletics Per Pupil, Aver Yrs Experience of Teachers

Next, inspect the Model Summary table (above) for the values reported in the column for R^2. This is a measure of the proportion of the variation across district test scores that is "explained by" the combination of all your independent variables. The variables we entered into this equation explain about 30% of the variation in the percentage of district students passing the state's tests. That's a fairly substantial proportion of explained variation as these statistics go in the real world, but much is left unexplained.

According to Cohen (1988), an R greater than .50 is interpreted as large, .50 to .30 as moderate, and .30 to .10 as small. Anything smaller than .10 is "negligible."[1] (Note, however, that even negligible effects may be important if they can be changed at little cost to society, a government agency, or a nonprofit organization.) We've got a "large" overall effect here.

Adjusted R^2 compensates for the fact that sample size and the number of independent variables in the equation affect R^2. The adjustment comes in handy (i.e., tends to differ from R^2) with small samples and a large number of independent variables. Report adjusted R^2 when it differs substantially from R^2. It doesn't here, so stick with the unadjusted R^2 when reporting these results.

ANOVA[b]

Model		Sum of Squares	df	Mean Square	F	Sig.
1	Regression	29372.392	7	4196.056	20.720	.000[a]
	Residual	69056.404	341	202.511		
	Total	98428.796	348			

a. Predictors: (Constant), Teacher Turnover Rate, Aver Salary for New Teachers, Percent of Teachers w Masters Degree, District 2005 Expend on Gifted Per Pupil, Total Enrollment Count, District 2005 Expend on Athletics Per Pupil, Aver Yrs Experience of Teachers

b. Dependent Variable: Grades 3-11 All Tests Taken 2006

The ANOVA table tells you whether the multiple correlation (R) is statistically significant, which it is at a reported Sig. = .000. (By the way, it's not "highly" significant, any more than a woman can be "somewhat" pregnant.)

Coefficients[a]

Model		Unstandardized Coefficients		Standardized Coefficients	t	Sig.
		B	Std. Error	Beta		
1	(Constant)	56.879	6.915		8.225	.000
	Total Enrollment Count	-8.387E-5	.000	-.080	-1.627	.105
	District 2005 Expend on Athletics Per Pupil	.004	.006	.037	.702	.483
	District 2005 Expend on Gifted Per Pupil	.030	.011	.126	2.585	.010
	Aver Salary for New Teachers	.000	.000	.062	1.190	.235
	Aver Yrs Experience of Teachers	.504	.307	.110	1.642	.101
	Percent of Teachers w Masters Degree	.090	.099	.046	.914	.361
	Teacher Turnover Rate	-.418	.065	-.401	-6.389	.000

a. Dependent Variable: Grades 3-11 All Tests Taken 2006

95.0% Confidence Interval for B		Correlations		
Lower Bound	Upper Bound	Zero-order	Partial	Part
43.277	70.481			
.000	.000	.009	-.088	-.074
-.008	.017	.246	.038	.032
.007	.052	.274	.139	.117
.000	.001	.052	.064	.054
-.100	1.107	.410	.089	.074
-.104	.285	.062	.049	.041
-.547	-.289	-.509	-.327	-.290

The Coefficients table tells you which of the independent variables best predicts districts' test scores. The *unstandardized regression coefficients* (*B* in the first numeric column in the table above) tell you how much of a unit change in a particular independent variable is associated with a change in the dependent variable.

The interpretation of the *B* value of .504 for "Aver Yrs Experience of Teachers" goes as follows: Every increase of an average of 1 year of experience among teachers in school districts is associated with about a 0.5-percentage-point increase in the proportion of public school kids in those districts who pass the TAKS tests (when holding constant, by the way, all other independent variables entered into the regression analysis).

Remember, however, that the size of *B* is in part a function of the scale (the type of units) in which the variables are measured. The interpretation of counts (e.g., total enrollment) and expenditure variables, for example, can be troubled by issues of scale, which may require transformations of such variables. We see in the output above, for example, that the regression coefficient associated with total enrollment is −8.4E-005. This is scientific notation for a very small number. The actual decimal point is five digits to the left of −8.4. That is to say, each additional (one!) student in a district is associated with a −.000084 decrease in the proportion of students who pass the state tests. Problems of scale and interpretation would have also likely arisen if we had used total expenditures rather than per pupil expenditures for athletics and gifted programs.

Why? Well, expenditures are often recorded in dollars, one buck at a time. In the case at hand, the effect of a $1 increase in expenditures across the entire district on the percentage of a district's students who pass the state's test is likely to be infinitesimal (although—and this may be difficult at first to understand—statistically significant).

To adjust for this problem of scale, we would want to transform the above total enrollment counts by dividing them by, say, 1,000. This will likely create a more easily interpretable regression coefficient but will require your written narrative of the results to read,

> For every increase of 1,000 pupils in a district, we find a corresponding decrease of 0.08 percentage point of students who pass the state's tests, which is substantively trivial and may be an artifact of the poor test performance we observe in the state's largest city, Houston.

(I haven't actually examined the performance of Houston's public schools in this data set but could do so if I were a little more ambitious.) The big impacts on test scores appear to arise from teacher turnover rates and teacher experience if we look only at the unstandardized regression coefficients.

But again, the interpretation of several of these regression coefficients is troubled by scale, range, and the unit in which they are measured. I don't (or shouldn't) want to know the effects of a single additional dollar in per pupil expenditures or salaries for those variables whose range is in the thousands of dollars. I would have to transform the values, say, of the teacher salary variable and the total instructional expenditures into thousands of dollars before entering them into a revised regression equation. These variables are also not normally distributed, but their regression coefficients will clearly be more easily interpretable. Note that I don't transform per pupil expenditures on gifted programs. I will later show what would have happened had I done so.

Before transforming these variables and rerunning the regression, let's return to the Coefficients table for an interpretation of the standardized regression coefficients, otherwise called **betas β**. These coefficients are calculated after SPSS (or any other statistical software program) standardizes all the variables in the equation (including the dependent variable).

Q. How does SPSS do this?

A. It subtracts the mean from each observation on that variable and then divides the results by the variable's standard deviation. Got it? We've seen this type of transformation on numerous prior occasions in this book.

What's more important for you to understand is that such transformations create variables, all of which have a mean of 0 and a standard deviation of 1, thus placing each variable on the same scale. (If you don't understand how the above calculation achieves this result, trust me.) Standardizing the variables in this way allows you to assess the relative influence of the independent variables on the dependent one, when controlling for all independent variables. In the Coefficients table above, teacher turnover rate remains important ($\beta = -.401$), average years of teacher experience declines in importance (from a B of .504 to a β of .110), and per pupil district expenditure on gifted programs increases in importance (from a B of .030 to a β of .126) when all the variables are standardized to have means of 0 and standard deviations of 1.

Beyond providing such a comparative rubric, betas have a substantive interpretation, although one that requires you to "plug in" the original standard deviations (the ones before SPSS standardized the variables). In general, betas tell you how much an increase of 1 standard deviation of an independent variable is associated with an increase of 1 standard deviation of the dependent variable (when taking all the other independent variables in the equation into account).

In the example in hand, a decrease of 15.10 in a district's teacher turnover rate (the standard deviation for teacher turnover rates) is associated with an increase of 6.48 percentage points of a district's students passing the state's tests (.401 × 16.15, i.e., the beta coefficient [β] times the standard deviation of test scores). To get a sense of the effect size of turnover rates, consider the fact that an average of about 63% of students in Texas school districts pass these standardized tests. Increasing this percentage by another 6.48 percentage points would be substantial, especially for those districts at the bottom of the test score distribution. Clearly, achieving this outcome wouldn't be possible for all the districts with an already low teacher turnover, but what might it accomplish for the 13% of all districts with teacher turnover rates above 35%? Reducing these districts' teacher turnover rates by 15 points would, if our model is correct, increase their test scores by 6.48 percentage points, which would likely be a substantial improvement over current performance levels. If you wanted to, you could find the mean test scores for all districts with 35% or greater teacher turnover and contrast this with the 6.48-percentage-point improvement predicted by these multiple regression results. (All these figures are real, generated by simple descriptive statistics used in conjunction with the standardized regression coefficients, betas.)

Incidentally, the Part Correlation column—if you square it—tells you how much of the total variance in the dependent variable is uniquely contributed by each independent variable, when holding all other independent variables constant. Note that the sum of these squared values does not equal the R^2 of the Model Summary table. The total variance explained there also includes shared contributions (as well as unique ones).

After transforming total enrollments and average new teacher salaries into thousands, rerunning the regression analysis, and adding collinearity diagnostics to our request, we arrive at the following Coefficient table, which makes the interpretation of the two transformed variables more meaningful from a policy perspective and more easily communicated to a nonstatistical audience.

Coefficients[a]

Model		Unstandardized Coefficients		Standardized Coefficients	t	Sig.
		B	Std. Error	Beta		
1	(Constant)	56.879	6.915		8.225	.000
	District 2005 Expend on Athletics Per Pupil	.004	.006	.037	.702	.483
	Distrrict 2005 Expend on Gifted Per Pupil	.030	.011	.126	2.585	.010
	Aver Yrs Experience of Teachers	.504	.307	.110	1.642	.101
	Percent of Teachers w Masters Degree	.090	.099	.046	.914	.361
	Teacher Turnover Rate	-.418	.065	-.401	-6.389	.000
	enroll_in_1000s	-.084	.052	-.080	-1.627	.105
	new_salary_in_$1000s	.192	.161	.062	1.190	.235

a. Dependent Variable: Grades 3-11 All Tests Taken 2006

95.0% Confidence Interval for B		Correlations			Collinearity Statistics	
Lower Bound	Upper Bound	Zero-order	Partial	Part	Tolerance	VIF
43.277	70.481					
-.008	.017	.246	.038	.032	.722	1.385
.007	.052	.274	.139	.117	.865	1.156
-.100	1.107	.410	.089	.074	.461	2.168
-.104	.285	.062	.049	.041	.805	1.243
-.547	-.289	-.509	-.327	-.290	.521	1.919
-.185	.018	.009	-.088	-.074	.851	1.175
-.125	.509	.052	.064	.054	.768	1.302

Each increase of 1,000 students in a district is associated with a decline of 0.084 percentage point in tests passed. Each increase in the average salary for new teachers of $1,000 is associated with an increase of 0.19 percentage point in tests passed. The coefficients for both variables, however, may be the result of the "luck of the draw" of our sample. They are not statistically significant, and I wouldn't put much store by them as levers to increase test performance across districts.

Before moving on to hierarchical multiple regression, consider one last point about scale, ranges, and units of measurement in multiple regression. What would have happened had we (carelessly) transformed per pupil district expenditure on gifted programs into thousands of dollars? (You will see in a moment why I consider this careless even though I have repeatedly talked about transforming raw counts and dollar figures in a similar fashion.)

Coefficients[a]

Model		Unstandardized Coefficients		Standardized Coefficients			!
		B	Std. Error	Beta	t	Sig.	
1	(Constant)	56.879	6.915		8.225	.000	
	District 2005 Expend on Athletics Per Pupil	.004	.006	.037	.702	.483	
	Aver Yrs Experience of Teachers	.504	.307	.110	1.642	.101	
	Percent of Teachers w Masters Degree	.090	.099	.046	.914	.361	
	Teacher Turnover Rate	-.418	.065	-.401	-6.389	.000	
	enroll_in_1000s	-.084	.052	-.080	-1.627	.105	
	new_salary_in_$1000s	.192	.161	.062	1.190	.235	
	gifted_in_$1000s	29.574	11.439	.126	2.585	.010	

a. Dependent Variable: Grades 3-11 All Tests Taken 2006

The unstandardized regression coefficient for per pupil expenditures on gifted programs is the last row of the first column in the Coefficients table above. Wow! Every unit increase in per pupil expenditures on gifted programs is associated with an increase in test scores by 29.6 percentage points! How can that be? (Note, by the way, that the beta and Sig. for these transformed variables do not differ from the untransformed variety.) The answer lies in the unit in which this transformed variable is now expressed—that is, in thousands of dollars.

Still puzzled? What's the problem with expressing per pupil expenditures on gifted programs in thousands of dollars? The answer is to be found in simple, descriptive statistics. To wit, what is the mean per pupil expenditure on gifted programs across districts in Texas in 2006? Answer: About $50. Three quarters of all Texas school districts in our sample spend less than $60 per pupil on gifted programs.

Would you propose to the governor of Texas that we increase mean per pupil expenditures on gifted programs by $1,000 to achieve an extraordinary expected increase of 29.6 percentage points in tests passed? Well, the payoff looks good, but the investment is 20 times greater than the current level of expenditures on such programs. How long would you keep your job as an analyst for the Texas Department of Education if you recommended this course of action? Or how much longer would you retain your job as an advisor to the governor if you didn't spot this problem in someone else's recommendation for such an increase in expenditures on gifted programs?

There are several morals to this little story. First, always think about the units in which your variables are measured. Second, don't forget about the simple, descriptive statistics such as mean and range that enable you to place any statistic in its proper context. And third, think about what you're doing instead of following some textbook prescription about transforming expenditures, revenue, or budget numbers into units such as thousands of dollars.

Hierarchical or Sequential Multiple Regression

You may recall that hierarchical multiple regression permits you to assess the impact of a set of independent variables on a dependent variable after holding constant a block of other variables that you enter into the regression first (in contrast to all at the same time, as we did above).

For example, let's say that you wanted to know how some of the independent variables above vary with test scores when controlling for the socio-demographic characteristics of school districts. The proportion of a district's students who are black or Hispanic and the proportion who are economically disadvantaged may influence test scores so as to substantially diminish the effects of the conditions over which the state and school districts are more likely to have some control (as we sought to test above).

Step 1: Click Analyze/Regression/Linear.

Step 2: Move the continuous version of the tests score variable into the Dependent: box.

Step 3: Move the percent black, percent Hispanic, and the percent economically disadvantaged variables into the Independent: box as Block 1 of 1.

Step 4: Click on Next, and enter three of the independent variables of the standard mode we used earlier in this example into the Independent: box as Block 2 of 2. These are years of teacher experience in the district, teacher turnover rates, and per pupil expenditures on gifted programs.

Step 5: Make sure the Method box is set to Enter, which will enter the variables within each block simultaneously.

Step 6: Click Statistics, and select "Estimates," "Model fit," "R Square Change," "Descriptives," and "Part and Partial correlations." Click Continue.

Step 7: Select Options/Missing Values/Pairwise if not already chosen, and click OK.

Part of the output from these procedures includes the Model Summary table below:

Model Summary

Model	R	R Square	Adjusted R Square	Std. Error of the Estimate	Change Statistics				
					R Square Change	F Change	df1	df2	Sig. F Change
1	.583[a]	.340	.335	13.712	.340	69.248	3	403	.000
2	.657[b]	.431	.423	12.777	.091	21.390	3	400	.000

a. Predictors: (Constant), Economically Disadvantaged Studetns, Percent, Black Student, Percent, Hispanic Students, Percent

b. Predictors: (Constant), Economically Disadvantaged Studetns, Percent, Black Student, Percent, Hispanic Students, Percent, District 2005 Expend on Gifted Per Pupil, Teacher Turnover Rate, Aver Yrs Experience of Teachers

Model 1 includes the first block of variables (%black, %Hispanic, %economically disadvantaged). These variables explain about 34% of the variation in test scores across Texas school districts in our sample. This is a "strong" effect. The block of variables is significantly related to test scores, not a result of the random sampling process ($p < .001$).

Model 2 includes the second block of variables (per pupil expenditures on gifted programs, teacher turnover rates, and average years of teachers' experience). This block is also significantly related to test performance, even after controlling for the economic, racial, and ethnic characteristics of the sample school districts. These variables can explain another 9% of the variation in test score performance, again after holding constant the sociodemographic variables specified in Model 1.

Coefficients[a]

Model		Unstandardized Coefficients		Standardized Coefficients	t	Sig.
		B	Std. Error	Beta		
1	(Constant)	82.397	1.891		43.567	.000
	Black Student, Percent	-.318	.042	-.361	-7.630	.000
	Hispanic Students, Percent	-.161	.034	-.267	-4.732	.000
	Economically Disadvantaged Studetns, Percent	-.190	.045	-.240	-4.192	.000
2	(Constant)	81.638	3.924		20.804	.000
	Black Student, Percent	-.212	.042	-.240	-4.991	.000
	Hispanic Students, Percent	-.112	.033	-.187	-3.423	.001
	Economically Disadvantaged Studetns, Percent	-.160	.043	-.202	-3.697	.000
	Distrrict 2005 Expend on Gifted Per Pupil	.019	.009	.080	1.990	.047
	Aver Yrs Experience of Teachers	.144	.235	.031	.613	.540
	Teacher Turnover Rate	-.300	.053	-.288	-5.693	.000

a. Dependent Variable: Grades 3-11 All Tests Taken 2006

The Coefficients table above reports the size and direction of the standardized and unstandardized regression coefficients and their respective statistical significance. From a policy analytic perspective, I want to focus on the variables in Model 2 because I presume (a) that the socio-demographic characteristics of school districts are important predictors of test performance, but (b) there's little that school districts and the state can do about them.

So what is the relative effect of Model 2 variables on test performance? Teacher turnover rates remain a moderately important variable, as can be seen from several of the numbers produced in this table. The *B* coefficient (unstandardized) tells me that I would predict a decline of about 1/3 of a percentage point in the proportion of a district's students passing the state's test for every increase of 1% in teacher turnover rates. Here's where it is useful again to return to our simpler summary statistics to help us give meaning to that regression coefficient and to provide interpretative context.

The average (i.e., mean) turnover rate among sample school districts is about 21%, as displayed in the Descriptive Statistics table below. The standard deviation for teacher turnover (16.15) tells us, assuming that this variable is normally distributed, that the turnover rate for the middle two thirds of all school districts ranges from 5% to 37% (i.e., 21 − 16 = 5; 21 + 16 = 37). Lowering teacher turnover rates from the mean of 21% to the 33rd percentile of 5% would reduce turnover by 17 percentage points on average across all school districts. Using the regression coefficient (*B*) of −.30 and multiplying it by a 17-point reduction in turnover (assuming, of course, that we knew how and had the resources to reduce teacher turnover by 17 points) would lead us to predict an increase in average test score performance of 5.1 percentage points (−.30 × 17 + 5.1). That would be a pretty dramatic result in light of the mean percentage of kids in school districts who pass the TAKS tests (i.e., 63%).

Descriptive Statistics

	Mean	Std. Deviation	N
Grades 3-11 All Tests Taken 2006	62.95	16.818	410
Black Student, Percent	11.918	19.0671	411
Hispanic Students, Percent	33.22	27.953	411
Economically Disadvantaged Studetns, Percent	54.150	21.2213	411
Distrrict 2005 Expend on Gifted Per Pupil	51.40	71.690	408
Aver Yrs Experience of Teachers	11.31006	3.660058	411
Teacher Turnover Rate	21.21937	16.150351	408

We could conduct a similar set of calculations for per pupil expenditures on gifted programs and on average years of teachers' experience. It is perhaps surprising to note that the influence of teacher experience becomes negligible when controlling for all other variables in the regression analysis. While the zero-order correlation between teacher experience and test performance was a moderately strong .41, the partial correlation (a fifth-order partial correlation if you're counting) falls to .03 and is no longer statistically significant (*p* = .54).

DICHOTOMOUS (DUMMY) ● INDEPENDENT VARIABLES

We will shortly turn to the situation in which you have a dependent variable that can take on only two values by using logistic regression. As we saw in the hierarchical regression example above, however, you can also find yourself in a situation in which you have one or more dichotomous *independent* variables. These variables take on the ignominious title of "dummy" variables when their two categories are coded 0 and 1. Indeed, make sure that all your independent dichotomous variables are so coded before entering them into a regression equation. (You may recall that the mean of a dummy variable is also the proportion of observations that are coded 1.) Their interpretation is often stated as the consequence of moving from the absence of a condition to the presence of that condition. Although somewhat odd, the regression coefficients associated with dummy variables would be interpreted as the effects of moving from nonmale to male, from nontall to tall, or from not smiling to smiling.

Hopefully, this makes sense to you. There is, however, a slightly more complicated rendition of dummy variables in regression analysis in which you can recode any categorical variable with three or more possible conditions to a set of dummy independent variables. This is not rocket science, but there is a small trap that awaits the unsuspecting analysts who recode their categorical variables improperly. Here's a hint: A variable with four categories should be recoded into three (and only three) dummy variables before it is entered into a regression equation. Explanation via example will follow.

Let us say that we want to include in our regression analysis a categorical measure of the race/ethnicity of respondents, which is coded as follows:

White   1

Black   2

Hispanic 3

Others   Missing

This categorical variable should be entered into the regression equation as two dummy variables that you create by recoding the responses to the above variable in the following way (note that these are not the SPSS commands per se):

Dummy1 = 1 if black, otherwise = 0.

Dummy2 = 1 if Hispanic, otherwise = 0.

The regression coefficients of each of these dummy variables would be interpreted as the effect of, say, being black, on some dependent variable (let's say, the index of satisfaction toward the quality of county services) in comparison with the one category that we did not make a dummy variable of—white. Similarly, the regression coefficient in this example for Dummy2 would be the effect of being Hispanic on satisfaction with services in comparison with the effect of being white. Values of 0 on these two dummy variables will identify respondents who are white.

If you had created three dummy variables and entered them simultaneously into the regression equation, you would have created three independent variables that are perfectly linearly related. It is mathematically impossible to calculate regression coefficients under these conditions.

In the now familiar example of the Orange County public perception data set, a regression equation in which dummy variables for being black and Hispanic are entered would produce the following regression coefficient results.

The unstandardized regression coefficient for "ethnic_black" is straightforwardly interpreted as blacks scoring 3.715 more points on the satisfaction index than whites. Hispanics are 3.251 points less pleased than whites with a summary measure of satisfaction with county contacts during the past year. The differences, of course, aren't very large. (Interestingly, I tried to throw in a third dummy variable for "ethnic_white" into the equation, but SPSS excluded one of the other dummy variables for me, without my consent. I had so hoped to describe a computational collapse.)

LOGISTIC REGRESSION ●

(*Note:* This procedure cannot be performed using the student version of SPSS.)

This technique is drawn from your statistical tool kit when you want to predict a dependent variable that has only two conditions (e.g., on welfare or not on welfare). Another way of describing this situation is that you have a dependent variable that can take on only one of two values: you either are or you ain't something. In statistical terms, this procedure requires that every observation (i.e., case, respondent, observation) of your dichotomous dependent variable has a value of 0 or 1.

Like standard multiple regression, logistic regression results are affected by sample size, mulicollinearity, and outliers. As a consequence, we should be alert to these conditions and inspect the data for possible problems there. The algorithms used to calculate its results, however, are not based on **ordinary least squares (OLS)** techniques (which rely on the sum of square differences from means) but rather on algorithms called maximum likelihood estimates. As a consequence, we don't have to worry about assumptions concerning normal distributions, which dichotomies would be hard-pressed to satisfy. Logistic regression is similarly comfortable with ignoring the normal distribution assumption for independent variables in its equation.

In our increasingly well-analyzed case of Texas school districts, let's assess the effects of several of our variables on an outcome other than test scores: the proportion of a school district's high school students who are at risk of dropping out of school (for details concerning how these figures were determined, see the Codebook for the Texas Academic Excellence Indicator System (TAEIS) that accompanies the data files for this text).

Procedurally, we want to recode this at-risk-to-drop-out variable such that districts in which fewer than 42% of high school students are at risk of dropping out are coded as "0" (on our new dichotomous dependent variable) and districts in which greater than or equal to 42% are at risk are coded as "1." (This roughly divides the districts into two equal parts.) Obviously, we would not have needed to transform our dependent variable and could have used standard or hierarchical multiple regression. There are a couple of interesting test statistics [odds ratios], however, that are provided in logistic regression that do commend its use, which we will see later. This example is only for illustrative purposes, although clearly interpretable, as you will see below.

Let's select the following subset of independent variables for our model:

- Teacher turnover
- Teacher experience
- Per pupil expenditures for instruction
- A dummy variable of the percentage of teachers who are Hispanic, where districts with fewer than 10% Hispanic teachers are coded as 0 and districts with 10% or more Hispanic teachers are coded as 1 (hisp_teachers_dichot)

Step 1: Click Analyze/Regression/Binary Logistic.

Step 2: Move the new dichotomous (dummy) version of "percent at-risk dichotomy" (0 = *less than 42%*, 1 = *42% or higher at risk*) into the Dependent: box.

Step 3: Move all your independent (predictor) variables into the Covariates box.

(Make sure that Enter is displayed in Methods.)

Step 4: Because you have a categorical independent variable (hisp_teachers_dichot), click on Categorical button at the upper right of the box, and move that variable into the Categorical Covariates box.

Step 5: Still within the Categorical dialog box, highlight your categorical variable (and any others in turn if you were to have more than one in another situation), and click the First button in the Change Contrast section. Click Continue. Click Options. Select Casewise Listings of Residuals and change Outside Outliers to 3 std. dev. Click Continue.

Step 6: Click Options, and select "Classification plots," "Hosmer-Lemeshow goodness of fit," "Casewise listing of residuals," and "CI for Exp (B)." Click Continue and OK.

Some of the output from this procedure is shown below. The first set of tables is straightforward and not the focus of your analysis and interpretation.

Examine them nonetheless to make sure that everything about your variables appears in order (e.g., not too many missing observations).

Block 0: Beginning Block

Block 0: Beginning Block

Classification Table[a,b]

Observed			Predicted		
			Percent at risk dichotomy		
			Fewer than 42 pecent	42 percent or greater	Percentage Correct
Step 0	Percent at risk dichotomy	Fewer than 42 pecent	210	0	100.0
		42 percent or greater	198	0	.0
	Overall Percentage				51.5

a. Constant is included in the model.

b. The cut value is .500

Variables in the Equation

		B	S.E.	Wald	df	Sig.	Exp(B)
Step 0	Constant	-.059	.099	.353	1	.553	.943

Variables not in the Equation

			Score	df	Sig.
Step 0	Variables	DPFEAINSK	.586	1	.444
		DPSTEXPA	19.779	1	.000
		DPSTURNR	26.727	1	.000
		hisp_teachers_dichot(1)	50.819	1	.000
	Overall Statistics		65.652	4	.000

The above tables provide results before any independent variables are entered into the logistic regression equation. The classification table, for example, shows the overall percentage of correctly classified cases (51.5%) before we use our knowledge of independent variables to classify cases. SPSS selected this value because it represents the category with the higher percentage of districts in it. That is to say, if we had to guess into which category a district fell without any other information about that district, we'd pick the category that has the larger number of observations in it. Our objective in the following tables is to see how much better we can predict whether a district is likely to fall into the low or high levels of dropout risk, given knowledge of our independent variables. Block 1 displays the results of this assessment.

Block 1: Method = Enter

The Omnibus Tests of Model Coefficients table (below) provides an assessment of how well all the independent variables do in predicting our dichotomous outcome variable, above and beyond the results from Block 0. You should report the chi-square value, degrees of freedom, and Sig., which in this case are 207.82, 4, and <.001, respectively.

Omnibus Tests of Model Coefficients

		Chi-square	df	Sig.
Step 1	Step	71.537	4	.000
	Block	71.537	4	.000
	Model	71.537	4	.000

Model Summary

Step	-2 Log likelihood	Cox & Snell R Square	Nagelkerke R Square
1	493.718[a]	.161	.214

a. Estimation terminated at iteration number 4 because parameter estimates changed by less than .001.

Hosmer and Lemeshow Test

Step	Chi-square	df	Sig.
1	14.313	8	.074

In the Model Summary table, the Cox and Snell R^2 and the Nagelkerke R^2 values are interpretable as the percentage of variation in the dependent variable that is explained by your independent variables (again, assuming that our theory or beliefs about causal relations are correct). In this particular case, instructional expenditures, teacher experience, the presence of Hispanic teachers, and teacher turnover rates explain from about 16% to 21% of the variance in dropout risk rates. This is not a huge effect, but don't despair. As a former governor of Texas was fond of saying, this is "hard work." Remember as well that these summary statistics tell the story for the entire set of sample school districts. These conditions may make a relatively bigger difference for those school districts with large percentages of students at risk of dropping out.

The Hosmer and Lemeshow Test also provides an assessment of the model as a whole. Like a few other tests (e.g., Levene's test of variance equality and the one-sample K-S test), the Hosmer and Lemeshow null hypothesis is that the model fits, which you hope not to reject. Therefore, look for the Sig. to be above .05, which it is in this particular analysis.

Classification Table[a]

Observed			Predicted		
			Percent at risk dichotomy		Percentage Correct
			Fewer than 42 pecent	42 percent or greater	
Step 1	Percent at risk dichotomy	Fewer than 42 pecent	179	31	85.2
		42 percent or greater	95	103	52.0
	Overall Percentage				69.1

a. The cut value is .500

The Classification table (above) provides an assessment of how well you can predict each category of your dichotomous dependent variable. These percentages of correct classifications can be compared with the naive predictions of Block 0. Based on knowledge of your independent variables, your model correctly predicts 85.2% of low at-risk districts and 52% of high at-risk districts. Your overall ability to make a correct prediction now stands at 69.1%, in contrast to the 51.5% in the model that did not have the aid of any independent variables. Unfortunately, our model does better in predicting the districts that have lower risks than those with higher ones, which is probably of greater concern to public officials in Texas.

The Variables in the Equation table gives you an assessment of the relative importance of the independent variables entered into the model (see below).

Variables in the Equation

		B	S.E.	Wald	df	Sig.	Exp(B)	95% C.I. for EXP(B)	
								Lower	Upper
Step 1[a]	DPFEAINSK	.000	.000	.020	1	.889	1.000	1.000	1.000
	DPSTEXPA	-.033	.042	.602	1	.438	.968	.891	1.051
	DPSTURNR	.027	.010	7.348	1	.007	1.027	1.008	1.048
	hisp_teachers_dichot(1)	1.612	.271	35.398	1	.000	5.012	2.947	8.524
	Constant	-.691	.681	1.028	1	.311	.501		

a. Variable(s) entered on step 1: DPFEAINSK, DPSTEXPA, DPSTURNR, hisp_teachers_dichot.

Casewise List[a]

a. The casewise plot is not produced because no outliers were found.

The test for statistical significance (analogous to the chi-square test) is in the Wald test column. The more readily interpretable columns are elsewhere, beginning with our old friend, the Sig. column. In this model, the percentage of Hispanic teachers and teacher turnover rates are "significantly" related to dropout risk. Per pupil expenditures on instruction and the mean years of teacher experience in a district appear unrelated to this risk (remember this when controlling for all the other independent variables in the model).

Look at the B column to interpret the two statistically significant variables. One more percentage point of teacher turnover in a district is associated with a 2.7% greater likelihood of being a high at-risk district. Perhaps surprisingly, moving from fewer than 10% Hispanic teachers to greater than 10% Hispanic teachers is associated with a 161.2% greater likelihood of being a high at-risk district. This "positive" relationship suggests that the causal mechanism I had presumed to be at work (e.g., Hispanic teachers are positive role models for at-risk kids) may not be at work. More plausible theories may suggest different causal mechanisms.

Exp (B) and the columns for 95.0% C.I. for EXP (B) report odds ratios (OR) for each independent variable. These odds ratios are interpreted as the increase (or decrease) in the chances of being in one outcome category when the value of the predictor variable increases by one unit. The odds of being in a high at-risk district become 1.027 times greater for every increase of 1 percentage point in teacher turnover (which is the equivalent of saying that each increase of 1% in teacher turnover corresponds to a 2.8% increase in the percentage of high-risk students). This apparently small number might be important from a policy perspective if school districts know how to reduce teacher turnover rates substantially. Recall that teacher turnover among Texas school districts ranges from 0% to 100%, with a median turnover rate of 16%. Reducing a district's turnover rate by 20 percentage points would have a corresponding effect (if our model is correct) of reducing the likelihood of being a high at-risk district by nearly 60%.

Note that SPSS also provides a 95% confidence interval for these odds-ratio effects. The "true" effect size of teacher turnover in the population would be found between 1% and 4% in 95 of 100 hypothetical samples of equal size and design drawn from that population.

Finally, you can observe that this logistic regression model has no outliers, which you should also report in a technical appendix. This will hopefully ward off the statistical geeks who want to challenge your results on this score.

CONCLUSION ●

Regression analysis is a very versatile tool, enabling you to answer a host of different questions. For example, it allows you to assess the extent to which one independent variable is related to a dependent variable when controlling for other independent variables. It enables you to rule out alternative explanations. It enables you to predict the level of a variable on the basis of a level or change in another. It even permits you to assess the relative importance of some variables (or blocks of them) in comparison with others. It offers summary metrics of the extent to which a set of independent variables explains variation in a dependent variable. And the tool even comes with a variety of attachments to use in special circumstances—that is, from dummy categorical independent variables to dichotomous dependent ones.

Extracting meaning from regression statistics, however, requires you to be mindful of the metrics or units in which variables are measured, transforming them in some instances while leaving others in their virgin state. Summary descriptive statistics provide the context in which to interpret these statistics. Don't leave them behind.

Finally, regression is best used when many of its assumptions and data requirements are met. Assessing the extent to which they are met or violated is the task of a set of diagnostic tools to which we turn in the next chapter, as well as some of the corrective steps you may take if these instruments detect substantial departures from those assumptions.

NOTE ●

1. Cohen (1988) also considered whether variance explained (the correlation squared) might be a suitable scale to represent magnitude of linearity. He argued against doing so because a correlation of .10 corresponds to explaining only 1% of the variance, which he thought did not convey adequately the magnitude of such a correlation.

To practice and reinforce the lessons of this chapter of the book, turn to Exercise 8 in the *Student Workbook* (available at http://www.sagepub .com/pearsonsp/), but only after swallowing and digesting the fruits of the next chapter in the book, Chapter 12.

CHAPTER **12**

DETECTING AND
CORRECTING VIOLATIONS
OF REGRESSION ASSUMPTIONS

This chapter is the geekiest of all you will confront in this book. It examines the assumptions on which regression statistics stand (or wobble). And there are quite a few such assumptions. Indeed, there are so many that programs such as SPSS provide a host of diagnostic tools to assess whether (and how badly) your data may violate them. Check your assumptions at the door, one might say, because you're about to be led through the world of multisyllabic terms that can utterly impress and befuddle audiences who have not read a statistics textbook of this kind (in other words, most of the world). Most of what follows is more technical than substantive (although I'll try to show how residuals can be used to identify cases that deserve further investigation and may produce a gold mine of insights).

Well, let's get on with it. What are these assumptions?

SAMPLE SIZE ●

Some statisticians suggest as a general rule of thumb that you include only as many independent variables as 1/10 the number of cases or observations you have in your data set. In other words, if you have 50 respondents in your data set, include no more than five independent variables in your regression equation (Elliott & Woodward, 2007, p. 101). This advice can be turned on its head to provide guidelines concerning how large a data set should be in order to use regression tools at all. The guideline above can be restated as 10 observations for each independent variable you include in your regression equation.

Other statisticians differ somewhat on this question. Stevens (1996, p. 72) suggests 15 subjects per predictor. Five independent (i.e., predictor) variables would require you to have 75 subjects or observations according to this formula. Tabachnick and Fidell (2007, p. 123) recommend 50 cases plus eight times the number of independent variables. This would require 90 cases for a regression equation with five independent variables.

These rules of thumb, however, ignore the fact that small effects in the population will be harder to detect than large effects. (Remember, a small effect can be substantively important.) Field (2005), drawing on others' work, introduces the expected size of the effect into such guidelines, as shown in Figure 12.1.

Obviously, samples of 1,000 or more observations are more than adequate for the type of regressions we will call on. Files of 400 or more are fine, except for detecting only the smallest effects.

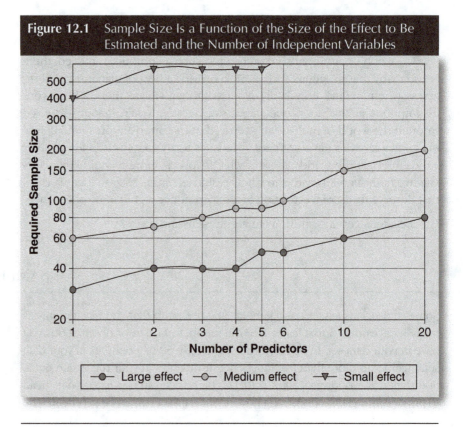

Figure 12.1   Sample Size Is a Function of the Size of the Effect to Be Estimated and the Number of Independent Variables

SOURCE: Field (2005).

MULTICOLLINEARITY •

Multicollinearity refers to the relationships among independent variables. The algorithms underlying regression statistics may not be reliable when your equation includes two or more independent variables whose bivariate correlation coefficient is larger than $|.70|$. You can certainly eyeball the correlation table that SPSS generates in multiple regression to look for correlations that exceed this level. If you discover this situation, you may want to omit one of the variables from the equation or create a composite or index measure that combines two (or more) highly related variables and rerun the regression with this new variable(s).

Many statistical software packages will also generate specific statistical tests for multicollinearity. SPSS reports two such tests in the Coefficients table: **Tolerance** and the **variance inflation factor (VIF)**. Tolerance is a measure of how much of the variance of each independent variable is *not* explained by the other independent variables in the equation $(1 - R^2)$. The VIF is calculated as 1 divided by the tolerance (which makes it redundant to report both). Rules of thumb exist for their interpretation: If the tolerance is .10 or less or if the VIF is 10 or greater, you may have multicollinearity, and your regression coefficients could be wacky, unreliable, not to be trusted, never used to draw a conclusion of any kind whatsoever, and so on. You get the picture. This is a bad thing. Fortunately, it rarely happens, and you can always correct the problem by taking one of the two steps noted above.

OUTLIERS •

Multiple regression statistics are based on formulas that use variables' means in their calculations, the famous sums-of-squared departures from the mean. And you may recall that means are not a fair measure of central tendency if they include extreme values (either very high or very low), otherwise known as outliers. These can be detected in your initial examination of the variables in your data set, and—as noted elsewhere—should not necessarily be summarily removed (especially if there are relatively few outliers in your file). They may be the result of an error in reporting, recording, or coding the data or the consequence of falsehoods, fabrications, or ignorance. They may also help reveal some interesting insights or identify subjects or observations that deserve our applause or derision. As we have seen before, outliers in bivariate relationships can be revealed through your inspection of their scatterplots.

You may realize, however, that outliers cannot be easily displayed in the multidimensional space of a regression equation with two or more independent variables. They can in such a situation, however, be revealed in the scatterplot of standardized residuals on the standardized predicted values of your dependent variable. These may be considered **multivariate**—instead of univariate or bivariate—**outliers**. Standardized residuals that are above 3.0 or below −3.0 standard deviations may identify multivariate outliers that you may have to deal with. If you find few such outliers in a large data set, they may not do great harm to your regression coefficients, but they may nonetheless be worth more careful examination for what they reveal about mistakes, lies, or extraordinary people, organizations, or events.

Indeed, not only is an examination of residuals used to detect whether outliers may be causing mischief with your regression estimates, residuals can also be used to check for homoscedasticity, linearity, and normality, additional assumptions made by your regression statistics.

Finally, there are several formal tests for the effect that outliers may have on regression results: **Mahalanobis distance (d)**, **Cook's distance**, and **centered leverage value**. We provide an example of how to request these statistics and interpret them below.

● HOMOSCEDASTICITY

Derived from the Greek *homo*, for same or similar, and *skedastikos*, for dispersion (or is it a rash on your elbow?), regression assumes that the variance of residuals when plotted against the predicted values of your dependent variable is relatively the same across all those predicted values. The violation of this assumption (also known as heteroscedasticity) causes the standard errors of the regression coefficients to be underestimated, thus sometimes making nonsignificant relationships appear to be statistically significant. (In the case of simple regression, the assumption of homoscedasticity can be assessed by a visual examination of the scatterplot of the independent and dependent variables. The assumption would be met if the spread of observations looks relatively the same across the entire range of values of your independent variable).

To "fix" this problem, you can either make nonlinear transformations of the variables (e.g., take their log) or use a weighted least squares estimation technique. The latter technique assigns weights to observations that are the reciprocal of their variances or distance from the mean of the distribution for that variable. This means that observations with large variances have a quieter voice in the analysis than observations that are near the mean of the variables.

● LINEARITY

Like the Pearson correlation coefficient (r), regression also tests for linear relations. Nonlinear relations may cause your regression estimates to appear as if there is no relationship when in fact there can be a strong one, albeit nonlinear (e.g., it could be curvilinear, exponential, or quadratic). A test of normality is found in the normal probability-probability (P-P) plot of regression standardized residuals (I'm not making these names up!), which we'll request shortly.

Nonlinearity, as well as heteroscedasticity, can be revealed through a visual inspection of the plot of the standardized residuals (**ZRESID**) on the standardized predicted values of the dependent variable (**ZPRED**), as illustrated in Figure 12.2 (from Field, 2005, p. 203).

Figure 12.2 Using Plots of ZPRED on ZRESID to Detect Heteroscedasticity and Nonlinearity

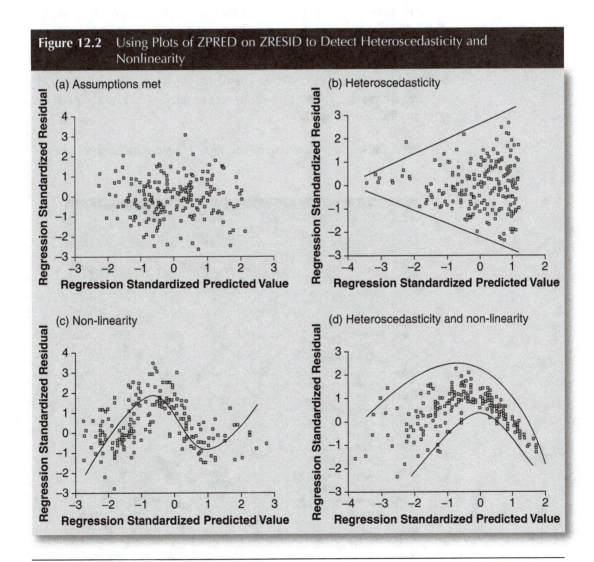

SOURCE: Field (2005).

● NORMALITY

Before you conduct any multivariate analysis, you should examine your variables' distributions, as we demonstrated in Chapter 5. You start with descriptive statistics, examining means, medians, skewness, and kurtosis. It is also often useful to eyeball the histograms of these variables in comparison with a normal curve that you can request SPSS to superimpose on them. Any uncertainties can be resolved through requests of the Kolmogorov-Smirnoff (K-S) one-sample test for normality.

The one-sample K-S tests whether a single variable is normally distributed. Unlike many Sig., a small value (i.e., <.05) is bad news because the K-S null hypothesis postulates that the distribution *is* normal, a conclusion you would rather *not* reject. Therefore, if the value of p (i.e., Sig.) is <.05, you will reject the null hypothesis that the distribution is normal.

The following procedure is used to conduct such a test (using the "Welfare and Economics" file):

Step 1: Click Analyze/Nonparametric Tests/1-Sample K-S as shown here.

Step 2: Move the "out of labor force" variable into the variable list. (Make sure "Normal" is checked in the Test distribution box.)

Step 3: Click Options, and select "Descriptive." Click Continue and OK.

The output from a one-sample K-S for this variable should look something like the following:

One-Sample Kolmogorov-Smirnoff Test

		%_out_of_lab _force_16plu s
N		47
Normal Parameters[a,b]	Mean	36.453
	Std. Deviation	3.0428
Most Extreme Differences	Absolute	.185
	Positive	.185
	Negative	-.127
Kolmogorov-Smirnoff Z		1.269
Asymp. Sig. (2-tailed)		.080

a. Test distribution is Normal.

b. Calculated from data.

The K-S Z test statistic (the second from the bottom row of information in the table above) is calculated (by SPSS) as the product of the square root of the number of valid observations and the largest absolute difference between the empirical (i.e., calculated from the data itself) and theoretical (i.e., calculated from the known mathematical properties of the normal distribution) cumulative distribution function. This won't be on the test either.

You can see from the last row of the table above that we cannot confidently reject the hypothesis that this distribution is normal, but we came pretty close (if the value in the last row had been <.05 instead of .08).

The K-S test, however, only detects univariate departures from normality. There are two tools available to examine potential multivariate departures from normality. The first of these is the normal P-P plot of the expected cumulative probabilities (Y-axis) on the observed cumulative probabilities (X-axis). If the points lie close to the straight diagonal line from bottom left to top right, you can feel confident that this assumption has not been violated. We will display one such plot below.

The second tool for checking multivariate normality is again the scattergram of standardized residuals (SPSS's ZRESID) on standardized predicted variables (ZPRED). Points that resemble those in Chart (a) of Figure 12.2 allow you to move along.

Violations of this assumption, however, are not as damning with samples of $n > 100$ because of the central limit theorem, which proves that the standard error of the sampling distribution tends to be normally distributed even when the empirical distributions of the variables are not.

● INDEPENDENCE OF RESIDUALS

Look in the plot of residuals and the predicted dependent variable for any patterns. Finding them will suggest that clusters of observations may not be independent of each other, as perhaps might occur when you randomly sample people from within the same housing unit (e.g., fraternities). This problem may also arise in time-series observations because an observation at time $t + 1$ will often be quite dependent on the value of observations at time t. A violation of this assumption will not affect the calculation of the regression coefficients but will affect the calculation of the standard errors of these coefficients, thus distorting your assessment of statistical significance.

Autocorrelation, the term for the violation of the independence-of-residuals assumption, occurs when the residuals of any two observations are correlated. The *Durbin-Watson statistic* tests for the presence of autocorrelation (also known as **serial correlation**). This statistic can vary between 0 and 4. Its size depends in part on the number of independent variables in the model and the number of observations. As a general rule of thumb, values less than 1 and greater than 3 are a cause for concern and possible corrective action on your part. These procedures will be examined in greater detail in Chapter 13.

● FULL MODEL SPECIFICATION

Regression equations also assume that you've included all the relevant explanatory variables in your model. Not doing so will produce regression coefficients that can be considerably misleading because you are not controlling for something that may be affecting the independent and dependent variables. Failing to include a variable for how hot the weather is will show a marked relationship between ice cream consumption and crime rates, for example. You can easily demonstrate the consequences of excluding relevant variables by comparing the results of two regression analyses that differ only in the exclusion of one variable known to be related to the dependent and independent variables.

One likely line of attack from opponents of your analysis is that some important variable(s) is (are) missing from your analysis (either because they weren't collected or because you failed to include them in your model). These opponents will argue that the results you find for any particular variable are incorrect (assuming, of course, that the excluded variables are related to both the dependent and the independent variables in your analysis). If the variables were not measured in the first place, this type of argument cannot be supported or rejected, but it can cast doubt in some people's minds about your analysis. Such a critique was used in rejecting the first article I sought to have published from my PhD dissertation. I've resented full-model specifications ever since.

Do not, however, envision your goal as selecting the set of independent variables that explain the most variance in your dependent variable. This is a trap that one can fall into when requesting a giant correlation matrix of all variables in your file and cherry picking the ones with the highest bivariate correlations with your dependent variable. Statisticians argue that such a strategy will increase the probabilities of rejecting the null hypothesis when you should not. More important, in my opinion, such a mechanical approach will exclude variables that it is important to know have no or little effect on outcomes of interest to you or your client. There is often an important story to be told in the discovery of factors that you and many others believe to be related to your dependent variable but that turn out not to be. You will miss this story if you look only for variables that are highly related to your dependent variables.

AN EXAMPLE OF REGRESSION DIAGNOSTICS •

Let's return to a slightly different regression equation from the one we requested in the previous chapter, while calling on SPSS to provide its diagnostics of the assumptions on which regression rests. I will repeat the steps we executed in the previous chapter but add commands to request these diagnostic tools.

Step 1: Open the Texas Indicator System data set, and click Analyze/Regression/Linear.

Step 2: Move the continuous version of districts' test scores ("Grades 3–11 All Tests Taken") into the Dependent: box.

Step 3: Move the following four independent variables into the Independent: box:

Percentage of economically disadvantaged students
Average years of teachers' experience
2005 per pupil instructional expenditures
Teacher turnover rates

Step 4: Make sure that Enter is selected for Method. This calls on SPSS to enter all the independent variables simultaneously, otherwise known as standard multiple regression.

Step 5: Click on Statistics, and select all except "Covariance Matrix."

In the Residuals section, select "Casewise diagnostics" and "Outliers outside 3 standard deviations." Click Continue.

Step 6: Click on the Plots button. Move ZRESID into the Y box. Move ZPRED into the X box.

Select the "Normal probability plot" option in the Standardized Residual Plots section. Click Continue.

Step 7: Click on the Save button. Check "Standardized" in the Predicted Values section. Check "Standardized" in the Residuals section. Check "Mahalanobis," "Leverage values," and "Cook's" in the Distances section, which will identify the multivariate outliers. Click Continue and OK.

Let's focus below on that part of this new output that diagnoses possible departures from regression assumptions.

Model Summary[b]

Model	R	R Square	Adjusted R Square	Std. Error of the Estimate	Change Statistics				Durbin-Watson
					e	df1	df2	Sig. F Change	
1	.634[a]	.402	.396	13.066	'2	4	402	.000	1.869

a. Predictors: (Constant), Teacher Turnover Rate, District 2005 Expend on Instruction Per Pupil, Economically Disadvantaged Students, Percent, Aver Yrs Experience of Teachers

b. Dependent Variable: Grades 3-11 All Tests Taken 2006

The model summary table above reports the Durbin-Watson statistic, which provides a test for the assumption of independent residuals. It is fairly close to 2.0, which we will report in a technical summary of our analysis, concluding that we found no evidence for autocorrelation. The range of values for this statistic that indicates no multicollinearity for $n = 100$ and $k = 5$ (the highest values available in Berman, 2007, p. 292) is 1.78 to 2.22, within which 1.86 falls.

Coefficients[a]

Model		Unstandardized Coefficients		Standardized Coefficients	t	Sig.
		B	Std. Error	Beta		
1	(Constant)	76.065	4.143		18.360	.000
	Economically Disadvantaged Students, Percent	-.307	.033	-.387	-9.334	.000
	District 2005 Expend on Instruction Per Pupil	.002	.001	.122	2.914	.004
	Aver Yrs Experience of Teachers	.274	.243	.060	1.128	.260
	Teacher Turnover Rate	-.345	.053	-.331	-6.481	.000

a. Dependent Variable: Grades 3-11 All Tests Taken 2006

Collinearity Statistics	
Tolerance	VIF
.863	1.158
.855	1.170
.532	1.880
.569	1.757

The Coefficients table above also provides evidence—in the tolerance and VIF statistics—that our four independent variables are not so strongly related to one another as to raise the red flag of multicollinearity. Recall that we look to see if the VIF is greater than 10 and the tolerance less than .10 as an indication of multicollinearity. Again, report one of these statistics and the guideline for its interpretation in a technical report or footnote, and move on if your results are similar to those here.

If the tolerance and VIF values are not within acceptable ranges, consider creating index variables by combining highly related independent variables. Recall from Chapter 4 that you can assess whether any highly correlated variables "hang together" by reaching into your statistical tool box for Cronbach's alpha. If the calculated alpha for any such variables is .70 or above, which is the minimal but acceptable level of the internal reliability recommended for such indexes, create an index of them and then rerun the prior analysis, again reporting in a footnote or technical report why and how you calculated the index.

The Casewise Diagnostics table (below) lists the case numbers for those observations whose standardized multivariate residuals are above 3.0 or below −3.0. You will observe eight of these observations. These cases might be considered multivariate outliers and may have an undue influence on the regression results, which we will assess shortly.

Casewise Diagnostics[a]

Case Number	Std. Residual	Grades 3-11 All Tests Taken 2006	Predicted Value	Residual
33	3.248	81	38.57	42.433
97	4.861	84	20.49	63.512
169	3.048	81	41.18	39.822
171	4.377	90	32.81	57.187
178	3.292	74	30.98	43.016
336	-3.611	22	69.17	-47.174
346	-4.350	15	71.83	-56.832
388	-3.218	19	61.04	-42.041

a. Dependent Variable: Grades 3-11 All Tests Taken 2006

These cases, however, may have substantive implications. Consider Case 97, for example, which is the second from the top. The absolute value of its residual is the largest in the entire set of 10 cases. What is interesting about this case substantively?

The predicted value (fourth column) for Case 97 shows that given knowledge of that district's teacher turnover rate, instructional expenditures per pupil, average years of teachers' experience, and economic status of students, our regression equation would have predicted that only 20.5% of that district's students passed the state's standardized tests. On the contrary, 84% of its students passed these tests. Incredible!

What we don't know without further investigation is whether the reported performance of this district's students is a function of a reporting error, cheating, or something special about the district (e.g., one highly specialized magnet school for smart, poor kids) or the result of outstanding performance that needs to be better understood in the hope of exporting its lessons to other districts. We take far too little advantage of this type of analysis, that is, using multivariate statistics to identify a handful of exceptional cases in order to examine them in sufficient depth as to provide clues about how we might better understand and—if found valid— replicate their success elsewhere.

The other side of the coin represents those districts that fell below −3.0 standardized residuals below the mean. The worst culprit here is Case 346. Instead of 71.8% of its students passing the tests (as we would have predicted from that district's values on our four independent variables), only 15% did. "Why such underachievers?" you might ask in a more detailed examination of that district.

Now, statistical geeks are often less worried about the substantive potential of these residuals than by the fact that outliers such as these 10 districts can distort or bias regression coefficients and tests of statistical significance. There are three diagnostic statistics to examine whether any of these outliers degrade our regression results:

Mahalanobis distance: Any case with a value in excess of 25 in a sample of 500 or more or 15 in samples of less than 100 presents an undue (bad) effect on the regression results.

Cook's distance: Any case with a value greater than 1 may be influencing the regression mode.

Centered leverage value: Values greater than three times the average of this value may be unruly influencers.

Residuals Statistics[a]

	Minimum	Maximum	Mean	Std. Deviation	N
Predicted Value	18.92	91.67	62.92	10.648	408
Std. Predicted Value	-4.128	2.692	-.004	.998	408
Standard Error of Predicted Value	.666	4.066	1.328	.562	408
Adjusted Predicted Value	15.76	91.61	62.96	10.676	407
Residual	-56.832	63.512	.064	12.715	407
Std. Residual	-4.350	4.861	.005	.973	407
Stud. Residual	-4.403	5.039	.005	.985	407
Deleted Residual	-58.227	68.242	.064	13.034	407
Stud. Deleted Residual	-4.507	5.199	.005	.994	407
Mahal. Distance	.058	38.322	3.947	4.975	408
Cook's Distance	.000	.378	.005	.023	407
Centered Leverage Value	.000	.094	.010	.012	408

a. Dependent Variable: Grades 3-11 All Tests Taken 2006

The summary table above suggests that at least one case violates each of the guidelines for Mahalanobis distance and centered leverage value. To find these cases requires you to go to the actual values that each case was assigned on these statistics, which you saved in the steps above and which now appear as new variables at the bottom of your list of variables in SPSS's Variable View screen.

There are many ways in which to do this. Here's one:

Select only those eight cases whose saved standardized residuals are greater than 3.0 or less than −3.0, and then generate a report that lists those cases and their values on these two statistics.

Step 1: Click Data/Select Cases/If.

Step 2: Turn on "If condition is satisfied," and click on the If button.

Step 3: In the blank variable dialog box, type "ZRE_1 ≤ −3.0 OR ZRE_1 ≥ 3.0." Click Continue and OK.

Now you have only eight cases (with extreme values for their standardized residuals) available for further inspection. To list which school districts violate either the Mahalanobis distance or the centered leverage value rules of thumb, do the following:

Step 1: Click Analyze/Reports/Case Summaries.

Step 2: Move the three statistics that now appear as new variables toward the bottom of your Variable View screen into the Variables: list. Move the district ID number into the Grouping Variables box (not shown below), and click OK.

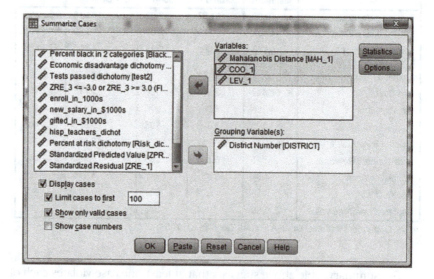

Inspecting the results of the Case Summaries request, we can see that one case exceeds the recommended threshold value for the Mahalanobis distance (i.e., 25) and three cases exceed the threshold value for the centered leverage value (3 × 0.01 = 0.03). But only one case exceeds these values for both statistics, District 57809. You may want to examine this district in more detail and, depending on that examination, exclude this district from your analysis, although it is very unlikely that a single case among more than 400 will affect the results dramatically. You might try it and see if it does. If not, you may want to leave the district in any analysis you report and save the juicy results of your investigation into outliers for a footnote or technical appendix.

Case Summaries[a]

			Mahalanobis Distance	Cook's Distance	Centered Leverage Value
District Number	15826	1	21.65066	.13199	.05333
		Total N	1	1	1
	57809	1	27.14344	.37817	.06686
		Total N	1	1	1
	101813	1	8.23750	.04425	.02029
		Total N	1	1	1
	101823	1	14.11972	.15390	.03478
		Total N	1	1	1
	101853	1	11.78812	.07278	.02903
		Total N	1	1	1
	212802	1	4.17506	.03408	.01028
		Total N	1	1	1
	220806	1	8.72656	.09514	.02149
		Total N	1	1	1
	233801	1	9.36834	.05568	.02307
		Total N	1	1	1
	Total	N	8	8	8

a. Limited to first 100 cases.

As noted above, we can see whether our regression equation is multi-variate normal by inspecting both the normal P-P plot and the scatterplot of standardized residuals and standardized predicted values, which are displayed below:

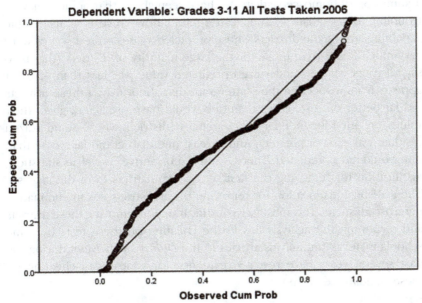

Normal P-P Plot of Regression Standardized Residual

Dependent Variable: Grades 3-11 All Tests Taken 2006

Both of these graphical diagnostic tools suggest departures from some assumptions. We might have suspected this possibility of trouble with the normality assumption in the inspection of the univariate statistics and the K-S test for the five variables in our equation. Only the "percentage of economically disadvantaged students in districts" variable behaves normally.

You could seek to transform all these variables and check (through descriptive statistics, histograms, and the one-sample K-S test) whether the newly transformed variables more closely approximate a normal distribution.

If not, fall back on your untransformed variables and proceed. If the transformed variables are "better behaved," run parallel analyses with untransformed and transformed variables, and determine whether your substantive conclusions differ between the two sets of analyses.

If not, return to your untransformed variable analysis, which you will use in your written and oral presentations, with due note of the fact that you transformed the variables to achieve more normal distributions but the results do not differ substantively from the ones you are reporting.

If you uncover different results, you can interpret these transformed variables, which may introduce a level of complexity that is unnecessary given the central limit theorem's help. The theorem proves theoretically (and simulations have demonstrated empirically) that the sample distributions of such variables will be normally distributed when the number of observations is above, say, 100. It's this hypothetical distribution on which we rely for determining confidence intervals and levels of statistical significance.

The scattergram above also suggests that our file violates the assumption of homoscedasticity. We have seen above that outliers may be troubling our statistics. The scattergram above reveals considerable variability among the districts whose predicted values on test scores were very much lower than those for the large majority of districts (that is to say, districts whose standardized predicted value was less than −2.0). It appears from inspecting the scattergram that about five of these districts did far better on test scores than one would have predicted, given their values on our four independent variables (districts whose standardized residual was +2.0 or greater). And at least one district did far worse than one would have predicted. There is some substantive, as well as statistical, justification for removing the first set of five districts from the analysis. The statistical justification for removing these districts lies in eliminating heteroscedasticity. The substantive justification for removing these districts and rerunning the analysis lies in the cheating on these tests by some schools in Texas (numerous articles in the *Dallas Daily News* during the past several years have revealed evidence for widespread cheating on these standardized tests).

CONCLUSION ●

As we saw in the previous chapter, regression is an all-purpose tool, capable of being used in a variety of circumstances to answer a variety of different questions. The small price you (or other analysts) should pay for this versatility is the careful attention you must devote to the assumptions on which regression is based. Fortunately, statistical software packages such as SPSS provide a host of diagnostics for assessing how closely your data approximate those assumptions and requirements.

There are a variety of statistical corrections that you can make to compensate for any detected assumption violations. But these too come at a price, the price of making your exposition of the results impenetrable, boring, and befuddling, particularly to the lay public. The general solution to this possible problem is severalfold:

- Make the appropriate transformations or corrections to the data.
- Rerun the analysis and the diagnostic tests as well.
- If the diagnostics show no improvement, inform the reader of the potential problem but return to the original data, which are usually easier to interpret.
- If the second set of diagnostics appears to overcome the violations, rerun the analysis.
- If the second set of analyses differs from the original, uncorrected data, report these results.
- If the second set of analyses does not differ from the original, uncorrected data, report the original results in the main report or memo to your audience but show and interpret the work you did in diagnosing and correcting the problems, even if to no substantive avail, in a technical report or appendix.

These steps will help persuade both lay and technical audiences that you are a careful carpenter who knows how to use your tools and materials appropriately. And you can look for evidence of use in others' work for the purpose of judging how well they've wielded their statistical tools. And try to work the word *outlier* into the next cocktail party you attend, making sure you distinguish it from Malcolm Gladwell's book of the same title.

To practice and reinforce the lessons of this and the prior chapter of the book, turn to Exercise 8 in the *Student Workbook* (available at http://www.sagepub.com/pearsonsp/).

CHAPTER 13

TIME-SERIES ANALYSIS, PROGRAM ASSESSMENT, AND FORECASTING

I t is common for public managers and nonprofit executives to collect observations over a period of time, be it in years, months, weeks, or days. Unemployment rates, welfare caseloads, ticket sales, tax revenues, and expenditures are all examples of data that can be recorded and stored as observations across time. Such data files require what is called time-series analysis.

Although there are several techniques for conducting time-series analysis, we will concentrate on regression-based techniques in this chapter. Such techniques can be used to forecast future values of an outcome variable, analyze the relationships among variables over time, and evaluate program interventions.

As with all regression analysis, however, the analytic power of regression-based time-series analysis comes at a price: careful attention to the assumptions on which these techniques are based. We ask the same kinds of questions we face with regression analysis of cross-sectional survey data. For example, Is the dependent variable continuous? Is/are the independent variable(s) continuous or dichotomous dummy variables? Are troublesome outliers present? Are the variables normally distributed? Is the spread of the residuals uniform across the range of predicted values on the dependent variable? Are the independent variables highly correlated with each other?

● TIMES-SERIES ANALYSIS PRESENTS UNIQUE ANALYTIC CHALLENGES

Time-series analysis, however, also presents additional concerns for the data analyst because of one or more of the following characteristics that typify time series:

- Observations in time often display strong *seasonal* or *cyclical patterns* that can dominate or mask any relationship that you want to estimate, any long-term trend you would like to understand, or any short- and long-term program effects that you would like to evaluate. Examples of such cyclical patterns include absences from work, which tend to be highest on Fridays of each week; farm incomes that are highest during the periods in which crops are harvested; and violent crimes that spike during summer months. Fortunately, there are techniques for removing short-term fluctuations or cyclical effects from time-series data through the creation of moving averages or through seasonal adjustments of the data.

- One observation in a time series is likely to be highly related to the observation before and after it. This phenomenon in a statistical sense is called autocorrelation or serial correlation. Its presence causes estimates of statistical significance to be exaggerated and makes the unsuspecting analyst conclude that the variables are statistically related to one another when they are in fact only spuriously related as a consequence of their joint relationship to the underlying, time-dependent processes.[1] Fortunately, there are steps that you as an analyst can take to test for autocorrelation and to remove it from your data.

- Programs or events that take place at a particular time may produce results only after a lapse of time. These effects may also be short-lived or, conversely, build momentum or reach a tipping point that generates multiplicative effects in the long run. In other words, the effects may not appear immediately after a program intervention or may not be monotonic or linear. Here again, techniques exist for detecting these conditions and for applying the appropriate adjustments through steps such as the use of lagged variables, taking the log of the dependent variable, or introducing new variables to assess program effects that are short, cumulative, or temporary.

Let's illustrate each of these special problems in time-series analysis, starting with the challenges presented by cyclical patterns.

DETECTING AND REMOVING ●
SEASONAL/CYCLICAL EFFECTS

Meier, Brudney, and Bohte (2009, pp. 365–368) provide a case of seasonal effects for us to examine (which I have modified here). A city's director of public works is troubled by his sanitation workers' absences from work. He knows that shorthanded crews do not work as efficiently as fully staffed crews and that it is difficult to forecast the need for and availability of substitute workers. He would prefer to minimize the use of substitute workers and short-staffed crews by reducing the number of absences among his full-time sanitation workers. He, therefore, creates an incentive program whereby unused sick leave at the end of each fiscal year can be "cashed in" as a bonus.

Obviously, the director of public works would like to know if his incentive program is achieving its objective. So he collects data on employee absences for 30 workdays after he announces the new incentive program. That is to say, he creates a time series with which to analyze the results of his program announcement.

These fictional data are included in the file "Sanitation Absenteeism," which you should open in SPSS to follow the steps below. Let's first display worker absences graphically.

Step 1: Click Graphs/Scatter/Dot.

Step 2: Select Simple Scatter (if not already selected), and click Define.

Step 3: Move the variable ABSENCES into the box for *Y*-axis and the variable DAY_NUMBER into the *X*-axis box. Click Continue and OK.

Step 4: Edit the chart in Chart Editor to draw a line connecting the observations, and show the data labels (to identify which days of the week are the spikes and troughs in the series) by clicking on one of the circles and selecting Elements and clicking on the Interpolation line (to connect the circles).

The resulting graph should look something like Figure 13.1. The numbers in the boxes next to each circle on the graph represent the day of the week (1 = *Monday*, 2 = *Tuesday*, etc.). We can see from this chart that most absences during this period occur on Fridays and Mondays of each week, while Wednesdays and Thursdays have the fewest absences. It is also the case that each cycle is defined by a week or five successive days. Absences on Monday are high, decline on each successive day to reach their lowest

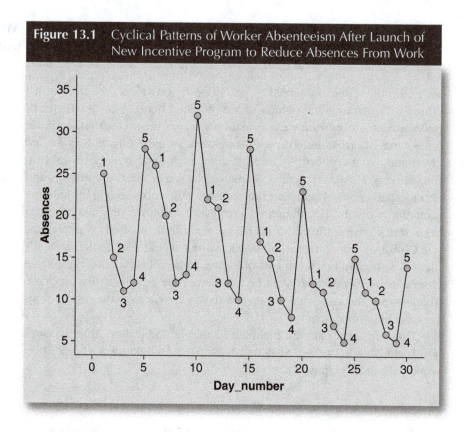

Figure 13.1 Cyclical Patterns of Worker Absenteeism After Launch of New Incentive Program to Reduce Absences From Work

point each Thursday, and then spike to the highest level each week on Friday, repeating a similar pattern each following week. It is somewhat difficult, however, to detect from the graph above whether the program announcement produced fewer employee absences. In fact, the absences at first appear to have grown during the first 2 weeks after the director's announcement.

You have at least two tactics available to you to make the effect of the new bonus program more visible.

Moving Averages/Smoothing

The first tactic is to remove the short-term cyclical effects in this pattern by calculating a moving average of observations that is equal in length to the number of observations that characterize each cycle—in this case, 5 days. In effect, you create a new variable from the average values of five adjacent observations, and you accomplish what is called "smoothing" the time series, thereby removing the short-term cyclical pattern.

Step 1: Click Transform/Create Time Series.

Step 2: Move the variable for which you would like to calculate a moving average (e.g., Absences) into the variable box, and select Centered Moving Average from the Difference drop-down list. In the case at hand, change the Span to 5. Rename the variable ABSENCES_MA. Click on the Change button. Click OK.

You can see this new variable in the Data View screen of the SPSS.sav file, which should look something like the following (without the bracket, which I've inserted and commented on below):

*sanitation absences v2_1.sav [DataSet2] – PASW Statistics Data Editor

File   Edit   View   Data   Transform   Analyze   Direct Marketing   Gr

	Week	Day	Absences	Day_number	Absences_ma
1	1	1	25	1	.
2	1	2	15	2	.
3	1	3	11	3	18.2
4	1	4	12	4	18.4
5	1	5	28	5	19.4
6	2	1	26	6	19.6
7	2	2	20	7	19.8
8	2	3	12	8	20.6

Note, as the bracket indicates, that the mean of the first 5 observations on ABSENCES becomes the first value of the third case (18.2). The mean of the next 5 observations appears as the moving average value for the fourth case (18.4).

Step 3: A scattergram of this new variable across time is shown in Figure 13.2.

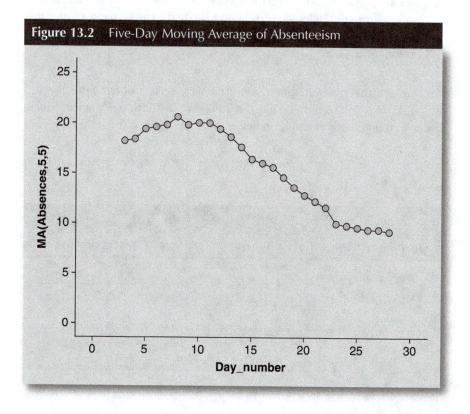

Figure 13.2   Five-Day Moving Average of Absenteeism

The visual display of a five-term moving average (Figure 13.2) strongly suggests that the new bonus incentive program cut the incidence of absenteeism after an initial period of about 2 weeks, when the program appeared to have no effect.

There is a problem, however, with this interpretation that is not uncommon in evaluating program effects through the use of time series. To wit, the data were collected from the point at which the new program was initiated. We know nothing about the pattern of absences before the program began. What, for example, would you conclude if the data displayed the pattern shown in Figure 13.3?

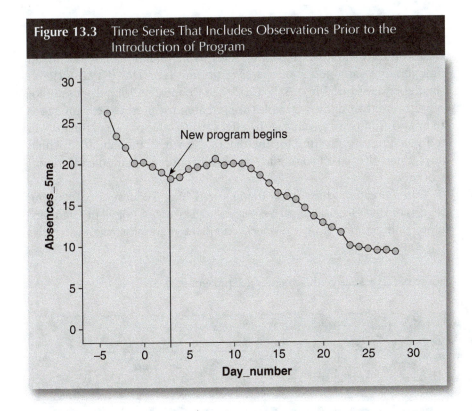

Figure 13.3 Time Series That Includes Observations Prior to the Introduction of Program

You might say that the new program actually slowed a longer-term decline in absences for nearly 2 weeks, after which the decline in absences continued at its preprogram pace. The short and sweet lesson of this illustration is that you can be much more confident about your conclusions if you collect data prior to a program or policy intervention. We will return to this type of "interrupted time-series analysis" later in the chapter.

Regression Controls for the Short-Term Cyclical Effects

A second tactic for assessing the effects of a program produces more precise estimates of how much of an effect the bonus program had, while providing us with the diagnostics tools useful in knowing whether these regression estimates are biased or inflated. This tactic does not smooth the data to eliminate short-term cycles. Instead, it uses all the data available by controlling for the short-term cyclical effects reflected, in this case, by the days of the week.

In this latter regard, you create four dummy variables from the indicator for the day of the week (Monday, Tuesday, etc.) and enter these dummy variables into the regression equation along with an independent variable for the passage of time (i.e., DAY_NUMBER) and the dependent variable, ABSENCES. (See Chapter 11 for a discussion of how to create dummy variables for a categorical variable with more than two nonmissing values.) In effect, the equation we estimate will tell you, after controlling for the day of the week, the extent to which days since the passage of time affect absenteeism among sanitation workers.

After creating these new dummy variables, request the following regression analysis, using Analyze/Regression/Linear. Ask for all the statistics, plots, and options from the more complete regression analysis in the previous chapter.

Some of the results of this analysis are presented below.

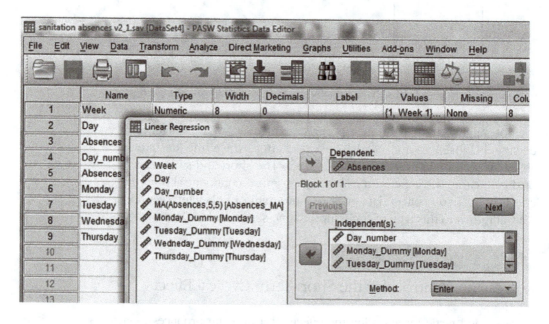

By inspecting the correlation table (not shown here), we can feel confident that our model is not troubled by multicollinearity. No relationship among the independent variables exceeds an absolute value of .25. (Remember that our rule-of-thumb standard here is |.70|.) The collinearity statistics in the Coefficients table (tolerance and VIF [variance inflation factor]) are also well within their recommended limits, further supporting the conclusion that our model has not violated this assumption.

Not surprisingly, the model appears not to be troubled by univariate outliers. While the histogram of the dependent variable is not perfectly bell-shaped, the mean and median are reasonably close together, and the kurtosis and skewness are relatively close to their respective standard errors, all suggesting the absence of troubling outliers and a fairly normal distribution. The residual statistics table (also not shown here) reveals Mahalanobis and Cook's distances and centered average values that are within suggested limits for outliers and normality (see Chapter 12 for a discussion of these guidelines).

Coefficients[a]

Model		Unstandardized Coefficients		Standardized Coefficients	t	Sig.	95.0% Confidence Interval for B	
		B	Std. Error	Beta			Lower Bound	Upper Bound
1	(Constant)	31.413	1.651		19.026	.000	28.006	34.821
	Day_number	-.462	.064	-.550	-7.243	.000	-.593	-.330
	Monday_Dummy	-6.347	1.740	-.350	-3.647	.001	-9.938	-2.755
	Tuesday_Dummy	-9.385	1.732	-.517	-5.419	.000	-12.960	-5.811
	Wednesday_Dummy	-14.590	1.726	-.803	-8.453	.000	-18.152	-11.028
	Thursday_Dummy	-14.962	1.723	-.824	-8.686	.000	-18.517	-11.407

a. Dependent Variable: Absences

In the partially reproduced Coefficients table above, we see that the unstandardized regression coefficient (*B*) for the passage of time (Day_number) is −.46 (Sig. = .000). In other words, absences declined by about one person every 2 days over the entire 30-day period. The dummy variables for days of the week also provide coefficients that indicate how many fewer (because of the negative coefficients) absences occurred each day of the week in comparison with the omitted day (Friday). This can be interpreted as the persistence of these "seasonal" effects even after the announcement. When controlling for the effects of the new program, we find six fewer absences on Mondays in comparison with Fridays, nine fewer absences on Tuesdays in comparison with Fridays, and so on.

Model Summary[b]

Model	R	R Square	Adjusted R Square	Std. Error of the Estimate	Durbin-Watson
1	.930[a]	.865	.837	2.981	1.254

a. Predictors: (Constant), Thursday_Dummy, Day_number, Wednesday_Dummy, Tuesday_Dummy, Monday_Dummy

b. Dependent Variable: Absences

The Model Summary table (above) shows that the combination of our independent variables explains about 84% of the variance in absenteeism (using the adjusted R^2 statistic).

Beware, however, that the Durbin-Watson statistic of 1.254 departs from our recommended value of 2.0. As you may recall, substantial departures (either more or less) from 2.0 may indicate the presence of auto- or serial correlation, which will exaggerate the explanatory prowess of the model's independent variables. Unfortunately, SPSS does not provide a test of the Durbin-Watson's statistical significance. To assess this requires you to consult a table of critical values, below or above which the presence of autocorrelation will be indicated. These critical values are determined by the number of observations (30 in this example) and the number of independent variables (5 in this example). Consulting a table for the Durbin-Watson distribution (Berman, 2007, p. 292) shows a lower critical value of 1.07 and an upper critical value of 1.83 for a p value of .05.

Plugging these values into the chart below from Berman (2007, p. 247) suggests that our value of 1.254 falls into that inconclusive lower region of 1.07 to 1.83.

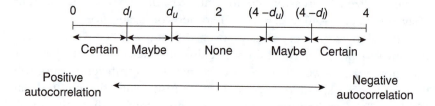

A plot of time against the equation's standardized residuals (Figure 13.4), which we saved as part of this regression analysis, shows a suspicious snakelike pattern, which is also indicative of autocorrelation. A conservative or prudent analyst would adjust the data to eliminate the autocorrelation, the steps for which we will turn to in the next example.

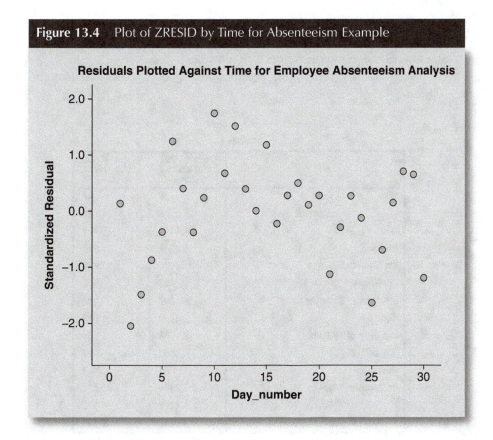

Figure 13.4 Plot of ZRESID by Time for Absenteeism Example

DETECTING AND CORRECTING FOR AUTOCORRELATION ●

The substantive question we're interested in answering in the following example is the extent to which the gross domestic product (GDP) in the United States between 1960 and 2006 affects the percentage of residents above the age of 16 who are defined as "out of the labor force" (i.e., people who are unemployed and *not* looking for work, sometimes referred to as "discouraged" workers). This data set is labeled "Welfare and Economics."

First, run some descriptive statistics on these two variables:

- GDP_in_trillions
- Percent_out_of_labor_force_plus16

Request a one-sample Kolmogorov-Smirnoff (K-S) statistic to formally test whether their distributions are normal. And plot each of these two variables over time, using the Scatter/Dot function.

Your summary descriptive statistics might look something like the following:

Statistics

		GDP in 2000 dollars in trillions	%_out_of_lab _force_16plu s
N	Valid	47	47
	Missing	0	0
Mean		6.1341	36.453
Median		5.4238	35.970
Std. Deviation		2.56808	3.0428
Skewness		.452	.363
Std. Error of Skewness		.347	.347
Kurtosis		-.938	-1.512
Std. Error of Kurtosis		.681	.681
Minimum		2.50	32.9
Maximum		11.32	41.3
Percentiles	25	3.8986	33.557
	50	5.4238	35.970
	75	8.0317	39.621

The mean percentage of U.S. residents (above the age of 16) who are not working and not looking for work is 36.5% during the period 1960 through 2006. The median is a nearby 36%. The lowest percentage out of the labor force is 32.9; the highest, 41.3. Skewness and kurtosis are fairly close to their respective standard errors, suggesting that our formal test of whether this variable is normally distributed will confirm our suspicions here that it is normally distributed.

The mean GDP (standardized to 2000 dollars) is $6.13 trillion over the course of these 47 years. GDP ranges from a low of $2.5 trillion to a high of $11.3 trillion. Kurtosis and skewness statistics relative to their standard errors appear to suggest a normally distributed variable. Ditto here for the likelihood of the K-S statistic confirming our suspicions of a normal distribution.

The one-sample K-S statistics indicates that neither of these distributions significantly departs from a theoretical normal distribution, as reflected in the table below:

One-Sample Kolmogorov-Smirnoff Test

		%_out_of_lab_force_16plus	GDP in 2000 dollars in trillions
N		47	47
Normal Parameters[a,b]	Mean	36.453	6.1341
	Std. Deviation	3.0428	2.56808
Most Extreme Differences	Absolute	.185	.120
	Positive	.185	.120
	Negative	-.127	-.079
Kolmogorov-Smirnoff Z		1.269	.820
Asymp. Sig. (2-tailed)		.080	.512

a. Test distribution is Normal.

b. Calculated from data.

It is, however, useful to see a picture of the levels of both of these variables over this period of time, which we can generate through the Graphs/Scatter/Dot command in which GDP and the percentage of U.S. residents out of the labor force are entered as dependent (*Y*-axis) variables and the variable for year is entered as the *X*-axis variable. Requesting each of these graphs (and editing them for presentation here) should produce something that looks like Figures 13.5 and 13.6.

Figure 13.5 Percentage of People Out of the U.S. Labor Force, 1960–2006

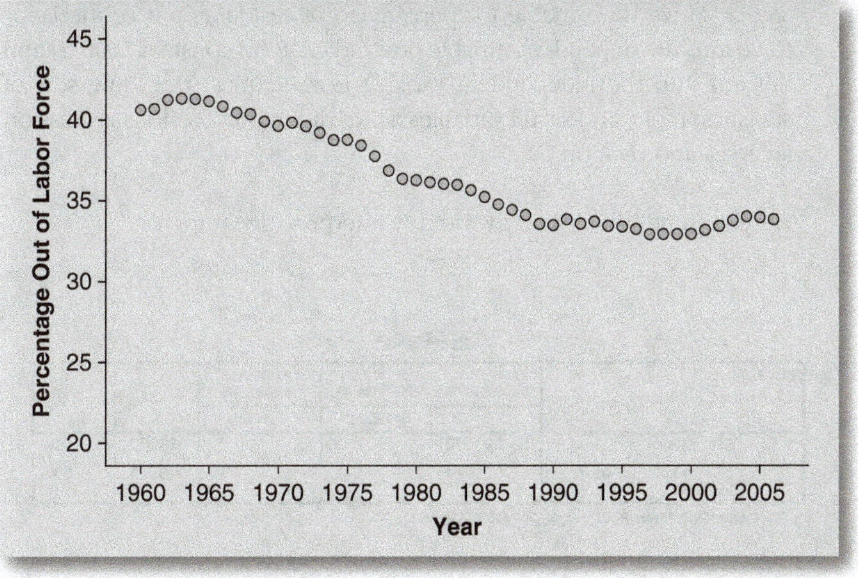

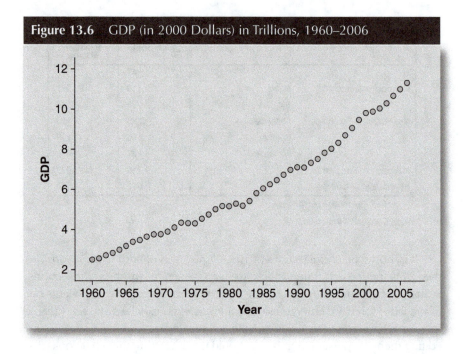

Figure 13.6 GDP (in 2000 Dollars) in Trillions, 1960–2006

Okay, let's examine the relationship between GDP and percentage of U.S. residents out of the labor force during this 47-year period by using regression analysis.

Step 1: Click on Analyze/Regression/Linear.

Step 2: Move the variable for percentage of residents out of the labor force into the dependent variable box and GDP (in constant 2000 trillion dollars) into the independent variable box. Request the same sets of statistics, plots, and saved variables as we did in our previous regression analysis, and click on OK.

Here is some of that output with my interpretative remarks:

Coefficients[a]

Model		Unstandardized Coefficients		Standardized Coefficients	t	Sig.
		B	Std. Error	Beta		
1	(Constant)	42.979	.516		83.273	.000
	GDP in 2000 dollars in trillions	-1.064	.078	-.898	-13.686	.000

a. Dependent Variable: %_out_of_lab_force_16plus

Ignore the constant. It has no meaningful interpretation in this example. The unstandardized coefficient for the effect of GDP on labor force participation is –1.06. That is to say, for each increase of $1 trillion in GDP, we see a corresponding decrease of a little more than 1 percentage point in U.S. residents out of the labor force.

Model Summary[b]

Model	R	R Square	Adjusted R Square	Std. Error of the Estimate	Durbin-Watson
1	.898[a]	.806	.802	1.3540	.051

a. Predictors: (Constant), GDP in 2000 dollars in trillions

b. Dependent Variable: %_out_of_lab_force_16plus

Levels of GDP explain about 80% of the variation in the percentage of U.S. residents who are out of the labor force. The Durbin-Watson statistic, however, is troublesome. If we were to look up the lower and upper critical values for this statistic at $p = .05$ for one independent variable and 47 observations, we'd find 1.49 and 1.58, respectively. Our 0.051 is well below the lower critical value, strongly suggesting the presence of autocorrelation.

The plot of standardized residuals over time in Figure 13.7 has a troublesome "snakelike" pattern that also suggests autocorrelation. (Note that we plot residuals against a measure of time. It's not a plot of standardized predicted values against standardized residuals as we've seen previously.)

But how do you correct for the autocorrelation that may be exaggerating the relationship between the GDP and labor force participation?

There are two widely used solutions to the problem of autocorrelation:

1. Introduce time as a variable in the time-series regression equation.

or

2. Use first-order differences between successive years on your independent and dependent variables.

This first tactic is predicated on the reasonable argument that you're removing the dependency of each year's observation on the previous year's observation by explicitly introducing time into the equation. (There is incidentally a two-step version of this, in which you regress your dependent

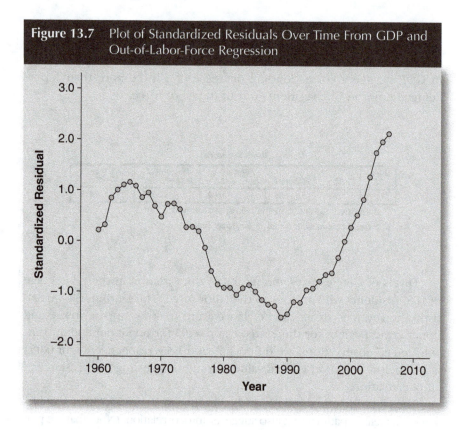

Figure 13.7 Plot of Standardized Residuals Over Time From GDP and Out-of-Labor-Force Regression

variable on a measure of time [e.g., year] and save the residuals for further analysis. Your residuals will have had the effects of Father Time removed from the series for further analysis.)

The second tactic employs first differences between successive observations in the time series (i.e., the observations I have for Time 3 is the difference between that variable at Time 3 and Time 2). This tactic is based on another reasonable presumption: If two variables are truly related to each other over time, then their increases or decreases from one time period to the next (e.g., the differences from one year to the next) should also be related.

Let's demonstrate how to take first differences and see if our conclusions differ from the prior analysis and if we can eliminate the pesky problem of autocorrelation.

Step 1: Click Transform/Create Time Series.

Step 2: Move both variables into the Variables box:, and make sure that the Function is "Difference" and the Order is "1." Click OK.

Step 3: Repeat the same regression analysis as above, using the first difference variables.

Part of your output should look something like the following:

Descriptive Statistics

	Mean	Std. Deviation	N
DIFF (Percent_out_of_labor_force_16plus,1)	-.148	.2899	46
DIFF(GDP_in_trillions,1)	.1917	.12023	46

On average, the percentage of residents out of the labor force declined by .15 each year during this 47-year period, while GDP increased each year by $0.19 trillion. Changes in GDP from one year to the next are only weakly related, however, to yearly changes in the percentage of residents out of the labor force, as the table below demonstrates.

Coefficients^a

Model		Unstandardized Coefficients		Standardized Coefficients	t	Sig.
		B	Std. Error	Beta		
1	(Constant)	-.089	.081		-1.089	.282
	DIFF(GDP_in_trillions,1)	-.309	.360	-.128	-.856	.397

a. Dependent Variable: DIFF(Percent_out_of_labor_force_16plus,1)

Substantively, an increase of GDP of $1 trillion in a single year (about five times the average yearly increase in GDP across this period of time) would be associated with a drop of about 1/3 of a percentage point in people out of the labor force. Another way to phrase this would be to say that an average yearly increase in GDP ($0.19 trillion) would result in a decline of 0.06 percentage point of people out of the labor force ($-0.309 \times 0.19 = 0.06$). Small, but better than nothing, you might conclude.

Model Summary[b]

Model	R	R Square	Adjusted R Square	Std. Error of the Estimate	Durbin-Watson
1	.128[a]	.016	-.006	.2908	.933

a. Predictors: (Constant), DIFF(GDP_in_trillions,1)

b. Dependent Variable: DIFF(Percent_out_of_labor_force_16plus,1)

Our model summary is no more impressive in terms of effect sizes. Year-to-year differences in GDP explain less than 2% of the variation in year-to-year changes in the percentage of people out of the labor force. A table of critical values for the Durbin-Watson statistic with one independent variable and 46 observations shows lower and upper values of 1.48 and 1.57, respectively, which suggests that our first-order differencing failed to eliminate the problem of autocorrelation.[2] An alternative strategy would be to transform the variables by taking their log and rerunning the regression analysis. That task lies ahead for the adventurous and ambitious reader.

● EVALUATING PROGRAM INTERVENTIONS

As Berman (2007, pp. 249–252) writes, program interventions or policy changes can result in a number of different effects, all of which can be modeled in a regression analysis.

● *Pulse:* An effect that occurs only during a brief period of time, after which the outcome returns to levels prior to the intervention

● *Period:* An effect that lasts somewhat longer than a pulse effect but, like it, sees outcomes returning to pre-intervention levels

● *Step:* A lasting effect that changes the outcome variable to a new level, at which it remains for a considerable length of time

● *Increasing or cumulative:* A lasting effect that grows in impact with the passage of time

● *Lagged:* An effect that may take any of the forms above but that only appears after some period of time after the program or policy intervention begins

These effects can be illustrated as follows:

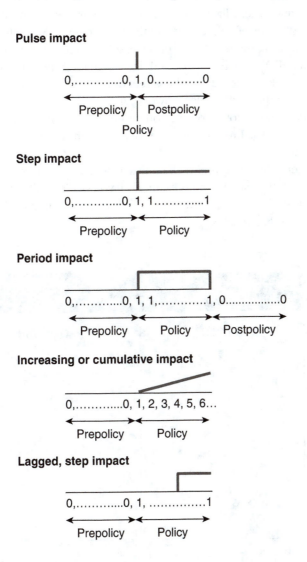

Pulse impact

0,.............0, 1, 0............0

Prepolicy | Postpolicy

Policy

Step impact

0,.............0, 1, 1..............1

Prepolicy | Policy

Period impact

0,.............0, 1, 1,.............1, 0................0

Prepolicy | Policy | Postpolicy

Increasing or cumulative impact

0,.............0, 1, 2, 3, 4, 5, 6...

Prepolicy | Policy

Lagged, step impact

0,.............0, 1, ...1

Prepolicy | Policy

Let's illustrate how we might model these effects in another example modified from Meier et al. (2009, pp. 427–428).

In this fictional story, Goose Pimple, Vermont, officials have noticed increasing petty lawlessness in town, as reflected in more illegal parking. They decide to hire a parking enforcement officer (PEO; previously known as a "meter maid") and expect that he will have an immediate, but lasting, effect (i.e., step effect) and a longer-term cumulative impact after he figures out where and when likely offenses are to occur (i.e., increasing effect). Unlike the director of public works in the first example, Springfield officials began monitoring the number of tickets issued 8 weeks prior to hiring and training the PEO. They then collected data on the number of tickets issued for the 8 weeks after he hit the streets and ask you, their analyst, to determine whether their policy is "working."

Your data can be found on the course Web site as the Excel file "Parking Tickets." First step: Import this Excel data file into SPSS, and save as an SPSS.SAV file.

Now, generate a graph of parking tickets across the 16 weeks for which you have data. (Consult previous examples if you don't recall how to request such a graph from SPSS.) After some editing, your graph should look something like Figure 13.8.

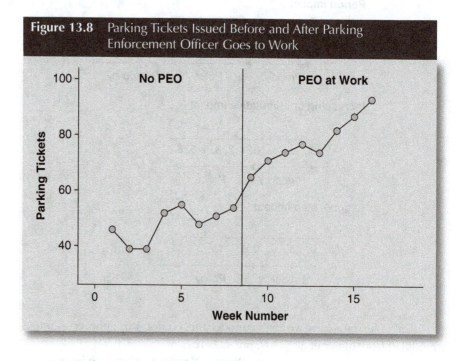

Figure 13.8   Parking Tickets Issued Before and After Parking Enforcement Officer Goes to Work

Notice in the Excel file (or SPSS Data View) how the two program effects being evaluated here (step and cumulative) are constructed below:

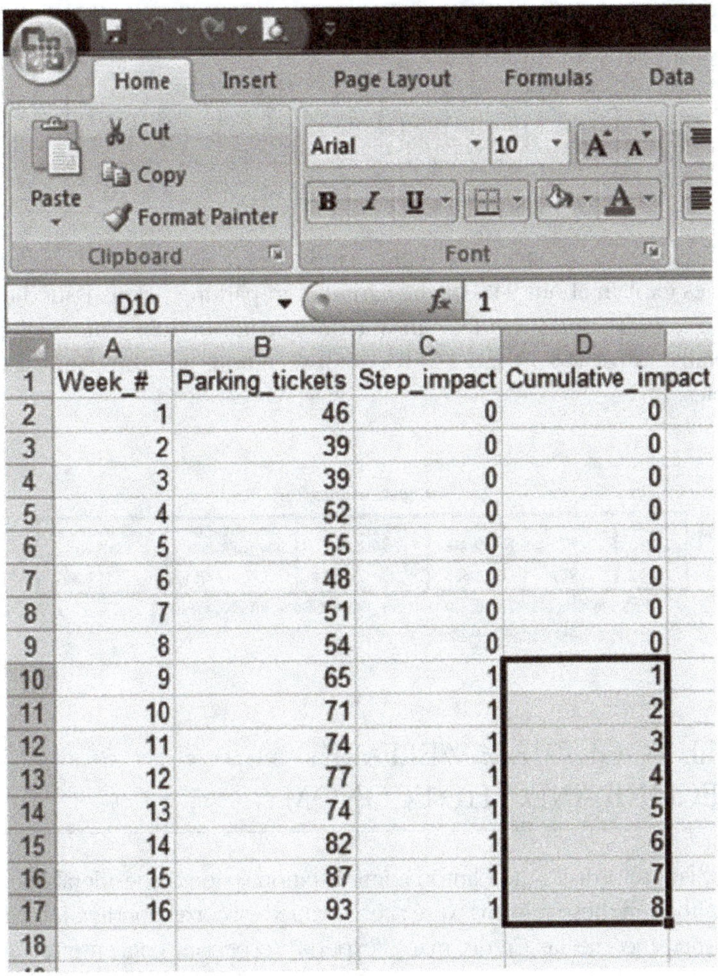

	D10		f_x	1
	A	B	C	D
1	Week_#	Parking_tickets	Step_impact	Cumulative_impact
2	1	46	0	0
3	2	39	0	0
4	3	39	0	0
5	4	52	0	0
6	5	55	0	0
7	6	48	0	0
8	7	51	0	0
9	8	54	0	0
10	9	65	1	1
11	10	71	1	2
12	11	74	1	3
13	12	77	1	4
14	13	74	1	5
15	14	82	1	6
16	15	87	1	7
17	16	93	1	8
18				

With Parking_tickets as the dependent variable, request SPSS to calculate the appropriate regression statistics, graphs, and diagnostics to assess the effects of hiring a PEO in contrast to the longer-term effects of the passage of time.

We can see from the Correlations table (not shown here) that we may have a problem with multicollinearity insofar as all independent variables are related to each other above the general guideline of [.70]. Fortunately, the formal tests for collinearity (tolerance and VIF) are within suggested limits (see far right of the Coefficients table). (Tolerances are not less than .10, and VIFs are not greater than 10.)

Coefficients[a]

Model		Unstandardized Coefficients		Standardized Coefficients	t	Sig.	Collinearity Statistics	
		B	Std. Error	Beta			Tolerance	VIF
1	(Constant)	40.179	3.157		12.728	.000		
	Week_#	1.738	.625	.482	2.780	.017	.124	8.095
	Step_impact	7.881	4.099	.237	1.923	.079	.244	4.095
	Cumulative_impact	1.798	.884	.300	2.033	.065	.171	5.857

a. Dependent Variable: Parking_tickets

The model summary table (below) indicates that our three independent variables explain about 94% of the variation in parking tickets issued during this 16-week period. The Durbin-Watson statistic of 1.853 falls within the acceptable range of 1.73 and 2.27 for 16 observations and three independent variables.

Model Summary[b]

Model	R	R Square	Adjusted R Square	Std. Error of the Estimate	Durbin-Watson
1	.977[a]	.955	.944	4.051	1.853

a. Predictors: (Constant), Cumulative_impact, Step_impact, Week_#

b. Dependent Variable: Parking_tickets

● PULLING IT ALL TOGETHER: WELFARE CASELOAD DECLINE AND THE ECONOMY

The welfare reforms of the Clinton administration sparked considerable controversy. Although these reforms were accompanied by corresponding increases in the Earned Income Tax Credit, many "experts" (especially concentrated among those who might be considered "liberal") predicted dire consequences for welfare recipients and their children. So strong were such sentiments that two highly placed and well-respected members of the Department of Health and Human Services resigned in protest, returning to their tenured university positions. Even those who believed that the reforms were necessary were soon surprised at how dramatic their apparent effects were in reducing welfare caseloads. As the Bush administration assumed the mantle of power in January 2001, welfare rolls were about half of what they had been prior to the reforms of 1996. Many people at that time, however, were unclear about the extent to which the welfare reforms produced these results or whether the booming economy of the late 1990s was the principal cause of this decline.

Time-series data exist through 2006 to provide an opportunity to answer that question. Such analysis, however, requires special attention to the pitfalls of time-series analysis, especially where serial correlation is likely to be present. Insofar as variables tend to increase (or decline) with time—often as a result of processes of inflation and population growth—time-series analysis will often appear to reveal strong relationships among these variables when in fact they are the spurious result of shared temporal processes.

Begin such an analysis with descriptive statistics and graphical displays of the principal dependent and prospective independent variables. The descriptive statistics suggest that our primary variables are normally distributed, but their histograms (not shown here) suggest that percentage of residents on welfare and percentage out of the labor force are bimodally distributed.

Statistics

		unempl_% _16plus	%_out_of_lab _force_16plus	GDP in 2000 dollars in trillions	Percent_ welfare_ recipients
N	Valid	47	47	47	47
	Missing	0	0	0	0
Mean		5.868	36.453	6.1341	3.7256
Median		5.600	35.970	5.4238	4.4713
Skewness		.703	.363	.452	-.416
Std. Error of Skewness		.347	.347	.347	.347
Kurtosis		.571	-1.512	-.938	-1.552
Std. Error of Kurtosis		.681	.681	.681	.681
Minimum		3.5	32.9	2.50	1.40
Maximum		9.7	41.3	11.32	5.47

A one-sample K-S test provides a more formal assessment of their normality. (Recall that the K-S statistic's null hypothesis is that the distributions are normally distributed, and we would hope not to reject that hypothesis.) The Sig. values for K-S indicate that our dependent variable is not normally distributed and comes close to declaring the same thing for percentage of residents out of the labor force.

One-Sample Kolmogorov-Smirnov Test

		unempl_% _16plus	%_out_of_lab _force_16plu s	GDP in 2000 dollars in trillions	Percent_ welfare_ recipients
N		47	47	47	47
Normal Parameters[a,b]	Mean	5.868	36.453	6.1341	3.7256
	Std. Deviation	1.4274	3.0428	2.56808	1.40660
Most Extreme Differences	Absolute	.116	.185	.120	.251
	Positive	.116	.185	.120	.141
	Negative	-.049	-.127	-.079	-.251
Kolmogorov-Smirnov Z		.797	1.269	.820	1.719
Asymp. Sig. (2-tailed)		.548	.080	.512	.005

a. Test distribution is Normal.

b. Calculated from data.

Let's pause here and see if any transformations of our dependent variable will help change its distribution. Although not shown here, taking the natural log, square root, square, and inverse of this variable does not produce a normally distributed variable. Mumble something about the central limit theorem, and plunge right ahead with the original dependent variable. Let's turn to something more aesthetically appealing: a graph (Figure 13.9).

Figure 13.9 is surely worth a thousand words (or at least the next 191). President Kennedy entered office with fewer than 2% of U.S. residents on welfare. When President Nixon assumed office 8 years later, the proportion had nearly doubled, thanks largely to President Johnson's Great Society programs. The rate of increase continued its steady climb until the first year of Nixon's second term in 1973. The percentages moved up and down somewhat thereafter, but within a relatively narrow band, until the beginning of a second wave of increases in 1990, which reached their historical peak in 1993, Bill Clinton's first year in office.

The vertical line in Figure 13.9 marks 1996, the year in which new welfare reform was enacted. This program replaced an emphasis on job training and education with an emphasis on "work first" and the clear message that welfare was to be limited to no more than 5 years of eligibility (although states had

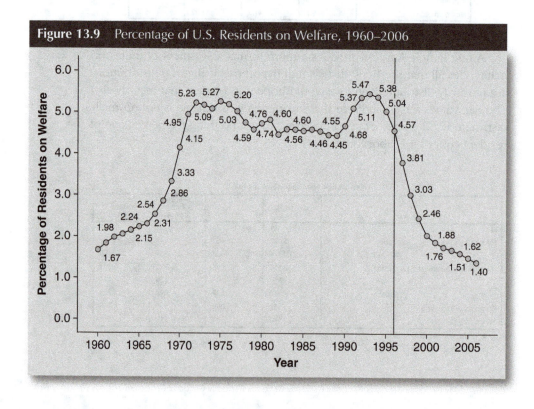

Figure 13.9 Percentage of U.S. Residents on Welfare, 1960–2006

some flexibility here). Interestingly, welfare rolls had already begun to decline prior to the enactment of the new law. But this is not an uncommon pattern as some states—permitted to depart from federal guidelines—adopt changes that are subsequently picked up by federal legislation that mandates other states to follow. And what was happening with the economy during this period of time?

Figure 13.10 displays several available, and commonly reported, economic indicators. It's hard to tell from eyeballing these two charts, however, just what the effects of economics on welfare use might be. Let's turn to regression analysis for that answer.

We are interested here in estimating both the step and the cumulative effects of welfare reform (when controlling for economic conditions). You will first have to create two new variables for these two types of program effects. Also, create a variable to represent time trends—that is, a variable with values 1, 2, 3, 4, 5, 6, and so on for each year in the file.

After creating these three new variables, I entered them into a regression analysis with percentage of residents on welfare as my dependent variable

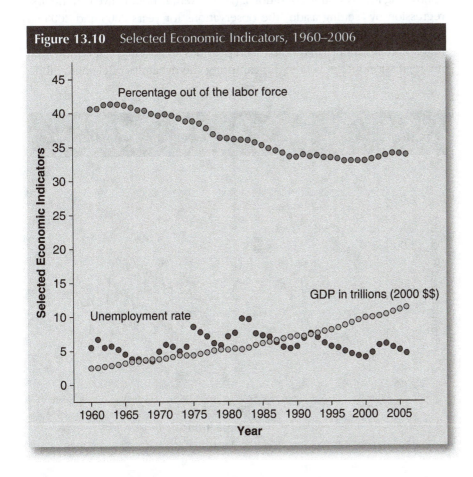

Figure 13.10 Selected Economic Indicators, 1960–2006

and the three new variables, as well as the unemployment rate, GDP in constant 2000 trillions of dollars, and the percentage of residents over 16 who were considered out of the labor force (i.e., those people out of work and not looking for a job). It would be easy to jump into an interpretation of the correlation and regression coefficients, but that would be unwise given the statistical challenges that time-series data present for regression.

Indeed, the Durbin-Watson statistic for this regression equation is 0.420, which is far below the acceptable lower critical value of 1.26 for $n = 47$ and $k = 6$. Our somewhat snakelike plot (Figure 13.11) of standardized residuals against time is an equally troublesome indication of autocorrelation. Our VIF statistics are beyond the acceptable limits for all but the step-impact and unemployment variables. We appear not to have any multivariate outliers. And our probability-probability (P-P) plot (not shown here) isn't too bad for our normality assumptions, but that's the least of our troubles here.

We've got to conduct some major surgery on these variables if we are to produce a believable story about the effects of the welfare reforms when controlling for economic conditions. (By the way, I should have run the first regression by "setting aside" the observations for years 2005 and 2006 so that I can later compare these levels with those predicted from my regression equation. This comparison provides an informal test of how well my regression model is doing in capturing the dynamics of change. I'll do

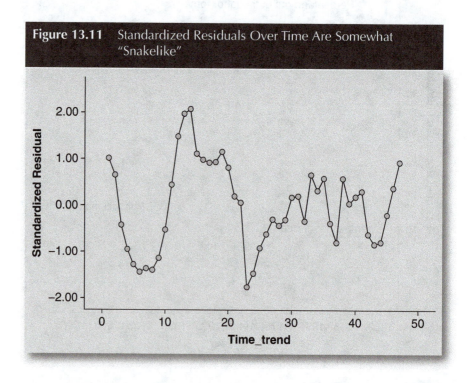

Figure 13.11   Standardized Residuals Over Time Are Somewhat "Snakelike"

that in the analysis from this point forward and demonstrate later what those comparisons are.)

One tactic to correct for autocorrelation is to take first differences of your measures. A second tactic is to use weighted least squares techniques, but let's see if we can eliminate the pesky problem of autocorrelation through first differencing our substantive measures (we'll leave the policy impact variables and time trend alone).

Step 1: Click Transform/Create Time Series.

Step 2: Move the dependent variable and the three economic variables into the Variables box:, and make sure that the Function is "Difference" and the Order is "1."

Step 3: Repeat the same regression analysis as above.

SPSS doesn't enable you to request a plot of standardized residuals against time, so you have to save these residuals from the regression analysis and request a separate scatterdot, an edited version of which is presented in Figure 13.12.

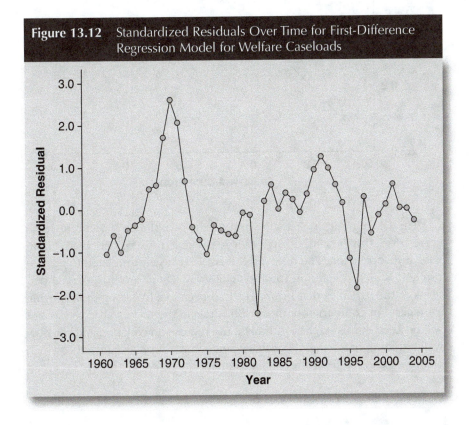

Figure 13.12 Standardized Residuals Over Time for First-Difference Regression Model for Welfare Caseloads

The graph fails to reveal the snakelike pattern that would be indicative of heteroscedasticity and nonlinearity. No residual exceeds ±3.0, so multivariate outliers are also not present. Tolerance statistics are well within standards to rule out multicollinearity. The P-P plot is similarly reassuring in this regard.

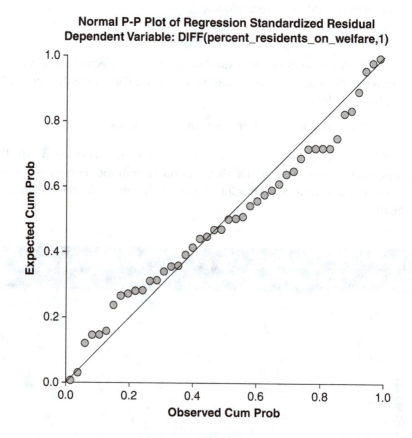

Normal P-P Plot of Regression Standardized Residual
Dependent Variable: DIFF(percent_residents_on_welfare,1)

The Durbin-Watson statistic improves but continues to indicate serial correlation. I can't think of any other reasonable transformations to elimi-nate autocorrelation. The time trend variable is largely unrelated to welfare use and is incorporated in the model anyway. There are no seasonal pat-terns to the variables that I can detect and remove by taking their moving averages. I'm going to note these difficulties in the technical appendix but will proceed at this stage to formulate the regression equation and see how well it does in predicting the welfare percentages for 2005 and 2006, which we have excluded from the model estimation below.

Model Summary[b]

Model	R	R Square	Adjusted R Square	Std. Error of the Estimate	Durbin-Watson
1	.771[a]	.594	.529	.22448	.820

a. Predictors: (Constant), Cumulative_fct, DIFF(Percent_unempl__16plus,1), DIFF(Percent_out_of_labor_force_16plus,1), Time, DIFF(GDP_in_trillions,1), Step_function

b. Dependent Variable: DIFF(Percent_welfare_recipients,1)

The step-function variable appears to make a substantial contribution to year-to-year differences in the percentage of U.S. residents on welfare. I would predict a decline of 0.84% in welfare use from one year to the next after passage of the legislation in 1996 when controlling for all other variables. The cumulative impact is surprisingly positive, with year-to-year change in welfare use when controlling for other factors. This is a rare instance in which a zero-order relationship changes signs when controlling for other variables in the equation, as you can see in the correlation column comparison with partial correlations. This suggests a longer-term, largely suppressed, tendency for welfare use to increase a small, but increasing, amount each year after passage. It's an odd finding to be sure and may be the result of the very high correlation between the step- and cumulative-function variables ($r = .86$). This level of multicollinearity can cause signs to flip and is very likely an artifact of this statistical problem rather than some quirky, inexplicable substantive result.

Coefficients[a]

Model		Unstandardized Coefficients		Standardized Coefficients	t	Sig.	Collinearity Statistics	
		B	Std. Error	Beta			Tolerance	VIF
1	(Constant)	.258	.104		2.479	.018		
	Time	-.010	.004	-.399	-2.458	.019	.397	2.517
	Step_function	-.794	.186	-1.033	-4.269	.000	.178	5.608
	Cumulative_fct	.092	.025	.765	3.657	.001	.239	4.189
	DIFF (Percent_out_of_labor_force_16plus,1)	.249	.133	.225	1.874	.068	.724	1.382
	DIFF(Percent_unempl__16plus,1)	.106	.069	.301	1.553	.128	.277	3.605
	DIFF(GDP_in_trillions,1)	.369	.619	.138	.596	.555	.194	5.164

a. Dependent Variable: DIFF(Percent_welfare_recipients,1)

This finding may also suggest that we exclude the cumulative function from the analysis and stick with an estimate of just the step impact. Large changes in sign or counterintuitive findings often call for such an adjustment in our statistics. The following analysis includes the cumulative-impact variable. (I could have compared these results with an analysis in which the cumulative effect variable is excluded to see, for example, whether the predictions improve. If they do, it would be justifiable to exclude the cumulative effect from the regression equation and recalculate our predicted values for the dependent variable.)

Year-to-year changes in unemployment rates and the percentage of discouraged workers has an understandable impact on year-to-year changes in the percentage of residents on welfare.

Year-to-year changes in GDP also has a counterintuitive interpretation, although it is far from statistically significant and moves from an intuitive negative correlation as a zero-order correlation to a negligible but positive partial correlation.

Beware that the first differences will require some careful application when using these variables to predict future values. They are predicted values in light of the prior year's value, so we'll have to take that into account, as we do below.

The predictive regression equation is as follows:

$$\hat{Y}_{\text{diff 2005}} = 0.25 - 0.84(\text{Step impact}) + 0.11(\text{Cum. impact}) - 0.01(\text{Time trend}) + 0.11(\text{Unemployment}_{\text{diff}}) + 0.23(\text{Out of lab force}_{\text{diff}}) + 0.38(\text{GDP}_{\text{diff}}).$$

Plugging in the values for each of these variables (remember to use the first difference values in 2005 for the unemployment rates and percentage out of the labor force variables), we arrive at the following values:

$$\hat{Y}_{\text{diff 2005}} = 0.25 - 0.84(1) + 0.11(8) - 0.01(45) + 0.11(-0.4) + 0.23(-0.10) + 0.38(0.33) = -0.49$$

Also remember that our dependent variable is a first difference. To find our predicted level of residents on welfare requires us to subtract 0.49 from the percentage of residents on welfare in 2004 (1.62). Our predicted value for the 2005 percentage of residents on welfare is, therefore, 1.13.

Our equation for the predicted value of the percentage of residents on welfare in 2006 can be expressed by the following equation:

$$\hat{Y}_{\text{diff 2006}} = 0.25 - 0.84(1) + 0.11(9) - 0.01(46) + 0.11(-0.5) + 0.23(-0.10) + 0.38(0.32) = -0.51.$$

Our predicted value for the 2006 percentage of residents on welfare is 1.51 − 0.51 = 1.0%. These predictions compare with the actual percentages of 1.51 and 1.40. Our model "overshoots" its mark in predicting more rapid declines in welfare use than were actually realized. We may be observing what are called "floor effects," where it becomes increasingly difficult to move toward 0% (similarly, there are "ceiling effects," which make most outcomes difficult to achieve 100%).

To complete the next stage of the analysis, we will include the 2005 and 2006 data and reestimate a regression equation so that we can predict levels of welfare use in 2007, 2008, and 2009, assuming a yearly decline of 3% in the three economic indicators that are included in the regression analysis. We might want to use an Excel spreadsheet for this purpose. But first, the new regression estimates (using first differences for the dependent and economic variables). The coefficients table is reproduced below:

Year	Time	Step Impact	Cumulative	Unempl'mt	Unempl_Diff	Out_of_Labor	Out_Diff	GDP	GDP_Diff	Predicted_Y
2006	47	1	10	4.60	-0.50	33.80	-0.13	11.32	0.32	1.40
2007	48	1	11	4.74	0.14	34.81	1.01	10.98	-0.34	1.29
2008	49	1	12	4.88	0.14	35.86	1.04	10.65	-0.33	1.08
2009	50	1	13	5.03	0.15	36.93	1.08	10.33	-0.32	0.79

Here's a comparison of the new regression equation (with 2 more observations) with the prior equation:

New:

$$\hat{Y}_{diff} = 0.25 - 0.79(\text{Step impact}) + 0.09(\text{Cum. impact}) - 0.01(\text{Time trend}) + 0.11(\text{Unemployment}_{diff}) + 0.25(\text{Out of lab force}_{diff}) + 0.37(\text{GDP}_{diff}).$$

Old:

$$\hat{Y}_{diff2005} = 0.25 - 0.84(\text{Step impact}) + 0.11(\text{Cum. impact}) - 0.01(\text{Time trend}) + 0.11(\text{Unemployment}_{diff}) + 0.23(\text{Out of lab force}_{diff}) + 0.38(\text{GDP}_{diff}).$$

The differences between the two equations are rather small. Using the newest model and predicting yearly "declines" in our economic measures of 3% (i.e., the country would be "worse off" on each of the three measures) would produce the following predictions for the percentage of residents on welfare:

Coefficients[a]

Model		Unstandardized Coefficients		Standardized Coefficients	t	Sig.	Collinearity Statistics	
		B	Std. Error	Beta			Tolerance	VIF
1	(Constant)	.258	.104		2.479	.018		
	Time	-.010	.004	-.399	-2.458	.019	.397	2.517
	Step_function	-.794	.186	-1.033	-4.269	.000	.178	5.608
	Cumulative_fct	.092	.025	.765	3.657	.001	.239	4.189
	DIFF (Percent_out_of_labor_force_16plus,1)	.249	.133	.225	1.874	.068	.724	1.382
	DIFF(Percent_unempl_16plus,1)	.106	.069	.301	1.553	.128	.277	3.605
	DIFF(GDP_in_trillions,1)	.369	.619	.138	.596	.555	.194	5.164

a. Dependent Variable: DIFF(Percent_welfare_recipients,1)

Graphically, this continuation of welfare caseload declines would look something like Figure 13.13.

Finally, what would have happened in a "It's a Wonderful Life" world in which the welfare legislation was not passed in 1996 and we continued as we had before? This requires us to fit a regression model to the series from 1960 through 1996 and then predict the percentage of welfare recipients based on that model for 1997 to 2006.

Obviously (hopefully), this new regression model will *not* include step- and cumulative-impact variables ("You were never born George Bailey."). We will stick with our first difference variables. But it's not clear whether a model with the three economic indicators provides a better or worse fit to the data than does a model with a more limited number of variables. Although not shown here, regression equations with a time trend variable and different combinations of the three economic indicators discovered that the model with only first differences in unemployment explained more of the variance in the first-difference transformation of percentage on welfare. Explaining more of the variance in the dependent variable will also mean that that model does the best job in predicting future values of welfare use. So that's how I backed into that choice. Parts of this would probably be useful to include in the policy memo but more so in the technical appendix. It is also the case that the overall model does not explain as much of the variation in welfare use prior to the implementation of TANF

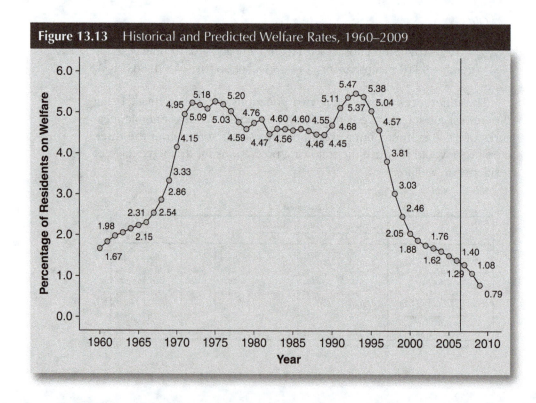

Figure 13.13   Historical and Predicted Welfare Rates, 1960–2009

(Temporary Assistance for Needy Families) as did the regression equation for the full data series (adjusted R^2s of .53 vs. .20 in the Model Summary table below).

Model Summary[b]

Model	R	R Square	Adjusted R Square	Std. Error of the Estimate	Durbin-Watson
1	.598[a]	.357	.328	.26276	.605

a. Predictors: (Constant), DIFF(Percent_unempl__16plus,1), Time
b. Dependent Variable: DIFF(Percent_welfare_recipients,1)

Coefficients[a]

Model		Unstandardized Coefficients B	Std. Error	Standardized Coefficients Beta	t	Sig.	Collinearity Statistics Tolerance	VIF
1	(Constant)	.296	.081		3.637	.001		
	Time	-.012	.003	-.513	-4.188	.000	.995	1.005
	DIFF(Percent_unempl__16plus,1)	.096	.043	.273	2.225	.031	.995	1.005

a. Dependent Variable: DIFF(Percent_welfare_recipients,1)

Our Durbin-Watson statistic still indicates serial correlation, which we should caution our readers about in the technical appendix, but our collinearity statistics are well within the suggested limits. A plot of standardized residuals against time is not too snakelike, suggesting no problems with nonlinearity or with heteroscedasticity. Nor do there appear to be multivariate outliers exceeding ±3.0 in standardized residuals (Figure 13.14).

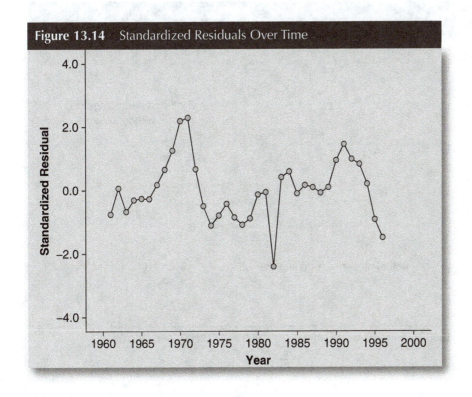

Figure 13.14 Standardized Residuals Over Time

The regression results provide us with the following regression equation:

$$\hat{Y}_{diff} = 0.26 - 0.01(\text{Time trend}) + 0.09(\text{Unemployment}_{diff}).$$

I find it somewhat easier to run these simple formulas in Excel and import the results (via cut-and-paste steps) into the Data View file in SPSS. Here are the results of those calculations in Excel:

Year	Time	Unempl'mt	Unempl_Diff	%_on_Welfare	Predicted_Y
1996	37	5.4	-0.2	4.57	
1997	38	4.9	-0.5	3.81	4.50
1998	39	4.5	-0.4	3.03	4.48
1999	40	4.2	-0.3	2.46	4.46
2000	41	4.0	-0.2	2.05	4.44
2001	42	4.7	0.7	1.88	4.35
2002	43	5.8	1.1	1.76	4.30
2003	44	6.0	0.2	1.69	4.37
2004	45	5.5	-0.5	1.62	4.43
2005	46	5.1	-0.4	1.51	4.41
2006	47	4.6	-0.5	1.40	4.41

I prefer SPSS's graphical facilities, however, so I'll plot these predicted values of welfare use (if welfare legislation had not been passed) as shown in Figure 13.15.

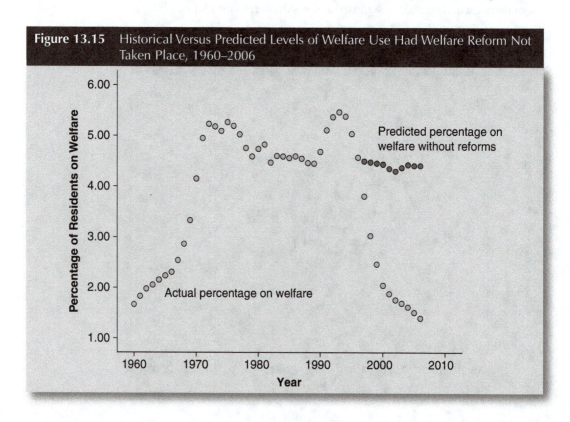

Figure 13.15 Historical Versus Predicted Levels of Welfare Use Had Welfare Reform Not Taken Place, 1960–2006

If you are a fan of reduced welfare rolls, you can't help but love the 1996 reforms and make Bill Clinton into a hero. And you might conclude, "It's the law, stupid, not the economy."

NOTES ●

1. In budgeting, this phenomenon has its own special status as "incrementalism," where next year's budget is created with a firm eye on this year's budget, with small incremental adjustments made to each line item.

2. The alternative tactic of regressing time (e.g., year) on both variables, saving the residuals, and then regressing these residuals on each other was no more successful in eliminating autocorrelation in this case.

> To practice and reinforce the lessons of this chapter of the book, turn to Exercise 9 in the *Student Workbook* (available at http://www.sagepub .com/pearsonsp/).

CHAPTER 14

PRESENTING PERSUASIVE STATISTICAL ANALYSES

Y ou have worked hard to get to the point of understanding the power and limitations of statistics and the procedures for generating them (assuming, of course, that you've read the prior 13 chapters and completed the exercises in the workbook). Although this is the final chapter, it might be fair to say that you are only a little over halfway toward your ultimate objective of principled and persuasive statistical analysis. The challenge now is to communicate that analysis effectively. Paradoxically enough, statistics can get in the way of that objective.

Here's why. You have learned a considerable amount of the vocabulary of statistics, which many members of the audiences for your analyses do not understand. Even worse, some of the statistical vocabulary you have learned includes words that have widely understood everyday meanings that do not correspond to their statistical meaning. Your temptation will be to use these words with meanings that you've come to understand, not fully appreciating the fact that the meanings of these words are not widely shared by the audiences with whom you'll be communicating your results.

It is as if you have begun to speak in statistical tongues but don't realize it. You probably talk about "variables" at the drop of a hat. You use mnemonic variable names instead of the concepts you believe these variables measure. Despite this book's exhortations, you may even allow statistical significance to blind you from the meaning and importance of your findings. You have worked so hard at generating statistics that you believe that they must speak for themselves and don't require further organization and selective emphasis on your part. You are increasingly likely to want to describe all the subtle and nuanced understanding of statistics that you've acquired, not realizing that your complex presentation may lead to frustration or decision paralysis on the part of those to whom you are presenting your results. In short, you've acquired some bad habits along the way that you need to become aware of in this final chapter so that you can overcome or compensate for them. Among these is the more generic problem of the "curse of knowledge."

● THE CURSE OF KNOWLEDGE AND HOW TO AVOID IT

As Chip Heath and Dan Heath (2007) argue in *Made to Stick: Why Some Ideas Survive and Others Die*, you must confront the enemy of persuasive argumentation, the "curse of knowledge" (a concept originated by Camerer, Loewenstein, & Weber, 1989). In short, you now know more about statistics than most of the people to whom your analysis will likely be presented.

Note that I am limiting the discussion in this section to nontechnical audiences of your analysis. You may also have a second type of audience, the statistical wonks or staff who will study the details of your analysis to judge its credibility. These two audiences have quite different needs and wants. We will turn to the more technical audiences in a later section of this chapter.

You may not know how much you know or how little your policy or public audiences do. But you will very likely fall into the trap of believing that certain things are obvious. They are not obvious to the people to whom you're conveying your results.

One of the most dramatic illustrations of the problem of the curse of knowledge arises from an experiment that was conducted as part of a 1990 PhD dissertation at Stanford University by Elizabeth Newton (Heath & Heath, 2007, pp. 19–20). Ms. Newton assigned her subjects to one of two roles: (1) "tappers," who were given a list of 25 well-known songs (e.g., "Happy Birthday to You") and asked to pick one and tap out the rhythm on a tabletop, and (2) "listeners," who were asked to guess the song on the basis of the tapping. The tappers knocked out the rhythms of 120 songs altogether. The listeners correctly identified only 2.5% of them: 3 of 120.

Interestingly, Newton asked the tappers before the tapping began what percentage of the tunes would be correctly identified by the listeners. They had predicted 50%, far more than 2.5%. What explains this discrepancy? Heath and Heath (2007) write,

> It's hard to be a tapper. The problem is that tappers have been given knowledge (the song title) that makes it impossible for them to imagine what it's like to lack that knowledge.

. . . There are, in fact, only two ways to beat the Curse of Knowledge reliably. The first is not to learn anything. The second is to take your ideas and transform them. (p. 20)

It's too late to pursue the first strategy (although I fear that some students erase any long-term memory of statistics after the final paper or test is submitted). It's the second strategy that we will pursue in this chapter: communicating the results of your statistical analysis to both statistical and non-statistical audiences. To paraphrase Musso, Biller, and Myrtle (2000, p. 645), your task in communicating your statistical results is to tell your clients what *they* need to *know* and *do* and *why*, not what *you* know.

WRITTEN AND ORAL PRESENTATIONS ● THAT STICK: THE SIX RULES OF SUCCESs

Heath and Heath (2007) direct their attention to the generic topic of designing communication that will "stick." But their advice can be applied to communicating statistical analysis to lay and policy audiences. As such, they offer six principles that can be used to transform your analysis in ways that are more likely to have an intended impact, changing others' behavior or thinking about an issue. The Heath brothers craft these principles into the acronym *SUCCESs* (recall the usefulness of "chunking" information into these easy to remember devices that we discussed in Chapter 3), which stands for the following characteristics of effective communication:

Simple

Unexpected

Concrete

Credible

Emotional

Story based

Let us discuss each of these characteristics briefly, as they may apply to statistical analysis presented to a political or lay public, say, in a policy memo or brief (to which we will return in more detail in the next section of this chapter).

Simple

You have undoubtedly heard the sage advice that is encapsulated in yet another acronym: KISS ("Keep it simple, stupid."). Well, you're not stupid. Quite the opposite. And, perhaps paradoxically, achieving simplicity is difficult.

Keeping an argument simple can be (more likely) achieved by following several guidelines:

- First, determine what the core finding, argument, or recommendation of your analysis is (depending on the objectives of your audience or client).

- Lead with these core arguments but make them compact and compelling. Grab your readers' attention, and convey the points quickly. Whatever the specific needs and wants of your audiences, their time is a scarce resource.

- Don't "bury the lead." Most of your audience do not want or need to receive the core of your argument in a novel-like denouement near the conclusion of your exposition. Put it up front.

- Use the journalists' dictum of the inverted pyramid, in which the most important points are put first. Do not assume that your readers will read every beautifully crafted word you include in your text. They won't. According to a study of state health policymakers, only 27% read health policy analyses in detail (Sorian & Baugh, 2002, p. 266).

Unexpected

The audiences for whom you write policy memos are busy people, bombarded with what they see as an overload of information. Part of the problem the analyst faces is to get the attention of an audience or client. And one way to do so is to frame the core argument in ways that are unexpected, break an expected pattern, and are interesting.

We can frame or present something that surprises by jolting what our readers expect, by posing our core arguments in contrast to widespread stereotypes or beliefs. Or we can try to determine what in our core argument is counterintuitive. But this also has to be done in ways that are "postdictable." That is to say, although your audience may not have seen it coming, they can, in retrospect, see how the outcome was not so surprising after all.

Note a danger in crafting messages that are surprises: The surprise can be viewed as gimmicky. This will likely be the case when the surprise is not germane to the message.

Consider the following two examples of how to craft an argument that counters the widespread belief among Americans that the United States spends too much on foreign aid. The first is a message crafted by the Intercommunity Peace and Justice Center, a Catholic advocacy group. The second is crafted by Heath and Heath (2007, pp. 77–79) to illustrate the effect of several of their principles, including simplicity and unexpectedness (as well as concreteness, credibility, and emotion, to which we turn after this example).

Message 1: Americans persist in thinking we spend too much on foreign aid despite honest efforts to inform the public by the State Department and other government agencies. Even President Bush's proposed increases, though welcome, will not make the United States generous in its foreign assistance. In fiscal year 2003, the Bush administration will spend about $15 billion in foreign aid, but over $7 billion of this amount—almost half—will be military, not economic assistance. The $8 billion in foreign economic assistance is, according to a recent estimate by the Congressional Budget Office, less than the costs of one month of war in Iraq. Of all the industrialized nations, the United States spends proportionally the least amount on foreign aid, and has for many years. All of sub-Saharan Africa receives just over $1 billion of economic assistance, about the costs of a B-2 bomber. Our foreign aid programs do not support our belief that we are a nation known for its good works around the world. (Heath & Heath, 2007, p. 77)

This statement has several flaws. First, it buries the lead, which is the last sentence. The last sentence also does a better job than the first one in piquing attention and interest because it contradicts what many people believe to be the case. The paragraph provides concrete and credible (two other principles) statistics that are contrary to common beliefs. But billions of dollars are difficult to get one's heart and mind around, and the attempt to compare these billions with the costs of a B-2 bomber does not quite work either, although it's an often-referenced comparison. It has little emotional resonance and is probably overused. Some people may think that B-2 bombers are good things. It may be better to use comparisons with more frivolous expenses that readers would be more hard-pressed to justify. See below how Heath and Heath (2007) reconstruct these raw materials, adding one or two more elements, to make a more memorable presentation of the same argument:

Message 2: Our foreign-aid programs do not support our belief that we are a nation known for its good works around the world. The public believes we spend a great deal more money helping other countries than we actually do. Polls suggest that most Americans think the federal government spends about 10 to 15 percent of its budget on foreign aid. The truth is that we spend less than 1 percent, the lowest of any industrialized nation.

All of sub-Saharan Africa receives just over $1 billion in economic aid. If everyone in the United States gave up one soft drink a month, we could double our current aid to Africa. If everyone gave up one movie a year, we could double our current aid to Africa and Asia. (Heath & Heath, 2007, p. 78)

And the second message required only 125 words instead of 160.

Concrete

Cognitive psychologists have demonstrated the relative ease of remembering concrete items in contrast to abstract ideas (an "apple" or "hammer" vs. "beauty" or "equity"; Rubin, 1995). Not only are concrete items more memorable, but they also can be more understandable and interesting (Sadoski, Goetz, & Rodriguez, 2000). The trick lies, however, not in concreteness alone but in the way in which people assign meaning to concrete terms. Here's another story from Heath and Heath (2007) to illustrate this and other principles.

Art Silverman worked in 1992 for the Center for Science in Public Interest (CSPI), a nonprofit organization that seeks to educate the public about nutrition. The organization conducted a study of medium-sized movie popcorn servings in 12 theaters in three major cities that year, only to discover that the average bag of buttered popcorn included 37 grams of saturated fat. Silverman was well aware of the U.S. Department of Agriculture's recommendation that diets include no more than 20 grams of saturated fat per day. The 20 and 37 grams were surely concrete figures, but Silverman realized that few people really understand what those figures mean. Comparing 20 with 37 grams of saturated fat in a bar chart wouldn't help much either. His solution was concrete, visual, and meaningful to the audiences CSPI sought to reach.

CSPI held a press conference on September 27, 1992, in which they reported, "A medium-sized 'butter' popcorn at a typical neighborhood movie theater contains more artery-clogging fat than a bacon-and-eggs breakfast, a Big Mac and fries for lunch, and a steak dinner with all the trimmings—combined!" CSPI presented the full assortment of these dishes on a table for the television media at the press conference to film. The story was aired on CBS, NBC, ABC, and CNN. It was featured in *USA Today*, the *Los Angeles Times*, and *The Washington Post*. It became fodder for jokes on the Leno and Letterman shows. Buttered popcorn sales fell. Soon after, several major movie chains discontinued their use of coconut oil, the major culprit in the story. Now, that's a sticky story.

Credible

Credible arguments rest on the trust that we have in the source of the argument. The source can be a friend or a relative (if we trust their judgment, knowledge, and information), experts, celebrities, and people who can provide believable testimonials based on their experiences. In the absence of these sources, we can help build a credible argument on the basis of other guidelines:

- Details can be powerful. But note, as above—not just any old details. They should be concrete, tangible, vivid, and meaningful to the audience.

- Statistics can lend credibility too! But be careful of the scale in which you report your statistics. It is better to combine raw numbers with the sensory perception of those numbers. Illustrating the power of the nuclear warheads on a single U.S. or Soviet nuclear submarine, as leaders of the Beyond War movement did in the 1980s, by pouring 10 BB pellets into an empty metal bucket—which they equated to 10 times the power of the bomb dropped on Hiroshima—was a good overture to the 5,000 BBs they poured into the bucket to represent the total fire power possessed by the two superpowers during the height of the Cold War. In other words, transform your numbers through analogy or metaphor but do so in ways that can easily map onto a human scale of perception.

- A third way to lend internal credibility to your argument is through a particular type of example. The "stickiness" of a report that a company delivers 98.84% of its packages on time may pale in comparison with the report that the company delivered every copy of the fifth *Harry Potter* book to every bookstore in India at 8 a.m. on the morning of its release (Heath & Heath, 2007, p. 152). This example also relates to the power and memorability of stories, in contrast to statistics alone.

- Credibility may be hard to achieve, but it's easily destroyed. Poorly written and poorly proofread work will surely and quickly do so.

Emotional

This principle may be the hardest to apply in the context of policy memos and briefs that are based on principled statistical argument. The gist of this principle is to use words or images to make people care about something they don't currently care about by associating it with something they do care about. The difficulty in tapping into emotions in part lies in the fact that words and images mean different things to different people and change with time.

The idea of "sportsmanship," for example, may have once moved parents and children to play by the rules. It apparently hasn't for quite some time. Interestingly, "honoring the game" is used now to evoke the same behaviors that appeals to sportsmanship once did (Heath & Heath, 2007, pp. 175–176). Appeals to self-interest work, as can altruistic appeals, appeals to one's identity ("What would someone like me do?"), and framing your story as if your audience "were there."

Story Based

Much of the power of an argument lies in its telling as a story. Humans may be hardwired to remember stories, as suggested by the tens of thousands of years of oral history that preceded humans' acquisition of writing. Stories fall into several genres. The first is the challenge plot, illustrated famously by the inspirational story of David and Goliath and mimicked in a more contemporary version in the Subway commercial of Jared, who reduced his weight from 425 to 180 pounds on what he called the "Subway diet." Such stories inspire and show the way to an outcome. So might a story in the context of some of the exercises and examples provided throughout this book if our statistical analysis could identify poor school districts that perform far above what we would expect of them and then "tell their stories," providing both inspiration and a model for how to improve to the level of those districts.

Second, connection plots such as the parable of the Good Samaritan (Should it be any surprise to us that religious texts are filled with stories?) inspire us to help others, often quite unlike ourselves.

Third, creativity plots involve someone making a mental breakthrough, as Newton did when the alleged apple fell on his head, thus inspiring the idea of gravity.

Of course, writing good stories is difficult. But consider how you might use the story of a case with a large regression residual to make a point, both about the disadvantages that school districts with poor students and inexperienced teachers face as well as about the heroic efforts that might help overcome those structural disadvantages.

WRITING POLICY MEMOS AND BRIEFS ●

In general, the first challenge of any analysis is to analyze a complex issue credibly and competently and arrive at sound, evidence-based recommendations or to provide information in ways that inform clients' decisions. This is what Heath and Heath (2007) call the "Answer stage" of getting your message across. The previous 13 chapters dealt mostly with this stage. The second stage, the "Telling Others stage," calls on you to communicate both the analysis and the recommendations to a nontechnical audience while protecting these recommendations against methodological challenges.

Consider, as we have throughout most of this text, the challenge facing analysts of statewide academic test performance scores. This is a policy issue about which there is considerable debate, controversy, and disagreement. The stakes are high for states, districts, schools and the public officials responsible for overseeing these systems, and the students who attend these schools. It is, therefore, a highly charged political arena in which numbers matter.

Let us say that you were commissioned by the Governor of Texas to analyze the data collected by the state's Department of Education on test performance and district and student characteristics and to report your findings and recommendations to the governor or a governor's aide. You would likely communicate your analysis and recommendations in the form of a *policy memorandum* or *brief* that might seek to answer questions such as the following:

1. What aspects of district finances and instructional characteristics appear to be most highly associated with district school performance (as measured by student test results) when taking into account the district students' social, economic, and demographic characteristics? Are there conditions that do not appear to be associated with test performance that are surprising or that suggest areas where fewer resources should be allocated?

2. Where would you recommend that the governor ask school districts and the state legislature to place a greater or lesser commitment of resources in order to increase TAKS test scores for all students or for students in poorly performing districts? How much of an effect on test scores are your recommendations likely to have? Why? How much are they likely to cost and with what payoff?

3. Which school districts appear to be underperforming, given what you would expect to find in a district with similar staff resources, finances, and student social, economic, and demographic characteristics?

4. Similarly, which districts appear to be overachieving, based on what we would predict their test performance scores to be in light of their meager finances, limited staff resources, and challenging student social, economic, and demographic characteristics?

Answers to such questions arise during the processes that are described in the prior 13 chapters in this text. But these answers poorly inform how they are to be presented—in what order, with what emphasis, and so on. Those choices are guided in part by what the data themselves reveal.

We have tried to present throughout the book some theories about cognition, memory, and perception to guide the development of questions and your presentation of tables and graphs. We will sharpen and repeat some of these lessons here as they pertain to a particular written format, the policy memorandum or brief, to nonstatistical audiences (we turn in the next section to the ingredients of a technical report). These guidelines will encompass both general and specific prescriptions (for more on this topic, see Dobel, Elmore, & Werner, 2003; Miller, 2005).

Let's start, as we always should, with our audience or client and the audiences or clients on whom they depend. What is it that you need to know about your audiences? The first and most obvious answer is who they are. Unfortunately, this is not always clear. Once having established who they are, however, try to determine what their responsibilities, constraints, and opportunities are. And to whom are they accountable or beholden.

Second, you need to know what they need to know in order to make good or better decisions. It is helpful if you know what the nature of those decisions might be and work backward to consider what information would be required to inform such decisions. Information for policy decision needs to have some obvious characteristics: It should be relevant to the decisions at hand, timely, honest, realistic, clear (i.e., devoid of technical jargon), and accurate. Lay out the reasons for your recommendations. Dobel et al. (2003) also recommend that you provide the bad news as well as the good, but this may conflict with length objectives (keeping it short) and simplicity and may contribute to burying the lead.

Good writing of any kind requires time. There is no such thing as a good first draft. Ideally, you'll have enough time to draft a memo, set it aside, and then return to it, playing the role of someone who has never seen the document before. Proofread your draft at two levels: first, for the main ideas and their support and, second, for the details of grammar and spelling. There's no such thing as a small grammatical error. They can trump the most elegant and efficient argument because they communicate volumes in themselves. Grammatical and spelling mistakes say to the reader that the author is poorly schooled, careless, sloppy, uncaring, and/or not the brightest bulb in the box. Need I conclude that none of these impressions is good?

WRITING TECHNICAL REPORTS ●

The purpose of a *technical report* or *appendix* is to persuade the reader—whether a technical expert or someone who, like you, understands what good statistical practices are—that you followed sound procedures in data collection, editing, data transformations, and statistical analysis. Such a report should in general be transparent and provide sufficient detail, or references to such details, so that the reader can decide whether the data and their analysis justify the recommendations you provide.

A technical report or appendix should describe several key elements of the data:

• The study design: How were the data collected? From where were the data collected, who was included (and excluded or missed), and when were the data collected? (e.g., "A 30-minute phone interview of a random sample of 500 people drawn from the list of people whom the state of Connecticut awarded a driver's license within the past 3 months. Initial interviews and up to three follow-up calls were conducted by the Survey Research Lab of the University of Connecticut between January 15, 2009, and March 3, 2009.")

• Any assessments of the validity and reliability of the measures and, if not published elsewhere, the wording of the questions used in the analysis

• Explanations of any units of measurement that are unusual or complex

• The treatment of item nonresponses—that is, missing values, especially if any imputations for them were made

• Response rates, an assessment of nonresponse bias, and (if present) the steps taken to compensate for nonresponse bias (e.g., weighted file)

• Descriptive statistics for the variables used in the analysis (including at least the mean and standard deviation of each variable, presented in tabular format)

- Bivariate correlations, if multivariate models or equations are presented

- Detailed statistical results of any models tested, including the test statistics used (e.g., t test, **F ratio**), the number of observations on which the tests were conducted, confidence intervals, effect sizes, and p values (An equation or a table of coefficients with their respective ns and p values can efficiently display these regression models, as well as an accompanying arrow diagram of your model.)

- Assessments of the assumptions on which the statistical tests are based (e.g., identification of outliers, assessments of whether univariate or multivariate distributions are normal)

- Any data transformations conducted (e.g., removal of outliers, creation of indexes or scales) and the results of any statistics calculated on data that were transformed to better meet test assumptions (e.g., Do the results with and without outliers differ substantially?)

- The strengths and weaknesses of the research design, data, and methods

Note, however, that dumping output without providing any narrative as to what the output says about the technical aspects of the analysis demonstrates only that you know how to cut and paste output. It reveals nothing about your understanding of the statistics on which the policy recommendations of your memorandum are based. Indeed, the absence of narrative explanation in such a document probably conveys the impression that the author doesn't know what he's doing.

● CREATING EFFECTIVE POWERPOINT SLIDES

While the emphasis of this text is on written exposition, the results of policy analysis are very likely to be conveyed, in addition to a written memorandum or technical report, in the form of a PowerPoint presentation. This concluding section provides guidelines for creating effective PowerPoint presentations of technical and nontechnical materials.

There are at least three things to think about in preparing a PowerPoint presentation:

1. The content

2. The look, feel, and behavior of the slides

3. The presentation

Content

Don't start with PowerPoint. Make sure you answer several related questions before you launch the software:

1. What am I trying to accomplish in this presentation? Do I want someone to take an action, learn a new skill, make a decision, and so on?

2. What do I really want to say? (Don't allow yourself to be sidetracked by minor points or diversions that get in the way of your objectives.)

3. What are the key ideas that I must communicate?

4. What are my audience's wants, needs, and level of knowledge about my content?

Another way of thinking about these questions is to write down the key points you want your audience to take away from your presentation. And then think about how you can use PowerPoint or other media to achieve that end (e.g., a flip chart, a series of questions that you ask your audience to answer, a role-play, a breakup into small groups).

The Look, Feel, and Behavior of Your Slides

How should your slides look? There are a number of items to consider here. For example: What graphical elements do I want to include? Do I reinforce my organization's brand by incorporating logos onto the slides? And so on.

The Value of a Consistent Look

Whatever elements you choose to include, strive for consistency across all your slides so that changing the elements doesn't draw attention to the elements, instead of the content and your objectives. One way to achieve this consistency is through the use of the Slide Master.

Step 1: Open a new or existing presentation.

Step 2: On the View menu, click Master/Slide Master, and alter the elements as you wish, including the importation of graphical elements (e.g., the Fels logo that you pluck from its Web site and drag and drop at the lower right corner of the Master Slide). You may also select images or photos for the entire slide's background. (*Note:* Select a background that does not draw undue attention to it, instead of your content. Select an image that is consistent with the theme of your presentation.)

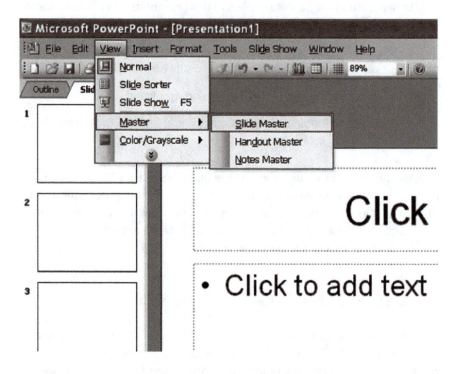

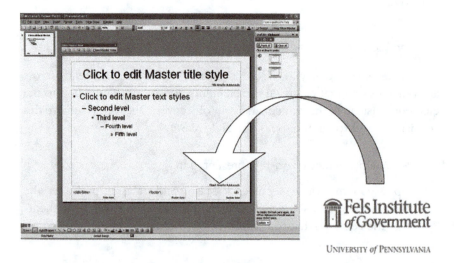

Step 3: If importing an image for the background of your slide presentation, you may want to first reduce the contrast and brighten the image in order to ensure that it does not dominate the content. Think subtle. To do this, click on the image and on the View menu, click Toolbars/Picture. You can use the icons for contrast and brightness to soften the background. Also, select the icon of what looks to my eyes as a black dog on a grid to move the image Behind Text.

Font Type and Size

- People read fonts without details on the ends of strokes (i.e., as the French would say, "sans serif") more quickly than those with serifs. In general, a font such as Arial can be more quickly read than Times New Roman.
- Similarly, avoid italics, which also tend to be more difficult to read.
- Use a font no smaller than 24 point.
- Use a 6 × 6 rule, in which you have a single idea per bulleted line, no more than six to eight words per line, and no more than six lines.
- Avoid ALL CAPS, except perhaps for titles.
- Use contrasting colors. Black lettering on light background works best.

Remember, consistency and content. Examine your objectives and design slides with that purpose in mind, as well as an appreciation for your audience's capacity, knowledge, and wants.

How Should the Slides Behave?

Just as in the look and feel of each slide, avoid using animation that directs the audience's attention to the movement rather than the content. In general, don't have words or objects fly in, materialize from a checkerboard pattern, or drop down. Cute animation is often distracting and, again, draws attention to the presenter (not favorably, by the way) rather than the message, content, and objective of the presentation.

Similarly, avoid the use of sound unless (and this is rarely ever the case) it enhances the message.

If you want to apply the same transition effects (e.g., each successive bullet appears with each new mouse click) to multiple slides, try this shortcut:

Step 1: On the View menu, click Slide Sorter.

Step 2: Select the slides you want to apply the transition effect to by clicking one slide and holding down the Ctrl key while you click each successive slide or by holding down the Shift key and moving the arrow keys to highlight a block of successive slides.

Step 3: On the Slide Show menu, click Slide Transition.

Step 4: In the Effect box, click the transition you want, as well as any other options.

Step 5: Click Apply.

It is often effective to have bulleted points appear one at a time in order to direct the audience's attention to one point at a time, without enabling them to read ahead and not listen to the point you are trying to make. This is accomplished by applying the Appear transition.

The Presentation of Your Presentation

You know what your objectives are in your presentation. You know your audience. You've got just the right content and have followed all the rules in the layout and use of transitions and animation. Yet you're not finished. You have to think about (*and practice!*) your presentation and follow a few more tips.

How Many Slides Should I Present?

The answer to this question depends in part on your objectives and the time your audience provides you. In general, allow 1 minute per slide, but err on the side of having one slide every 2 minutes (especially if you expect to engage your audience in a discussion during your presentation).

Learn how to navigate nonlinearly, so that you can move about your presentation as questions from your audience might require.

Here are some shortcuts for doing this:

Advance to the next slide	"N," Enter, Page Down, right arrow, down arrow, spacebar, or click the mouse
Return to the previous slide	"P," Page Up, left arrow, up arrow, or Backspace
End a slide show	Esc or hyphen
Stop or restart an automatic slide show	"S" or plus sign
Go to slide <number>	<number> + Enter
Return to the first slide	Depress both mouse buttons for 2 seconds

You may also want to direct attention away from the slides themselves in order to, say, engage in a discussion. You can easily turn the slides "off" by hitting the "B" key or period to blacken the screen. Hit the same keys to bring the screen back. Or if you prefer a white background, hit "W" or the comma.

Practice in front of an audience you've invited to play the role of the one to which you'll be making your real presentation. You'll hone your presentation skills, while being given an opportunity to provide succinct answers to questions you can expect (and not fear) to receive from your real audience.

One unscientific survey of 159 people found the following problems with many PowerPoint presentations (which offer a good list of dos and don'ts regarding the look and content of slides and the manner in which they are presented):

- The speaker read the slides to us: 60.4%
- Text so small, I couldn't read it: 50.9%
- Full sentences instead of bullet points: 47.8%
- Slides hard to see because of color choice: 37.1%
- Moving/flying text or graphics: 24.5%
- Annoying use of sounds: 22.0%
- Overly complex diagrams or charts: 22.0% (www.presentersuniversity. com/Courses_Annoying.php, accessed July 25, 2006)

We have all seen terrible slides and ever poorer presentations. This result can be achieved with or without PowerPoint. Use common sense. Effective presentation skills include good content, eye contact with your audience, good projection, and energy, as well as all the tips above. Just do it!

To practice and reinforce the lessons of this chapter of the book, turn to the final exercise in the *Student Workbook* (available at http://www.sagepub .com/pearsonsp/). This exercise also seeks to help you synthesize the skills and knowledge you've acquired since the midterm exercise.

APPENDIX A

FROM WHENCE DO DATA COME?

Key Statistical Sites From the U.S. Government

Here are some sources for data that are provided by the University of Pennsylvania's library (I've revised these somewhat), http://gethelp.library.upenn.edu/guides/general/stats/stats.html (accessed May 16, 2007).

MAJOR STATISTICAL SOURCES

- Statistical Abstract of the United States—all editions, 1878 to the present
  www.census.gov/compendia/statab

- FEDSTATS
  Provides easy access to statistics produced by more than 100 government agencies
  www.fedstats.gov

- STAT-USA/Internet
  Business, trade, and economic information data
  hdl.library.upenn.edu/1017/7046

- LexisNexis Statistical
  Statistical Universe indexes statistical data published in federal, state, and selected privately published titles, at the table level. In some cases, the full text of the documents is also available. It includes all *American*

Statistics Index (ASI) abstract and index records for statistical publications from the U.S. government, indexing from the *Statistical Reference Index* for nongovernmental publications, links to hundreds of full-text documents published from 1994 to the present, and some state and international publications.

hdl.library.upenn.edu/1017/7045

- Census Bureau

  www.census.gov

- Economics Statistics

  www.gpoaccess.gov/indicators/

Agriculture

- National Agricultural Statistics Service

  www.nass.usda.gov/Data_and_Statistics/

- Foreign Agricultural Service

  www.fas.usda.gov/

- *Census of Agriculture*—1992, 1997, 2002, and 2007.

  www.agcensus.usda.gov/

- USDA Economics and Statistics System—Mann Library, Cornell University

  www.mannlib.cornell.edu/usda

Crime

- Bureau of Justice Statistics, U.S. Department of Justice

  www.ojp.usdoj.gov/bjs/

- Criminal Justice Statistics, National Criminal Justice Service (NCJRS)

  www.ncjrs.org

- Federal Bureau of Prisons, U.S. Department of Justice

  www.bop.gov

- Federal Justice Statistics Resource Center (FJSRC)

Contains comprehensive information about suspects and defendants processed in each stage of the federal criminal justice system in a given year (1994–1996).

http://fjsrc.urban.org/

- *Sourcebook of Criminal Justice Statistics*

  www.albany.edu/sourcebook/

- TRAC: Transactional Records Access Clearinghouse—ATF Web site

  www.trac.syr.edu/tracatf/atfhome.html

- Uniform Crime Reports—Federal Bureau of Investigation, 1995 to the present

  www.fbi.gov/ucr/ucr.htm

- *Uniform Crime Reports*—University of Virginia, Social Sciences Data Center, data from 1990 to the present

  http://fisher.lib.virginia.edu/crime/

Defense

- Defense Almanac

  www.defenselink.mil/pubs/almanac/

- Facts and Reports—U.S. Department of Defense

  www.defenselink.mil/pubs/#FACTS

Economics

- Bureau of Economic Analysis, U.S. Department of Labor

  www.bea.doc.gov/

- Bureau of Labor Statistics, U.S. Department of Labor

  http://stats.bls.gov/

- Office of Policy, Research and Statistics, Social Security Administration

  www.ssa.gov/policy/

- *Budget of the United States Government*, FY 1996 to the present

  www.gpoaccess.gov//usbudget/index.html

- *County Business Patterns*—1993 to the present; from the Bureau of the Census

  www.census.gov/epcd/cbp/view/cbpview.html

- *Economic Census*

  www.census.gov/epcd/www/econ97.html

- *Economic Indicators*, 1995 to the present

  www.gpoaccess.gov/indicators/index.html

- *Economic Report of the President*, GPO Access, 1996 to the present

  www.gpoaccess.gov/eop/

- *Occupational Outlook Handbook* (latest)

  www.bls.gov/oco/

- *State Personal Income, 1969–2003*—University of Virginia, Social Sciences Data Center

  www.bea.gov/bea/regional/spi

Education

- National Center for Education Statistics
  - Surveys and Programs

    http://nces.ed.gov/Surveys/

  - Condition of Education

    http://nces.ed.gov/programs/coe

  - *Digest of Education Statistics*

    http://nces.ed.gov/programs/digest/

- Science Resources Studies Division, National Science Foundation

  www.nsf.gov/sbe/srs/stats.htm

Environment

- Envirofacts—EPA

  www.epa.gov/enviro/index_java.html

- National Geophysical Data Center (NGDC)
  www.ngdc.noaa.gov/ngdc.html

Health

- National Center for Health Statistics, Department of Health and Human Services
  www.cdc.gov/nchs/index.htm
- Centers for Disease Control and Prevention, Data and Statistics
  www.cdc.gov/scientific.htm
- Injuries, Illnesses, and Fatalities (IIF)—U.S. Department of Labor
  www.bls.gov/iif/

Housing/Urban Development

- Census Bureau
  - o Census Bureau Housing Topics
    www.census.gov/hhes/www/housing.html
  - o American Housing Surveys
    www.census.gov/hhes/www/housing/ahs/nationaldata.html
  - o Construction Statistics
    www.census.gov/mcd/
  - o New Residential Sales
    www.census.gov/mcd/
- HUD User—Data Sets
  www.huduser.org/datasets/pdrdatas.html

Immigration

- U.S. Citizenship and Immigration Services
  www.uscis.gov/graphics/index.html

- Immigration—U.S. Bureau of the Census
  www.census.gov/population/www/socdemo/immigration.html

Population

- Bureau of the Census, U.S. Department of Commerce
  www.census.gov

- U.S. Census—Research Guide
  http://gethelp.library.upenn.edu/guides/govdocs/census/census.html

- County and City Data Book, 2007—U.S. Bureau of the Census
  www.census.gov/statab/www/ccdb.html

- *Current Population Survey*—Bureau of Labor Statistics
  www.bls.census.gov/cps

Transportation

- Aviation Accident Statistics
  www.ntsb.gov/Aviation/Stats.htm

- Federal Highway Administration
  www.fhwa.dot.gov/

- Federal Railroad Administration
  www.fra.dot.gov/

- TransStats, Bureau of Transportation Statistics, U.S. Department of Transportation
  www.bts.gov/

- National Transit Database (FTA)
  www.ntdprogram.com/

- National Transportation Data Archive, U.S. Department of Transportation
  www.bts.gov/ntda

- National Transportation Safety Board
  www.ntsb.gov/

Business and Finance

- A guide to U.S. Economic Statistics
  http://gethelp.library.upenn.edu/guides/business/useconomicstats
  .html

- Business FAQs
  http://faq.library.upenn.edu/recordList?library=lippincott

International Statistics

http://gethelp.library.upenn.edu/guides/general/stats/intlstats.html

Opinion Polls

http://gethelp.library.upenn.edu/guides/polisci/polls.html

These data sources constitute what may be called a rudimentary national indicator system, and some federal agencies use these data sources to produce biennial chartbooks that describe conditions over time. Many of these sources of data, however, do not in themselves suggest what some one person or group should do in response to a worsening condition. As Kingdon (2003) writes, only when a promising solution exists does a condition actually become a problem worthy of attention by public or private agencies.

APPENDIX B

HOW TO SELECT
THE RIGHT STATISTICS[*]

Make a decision by reading from left to right.

Descriptions of Single Variables

	Level of Measurement	*Statistical Procedure*
To describe a single variable	Continuous and normally distributed[a]	Mean, median, mode, quartiles, histogram, *SD*, kurtosis, skewness, and boxplot
	Nominal and ordinal	Frequency table and bar chart

a. Large samples also tend to produce results that are not affected by departures from normal distributions.

[*](Adapted from Elliott and Woodward, 2007, pp. 245–247)

Group Differences or Comparisons of Independent Observations

	Level of Measurement	Statistical Procedure
Comparing a single sample characteristic to a standard or norm	Continuous and normal	Single-sample *t* test
	At least ordinal	Sign test
	Nominal or ordinal	Goodness of fit
Comparing two independent groups	Continuous and normal	Two-sample *t* test
	At least ordinal	Mann-Whitney
	Nominal or ordinal	Chi-square
Comparing more than two independent groups on one continuous dependent (response) variable	Continuous and normal	One-way (between groups) ANOVA
	At least ordinal	Kruskal-Wallis
	Nominal or ordinal	Chi-square
Comparing more than two groups on one *repeated* continuous dependent variable	Continuous and normal	One-way (within groups) ANOVA
	At least ordinal	Friedman's test
	Nominal or ordinal	Cochran's *Q*
Comparing the separate and joint effects of two categorical independent variables on one continuous dependent variable	Continuous and normal	Two-way (between groups) ANOVA
Comparing two or more group means after controlling for the effects of one or more other continuous independent variables (called covariates)	Continuous and normal	ANCOVA

Group Differences or Comparisons of Dependent Observations (i.e., Paired, Repeated, or Matched Data)

	Level of Measurement	*Statistical Procedure*
Comparing two groups	Continuous and normal	Paired *t* test (if directional)
		Wilcoxon signed-rank test (if nondirectional)
	At least ordinal	Sign test
	Nominal	McNemar

Relational Analysis of Independent Observations

	Level of Measurement	*Statistical Procedure*
To describe a relationship between two variables	Both are continuous and normal	Pearson correlation coefficient (*r*) and simple linear regression (*b*)
	Both are at least ordinal	Gamma, tau-*b*, and tau-*c*, and Spearman correlation rho (if nondirectional) and Somer's *d* (if directional)
	Both nominal	Cross-tabulations and chi-square, Cramer's *V* (if nondirectional) or lambda, Goodman and Kruskal tau, and/or uncertainty coefficient and odds ratio (if directional)

(Continued)

(Continued)

	Level of Measurement	Statistical Procedure
	Dependent (response) variable is dichotomous and independent (predictor) variable is continuous	Logistic regression
To describe a relationship between a dependent (response) variable and two or more independent (predictor) variables	Nominal and ordinal	Cross-tabulation with layers and partial measures of association as noted above
	Continuous and normal	Part and partial correlation and multiple regression

APPENDIX C

IN-CLASS QUESTIONNAIRE

This brief questionnaire will be used as a teaching tool in applied statistics. We will critique the questions, identifying common measurement problems in surveys (whether self-administered, such as this one, or face-to-face or via phone). We will also use the results to create a codebook and data files for analysis.

Please answer each question as best as you can and as completely as possible. Your responses will be held in confidence and will not be identified in class with your name. The student identification number requested below is required only for administrative purposes. We will learn how to add data to the files we create later in the semester, and this can only be done by linking the new data to the old data via this identification number.

Please enter the last four digits of your eight-digit student identification number here:

___   ___   ___   ___

1. In general, how strongly do you agree or disagree with each of the following statements (please circle the number that best represents your response):

Agree Strongly	Agree Somewhat	Disagree Somewhat	Disagree Strongly

a. The palms of my hands become sweaty when I even hear the word *statistics*.

4	3	2	1

b. Statistics is often boring and difficult to understand.

4	3	2	1

    c. I'm looking forward to learning how to use statistics to design better public policies.

      4   3   2   1

    d. I don't hate mathematics.

      4   3   2   1

    e. One can learn statistics only by actually doing it.

      4   3   2   1

    f. Statistics are a rhetorical tool for persuasion.

      4   3   2   1

    g. My prior education has prepared me to do well in this class

      4   3   2   1

    h. I like academic challenges.

      4   3   2   1

    i. It's not how hard you work that leads to success; it's how smart you work.

      4   3   2   1

2. How many courses have you taken in your program prior to this semester? _____

3. In what year were you born?   19_____

4. What is/was your undergraduate major?

    _____

5. What is/was your undergraduate GPA? _____.

6. How many undergraduate courses in statistics have you taken? _____ If *zero*, skip to Question 8.

7. If you took one or more undergraduate courses in statistics, what was your average letter grade in that/those course(s)? _____

8. What is your gender (please circle one number)?

        Male ... 1   Female ... 2

9. Do you have children below 18 years of age living at home with you?

        Yes ... 1   No ... 2

10. Are you a U.S. citizen?

        Yes ... 1   No ... 2

11. What ethnic/racial group do you consider yourself a member of?

White	1
Black/African-American	2
Hispanic/Latino	3
Asian/Pacific Islander	4
Other	5

12. I consider myself proficient in the use of the following software programs:

	Yes	No
a. SPSS	1	2
b. Microsoft Word	1	2
c. Microsoft Excel	1	2
d. Microsoft PowerPoint	1	2
e. Microsoft Access	1	2

13. How tall are you? _____ inches.

14. What is your height, as measured by a fellow student in class today?

           _____ inches.

15. What is the value of X in the following equation? _____

$$\frac{5}{2} = \frac{X}{6}$$

16. What is the mean of the following set of observations? _____

$$5, 2, 3, 10, 7, 3$$

17. What does "b" signify in the following regression equation (circle the letter corresponding to what you believe to be the correct answer)?

$$Y = a + bX = e.$$

    a. The independent variable
    b. The dependent variable
    c. The intercept
    d. The regression slope
    e. The error term
    f. None of the above

18. Please indicate whether the following statements are True or False.

    a. A high correlation demonstrates a causal relationship between two variables.

        True   False

    b. Measures of respondents' gender on a survey are considered ordinal rather than nominal or interval.

        True   False

    c. A relationship that is reported as being significant at "$p = .956$" is considered "statistically significant."

        True   False

GLOSSARY

Adjusted R^2   An adjusted regression estimate of the amount of variation in a dependent variable that is explained by one or more independent variables. The adjustment takes into account the influence of the number of independent variables on the amount of variance explained. It should be reported if substantially different from the unadjusted R^2.

Analysis of covariance (ANCOVA)   An ANCOVA assesses whether the mean of a continuous dependent variable differs among categories (or groups) of an independent variable when controlling for (or holding constant) one or more continuously measured independent variables.

Analysis of variance (ANOVA)   A statistical tool used to determine whether the mean of a continuous dependent variable differs among categories (or groups) of an independent variable.

Asymmetric   A type of measure of association that assumes or presupposes that two or more variables are causally related to one another. The magnitude of the association will often vary depending on whether the analyst assumes that X causes Y or Y causes X. This measure is also known as a **directional** measure of association.

Autocorrelation (also **serial correlation**)   A condition that often arises in time-series analysis when subsequent observations are highly correlated with one another; that is, observations on a variable at time $t + 1$ are affected by the values of that variable during the preceding time period, t.

Beta coefficient (β)   A regression coefficient calculated from standardized transformations of independent and dependent variables. These transformations enable comparisons of the relative influence of independent variables on a dependent variable that are not affected by the type of unit in which the variables are measured. Betas tell you how much an increase of 1 standard deviation of an independent variable is associated with an increase of 1 standard deviation of the dependent variable (when taking all the other independent variables in the equation into account). Betas are also known as "path coefficients."

Bonferroni correction   A method used to compensate for the possibility of finding statistically significant correlations by chance alone when requesting a large number of such correlations, say, in a correlation matrix. This procedure would, if requesting 100 significance tests simultaneously, call for an acceptable p value of .05/100 (if .05 would have otherwise been your acceptable level for rejecting the null hypothesis).

Boxplot   A graph that displays several key features of one or more distributions: median, outliers, and the 25th and 75th percentiles (the distance between which is called the interquartile range).

Categorical variable   A variable whose values designate an observation's membership in a discrete group or nominal category (e.g., male or female). Analysts typically assign numeric values to such categories (e.g., a "1" to *males* and "2" to *females*), but this assignment is arbitrary (i.e., females could just as well be assigned the value "1" on a variable for gender). The values are merely labels or numeric placeholders. They convey no information about quantity or rank. Being "female" is not twice the value of being a male. Seriously.

Centered leverage value   A test to detect multivariate outliers. A value greater than three times its average indicates the possibility that outliers are unduly influencing the results of a multiple regression.

Central limit theorem   A mathematically derived theorem that predicts that the distribution of means drawn from many random samples of size n from the same population will be normally distributed as n approaches 100, even when the variable whose mean is being estimated is itself not normally distributed in the population. This distribution of means—also known as a sampling distribution—can be demonstrated empirically to be normally distributed by drawing many random samples from a population with known characteristics (e.g., a jar into which you added an equal number of white and red beans). The standard deviation of the sampling distribution—also known as the standard error—can be calculated from a single random sample by dividing the sample standard deviation of a variable by $\sqrt{n}$.

Chi-square (χ^2)   A nonparametric test for assessing whether two categorical variables in a sample are related to each other. The measure has a possible minimum value of 0 but no upper limit. The size of the test, often used in conjunction with contingency tables (also known as crosstabs), is calculated as the sum of the squared differences between the observed and "expected" frequencies. The size of chi-square is a function of the differences between the expected and observed cell frequencies and the number of cells (row $\times$ column) in a contingency table. (Cramer's V corrects for this latter effect.) A "sledgehammer" of tests for the association between two categorical variables, chi-square makes very few assumptions about the variables being studied, but it does require that the table include no cell with expected cell frequencies less than 5. Fisher's exact test can be used in such circumstances when analyzing 2 × 2 tables with cells with fewer than 5 expected observations.

Confidence interval (CI)   The range of sample estimates within which you can expect to find the true population parameter in, say, 95 of 100 samples of similar size and design as the sample you have in hand.

Confidence level   The probability that your single sample estimate will include the true population parameter if you drew, say, 100 samples from the same population. The choice of level is yours, but a 95% confidence level is common.

Consumer price index (CPI)   An index created by the U.S. Bureau of Labor Statistics to measure monthly changes in the prices paid by urban consumers for a representative basket of goods and services. It can be used to transform "current" dollars" into "constant" dollars, thus removing the effects of the changing value of money in any financial time series.

Contingency table (also known as **crosstab**)   A table whose cells represent the frequency and/or percentage of observations that jointly share the characteristics defined by the row and column categories of the table.

Control variable   An independent variable whose influence on a dependent variable you want to account for, control, or hold constant while assessing the effect of other independent variables. Control variables may also represent alternative hypotheses or explanations for an outcome that you want to "rule out" or an influence you want to remove from the causes of the dependent variable. Experimental designs (otherwise called randomized control trials) seek to control for the influence of all unmeasured causes of an outcome by the random (and perhaps "blind") assignment of subjects to treatment and control groups in such a way that the two groups differ only in the assignment to one of these two groups, thereby isolating the effect of the treatment or intervention from all other possible causes of the outcome.

Cook's distance   A test to detect multivariate outliers. Any case with a value greater than 1 may be unduly influencing the results of a multiple regression.

Correlation   Generally speaking, the extent to which two variables are linearly related to each other. More specifically, the term is often used as a shorthand for the Pearson product moment correlation coefficient (r).

Cramer's V   A measure of association that often accompanies reports of chi-square because, unlike chi-square, it can range between 0 (indicating no relationship between two categorical variables) and +1.0 (representing a pair of variables whose values are perfectly matched).

Cronbach's alpha (α)   A measure of the extent to which variables believed to measure the same underlying concept are consistent or "hang together." It also measures the extent to which an index composed of such variables is said to demonstrate internal reliability. The minimal acceptable level to justify the combination of variables in a single index or scale is .70. The statistic has a possible range of values from 0 to +1.0.

Degrees of freedom (df)   The number of pieces of information that can vary independently of each other in calculating a statistic such as the sum of squared deviations from the mean. The values of $n - 1$ observations are "free to vary" in calculating that statistic. Conversely, if you know the values of $n - 1$ observations, you can deduce the value of the last unknown observation. Knowledge of eight values in a row or column of a Sudoku puzzle $(9 - 1)$ fully determines the value of the ninth cell of that row or column. Degrees of freedom are used in determining p values, or levels of statistical significance.

Dependent sample   A sample whose members (e.g., respondents, participants) are matched or paired in some way. In other words, one sample member's selection in the sample is dependent on some other member's selection. This condition arises under one of three circumstances: (1) repeated measures of the same respondents are taken (i.e., selection in the second wave of a panel study depends on selection into the sample in the first wave); (2) respondents are selected into a sample because they match some set of similar characteristics to someone already in the study (i.e., a matched-comparison group study); and (3) observations are made by two or more raters of the same objects or sample members.

Dependent variable   The variable that is presumed in an observational study to be the outcome of (i.e., dependent on) one or more independent (or causal) variables. In experimental designs, the dependent variable is the outcome that you believe your treatment(s) will produce.

Dichotomous variable (or dichotomy)   A variable that can take on only one of two values. Dummy variables are a special case of such a variable in which values of 0 and 1 are typically assigned to these two categories.

Eta-squared (η^2)   The proportion of variation in a continuous dependent variable that is explained by group membership in an independent variable in a t test or ANOVA.

Expected cell frequency   The number of observations you would expect to find in each cell of a contingency table if two categorical variables are not related. This frequency can be calculated by multiplying the row and column total for that cell and dividing that number by the total number of observations in the table.

Fisher's exact test   A measure of association used in 2 × 2 tables with expected cell frequencies less than 5. The test is a *p* value. Look for values less than .05 if you use that conventional criterion for statistical significance.

***F* ratio** (or *F* statistic)   In ANOVA and regression analysis, this statistic is the ratio of explained to unexplained variation. It has a known distribution that is used to determine whether at least one variable in regression analysis or one group in ANOVA is statistically significant, without identifying which variable or group.

Frequency distribution   A display of the number of observations found in each category of a variable. The display is often accompanied by the percentage of the total number of observations found in each category and the cumulative frequency that counts the number (and percentage) of observations that are found with the addition of each successive category or value.

Full model specification   A multivariate analysis (e.g., multiple regression) that includes all the independent variables that you believe exhaust the range of important causal determinants of your dependent variable. Hopefully, your beliefs are based on a review of the existing literature, sound theory, and at least an ounce of common sense.

Gamma (γ)   A symmetric measure of association between two ordinal variables. It has a possible range from −1.0 to +1.0, with 0 indicating the absence of a relationship; −1.0, a perfect, negative relationship; and +1.0, a perfect, positive relationship.

Heteroscedasticity (opposite of **homoscedasticity**)   Differences in the amount of variation in a dependent variable across different values in the independent variable(s). Pearson correlation coefficients, regression coefficients, and ANOVA are calculated in such a way that assumes these variances to be roughly equal across the range of the independent variables' values (a condition called "homoscedasticity").

Independent observations   Responses, measures, or observations that are not influenced by other responses, measures, or observations through processes such as imitation, discussion, or cooperation. A lack of independence will produce estimates or measures with less variation than is characteristic of the population from which the sample is drawn.

Independent samples   Samples drawn in such a way that any one member's selection is independent of another's selection. This is typically the case with simple random samples and classical experiments in which subjects are assigned randomly (and thus independently of each other) to treatment and control groups.

Independent variable(s) Variables that are presumed to cause an outcome or dependent variable. In classical experiments, these variables are the treatments that the investigator introduces. In nonexperimental research designs, variables are so designated because a plausible theory suggests this causal relationship, because the variable is known to have occurred before the dependent variable (i.e., temporal order can be a necessary condition for causation), or because many previous studies using a variety of methodologies are consistent with such a causal argument.

Inference or inferential statistics Any number of statistics that, based on a sample of observations, estimate the "true" value in the population from which the sample is drawn.

Interaction effect The effect of one independent variable that differs or varies depending on the values of a second (or third, fourth, etc.) independent variable. Interaction effects can be estimated in regression analysis by entering a variable that is the product of two or more independent variables.

Intercept (or constant) The predicted value of the dependent variable when independent variable(s) have the value of 0. In a bivariate regression analysis, the intercept is the value of Y where the regression line crosses the vertical (Y) axis. The intercept is not always interpretable because independent variables may not achieve a value of 0 in reality.

Internal validity Quite unlike the concept of validity as applied to measurement, internal validity is the degree to which the results of a study provide evidence of causal relationships. Experimental designs are typically better able to achieve this result than quasi- or nonexperimental designs.

Interquartile range Observations that fall within the middle 50% of all observations in a distribution—observations between the 25th and 75th percentiles of a distribution.

Interrater reliability A measure of the extent to which two or more raters, coders, or observers agree in their judgments, say, about the rank order of candidates or the assignment of numeric values or categories to open-ended responses.

Interval variable A variable whose values designate meaningful intervals and differences. For example, an IQ score of 110 is 10 interval points more than a score of 100.

Kendall's tau-*b* (τ-*b*) A nonparametric measure of association between ordinal variables. Its calculation includes observations that take on the same value for both variables. It has a range of values from –1.0 to +1.0, where 0 is indicative of the absence of a relationship. A value of –1.0 or +1.0 can only be obtained for tables with an equal number of rows and columns.

Kendall's tau-*c* (τ-*c*) A nonparametric measure of association between ordinal variables. Its calculation excludes observations that take on the same value for both variables. It has a range of values from –1.0 to +1.0, where 0 is indicative of the absence of a relationship. A value of –1.0 or +1.0 can only be obtained for tables with an equal number of rows and columns.

Kurtosis The degree to which a distribution is more peaked or flatter than a normal distribution.

Levene's test A test of the equality of variances on a dependent variable across categories of an independent variable. Its null hypothesis is that the variances are equal, a condition that standard ANOVA calculations assume to be the case. It is, therefore, a null hypothesis you hope *not* to reject—that is, hope for a *p* value *greater* than .05 (or use the unequal variance solutions that SPSS provides for no additional charge).

Lie Factor Quotient A quotient of the size of an effect as displayed in a graph (e.g., by the length of a line area of a bar) divided by the size of the effect in the data. Quotients less than 0.95 or greater than 1.05 indicate a graphical distortion of the statistic.

Logistic regression A regression analysis in which the dependent variable is a dummy dichotomous variable. Its calculations are based on maximum likelihood algorithms instead of ordinary least squares.

Mahalanobis distance (d) A test for the presence of multivariate outliers in a multiple regression analysis. Any case with a value in excess of 25 in a sample of 500 or more observations or 15 in samples of less than 100 observations may be unduly influencing the results of a multiple regression.

McNemar test A test applied to 2 × 2 tables for measures taken at two points in time.

Multicollinearity The extent to which independent variables are related to each other. Independent variables that are highly related to each other (above |.70|) can produce unreliable regression coefficients, including dramatic changes in the direction of a relationship. Relatively uncommon in most survey-based studies, multicollinearity can be mitigated by removing one or more highly correlated independent variables from the equation or combining such variables into a scale or index.

Multiple regression (R)   A summary measure of the extent to which two or more independent variables are linearly related to a dependent variable.

Negative relationship   A relationship or measure of association in which high values of one variable tend to be paired or found to occur with low values of another variable.

Nominal variable   A variable that is assigned values that are not numerically meaningful. See also **Categorical variables.**

Nonparametric statistics   Statistics that do not require or assume that variables are normally distributed or have interval measures with equal variances across different groups or categories. Many such statistics calculate the correlation between variables that are converted to ranks (e.g., from highest to lowest values), which also makes them immune to outliers in the data.

Nonresponse bias   Differences between sample estimates and population parameters that arise from the combination of (a) differences in the response rates of different groups in the sample and (b) correlations between group membership and other measures of interest in the study.

Normal distribution   A mathematically defined distribution with properties that have proven useful in developing and interpreting inferential statistics. Otherwise known as a bell-shaped curve, a normal distribution's mean and median are the same, 2/3 of all observations fall within about ±1 standard deviation from the mean, and 95% of all observations in such a distribution can be found within about ±2 standard deviations from the distribution's mean.

Ordinary least squares (OLS)   A technique for calculating a large family of statistics by minimizing the sum of squared differences between actual observations and what those statistics would predict on a dependent variable.

Outlier:

   Bivariate   An observation or case whose joint values on two variables mark it as unusual relative to other observations as displayed, for example, in a scatterplot.

   Multivariate   An observation or case that displays an unusual combination of values on a dependent and two or more independent variables. Such observations can be detected by (1) the identification of large standardized residuals (e.g., differences between predicted and actual values on a dependent variable in a regression equation that exceed ±3 standard deviations) and/or (2) an examination of case statistics such as Mahalanobis d, Cook's distance, or centered leverage value.

Statistical tools that employ ordinary least square algorithms (i.e., that seek to minimize the squared differences between predicted and observed differences) and/or whose calculations depend on observed differences from the mean of a variable's distribution can be strongly influenced by outliers and their interpretation thereby distorted, just as the mean value on a single variable's distribution can be a misleading measure of its central tendency if the distribution includes a substantial number of outliers.

Univariate An extreme observation relative to the distribution of all other values of a measure or variable. Different criteria can be used to identify such cases: (1) an observation that falls ±3 standard deviations from the mean of a variable's distribution or (2) observations that fall above or below 1.5 times a variable's interquartile range—that is, observations that fall above or below the "whiskers" of a boxplot.

Parameter A characteristic of a population, whether a measure of central tendency or a correlation. Sample statistics are estimates of population parameters derived from samples from that population.

Part correlation A measure of the amount of variation in a dependent variable that is explained (when squared) by a single variable after controlling for one or more other independent variables.

Partial correlation A measure of the linear relationship between an independent and dependent variable when controlling one or more other independent variables.

Pearson *r* (Pearson product-moment correlation) A measure of the linear relationship between two continuous variables. It has a possible range from −1.0 to +1.0, with 0 indicating the absence of a relationship; −1.0, a perfect, negative relationship; and +1.0, a perfect, positive relationship.

Phi (ϕ) A measure of association between two categorical variables in 2×2 contingency tables.

Positive relationship A relationship or measure of association in which high values of one variable tend to be paired or found to occur with high values of another variable.

Power The probability (.80 is an often recommended level) that a sample test will detect a statistically significant effect when it actually exists in the population from which the sample was drawn. Metaphorically, we would decide to set a guilty man free 20% of the times when the "power" of our evidence was .80.

Proportional reduction in error (PRE)   A type of measure of association that can be interpreted as the extent to which knowledge of the values of an independent variable improves the ability to predict a dependent variable, relative to some naive prediction such as the mean of the dependent variable.

***p* value**   The probability that the estimates from a single sample are the chance results of the "luck of the random draw." More formally speaking, it is the probability of rejecting the null hypothesis when it is actually true in the population from which a sample was drawn. Metaphorically, it is the probability of convicting an innocent man given the evidence you've assembled for his guilt. The choice of a specific level of *p* to reject the null hypothesis is up to the analyst, but .05 is an often-used criterion.

Quasi-experimental design   Any one of a number of research designs that include some, but not all, of the characteristics of a classical randomized control trial (i.e., experiment). These departures from a randomized control trial design diminish the ability of the study to authoritatively assess the causal impact of an independent (or treatment) variable on a dependent (or outcome) variable.

R^2 (the coefficient of determination)   The proportion of variation in a dependent variable that is explained by one or more independent variables.

Reliability   The extent to which a measurement produces the same result consistently. For example, a question on a survey about the date of your birth is said to be reliable if the same question produces the same answer when asked in a different survey tomorrow or a week from now. There are at least four types of reliability:

> **Internal reliability**   The extent to which measures or observations collected at the same time (e.g., in the same survey) "hang together" or appear to be measuring parts of some underlying phenomena. You are justified in combining these measures into a single scale or index if they have high internal reliability.

> **Interrater reliability**   An assessment of the extent to which, say, two or more people agree in the way in which they classify a response, for example, to an open-ended question on a survey.

> **Parallel form reliability**   A measure of the extent to which, say, two different tests or questionnaires measure the same concept.

> **Test-retest reliability**   The consistency of responses to the same question or measuring instrument over some period of time during which one assumes that the responses are not likely to have changed. Your date

of birth is very unlikely to change no matter how distant the repeated measurement of it, but attitudes and skills can.

Residual   The difference between the actual value that we observe on a dependent variable and the value you would predict that dependent variable to take on given knowledge of the values of one or more independent variables and their association with the dependent variable.

Sampling distribution   The distribution of, say, the mean of a variable as measured by repeated samples of the same size and design that are drawn from the same population. The larger and more numerous the samples, the more likely these means will be normally distributed, which can be demonstrated empirically or proven mathematically by the central limit theorem.

Skewness   A characteristic of a distribution that takes on positive values when the peak of a distribution is "off" to the left and the tail is long to the right (i.e., the positive side). It is negative when the peak is "off" to the right and the tail is long to the left. Highly skewed distributions are said to be not "normally distributed."

Social desirability effects   The errors in measurement that result from respondents giving answers that they believe are valued or widely accepted (e.g., voting) when the respondents' actual attitudes or behaviors differ from these norms.

Somer's *d*   A measure of association between two categorical variables.

Spearman's rank order correlation (*r*)   A nonparametric measure of association between the ranks of two variables.

Spurious correlation   The correlation between two variables that results from their joint dependence on a third variable.

Standard deviation   A common measure of the extent to which sample observations on a variable differ from one another. It is calculated as the square root of a sample variable's variance.

Standard error   Analogous to the standard deviation of a sampling distribution, the standard error is calculated in a single sample by dividing the sample standard deviation by the square root of the sample size. Any statistical estimate of a population parameter (e.g., a mean or correlation) will be found within about ±2 standard errors in 95 out of 100 samples of equal size and design. The range of an estimate's values as established by the standard error is the confidence interval for that statistic.

Standard score (standardization, *z* score)   A transformed variable created by subtracting the mean and dividing the standard deviation for each observation, thus creating a new variable with a mean of 0 and a standard deviation of 1. Such transformations enable you to compare the relative effects of independent variables across variables because they have equivalent units of measurement.

Suppressor variable   A variable that is positively related to one variable and negatively related to another in such a way as to make it appear as if these latter two variables have no or little bivariate relationship to each other.

Tolerance   A test of multicollinearity. It is the reciprocal of the variance inflation factor (1/VIF). Values of less than .10 suggest a troubling level of multicollinearity.

Validity   The extent to which a measure truly measures what it is intended to measure.

> **Construct validity**   A way of assessing a measure's validity by examining the relationship between that measure and others that are known or thought to be related to it.

> **Content validity**   The degree to which a measure captures the entire breadth of a concept. Asking students to define the meaning of content validity would hardly be a valid measure of one's understanding of statistics.

> **Face validity**   The extent to which a measure is thought to measure what it is intended to measure because it seems to do so "on the face of it." Asking someone the date on which they were born seems, "on the face of it," to produce a valid measure of the person's age.

> **Predictive validity**   A method for judging the validity of a measure by determining the extent to which your variable is empirically related to other variables you would expect if it were a valid measure.

As if it wasn't confusing enough, statisticians also use validity to mean two quite different things from the above types of measurement validity:

External validity   The degree to which the results from one study can be generalized to people or settings that are outside the study. To what extent, for example, can the results of a study of the effects of school vouchers on the test performance of African-American public school students in elementary schools in Milwaukee be generalized to, say, public high school students in that city or to elementary school students in other cities?

Internal validity   The extent to which the research design and analysis affords you the ability to confidently make assertions about causation.

Variance   The average sum of squared differences of each observation from its mean. It is a general tool for measuring the extent to which observations on a variable differ. In practice, it plays second fiddle to its offspring, the standard deviation.

Variance inflation factor (VIF)   A diagnostic test for the presence of multicollinearity. Values greater than 10 may indicate troubling multicollinearity.

Weights   A technique for making adjustments to a sample that has more observations from, say, particular socio-demographic groups that are known to exist in the sampling frame.

ZPRED   A standardization of predicted values of a dependent variable that are derived from a regression analysis.

ZRESID   A standardization of residual values that are derived from a regression analysis.

REFERENCES

Aaron, H. J. (1978). *Politics and the professors: The great society in perspective.* Washington, DC: Brookings Institution.

Abelson, R. P. (1995). *Statistics as principled argument.* Hillsdale, NJ: Lawrence Erlbaum.

Allison, P. (2001). *Missing data. Sage University paper series on quantitative applications in the social sciences* (No. 07-136). Thousand Oaks, CA: Sage.

Almquist, E., & Wyner, G. (2001). Boost your marketing ROI with experimental design. *Harvard Business Review, October,* 135–141.

Anderson, E., Brooks, S. N., Gunn, R., & Jones, N. (Eds.). (2004). Being here and being there: Fieldwork encounters and ethnographic discoveries. *Annals of the American Academy of Political and Social Science, 595*(1), 1–327.

Andreasen, A. R. (2002). *Marketing research that won't break the bank: A practical guide to getting the information you need.* San Francisco: Jossey-Bass.

Anscombe, F. J. (1973). Graphs in statistical analysis. *American Statistician, 27,* 17–21.

Bakan, D. (1966). The test of significance in psychological research. *Psychological Bulletin, 66,* 1–29.

Bassili, J. N. (2003). The minority slowness effect: Subtle inhibitions in the expression of views not shared by others. *Journal of Personality and Social Psychology, 84*(2), 261–276.

Berglas, N., Brindis, C., & Cohen, J. (June, 2003). *Adolescent pregnancy and childbearing in California* [PDF; Outside Source]. Sacramento, CA: California State Library Foundation.

Berk, R. A. (2004). *Regression analysis: A constructive critique.* Thousand Oaks, CA: Sage.

Berman, E. M. (2007). *Essential statistics for public managers and policy analysts.* Washington, DC: CQ Press.

Bishop, G. (2004). *The illusion of public opinion: Fact and artifact in American public opinion polls.* Lanham, MD: Rowman & Littlefield.

Blumberg, S. J. (2007). *National health interview survey.* Retrieved May 14, 2009, from www.cdc.gov/nchs/nhis.htm

Boruch, R. F. (1975). Coupling randomized experiments and approximations to experiments in social program evaluation. *Sociological Methods and Research, 4*(1), 31–53.

Boruch, R. F. (2004). Experimental design: Randomization and social experiments. In N. J. Smelser & P. B. Baltes (Eds.), *International encyclopedia of the social and behavioral sciences* (pp. 5096–5100). Oxford, UK: Elsevier.

Boruch, R. F. (Ed.). (2005). Better evaluation for evidence-based policy: Place randomized trials in education, criminology, welfare, and health. *Annals of the American Academy of Political and Social Science, 599*(1), 6–18.

Bracey, G. W. (2006). *Reading educational research: How to avoid getting statistically snookered.* Portsmouth, NH: Heinemann.

Bradburn, N., Sudman, S., & Wansink, B. (2004). *Asking questions* (Rev. ed.). San Francisco: Wiley.

Briggs, S. R., & Cheek, J. M. (1986). The role of factor analysis in the development and evaluation of personality scales. *Journal of Personality, 54,* 106–148.

Brooks, D. (2006). Harvard bound? Chin up. *New York Times.* Retrieved March 2, 2006, from http://select.nytimes.com/2006/03/02/opinion/02brooks.html

Camerer, C. F., Loewenstein, G., & Weber, M. (1989). The curse of knowledge in economic settings: An experimental analysis. *Journal of Political Economy, 97,* 1232–1254.

Campanelli, P. C., Martin, E. A., & Creighton, K. P. (1989). Respondents' understanding of labor force concepts: Insights from debriefing studies. In *Proceedings of the Fifth Annual Research Conference* (pp. 361–374). Washington, DC: Bureau of the Census.

Campbell, D. T., & Ross, H. L. (1968). The Connecticut crackdown on speeding: Time-series data in quasi-experimental analysis. *Law and Society Review, 3*(1), 33–54.

Campbell, D. T., & Stanley, J. C. (1963). *Experimental and quasi-experimental designs for research.* Chicago: Rand-McNally.

Cappella, J. N., Yzer, M., & Fishbein, M. (2003). Using beliefs about positive and negative consequences as the basis for designing message interventions for lowering risky behavior. In D. Romer (Ed.), *Reducing adolescent risk* (pp. 210–219). Thousand Oaks, CA: Sage.

Carver, R. P. (1978). The case against statistical significance testing. *Harvard Educational Review, 48,* 378–398.

Chen, H., & Rossi, P. A. (1985). Evaluating with sense: The theory-driven approach. In R. F. Conner & others (Eds.), *Evaluation studies annual review* (Vol. 9). Beverly Hills, CA: Sage.

Cohen, J. (1988). *Statistical power analysis for the behavioral sciences* (2nd ed.). Hillsdale, NJ: Lawrence Erlbaum.

Cohen, J. (1994). The Earth is round ($p < .05$). *American Psychologist, December,* 997–1003.

Conway, M., & Ross, M. (1984). Getting what you want by revising what you had. *Journal of Personality and Social Psychology, 47,* 301–309.

Cook, T. D. (2003). *Remarks upon accepting appointment as a Fellow of the American Academy of Political and Social Science.* Retrieved January 17, 2009, from www.aapss.org/videos/cook.rm

Cook, T. D., & Campbell, D. T. (1979). *Quasi-experimentation: Design and analysis issues for field settings.* Chicago: Rand-McNally.

Couper, M. (2001). The promises and perils of Web surveys. In A. Westlake, W. Sykes, T. Manners, & M. Riggs (Eds.), *The challenge of the Internet* (pp. 35–56). London: Association for Survey Computing.

Deutsch, M. (1967). *The disadvantaged child.* New York: Basic Books.

Dobel, J. P., Elmore, R., & Werner, L. (2003). *Memo writing. Teaching case resources from the Evans School of Public Affairs.* Seattle, WA: University of Washington.

Dorofeev, S., & Grant, P. (2006). *Statistics for real-life sample surveys.* Cambridge, UK: Cambridge University Press.

Draisma, S., & Dijkstra, W. (2004). Response latencies and (para)linguistic expressions as indicators of response error. In S. Presser, J. M. Rothgeb, M. P. Couper, J. T. Lessler, E. Martin, J. Martin et al. (Eds.), *Methods for testing and evaluating survey questionnaires* (pp. 131–147). New York: Wiley.

Ehlen, J., & Ehlen, P. (2007). Cellular-only substitution in the U.S. as lifestyle adoption: Implications for telephone survey coverage. *Public Opinion Quarterly, 71*(5), 717–733.

Elliott, A. C., & Woodward, W. A. (2007). *Statistical analysis quick reference guidebook.* Thousand Oaks, CA: Sage.

Esposito, J. L., Campanelli, P. C., Rothgeb, J., & Polivka, A. E. (1991). Determining which questions are best: Methodologies for evaluating survey questions. In *Proceedings of the American Statistical Association* (Survey Research Methods Section, pp. 46–55). Alexandria, VA: American Statistical Association.

Featherman, D. L., & Vinovskis, M. A. (Eds.). (2001). *Social science and policy-making: A search for relevance in the twentieth century.* Ann Arbor: University of Michigan Press.

Few, S. (2004). *Show me the numbers: Designing tables and graphs to enlighten.* Oakland, CA: Analytics Press.

Field, A. (2005). *Discovering statistics using SPSS* (2nd ed.). London: Sage.

Finckenauer, J. O. (1982). *Scared straight and the panacea phenomenon.* Englewood Cliffs, NJ: Prentice Hall.

Finckenauer, J. O., & Gavin, P. W. (1999). *Scared straight: The panacea phenomenon revisited.* Prospect Heights, IL: Waveland Press.

Forsyth, B., Rothgeb, J. M., & Willis, G. B. (2004). Does pretesting make a difference? An experimental test. In S. Presser, J. M. Rothgeb, M. P. Couper, J. T. Lessler, E. Martin, J. Martin et al. (Eds.), *Methods for testing and evaluating survey questionnaire* (pp. 525–546). San Francisco: Wiley.

Fowler, F. J., Jr. (1992). How unclear terms affect survey data. *Public Opinion Quarterly, 56,* 218–231.

Frieden, J. A., & Lake, D. A. (2005). International relations as a social science: Rigor and relevance. *Annals of the American Academy of Political and Social Science, 600*(1), 136–156.

Friedman, J., & Shapiro, I. (2004, April 23). *Tax returns: A comprehensive assessment of the Bush administration's record on cutting taxes.* Retrieved June 21, 2007, from www.cbpp.org/4-14-04tax-sum.htm

Goleman, D. (1995, January 15). An elusive picture of violent men who kill mates. *New York Times,* p. 22.

Groves, R. M., Fowler, F. J., Couper, M. P., Lepkowski, J. M., Singer, E., & Tourangeau, R. (2004). *Survey methodology.* Hoboken, NJ: Wiley.

Guttman, L. (1985). The illogic of statistical inference for cumulative science. *Applied Stochastic Models and Data Analysis, 1,* 3–10.

Heath, C., & Heath, D. (2007). *Made to stick: Why some ideas survive and others die.* New York: Random House.

Heckman, J., & Seligman, P. (1993). The Urban Institute Audit Studies: Their methods and findings. In M. Fix & R. J. Struyk (Eds.), *Clear and convincing evidence: Measurement of discrimination in America* (pp. 187–258). Washington, DC: Urban Institute Press.

Heerwegh, D., & Loosveldt, G. (2008). Face-to-face versus Web surveying in a high-Internet-coverage population. *Public Opinion Quarterly, October,* 1–11.

Hochstim, J. (1967). A critical comparison of three strategies of collecting data from households. *Journal of the American Statistical Association, 62,* 976–989.

Hooke, R. (1983). *How to tell the liars from the statisticians.* New York: Marcel Dekker.

Howell, W. G., & Peterson, P. E. (2004). Uses of theory in randomized field trials. *American Behavioral Scientist, 47,* 634–657.

Hox, J., & de Leeuw, E. (1994). A comparison of nonresponse in mail, telephone, and face-to-face surveys: Applying multilevel modeling to meta-analysis. *Quality and Quantity, 28,* 329–344.

Iannacchione, V. G., Staab, J. M., & Redden, D. T. (2003). Evaluating the use of residential mailing addresses in a metropolitan household survey. *Public Opinion Quarterly, 76,* 202–210.

Jaccard, J., & Becker, M. A. (2002). *Statistics for the behavioral science*s (4th ed.). Pacific Grove, CA: Brooks/Cole.

Julien, M., & Hanley, J. A. (2008). Profile-specific survival estimates: Making reports of clinical trials more patient-relevant. *Clinical Trials, 5,* 107–115.

Kingdon, J. W. (2003). *Agendas, alternatives, and public policies* (2nd ed.). New York: Longman.

Krosnik, J. A. (1991). Response strategies for coping with the cognitive demands of attitude measures in surveys. *Applied Cognitive Psychology, 5,* 213–236.

Krosnik, J. A., Holbrook, A. L., Berent, M. K., Carson, R. T., Hanemann, W. M., Kopp, R. J., et al. (2002). The impact of "no opinion" response options on data quality. *Public Opinion Quarterly, 66,* 371–403.

Krueger, A. B., & Zhu, P. (2004a). Another look at the New York City school voucher experiment. *American Behavioral Scientist, 47,* 658–698.

Krueger, A. B., & Zhu, P. (2004b). Inefficiency, subsample selection bias, and nonrobustness: A response to Paul E. Peterson and William G. Howell. *American Behavioral Scientist, 47,* 718–728.

Lavrakas, P. J., Shuttles, C. D., Steeh, C., & Fienberg, H. (2007). The state of surveying cell phone numbers in the United States. *Public Opinion Quarterly, 71*(5), 840–854.

Lee, E. S., & Forthofer, R. N. (2005). *Analyzing complex survey data* (2nd ed.). Sage University Paper Series on Quantitative Applications in the Social Sciences. Thousand Oaks CA: Sage.

Lessler, J. T., & Forsyth, B. H. (1996). A coding system for appraising questionnaires. In N. Schwarz & S. Sudman (Eds.), *Answering questions: Methodology for determining cognitive and communicative processes in survey research* (pp. 259–292). San Francisco: Jossey-Bass.

Light, R. J., Singer, J. D., & Willett, J. B. (1990). *By design: Planning research in higher education.* Cambridge, MA: Harvard University Press.

Link, M. W., Battaglia, M. P., Frankel, M. R., Osborn, L., & Mokdad, A. H. (2008). A comparison of address-based sample (ABS) versus random-digit dialing (RDD) for general population surveys. *Public Opinion Quarterly, 72,* 6–27.

Lipsey, M. W., & Wilson, D. B. (2001). *Practical meta-analysis.* Thousand Oaks, CA: Sage.

Loftus, E. F., & Palmer, J. C. (1974). Reconstruction of automobile destruction: An example of the inter-action between language and memory. *Journal of Verbal Learning and Verbal Behavior, 13,* 585–589.

Loftus, G. R. (1991). On the tyranny of hypothesis testing in the social sciences. *Contemporary Psychology, 36,* 102–105.

Loftus, G. R. (1994). *Why psychology will never be a real science until we change the way we analyze data.* Paper presented at the 102nd annual convention of the American Psychological Association, Los Angeles, CA.

Lykken, D. E. (1968). Statistical significance in psychological research. *Psychological Bulletin, 70,* 151–159.

Martin, E., & Polivka, A. E. (1995). Diagnostics for redesigning survey questionnaires. *Public Opinion Quarterly, 59*(4), 547–567.

Massey, D. S., Durand, J., & Malone, N. J. (2002). *Beyond smoke and mirrors.* New York: Russell Sage Foundation.

McCaughey, R. A. (1993). But can they teach? In praise of college professors who publish. *Teachers College Record, 95*(2), 242–257.

McCord, J. (2003). Cures that harm: Unanticipated outcomes of crime prevention programs. *Annals of the American Academy of Political and Social Science, 487,* 16–30.

McNeil, L. M., Coppola, A., Radigan, J., & Heilig, J. V. (2008). Avoidable losses: High-stakes accountability and the dropout crisis. *Education Policy Analysis Archives, 16*(3), 1–48.

Meehl, P. E. (1967). Theory-testing in psychology and physics: A methodological paradox. *Philosophy of Science, 34,* 103–115.

Meier, K. J., Brudney, J. L., & Bohte, J. (2009). *Applied statistics for public and non-profit administration.* Belmont CA: Thomson Wadsworth.

Miles, J., & Shevlin, M. (2001). *Applying regression and correlation: A guide for students and researchers.* London: Sage.

Miller, G. (1956). The magical number seven, plus or minus two: Some limits on our capacity for processing information. *Psychological Review, 63,* 81–97.

Miller, J. E. (2005). *The Chicago guide to writing about multivariate analysis.* Chicago: University of Chicago Press.

Miller, J. M., & Krosnick, J. A. (1998). The impact of candidate name order on election outcomes. *Public Opinion Quarterly, 62,* 291–330.

Montaquila, J. M., Brick, J. M., Hagedorn, M. C., Kennedy, C., & Keeter, S. (2008). Aspects of nonresponse in RDD telephone surveys. In J. M. Lepkowski, C. Tucker,

J. M. Brick, E. D. de Leeuw, L. Japec, P. J. Lavrakas et al. (Eds.), *Advances in telephone survey methodology* (pp. 561–586). New York: Wiley.

Moore, D. S., & McCabe, G. P. (2006). *Introduction to the practice of statistics* (5th ed.). New York: W. H. Freeman.

Morrison, D. E., & Henkel, R. E. (1970). *The significant test controversy: A reader.* Chicago: Aldine.

Musso, J., Biller, R, & Myrtle, R. (2000).Tradecraft: Professional writing as problem solving. *Journal of Policy Analysis and Management, 19,* 635–646.

Newton, E. (1990). *Overconfidence in the communication of intent: Heard and unheard melodies.* Doctoral dissertation, Stanford University, Palo Alto, CA.

Oakes, M. L. (1986). *Statistical inference: A commentary for the social and behavioral sciences.* New York: Wiley.

O'Muircheartaigh, C., Eckman, S., & Weiss, C. (2003). Traditional and enhanced field listing for probability sampling. On *Proceedings of the American Statistical Association, Survey Methodology Section* [CD-ROM] (pp. 2563–2567). Alexandria, VA: American Statistical Association.

Pager, D. (2003). The mark of a criminal record. *American Journal of Sociology, 108*(5), 937–975.

Pallant, J. (2005). *SPSS survival manual* (2nd ed.). Maidenhead, UK: Open University Press.

Payne, S. L. (1951). *The art of asking questions.* Princeton, NJ: Princeton University Press.

Pearson, R. W., Ross, M., & Dawes, R. (1992). Personal recall and the limits of retrospective questions in surveys. In J. Tanur (Ed.), *Questions about questions: Inquiries into the cognitive basis of surveys* (pp. 65–94). New York: Russell Sage.

Peterson, P. E., & Howell, W. G. (2004). Efficiency, bias, and classification schemes: A response to Alan B. Krueger and Pei Zhu. *American Behavioral Scientist, 47,* 699–717.

Petrosino, A., Turpin-Petrosino, C., & Buehler, J. (2003). Scared straight and other juvenile awareness programs for preventing juvenile delinquency: A systematic review of the randomized experimental evidence. *Annals of the American Academy of Political and Social Science, 589*(1), 41–62.

Presser, S., Couper, M. P., Lessler, J. T., Martin, E., Martin, J., Rothgeb, J. M., et al. (Eds.). (2004). Methods for testing and evaluating survey questions. *Public Opinion Quarterly, 68*(1), 109–130.

Presser, S., Rothgeb, J. M., Couper, M. P., Lessler, J. T., Martin, E., Martin, J., et al. (Eds.). (2004). *Methods for testing and evaluating survey questionnaires.* New York: Wiley.

Prewitt, K. (1987). Public statistics and democratic politics. In W. Alonso & P. Starr (Eds.), *The politics of numbers* (pp. 261–274). New York: Russell Sage Foundation.

Relman, A. S. (2007). *A second opinion: Rescuing America's health care.* New York: Century Foundation.

Rossi, P. H., Sampson, W. A., Bose, C. E., Jasso, G., & Passel, J. (1974). Measuring household social standing. *Social Science Research, 3,* 169–190.

Rozeboom, W. W. (1960). The fallacy of the null hypothesis significance test. *Psychological Bulletin, 57,* 416–428.

Rubin, D. C. (1995). *Memory in oral traditions: The cognitive psychology of epics, ballads, and counting-out rhymes.* Oxford, UK: Oxford University Press.

Sadoski, M., Goetz, E., & Rodriguez, M. (2000). Engaging texts: Effects of concreteness on comprehensibility, interest, and recall in four text types. *Journal of Educational Psychology, 92,* 85–95.

Salkind, N. J. (2006). *Tests and measurement for people who (think they) hate tests and measurement.* Thousand Oaks, CA: Sage.

Schmidt, F. L. (1996). Statistical significance testing and cumulative knowledge in psychology: Implication for training of researchers. *Psychological Methods, 1,* 115–129.

Shadish, W. R. (2004). Quasi-experimental designs. In N. J. Smelser & P. B. Baltes (Eds.), *International encyclopedia of the social and behavioral sciences* (pp. 12655–12659). San Francisco: Elsevier.

Shadish, W. R., & Cook, T. D. (1999). Comment—design rules: More steps toward a complete theory of quasi-experimentation. *Statistical Science, 14,* 294–300.

Sheatsley, P. (1983). Questionnaire construction and item writing. In P. Rossi, J. Wright, & A. Anderson (Eds.), *Handbook of survey research* (pp. 195–230). New York: Academic Press.

Shen, H. (2003). *Nonparametric regression for problems involving lognormal distributions.* Doctoral dissertation, University of Pennsylvania, Philadelphia.

Sherman, L. W. (2003). Misleading evidence and evidence-led policy: Making social science more experimental. *Annals of the American Academy of Social and Political Science, 589,* 6–19.

Simon, H. A. (1957). *Models of man: Social and rational.* New York: Wiley.

Singer, J. D., & Willett, J. B. (2003). Applied longitudinal data analysis: Modeling change and event occurrence. Oxford, UK: Oxford University Press.

Smith, A. F. (1991). Cognitive processes in long-term dietary recall. In *Vital and Health Statistics, Series 6, No. 4* (DHHS Publication No. PHS 92–1079). Washington, DC: Government Printing Office.

Sorian, R., & Baugh, T. (2002). Power of information: Closing the gap between research and policy. *Health Affairs, 21*(2), 264–273.

Stevens, J. (1996). *Applied multivariate statistics for the social sciences* (3rd ed.). Mahwah, NJ: Lawrence Erlbaum.

Strauss, V. (2007, March 26). Putting assessments to the test. *Washington Post,* p. B2.

Sudman, S., & Bradburn, N. (1982). *Asking questions: A practical guide to questionnaire design.* San Francisco: Jossey-Bass.

Szanton, P. (2001). *Not well advised: The city as client—an illuminating analysis of urban government and their consultants.* San Jose, CA: Authors Choice Press.

Tabachnick, B. G., & Fidell, L. S. (2007). *Using multivariate statistics* (5th ed.). Boston: Pearson.

Texas Education Agency. (2006). Validity. In *Technical digest 2004–2005.* Retrieved July 24, 2008, from http://ritter.tea.state.tx.us/student.assessment/resources/techdig05/chapter15.pdf

Tierney, J. P., & Grossman, J. B. (with Resch, N. L.). (1995). *Making a difference: An impact study of Big Brothers Big Sisters.* Philadelphia: Public/Private Ventures.

Tourangeau, R., Rips, L., & Rasinski, K. (2000). *The psychology of survey response.* Cambridge, UK: Cambridge University Press.

Tourangeau, R., & Smith, T. (1996). Asking sensitive questions: The impact of data collection, question format, and question context. *Public Opinion Quarterly, 60,* 275–304.

Tufte, E. R. (1990). *Envisioning information.* Cheshire, CT: Graphics Press.

Tufte, E. R. (2001). *The visual display of quantitative information* (2nd ed.). Cheshire, CT: Graphics Press.

Turner, C., Lessler, J., & Devore, J. (1992). Effects of mode of administration and wording on reporting of drug use. In C. Turner, J. Lessler, & J. Gfroerer (Eds.), *Survey measurement of drug use: Methodological studies* (pp. 177–220). Rockville, MD: National Institute on Drug Abuse.

U.S. General Accounting Office. (2003). *Youth illicit drug use prevention: DARE long-term evaluations on the effectiveness of the DARE elementary school curriculum in preventing illicit drug use* (GAO-03–172R). Retrieved July 17, 2009, from www.gao.gov/new.items/d03172r.pdf

Wallis, C., & Steptoe, S. (2007, June 4). How to fix No Child Left Behind. *Time Magazine,* pp. 34–41.

Ware, C. (2000). *Information visualization: Perception for design.* San Francisco: Morgan Kaufmann.

Warner, R. M. (2008). *Applied statistics.* Thousand Oaks, CA: Sage.

Weber, C. U., Foster, P. W., & Weikart, D. P. (1978). *An economic analysis of the Ypsilanti Perry Preschool Project.* Ypsilanti, MI: High Scope Educational Research Foundation.

Wienk, R. E., Reid, C. E., Simonson, J. C., & Eggers, F. J. (1979). *Measuring discrimination in American housing markets: The housing market practices survey.* Washington, DC: U.S. Department of Housing and Urban Development.

Winship, C., & Morgan, S. L. (1999). The estimation of causal effects from observational data. *Annual Review of Sociology, 25,* 659–706.

Yates, F. (1951). The influence of *Statistical Methods for Research Workers* on the development of the science of statistics. *Journal of the American Statistical Association, 46,* 19–34.

Ziliak, S. T., & McCloskey, D. N. (2008). *The cult of statistical significance: How the standard error costs us jobs, justice, and lives.* Ann Arbor: University of Michigan Press.

Zumbo, B. D., & Zimmerman, D. W. (1983). Is the selection of statistical methods governed by level of measurement? *Canadian Psychology, 34,* 390–400.

INDEX

ABOUT THE AUTHOR

Robert W. Pearson, PhD, is a senior fellow at the Fels Institute of Government at the University of Pennsylvania. He has previously served as executive director of the American Academy of Political and Social Science, associate dean at the H. John Heinz III School of Public Policy and Management at Carnegie Mellon University, program officer at the Social Science Research Council, assistant survey director at the National Opinion Research Center at the University of Chicago, and training consultant for SPSS, Inc. He has been on the faculties of Catholic University, Columbia University, and Barnard College. His publications have focused on three areas: (1) trends in higher education (e.g., the future of U.S. higher education, distance education, and the design of management programs for physician executives), (2) appropriate research designs (e.g., the comparative advantages and disadvantages of longitudinal surveys and the limitations of retrospective questioning in surveys), and (3) public policy and the social sciences (e.g., the mismatch between the nation's statistical system and the data required to test theories and inform public policy about persistent and concentrated urban poverty). He earned his doctorate in political science from the University of Chicago and his undergraduate degree from the University of Missouri, Columbia.

Supporting researchers for more than 40 years

Research methods have always been at the core of SAGE's publishing program. Founder Sara Miller McCune published SAGE's first methods book, *Public Policy Evaluation*, in 1970. Soon after, she launched the *Quantitative Applications in the Social Sciences* series—affectionately known as the "little green books."

Always at the forefront of developing and supporting new approaches in methods, SAGE published early groundbreaking texts and journals in the fields of qualitative methods and evaluation.

Today, more than 40 years and two million little green books later, SAGE continues to push the boundaries with a growing list of more than 1,200 research methods books, journals, and reference works across the social, behavioral, and health sciences. Its imprints—Pine Forge Press, home of innovative textbooks in sociology, and Corwin, publisher of PreK–12 resources for teachers and administrators—broaden SAGE's range of offerings in methods. SAGE further extended its impact in 2008 when it acquired CQ Press and its best-selling and highly respected political science research methods list.

From qualitative, quantitative, and mixed methods to evaluation, SAGE is the essential resource for academics and practitioners looking for the latest methods by leading scholars.

For more information, visit **www.sagepub.com**.